The Community's Response
to Drug Use

Related Titles

Deniker, Radouco-Thomas & Villeneuve *Neuro-Psychopharmacology*

Einstein *Beyond Drugs*

Einstein *Drugs in Relation to the Drug User*

Gottheil, McLellan, Druley & Alterman *Addiction Research and Treatment*

Gottheil, McLellan & Druley *Substance Abuse and Psychiatric Illness*

Nahas *Keep Off the Grass*

Nahas & Paton *Marihuana: Biological Effects*

Sobell, Sobell & Ward *Evaluating Alcohol and Drug Treatment Effectiveness*

Stillman & Willette *The Psychopharmacology of Hallucinogens*

The Community's Response to Drug Use

Edited by
Stanley Einstein

Pergamon Press
New York □ Oxford □ Toronto □ Sydney □ Frankfurt □ Paris

Pergamon Press Offices:

U.S.A   Pergamon Press Inc., Maxwell House, Fairview Park,
                       Elmsford, New York 10523, U.S.A.

U.K.   Pergamon Press Ltd., Headington Hill Hall,
                       Oxford OX3 0BW, England

CANADA   Pergamon of Canada Ltd., 150 Consumers Road,
                       Willowdale, Ontario M2J 1P9, Canada

AUSTRALIA   Pergamon Press (Aust) Pty. Ltd., P.O. Box 544,
                       Potts Point, NSW 2011, Australia

FRANCE   Pergamon Press SARL, 24 rue des Ecoles,
                       75240 Paris, Cedex 05, France

FEDERAL REPUBLIC   Pergamon Press GmbH, 6242 Kronberg/Taunus,
OF GERMANY   Pferdstrasse 1, Federal Republic of Germany

Library of Congress Cataloging in Publication Data

Main entry under title:

The Community's response to drug use.

   Bibliography: p.
   Includes index.
   1. Drug abuse—Social aspects—Addresses, essays,
lectures. 2. Drugs—Social aspects—Addresses, essays,
lectures. I. Einstein, Stanley.
HV5801.C576 1979   363.4'5   79-16278
ISBN 0-08-019597-0

Printed in the United States of America

Contents

Part I – Drug Use and Its Control

Chapter

1   HISTORICAL AND THEORETICAL CONSIDERATIONS
    FOR DRUG USE INTERVENTION
    A.G. Hess   3

2   AUSTRALIA AND NEW ZEALAND
    D.S. Bell   29

3   SINGAPORE AND THE SOUTHEAST ASIAN REGION
    L. Hon Koon   66

4   CANADA
    P.G. Erickson and R.G. Smart   91

5   UNITED STATES
    R. King   130

6   UNITED KINGDOM
    M.M. Glatt   146

7   ISRAEL
    M. Amir   171

Part II – Drug Education

8   DRUG ABUSE PREVENTION: ISSUES, PROBLEMS,
    AND ALTERNATIVES
    S. Einstein   201

Part III – Research

9   METHODOLOGY IN COMMUNITY RESEARCH
        M.A. Lavenhar   245

10   ADDICTION AS A COMMUNITY DISORDER
        I. Silverman   305

11   THE PHARMACEUTICAL INDUSTRY AND DRUG
        USE AND MISUSE
        M. Falco   317

12   ALTERNATIVES TO DRUGS: NEW VISIONS FOR
        SOCIETY
        A.Y. Cohen   339

Index   361

About the Contributors   368

I
Drug Use and
its Control

1 Historical and Theoretical Considerations for Drug Use Intervention

A.G. Hess

This book deals with two contestants, namely the community and drugs. Their struggle is nothing new; for thousands of years they have wrestled with each other. And this was by no means only an occasional skirmish. As the documented history of about eight thousand years shows, the association between mankind and drugs was universal: Drugs were used not only as medicine but also on a large scale for magic purposes, as aphrodisiacs, and for sheer pleasure.

Today's drug situation is in many aspects a continuation of history. The use of drugs within religions continues; Christian as well as Jewish rituals require alcohol consumption (wine drinking), and certain American Indian rituals call for mescaline (peyote). Also nonmedical drug use goes on today, and there prevails a general perception that this "social" use is larger than ever and it is continuously growing.(1)

Modern times have also brought with them certain new phenomena. The development of the large chemical industry has greatly increased the number of available drugs, while mass media and communications make universal the knowledge about drugs and their usage. Another relatively recent feature is the prevalent criminalization of nonmedical drug use, as can be found in varying degrees in the penal laws of many countries. This criminalization is part of the wider aspect of nonmedical drug use being defined as a social problem. It is this social problem that is the main thesis of this introductory article.

Taking cognizance of this situation, and in order to understand the present-day relationship between the community and drugs, it may be beneficial to look back over our long history of drug use and see how the problems of today present themselves in the light of past events.

HISTORICAL PERSPECTIVES ON THE OPIATES AND CANNABIS

Opiates

The known history of opium and the opiates can be traced to the

3

seventh century b.c. when the Sumerians used a script symbol
HUL.GIL which has been interpreted as indicating "the power of opium
to produce a sense of delight or satisfaction."(2) Among the Assyrians,
opium was one of the 115 most common vegetable drugs (Fig. 1.1). The
Assyrian word for poppy juice Arat Pa. Pa may be the origin of the
Latin word papaver for the poppy.(3) The Egyptians may have known
opium, and the biblical term me-rôsh may or may not have indicated the
"juice of the poppy."(4) The poppy was cultivated in the area now known
as Hungary about 1200 b.c. and traces have also been found near
prehistoric lake dwellings in Switzerland.(5) Homer's Helen of Troy
served Telemachos – when he was mourning his supposedly dead father
Ulysses – an Egyptian "drug potent against pain and quarrels and
charged with forgetfulness of all trouble," opium, as it appears.(6)

Opium was known in Greek culture; frequent pictorial representations of the poppy indicate a widespread use (Fig. 1.2). The poppy
depicted in the hands of Aphrodite, the goddess of love, appears as a
symbol of love and fertility. In medicine, opium was particularly
esteemed because of its capacity to induce sleep. Philosopher and
botanist Theophrastos (c.372-c.287 b.c.) described mekonion, the juice
of the poppy. An opponent to the medical use of opium was Erasistratos

Fig. 1.1. Drugs stood at the cradle of mankind – Assyrian relief showing
man holding poppies. From the Assyrian word for this plant Arat.Pa.Pa.,
the English term "poppy" is derived. Source: New York Public Library
Picture Collection (photo A.G. Hess).

Fig. 1.2. Golden sealring from the acropolis in Mycenae. Women present offerings to a seated tree-goddess (?). Among the offerings are three poppy pods. Source: P. Kritikos and S. Papathaki, Mikonos ke opiou istoria ke exaplosis en ti perichi tis anatolikis mesoyiov kata tin archeotita. Reprint from Archeological Journal, 1963; Athens, 1965, illus. 7, p. 100. Courtesy of Professor P. Kritikos, Athens, with grateful acknowledgment also to Professor A. Yiannakis, State University of New York at Brockport, for translation from Greek.

of Julis (304-254 b.c.) in Alexandria.(7)

In ancient Rome, the Greek physician Galen prescribed opium as an antidote against a large number of illnesses from poisoning to headache and depression, but he did not want it administered to children fearing that this might lead to "poisoning" of the human flesh.(8)

An important role was played by a beverage called theriac. It was regularly kept in the wealthy households of Rome as a panacea against many diseases.(9) As opium was linked to Aphrodite in Greece, so it was to Venus in Rome. According to Festus, a mixture of honey, milk, and poppy juice, called coccetum, was drunk by women at her feast and also by brides on their wedding day, as an aphrodisiac.(10)

After the conquest of Rome by the so-called barbarians, classical medical tradition continued in the East where theriac and other opium preparations continued to be used on a large scale in spite of warnings by physicians Rhazes and Avicenna in the tenth century.(11)

The use of opium spread further East and especially to India which was later to become its main producer (Fig. 1.3), and to China where opium was then not yet smoked but consumed by mouth. There the consumption increased so much in the Middle Ages that the last Mongol emperor, according to legend, had to plead for divine help, which was bestowed on him in the form of a "red rain" that destroyed the crop of the poppy.(12)

From the East opium returned to Europe in the Middle Ages. In the sixteenth century the German Paracelsus and his followers prepared laudanum, an opium preparation that became most popular.(13) We also learn that in the sixteenth century Festus opposed theriak, and that the city of Delft in the Netherlands prohibited its use.(14) A century later, opium was highly praised by various writers. John Jones wrote in 1700

Fig. 1.3. Indian opium fleet descending the Ganges River to Calcutta, c. 1880. In that city, the opium was loaded on British ships for export to China. Source: Scientific American, July 29, 1882. New York Public Library Picture Collection.

about the opium experience: "It is indeed so unexpressibly fine and sweet a Pleasure, that it is very difficult for me to describe, or any to conceive it, but such as actually feel it." He called the euphoria following the opium intake a "Heavenly Condition, as no worldly Pleasure was to be compared with it."(15)

It was relatively late – the second half of the sixteenth century – that the Europeans learned about a phenomenon which later came to be called "addiction", and which they then thought of only as something which occurs in Persia and India or other distant countries. Garcia da Orta (1563) may have been the first one to describe addiction in India.(16) He was followed soon after by the traveler Leonhart Rauwolf who reported about the phenomenon in Turkey and Persia.(17) Another traveler, Linschoten, dealt with addiction in the East Indies,(18) and finally, Kaempfer reported on drug abuse in China and Indonesia in the eighteenth century.(19)

These travel reports at first did not make much impact on the West, addiction being merely an outlandish curiosity, but, in the eighteenth century and perhaps already under the influence of the beginning romanticism, the exoticism of the "mysterious" powers of opium began to stimulate the imagination of the European literati; they began to experiment with the drug, which was easily obtainable from any apothecary.

But in the same period another type of literature – medical and pharmaceutical – begins to take an interest in opium. These publications do not report any more strange phenomena in faraway parts of the world, but deal realistically with medical problems at home. It is in this literature that a long struggle takes place and finally leads to the definition of addiction as a medical problem in the modern sense, that is, in terms of its two main components, dependence and tolerance. This struggle, which has not yet been fully researched,(20) may well have extended for over two centuries. For a long time, although physicians were cognizant of certain bad effects of opium such as "vomiting, hiccoughs, distresses, anxieties, convulsions, chiefly at or about the region of the stomach,"(21) the only real danger that was recognized was death from overdose; dogs and other animals were sacrificed far into the nineteenth century in experiments to determine exactly this danger. But addiction was not yet seen as a medical problem. Dependence on the "irresistible" drug was known since the travel writers; Jones, for example, describes withdrawal symptoms ("Great, and even intolerable distresses, anxieties, and depressions of spirit"), and how they can be relieved when the user "returns to the Pleasure of Opium."(22) And tolerance was equally known.(23) The forming of the opium habit, however, was not considered bad; on the contrary, it was seen as a protection against overdoses: "Habit or customary use, makes that quantity of opium safe, and even beneficial, which would otherwise be poison."(24) The beginning of recognizing the dangers of a habit may have been Awsiter's Essay on the Effects of Opium, Considered as a Poison (1763). Although it deals almost exclusively with dangerous physical effects of the drug, he already briefly states that spreading of the opium habit "must prove a general misfortune."(25) But like other eighteenth-century writers he is vague about tolerance and dependence, and fails to see a medical problem in them. Who really was the first writer clearly defining addiction as a medical problem is still unknown; we may have to proceed well into the nineteenth century in order to find him.

Medical and pharmaceutical warnings against opium did not hinder the spread of its use. The English romantic writer, Thomas De Quincey, described his experience in the widely read book Confessions of an English Opium-Eater (1821; repr. 1966). Other publications followed; the growing press of the nineteenth century began to pay a great deal of attention to the narcotic. These popularized writings enhanced the spread of drug use which in turn gained considerably by the invention and spread of several new opiates – codeine, morphine, and, at the end of the nineteenth century, heroin – and of the hypodermic needle. In America at the time of the Civil War,(26) morphine injections were widely applied, and morphine injections, it appears, gave added inspiration to contemporary writers. It seems that persons who had been given morphine injections for medical reasons became easily dependent on the drug when learning of the kind of medicine they had been administered. Frequently physicians were warned not to tell their patients of the nature of the medication. Opium being cheap, it was also taken for enjoyment by British workers when they could not afford alcoholic beverages.(27) Temperance preachers and society ladies devoted to the cause of temperance, turned to opium instead of alcohol.(28) In the form of various elixirs, it was also administered to infants in order to keep them quiet and manageable.(29) During the age of early industrialization, working mothers sometimes kept their little children quiet in this fashion all day and all night either while they were at work or while they themselves needed sleep. In 1862 Mayhew reported in London that the rental fee for two beggar children was one shilling without food but only nine pennies if food and a laudanum preparation were supplied to keep them contented.(30)

In America, opium use was characterized in the second half of the nineteenth century by another feature, the newly introduced custom of smoking the drug, while earlier, the drug had been taken either orally or by injection; smoking was brought to the West Coast of the United States by immigrated Chinese.(31) The smoking habit also received wide publicity (Figs. 1.4a-b), which contributed to the spread of it to the

Fig. 1.4. Chinese Opium smokers in their homeland and in America. a. Arrest by Chinese police of an opium-smoking priest-Chinese picture postcard, early 20th cent. Source: New York Public Library Picture Collection. b. Opium smoker in a Chinese laundry in Virginia City, Nevada. Part of a woodcut of several Chinese scenes after a sketch by C. L. Sears (the woman's head in the lower left corner belongs to a different scene). Source: Harper's Weekly, December 29, 1877, p. 1025.

indigenous population. The first white opium smokers were dubious underworld characters – gamblers, prostitutes and the like – which led to suspicion and initiated measures against the drug, mainly in the form of local ordinances against opium "dens" and opium smoking. The legislators of these ordinances began mistakenly to see opium smoking as cause for asocial behavior, although those whites who indulged in smoking had been criminals, gamblers, or prostitutes before smoking the drug. This is the beginning of the criminalization of drug use in the United States, a process to which we will come back later. Opium use by mouth or hypodermic needle was initially not frowned upon and only included later into the prohibitions.(32)

Cannabis

The history of cannabis is almost as long as that of opium. Early evidence of the use of cannabis are remnants of the plant found in Germany in a prehistoric urn that dates from the fifth century b.c.(33) In 2737 b.c. the Chinese Emperor Shen Nung described the plant and recommended it for female weakness, gout, rheumatism, malaria, beriberi, constipation, and absentmindedness.(34)

The "Indian" hemp plant was probably not of Indian origin but reached that country at an early date. In the susruta dating from before 1000 b.c. the drug appears as a medicine and its euphoric effect is also mentioned.(35) The Assyrians referred to hemp as azallu. They already knew that it could be used to make textiles and ropes and at the same time dispel the suppression of the spirit.(36)

The writings of Herodotus (484?-425?b.c.) give the impression that many people did not even know hemp as material used for fabrics in the Greek world of his day,(37) but he describes it as in use by the Scythians who were living all over the widely extended area between the river Danube and China. They took vapor baths as a cleansing ceremony after burials by inhaling vapors from hemp seeds that were thrown on hot stones: "The Scythians enjoy it so much that they howl with pleasure."(38)

Dioscorides described the plant for making ropes and medicine, though he did not mention any intoxicating qualities. Galen, in Rome, writes about a confectionary dessert containing cannabis. It elicited great pleasure and was occasionally indulged in.(39)

The Arabs also extensively used cannabis in the first centuries a.d. "The Thousand and One Nights are saturated with the odour of hashish."(40) Occasionally the popularity of the drug was opposed by priests and writers. Well known is Marco Polo's story about the "Old Man of the Mountain" who in a strong mountain fortress allegedly induced young men to assassinate his enemies by means of hashish.(41) There is no need to go into this story at length, except to note that the word "assassin" derived apparently from hashish and has been interpreted as meaning "hashish eater." Picturesque as the story is, it has been debunked for a number of years, a fact which did not stop the narcotics commissioner from using the story as "proof" of the allegedly criminogenic qualities of cannabis, when he spoke at the congressional hearings that led to the passing of the Marijuana Act of 1937.(42)

In Europe the hemp plant was not only known and used for making ropes and fibers, but also some of its effects on the human mind were known. This is shown, for example, by Rabelais's description in the sixteenth century of the plant ("Pantagruelion") which "begets bad blood and, on account of its excessive heat, goes to the brain and fills the head with painful and annoying fumes."(43) In the seventeenth century hemp growing started in America which supplied the raw material for the ever-growing need for hemp ropes for the British navy. One of the hemp growers, though not a very successful one, was George Washington who, it appears, was also familiar with the medicinal qualities of the drug.(44)

When Napoleon invaded Egypt in 1798, he found widespread hashish abuse in that country and attempted unsuccessfully to fight it with draconic penalties.(45) Due to the focus of attention of Napoleon's campaign, greater interest was shown to cannabis at home, in Europe. From 1840 to 1900, it was the topic of approximately 100 medical articles.(46) In 1839 Cannabis indica was introduced to European medicine by Sir William B. O'Shaughnessy, and, thanks to him, it found its way into the British pharmacopeia of 1864.(47) And in France, Moreau, interested in hallucinations, wrote his influential treatise, Hashish and Mental Illness, in 1845.(48) Cannabis also gained entrance into literature other than the medical one, a fact that – as we have already seen for opium – helped to propagate the drug and to hasten its spreading.   In France a Club des Hachichins existed around 1843. According to the description by the French writer Theophile Gautier, it met in an old, elegant, but dilapidated palace from the seventeenth century, the Hotel Lauzun (then Hotel Pimodan).(49) Here the members of the club enjoyed bizarre gourmet banquets. The hors d'oeuvre contained hashish which usually took effect at the end of the meal.(50) Prominent in this group were the writers Gautier, Balzac, Dumas, and occasionally Beaudelaire. The club also included poets, sculptors, architects, the above-mentioned psychiatrist Moreau de Tours, who may be "Doctor X" in Gautier's famous description of the club (Figs. 1.5a,b,c), and another physician, Dr. Louis Aubert-Roche who was familiar with the drug from long years in Egypt and the Orient.(51)

In Lands of the Saracen published in America in 1855, Bayard Taylor described the effect of hashish.(52) Taylor was followed by Fitzhugh Ludlow who, in 1857, published his autobiography, The Hasheesh Eater, showing influence by Taylor and De Quincey.(53)

Cannabis did not gain much ground in the Western world in the late nineteenth and early twentieth centuries. It being widely used in Great Britain's Indian Empire, the British government in 1894 started a vigorous investigation into cannabis resulting in seven elaborate volumes of report. The commission found modest use of the drug harmless.(54)

In the United States there was, it appears, only a small consumption limited mostly to Mexican workers who, since the beginning of this century, had been bringing "their little bags of 'mota' across the

Fig. 1.5. a. The meeting place of the Club des Hachichins, present-day view. The ancient Hotel Pimodan, now Hotel Laudun. b. Portrait of Charles Baudelaire, drawn by himself under hashish consumption. c. Jacques-Joseph Moreau de Tours in Turkish attire playing the piano, as drawn by Theophile Gautier under the influence of hashish. Source: Bo Holmstedt, "Introduction" to Jacques-Joseph Moreau, Hashish and Mental Illness, H. Peters and G. G. Nahas, ed. (Raven Press Publishers, 1973), figures 1, 3, 4. Courtesy of Professor B. Holmstedt and Dr. Alan M. Edelson, President, Raven Press.

border."(55) In the 1930s a government-sponsored propaganda wave started alleging that marijuana consumption led to the commission of crime. Evidence, however, on this point was meager. In 1937 the Federal Marijuana Act was passed which criminalized the use and possession of the drug.(56) In 1946, New York City undertook another investigation of marijuana, confirming the absence of danger by the drug if moderately used.(57) The penalties for drug abuse were severely aggravated by the Narcotics Control Boggs-Daniel Act of 1956 (Boggs-Daniel Act). When promoting this act, the government had changed its strategy; the claim that marijuana led to crime was no longer alleged but, instead, it was maintained that marijuana led to heroin use.(58)

AN INTERPRETATION OF THE HISTORICAL OBSERVATIONS

The brief history of two of the most important drugs may suffice for our discussion. As can be seen from over thousands of years, the use of the opiates and cannabis was widespread, but complaints against their use were seldom, and set far apart in time and geographic space. Of course, we have to be conscious of the fact that our knowledge of the history of drugs is still limited and that not all complaints may be known to us today.

The impression remains, however, that although during the relatively short span of time of about two centuries narcotic drugs have given us considerable trouble, mankind and these drugs lived together for thousands of years before in a rarely disturbed, peaceful coexistence. It may also be noteworthy that the few known complaints were not always directed to the same ill effects that we attach nowadays to the drugs. For example, complaints about opiates leading to "addiction" in the modern sense did not occur, as far as we know, until a few centuries ago. In the case of cannabis, there are hardly any complaints about it leading to crime or to the use of "hard drugs." In other words, while drug use was universal, and ubiquitous, it became a "social problem" only during certain periods, and, one may add, only in certain places. Even today the use of cocaine is not necessarily considered a social problem in parts of South America and, similarly, no great concern is voiced either by the community or by policymakers about the use of kava in the South Pacific region.

Several explanations for the relative absence of such complaints are possible. First, as far as the opiates are concerned, could it be that drug users in former ages did not become addicted, contrary to those living in more recent periods? Or, second, is it possible that drug abuse problems existed in former times but that the contemporaries were not aware of its bad effects? Finally, could it be that the nonmedical use of drugs was perceived in certain periods as a community problem, perhaps even without there being an objective basis for such a perception?

Before we attempt to answer these three questions, let us cast a glance at the concept of "community," since we will eventually be interested in the community's response to drug use. This response will obviously depend on whether drug use is or is not a "community problem"; thus we have to investigate what is meant by that term, whereby, as we shall see, we can equate it with the sociological concept of the "social problem."

The Concept of the Community

The term "community"(59) is used extremely frequently and often without an express definition. This does not mean however, that we lack definitions. The Oxford English Dictionary offers a total of 18 different definitions.(60) A study undertaken in 1955 reviewed no less than 94 definitions.(61) Some writers understand it in a biological sense while most others give it a cultural one. Certain authors delineate it by means of objective criteria, others insist on subjective ones. No doubt, the authors of this book will also vary in how they define this term. Frequently community is used as a synonym for society, though perhaps the term is limited to either the local or the national society, often implying or expressly stating that the members of the community show a certain sense of identification. The term is also identified with "group," "social system," "social organization," and so forth, and it is also used to refer to certain groups with common features or common interests, e.g., as a synonym for professional groups. One can well apply it to the "community of drug users," and the like.

With such a wide range in usage, it is suggested that authors should clearly define the operational meaning they attach to the term community in their writing. Or perhaps, still better, that they avoid the term altogether and replace it with a more precise one. In particular, when the word is used without being clearly defined the danger of semantic confusion appears to be quite real. Undefined, as the term is usually applied, it probably suggests to most readers, on the one hand, a rather large group such as of the size of a village, a city, or even a nation and, on the other, a group of considerable uniformity in thinking. It may suggest, in the Durkheimian sense, a "common conscience," or common recognition of values. This may indeed give an impression that is quite false; for example, when the term community is applied to modern multicultural groups, such a commonness in thinking may be absent in reality. Or while the use of the term may suggest in a certain case that a whole community rejects drug use, this may not be the case in reality, particularly nowadays when the drug in question is marijuana. Furthermore, as we shall see in the following, those active in defining drug use as a social problem and in attempting to change the existing situation, as well as those who themselves engage in nonmedical drug use, are frequently small groups, such as reform organizations stimulated by "moral entrepreneurs," or they are small, only loosely organized "retreatist" subcultures(62) or contracultures. To call these groups "communities" may also blur the picture.

The Sociology of Social Problems

Because of these ambiguities, we do not persist in the following to speak either of "community" or of "community problem." As to the latter term, we replace it by "social problem,"(63) an expression regularly found in the relevant literature. To be sure, this term, too, is sometimes ambiguous. It seems, however, to be used mainly for problems within those groups that are often called communities. As Lemert (1968) states, social problems can either be described very simply as "perplexing questions about human societies proposed for solution," or their definition becomes extremely complicated.(64) Frequently the term is explained in terms of such concepts as "cultural lag," "social disorganization," "social pathology," or "deviance," and for many decades the discussions on social problems have combined a great variety of different areas, from crime to war and from narcotics to minorities.

Recently, efforts toward a more systematic definition and toward a sociology of "social problems" have been undertaken, as will be discussed later. In order to understand these discussions, one should distinguish between conditions that are:

1. objectively "bad" (e.g, dysfunctional conditions, norm violations the "badness" of which is verifiable)

2. merely subjectively perceived as "bad" without varifiable basis

3. both objectively "bad" and subjectively perceived as such

Theories that combine objective and subjective elements often look, with regard to the subjective side, to social values as the criteria on the basis of which existing conditions are considered unsatisfactory and represented as a "social problem." However, different authors may define "values" in different ways and it may not always be clear who makes the decisions, and whose standards apply.

In particular, three theories deal with the three alternatives. According to Merton (1971), "the first and basic ingredient of a social problem consists of a substantial discrepancy between widely shared social standards and actual social conditions of social life."(65) He recognizes as social problems not only "those objective social conditions identified by problem-definers as at odds with social values," the so-called "manifest social problems," but also "all manner of other conditions that are in fact at odds with the declared values current of those who accept these conditions," the "latent social problems."(66) The manifest problems fall under (3) above; i.e., they have to do with a combination of objectively "bad" and subjectively perceived "bad" conditions, while the latent problems are merely problems in an objective sense, not yet subjectively seen as such. In either case the existence of "bad" conditions in an objective sense is required.

Another approach, Fuller and Myers' "value-conflict" theory states: "A social problem is a condition which is defined by a considerable number of persons as a deviation from some social norm which they cherish."(67) As the authors expressly expound, "sociologists must ... study not only the objective conditions phase of a social problem, but also the value judgments of the people involved in it"; i.e., "social problem" is defined in the sense of category (3), similar to Merton's "manifest social problems." Contrary to Merton, however, Fuller and Myers do not recognize a merely objective "latent" problem: conditions that are not defined as social problems are not social problems, at least not to the potential definers.

The most recent theory, that by Kitsuse and Spector, is of a dynamic nature: social problems are ongoing "activities," namely "the activities of groups making assertions of grievances and claims with respect to some putative conditions."(68) Thus attention is focused not on static conditions — whether existing objectively or only in the opinion of certain individuals — but on a process of making claims and on interactions and changes that occur in connection with this activity of claiming. The main actors are "protest groups," which can be either "value groups," that is altruistic, crusading reformers trying to change conditions for others, or "interest groups," composed of victims who attempt to bring about changes from which they themselves hope to profit. Their counterparts are "official organizations, agencies, or institutions" who react to the claims.

Kitsuse and Spector postulate a four-stage history of a social problem which may be summarized as follows:

Stage 1:   The problem is defined by some group(s);

Stage 2:   An official organization, etc., recognizes the problem and takes certain steps;

Stage 3:   One or several groups express dissatisfaction with the official handling of the problem and formulate new claims;

Stage 4:   After rejection of these new claims by the official organization, etc., the dissatisfied group(s) develop alternate modes of action in order to deal with the problem.

Of course this scheme represents the ideal, and the process may stop at any stage, without ever reaching stage four.

Noteworthy is that Kitsuse and Spector define a social problem merely in subjective terms: an assertion of grievances about putative conditions suffices, and the existence of an objectively verifiable condition is expressly not required. Perhaps a minor modification should be suggested to Kitsuse and Spector's postulates. According to Becker,(69) it is not always groups that start out the definition of a social problem. It may begin with a "moral entrepreneur," a crusading reformer who is profoundly disturbed by certain existing or imagined conditions and sets out to change them. If such an entrepreneur is then successful in getting groups to support his cause, we come to the first of the four stages in the natural history of a social problem, as defined by Kitsuse and Spector. The fact that the initiating group may be an "interest group" does not preclude the role of the moral entrepreneur. He may persuade value groups as well as interest groups. It is even conceivable that the moral entrepreneur is himself an interested victim of a situation which leads him to define a social problem.

It should be stressed that moral entrepreneurs as well as value groups or interest groups are not necessarily always outside the government; the definition process may well begin within a government. A government agent may be the moral entrepreneur; an agency may be one of the groups, which, when stage two is reached, frequently causes another government body to take action. This particularly applies to earlier periods and to cultures other than our own which may not provide free speech or other avenues to initiate reforms from outside the government. Indeed, in our own culture and not very far back it was frequently from within the American government, it appears, that the initiative in the drug abuse field was taken. This is rather obvious with respect to marijuana.(70) After first denying the drug's danger, the U.S. government reversed its position and suddenly claimed in the 1930s that the consumption of marijuana led to the commission of crime – a claim for which there was no factual basis – and that it therefore should be forbidden. The government became active to obtain the necessary legislation (stage one of the Kitsuse-Spector scheme), and eventually was successful when Congress passed the Marijuana Act in 1937 (stage two). Since then, the government approach was itself criticized, and organizations developed plans of their own (stages three and four).

Also, with regard to opiates it appears that a good deal of the defining and social action (which was mainly criminalization in this particular case) was initiated by the U.S. government, though this area needs further study. It may be suggested that the United States had considerable interest during the nineteenth century to obtain its slice of the Chinese market, and it had also strong reasons to find ways and means for appeasing the Chinese who had been humiliated by our anti-Chinese riots and legislation. The United States had to compete economically with England, the main supplier of opium. For the United States, opium was somewhat "sour grapes"; America having no access to the high quality Indian opium, could never hold its own against the British and it had little to lose in giving up the opium trade. By taking an anti-opium stance, especially internationally, the United States pleased the Chinese government in its support of the latter's fight against the drug. From its first treaty with China, which excluded from the protection of the U.S. government American citizens engaging in opium traffic, to the conferences of Shanghai (1909) and The Hague (1912), the United States adhered to an international anti-opium policy, and from that policy, it was only another, quite natural step, to forbid nonmedical opium consumption at home where there had been indeed a number of complaints. The prohibition took place with the Harrison Act of 1914.

It may be said that an important aspect of the definition of a social problem is that the definers believe that the needed social action is possible, and that the planned action be on a broad "social" scale, that is on a scale affecting more than a few individuals. For example, the mass destruction caused by a typhoon may lead a person or a group to a correct appraisal of the human misery caused by it, but if he or they believe that nothing can be done because this is a catastrophe of nature, it will not lead to the definition of a "social problem." Also, for example, a limited number of cases of a certain illness leading to the administration of medication to one or a few individuals is a definition of a medical problem, and not of a social problem. It would be different if the activities envisaged would include general sanitation measures, mass vaccinations, and the like.

Drug Use as a Social Problem

At the end of our historical excursion we had asked three questions in the search for an explanation for the relative absence of complaints about drug abuse in former centuries and their greater frequency in more recent times:

1. Could it be that drug users then did not become addicted as frequently as the more recent users?

2. Is it possible that drug "abuse" (i.e., nonmedical use) existed in former periods, but that the contemporaries were not aware of its bad effects?

3. Could it be that nonmedical drug use was seen as a social problem only during certain periods, and sometimes even when objectively bad effects on a social scale could not be observed?

Of course, whatever answers we give to these questions will have to be of a tentative nature. The existing source material is indeed scarce and spotty, and does not permit more conclusive replies, at least not at present. Nevertheless, it is interesting to raise these questions, not only in the hope that additional source documentation will throw light on them in the future, but also because our historical observations may, hopefully, throw some light on present-day conditions.

As to question 1., it intentionally speaks of "addiction," as comprising dependence plus tolerance. We have dealt with this question already in an earlier paper(71) in which we investigated it in the light of Wilkins' "deviance theory," an information theory-oriented labelling theory: Systems with information feedback may differ from systems without it or with only minimal feedback. Feedback may lead to a vicious curcuit of "deviation amplification." Individuals may be "cut off" by definition from the value system of the group and the defining act may provide information sets for these individuals so that they become alienated, begin to see themselves as deviants, and act accordingly. This increased deviance may lead to both more acts being defined as deviant and to more forceful action by the conformists, and thus the vicious circle may repeat itself in an amplifying manner.(72) Taking into account the scarcity of "feedback" available to the contemporaries of earlier periods, and the absence of a clear definition of addiction, we suggested, in the case of opiates, that fewer people may have then become addicted; they simply did not know there was such a thing as addiction.(73) And without such knowledge, no "moral entrepreneur" could make a fuss and persuade groups to define the matter as a social problem. That knowledge of the existence and danger of addiction favors addiction was also confirmed to a certain degree by the experience of physicians who warned their colleagues not to tell their patients the nature of the medication when these patients were given morphine injections.(74)

Question 2   may also be answered in the affirmative. As is clear from the preceding discussion of the nature of social problems, objectively "bad" conditions may well exist without necessarily leading to a perception by individuals or groups of the existence of a social problem. Certainly there prevail many objectively "bad" conditions in other areas of our culture, conditions which have been lingering for a long time without having any successful action ever taken against them; such is the case in the fields of public corruption, consumer deception, and − last but not least − tobacco smoking (something which is tolerated and often even encouraged in spite of its apparent dangers to human health). Such static "bad" conditions not defined as "social problems," also existed in former periods and other cultures.

In Western countries, nonmedical opium use was first considered not to be a problem at all. Then it became merely a medical problem, in as much as the addicts − a few persons among the upper class and among intellectuals − were considered as sick persons, not without a certain compassion.

The first appearance of a moral entrepreneur calling for social action against nonmedical drug use, has not yet been ascertained. He probably did not appear on the scene until sometime in the nineteenth century. For a certain time, narcotics users were looked at as "primary" deviants, normbreakers who were, however, still tolerable, but shortly they were perceived, in America at least, as intolerable deviants. The term "dope fiend" made its appearance.(75) As we have seen, criminalization soon reached national scope with the Harrison act of 1914. And a few years later "dope fiends" were not even considered as worthy of medical attention.(76)

Finally, the answer to question 3 is also yes, at least to a certain degree. Sometimes social problems can be defined upon the assumption of their being a "social evil," though without a factual basis, as Kitsuse and Spector stressed, and as we have already illustrated by describing the propaganda that led to the passing of the Marijuana Act of 1937. Incidentally, when a new campaign was started in the 1950s in order to raise the penalties, the government discarded its previous unsubstantiated argument that marijuana use led to crime, in favor of another equally unproven one, namely that marijuana use was a stepping stone toward the use of "hard" drugs.(77)

CONCLUSIONS

As far as our historical survey goes, it indicates that drug use and mankind coexisted for thousands of years without drug use being considered a social problem, or perhaps even considered "bad." Only during the last few hundreds of years did it come to be regarded as such. And even nowadays considerable nonmedical drug consumption is not seen as a problem at all (Fig. 6). This applies not only to most coffee, tobacco, and alcohol use in our culture but also, for example, to the use of peyote in the religious rites of the Navaho Indians, of kava in the South Pacific, of betel in India, and of coca in South Africa.(78) (See Fig. 1.6)

Whether or not drug use is a social problem depends not so much on the objective nature and real dangers of the drug consumption, but frequently on how this consumption is perceived (Fig. 1.7), and, particularly, on how it is perceived especially by certain "moral entrepreneurs" — individuals within a group who look unfavorably on the consumption of drugs, therefore call for social action, and are successful with their call. Such a defining process may occur with or without the presence of "bad" factors that can be objectively verified. Defining processes which take place on the basis of the mere assumption of such "bad" factors, are by no means rare, it appears. They occurred twice during the last 50 years in the United States with respect to marijuana. As we have seen, marijuana was first condemned because of its alleged criminogenic qualities which then turned out to be imaginary, and it was subsequently frowned upon a second time under the claim that marijuana use led to the consumption of "hard" drugs, a claim equally untenable, at least for the large majority of marijuana users.

We may wish to keep those observations in mind when dealing with drug matters in the future. To be sure, complaints about the damaging consequences of the use of certain drugs are by no means to be taken lightly. However, it appears questionable whether far-reaching social action should be started on the basis of such reports alone, without their thorough verification. The practical difficulty in such situations may often be that politicians do not necessarily follow the same thinking as do drug scientists. But without such a verification of claims, we may find ourselves "barking up the wrong tree." And, indeed, our "barking" may become expensive if the programs that are started are costly, as is so often the case, and it may also lead to a good deal of human suffering. Then, some time later, the dangers originally seen in the use of the drug may turn out to be nonexistent in reality.

Furthermore, the effects of our social action may be different from what we intended them to be. We live in an age of widespread information feedback. Feedback, however, gives great instability to information systems and may make the consequences of social action highly unpredictable. They may be, in fact, quite contrary to what was expected from the measures taken. This may happen particularly if criminal sanctions are used to control drug consumption. In the past, such criminalization has not always led to the disappearance, or even a

a.

b.

c.

Fig. 1.6. Drug use is worldwide; it may, or it may not be considered deviant. a. Coca leaf smoker from the Andes. Source: World Health, July 1967, p. 8. b. Hashish smokers in North Africa. Source: Ibid., p. 9. c. Heroin has replaced the traditional opium (see fig. 1.4) in Hong Kong. A heroin "divan" (= den) in a slum, c. 1959. The drug is inhaled and not injected as in the United States, the main method being called "Chasing the Dragon." Source: A. G. Hess, Chasing the Dragon (Amsterdam and New York: North-Holland Publishing Company and Free Press, 1965), p. 46. Photo, Hong Kong Police Narcotics Bureau.

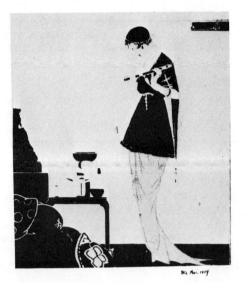

LA FUMÉE NOIRE

a.   Robe du soir de Redfern

b.

Fig. 1.7. Even in the twentieth century, the arts in the Western
countries deal sometimes with nonmedical drug use as something
appealing and attractive. a. French fashion design "Black Fume" by
Redfern of an evening gown, with the lady holding an opium pipe.
Source: Gazette du Bon Genre, March 1914. New York Public Library
Picture Collection. b. "Opium Smoker," porcelain statuette by Arno
Malinowski. Courtesy of Royal Copenhagen Porcelain Manufacture Ltd.

reduction, of the drug abuse. Often it has led to the emergence of black markets for illegal drugs, and to great profits illegally being made. The antisocial behavior of the drug users (who were formerly as law-abiding as the rest of us) may become impregnable due in part to their close association with criminals who were their source of supply for narcotics.

Criminalization which brings with it also the defining of drug use as "deviant" behavior, may indeed be the starting point of that vicious circuit known as "deviance amplification." The defining leads to the increase in deviant behavior, that increase in deviant behavior leads to more defining, this again leads to still more deviant behavior, and so forth ad infinitum, continuing the vicious circle.(79)

If there exists a high level of drug abuse in many countries at the present time as many claim, history may help to explain it. The alleged increase in drug consumption runs parallel, at least during the last 100 years, to an enormous development of the mass media, and, throughout this period, the media always gave great visibility to drug matters, be it opium, morphine, heroin, cocaine, marijuana, or LSD. Could it be that our drug explosion is a continuous, age-old vicious circle of deviation amplification?

NOTES

(1) Whether this perception is correct, nobody can assert due to lack of reliable statistics for times past as well as for the present.

(2) Neligan (1927), 2.

(3) Terry (1970 repr.), 54.

(4) Macht (1915), 477.

(5) Jermstadt (1921), 24.

(6) Homer Odyssey (1937 ed.), 49; Kritikos (1967), 5-10.

(7) Jermstadt (1921), 4.

(8) Treese (1964), 479; Jermstadt (1921), 11.

(9) Jermstadt (1921), 5, note 3.

(10) Ibid., 3.

(11) Neligan (1927).

(12) Jermstadt (1921), 117.

(13) Treese (1964), 479; Sonnedecker (1963), 10, note 23.

(14) Jermstadt (1921), 15.

(15) Jones (1701), 20.

(16) Sonnedecker (c. 1963), 9.

(17) Ibid., 7.

(18) Van Linschoten (1956 repr.), 145-146.

(19) Kaempfer (1712), 644ff., as translated from the original Latin.

(20) Sonnedecker (c. 1963) discusses a number of publications relevant to this struggle, but does not explore it fully.

(21) Jones (1701), 255.

(22) Jones (1701), 249 ff.

(23) See also, e.g., the first edition of the Encyclopaedia Britannica (1771), III, 416, which reports: "A moderate dose is commonly under a grain; . . . but custom will make people bear a dram or more," without criticizing the forming of a habit.

(24) James, Medical Dictionary, 12.

(25) Awsiter (1763), 5.

(26) The Civil War application of morphine may not have necessarily contributed by itself as much as is usually believed to the spreading of opiate use (Musto (1973), 3). For details on the history of narcotics in the United States see, besides Musto, also King (1972) and Lindesmith (1968).

(27) De Quincey (1966, 25) describes how cotton mill workers in Manchester "were rapidly getting into the practice of opium-eating, so much so that on a Saturday afternoon the counter of the druggists were strewed with pills of one, two, or three grains, in preparation for the known demand of the evening. The immediate occasion of this practice was the lowness of the wages, which, at that time, would not allow them to indulge in ale or spirits."

(28) Smith, W.G. (1832) as quoted in Terry (1928), 61; see also the survey by Oliver in the Annual Report of the Massachussetts Board of Health for 1871, as cited in Terry (1928), 7ff.

(29) Smith (1832) as cited ibid., 61.

(30) As quoted by Tobias (1967), 76.

(31) For a brief survey of the history of opium use in China, and especially in Hong Kong see Hess (1965), 13-34.

(32) Lindesmith (1968), 214.

(33) Reininger (1966), 142 & Reininger (1967), 14.

(34) Bloomquist (1968), 18-19, citing Taylor (1963), 11.

(35) Ibid., 19ff.

(36) Ibid., 22.

(37) "The Thracians make clothes from it very like linen ones – indeed, one must have much experience in these matters to be able to distinguish between the two, and anybody who has never seen a piece of cloth made from hemp, will suppose it to be of linen." (Herodotus, (1954 ed.)), 265.

(38) Ibid., 266.

(39) Bloomquist (1968), 23-24.

(40) Andrews (1967), Introduction.

(41) Polo (n.d.), Chap. 22, p. 48.

(42) Oteri (1967), 138.

(43) Rabelais (1966 ed.) 148.

(44) Washington, George, "Diary Notes," 34; Freemann (1948-1957), III, 107,117, 145, 179, 263.

(45) Bloomquist (1968), 29.

(46) Walton (1966), 449.

(47) Treese (1964), 197; Snyder (1970), 121.

(48) Moreau (repr. 1973).

(49) Holmstedt (1973), ixff.

(50) Gautier (repr. 1966), 163 ff.

(51) Holmstedt (1973), x.

(52) Taylor (1855).

(53) Ludlow (repr. 1970).

(54) Indian Hemp Drugs Commission. Report (1894).

(55) Bloomquist (1968), 32.

(56) Becker (1966); Solomon (1966) 481-496; Oteri (1967), 136-162.

(57) Reprinted in Solomon (1966), 277-410.

(58) Lindesmith in Solomon (1966) xxvi, xxviii; Leary (1966), 124 quoting comments from several.

(59) Sjoberg (1964), 114-115.

(60) Oxford English Dictionary (1971), I, 702. This would include subdivisions of definitions.

(61) Hillery (1955), 112.

(62) Cloward (1960), 25ff.

(63) The following discussion uses the articles by Rose (1964) and Lemert (1968).

(64) Lemert (1968), 452.

(65) Merton (1971), 799.

(66) Ibid., 806.

(67) Fuller & Myers (June 1941), 320; see also by the same authors (February 1941), 24.

(68) Kitsuse & Spector (1973), 407ff.; Spector &Kitsuse (1973), 145ff. When mentioned in the text, the names of the authors appear in alphabetical order, without that this refers necessarily only to the first of the two papers.

(69) Becker (1963), 147ff.

(70) Becker (1966); Solomon (1966) 481-496; Oteri (1967), 136-162.

(71) Hess (1971), 585ff.

(72) Wilkins (1965), 91ff.

(73) Hess (1971), 589.

(74) E.G. Wilson (1896), 105.

(75) The first known appearance occurred in the <u>New York Sun</u> in December 1896.

(76) Oxford Universal Dictionary (1933), 301.

(77) Lindesmith (1966), xxvi.

(78) Blum (1970), 99ff., 125ff.

(79) Wilkins (1965), 91ff.

BIBLIOGRAPHY

<u>Note</u>: Recent key reference works and anthologies on drugs are marked by an asterisk.

*Andrews, George & Simon Vinkenoóg. <u>The Book of Grass: An Anthology of Indian Hemp</u>. New York: Grove Press, 1967.

Aswiter, John. <u>An Esssay on the Effects of Opium. Considered as a Poison. . .</u> London: G. Kearsly, 1763.

Becker, Howard S. <u>Outsiders: Studies in the Sociology of Deviance</u>. New York: Free Press, 1963.

Becker, Howard S. "The Marihuana Tax Act" in Solomon, 94-102, 1966.

*Bloomquist, E.R. ed. <u>Marijuana</u>. Beverly Hills, California: Glencoe Press, 1968.

*Blum, Richard H. & Associates. <u>Society and Drugs</u>. San Francisco: Jossey-Bass, 1970.

Cloward, Richard A. & Lloyd E. Ohlin. <u>Delinquency and Opportunity: A Theory of Delinquent Gangs</u>. New York: Free Press, 1960.

DeQuincey, Thomas. <u>Confessions of an English Opium Eater and Other Writings</u>. New York: New American Library, repr. 1966.

East India, Royal Commission Opium. <u>Reports</u>. 7 volumes, 1894-1895.

<u>Encyclopedia Brittanica; or, a Dictionary of Arts and Sciences. . .</u> By a Society of Gentlemen in Scotland. 3 volumes, 1st edition. Edinburgh: A. Bell & C. Macfarquhar.

Freeman, Douglas S. <u>George Washington: A Biography</u>. 7 volumes. New York: Scribner, 1948-1957.

Fuller, Richard & Richard Myers. "Some Aspects of a Theory of Social Problems." <u>American Sociological Review</u> (February), 6:24-32, 1941.

Fuller, Richard & Richard Myers. "The Natural History of a Social Problem." <u>American Sociological Review</u> (June), 6:320-328, 1941.

Gautier, Theophile. "The Hashish Club." R.A. Gladstone, trans. Solomon 163-178, repr. 1966.

Gould, Julius & William L. Kolb, ed. <u>A Dictionary of the Social Sciences</u>. New York: Free Press.

Herodotus. <u>The Histories</u>. de Selincourt, Aubrey, Trans. Baltimore: Penguin, 1954 ed.

Hess, Albert G. <u>Chasing the Dragon: A Report on Drug Addiction in Hong Kong</u>. Amsterdam & New York: North-Holle Publishing Company and Free Press, 1965

Hess, Albert G. "Deviance Theory and the History of Opiates." International Journal of the Addictions 6(4):585-598, 1971.

Hillery, G.A. "Definitions of Community: Areas of Agreement." Rural Sociology, 20:111-123, 1955.

Holmstedt, Bo. "Introduction" to Moreau (repr. 1973), ix ff, 1973.

Homer The Odyssey: The Story of Odysseus. W.H.D. Rouse, trans. New York: New American Library, 1937.

James, Robert. A Medical Dictionary With a History of Drugs. 3 volumes. London: as quoted by Sonnedeckes (1963), 12, 1743.

Jermstadt, A. Das Opium: Seine Kultur und Verwertung. Vienna: A. Hartleben, 1921.

Jones, John. The Mysteries of Opium Revealed. London: Richard Smith, 1701.

Kaempfer, E. Amoenitatum, Exoticarum Politico-Physico-Medicarum Fasciculi V. Lemgovia: Meyer, 1712.

*King, Rufus. The Drug Hang-up: America's Fifty-Year Folly. Springfield, Illinois: Thomas, 1972.

Kitsuse, John I. & Malcolm Spector. "Toward a Sociology of Social Problems: Social Conditions, Value-Judgments, and Social Problems." Social Problems 20(4): 407-419, 1973.

Kritikos, P.G. & Papadaki, S. "A History of Opium in Antiquity." Bulletin of Narcotics. (October/December), 19(4):5-10, 1967.

Leary, Timothy. "The Politics, Ethics and Meanings of Marijuana." Solomon (1966), 121-140, 1966.

Lemert, Edwin M. "Social Problems." International Encyclopedia of the Social Sciences. New York: Macmillan & Free Press, 14, 452-458, 1968.

Lindesmith, Alfred R. "Introduction." Solomon (1966), xxv-xxviii, 1966.

Lindesmith, Alfred R. Addiction and Opiates. Chicago: Aldine, 1968.

Ludlow, Fitz High. The Hashish Eater. (org. publ. 1857). repr. Upper Saddle River, New Jersey: Literature House/Gregg Press, repr. 1970.

Macht, David I. "The History of Opium and Some of Its Preparations and Alcaloids." Journal of the American Medical Association (February 6). 64:447-448.

Merton, Robert K. "Social Problems and Sociological Theory." Merton, Robert K. & Robert A. Nisbet Contemporary Social Problems. 3rd ed. New York: Harcourt Brace Jovanovich, 793-845, 1971.

Moreau (de Tours), Jacques-Joseph. Hashish and Mental Illness. G.J. Barnett, trans.; H. Peters & G.G. Nahas, eds. New York: Raven Press, repr. 1973.

*Musto, David F. The American Disease: Origins of Narcotic Control. New Haven: Yale University Press, 1973.

Neligan, Anthony R. The Opium Question; with Special References to Persia. London: J. Bale, Sons & Danielsson, 1927.

Oteri, Joseph S. & Silverglate, Harvey A. "In the Market Place of Free Ideas: The Marijuana Tax Act," Simmons, 136-162, 1967.

Oxford English Dictionary, The Complete Edition of. 2 Volumes. Micrographic edition. Glasgow, etc.: Oxford University Press, 1971.

Rabelais, Francois. "The Herb Pantagrauelian," from the Third book of Pantagruel, repr. in Solomon (1966), 145-162, 1966 ed.

Reininger, W. "Historical Notes." Solomon (1966), 141-142, 1966.

Reininger W. "Remnants from Prehistoric Times." Andrews (1967), 14-15, 1967.

Rose, Arnold M. "Social Problem." Gould Kolb, 662-663, 1964.

*Simmons, J.L. ed. Marijuana: Myth and Realities. North Hollywood, California: Brandon House, 1967.

Sjoberg, Gideon. "Community" in Gould & Kolb, 114-115, 1964.

Smith, William G. An Opium: Embracing Its History, Chemical Analysis and Use and Abuse as a Medicine. New York, 1832.

Snyder, Solomon H. "What We have Forgotten about Pot − A Pharmacologist's History." New York Times Magazine (Dec. 13, 1970), 26-27, 121, 125-126, 129-134, 1970.

*Solomon, David ed. The Marihuana Papers. New York: New American Library, 1966.

Sonnedecker, Glenn.   Emergence of the Concept of Opiate Addiction. Madison, Wisconsin: American Institute of the History of Pharmacy, c. 1963.

Spector, Malcolm & John I. Kitsuse. "Social Problems: A Re-Formulation." Social Problems (Fall 1973):21(2):145-159, 1973.

Taylor, Bayard. The Lands of the Sararen; or Pictures of Palestine, Asia Minor, Sicily and Spain. (First American edition: New York: G.P. Putnam & Co., 1856 − In the British edition title and subtitle are reversed, 1855.

*Taylor, Norman. Narcotics: Nature's Dangerous Drugs. New York: Dell, 1963.

*Terry, Charles E. & Mildred Pelleus. The Opium Problem. New York: Bureau of Social Hygiene. (Montclair, New Jersey: P. Smith, repr.)

Tobias, J.J. Crime and Industrial Society in the Nineteenth Century. New York: Schocker Books, 1967.

Treese, George E. Pharmacy in History. London: Bailliere, Tindall & Cox, 1964.

Van Linschoten, J.H. Itineraria Voyage ofte Schipvaert . . . naer Oost ofte Portugaels Indien 1579-1592, repr. The Hague:Nijhoff,repr.1966.

Walton, Robert. "Therapeutic Application of Marihuana." Solomon 447-454, 1966.

Washington, George. "Diary Notes." Andrews (1967), 34, repr. 1967.

Wilkins, Leslie T. Social Deviance: Social Policy Action and Research. Englewood Cliffs, New Jersey: Prentice Hall, 1965.

Wilson, J.C. & A.A. Eshner. American Textbook of Applied Therapeutics. Terry & Pelleus (1970 repr.), 104, 1896.

2 Australia and New Zealand

D.S. Bell

HISTORY AND SOCIAL BACKGROUND

The use of alcohol in Australia and New Zealand is more extensive than that of any other drug and produces the largest drug problem in these communities. The first colony was practically baptized, bathed, and raised on rum; the early history of New South Wales, the mother colony, can be described in terms of the trade in rum that corrupted the law enforcement bodies and demoralized the early settlers.

In 1768 Captain Cook set out on a voyage of discovery in which he sailed round New Zealand and up the east coast of Australia, landing in 1770 on the coast where Sydney now stands. In 1776 the transportation of convicts from England to America was halted abruptly by the American Revolution. While the convicts were crowded into the hulks on the Thames and elsewhere to an increasingly intolerable degree, the search for a new dumping ground gained urgency. Persuaded by Lord Sydney, the English Parliament decided to dispose of their unwanted criminals by sending them to this new land. The first group of convicts and their guards founded the colony in 1788.

In the early days the ships that called at port were few and far between. Some of these visitors were American ships, carrying the rum that played a large part in the economy of the slave trade (Bacon, 1967). At each visit the sudden availability of rum resulted in widespread drunkenness, violence, and debauchery, a temporary state of lawlessness known as the "rum riots." In a short space of time rum became the focus round which the commercial, political, and recreational life of the colony revolved. The community was desperately short of practically all the material necessities, including coins of the realm. Barter had to take the place of monetary transactions and rum virtually became the currency. By 1802 the annual consumption of imported alcohol was almost six gallons of rum and three gallons of wine for every man, woman, and child of the 5,800 population (Dax, 1975).

The control of the colony passed increasingly into the hands of the New South Wales Corps, a body of men whose officers were selected in much the same way as the convincts they guarded, that is, more because of their failings than their quality. Some had been disgraced, some were evading active service in the Napoleonic Wars, some had bought their commission, and some were actually fleeing justice (Evatt, 1971, p. 25). Within the space of six years they extended their power to exercise the control of administering criminal justice. They were granted land and assigned convicts on a generous scale. Every officer belonged to the trading ring, which had first call on all merchandise sent out by the British government. In particular they obtained the practical monopoly of the sale of all imported spirits within the colony, the "rum monopoly."

Having exclusive control of the "rum currency," they were able to force others to accept rum at highly inflated prices in payment for services or goods. In a short time they richly deserved the title of the "rum regiment." They placed a value on the rum of four to five times the price they paid and they sold the products they purchased by barter to the King's stores at the highest rates. Those of their victims who drank freely what they were paid were soon in desperate straits.

> A pannikin of rum would bring oblivion of reality. Rum clouded memories of agonized screams that came from the flogging post. It deadened tortures of mind and body suffered in the rigours of this harsh land and softened the barbarity of exile. Rum made a man forget a failing farm, the muscle-straining back-breaking labour that none was fit for, half-starved convicts as most were, or had been, the very core of their lives torn out by slavery and the lash.
>
> Women drank with the men, seeking forgetfulness of home. Surrendered to misery, they were sunk in a morass of their own making and they drank themselves into a stupor to forget it (Pullen, 1975, p. 56).

The reign of the "rum corps" was to last only twenty years, but not before reaching the climax of the "rum rebellion." The governors of New South Wales, all naval men in this period, lacked the ability and the power to control the corps. In 1805 Governor Bligh, survivor of the mutiny on the Bounty, was appointed to bring order to the colony. Bligh suffered three mutinies against his authority during his lifetime. He was probably not the cruel tyrant that some historians and Hollywood have claimed, but rather was a strong man trying to administer his command firmly and impartially and making an effort to bring about essential reforms (Evatt, 1971, chap. 13). His strength brought him almost to success in controlling the "rum monopoly" and his impartiality put him above the possibility of corruption.

The only measure left to the officers of the corps to retain their privileges was mutiny. At their subsequent trial in London, Bligh's reputation was completely upheld. The corps was disbanded and the next governor to be appointed was a military officer who was accompanied by his own regular army unit. This man, Governor Macquarie, did not attempt to break the "rum monopoly." Instead he made it a privilege to be bought from the government. Sydney Hospital, known as the "rum hospital" and to this day sporting a rum puncheon in the center of its heraldic device, was built free of charge by three private individuals in return for a monopoly of the importation of 45,000 gallons of rum. The rumors were that they probably managed to import as much as three times this amount. By 1820 Governor Bourke pleaded in a letter to London that, "A lunatic asylum is an establishment that can no longer be dispensed with. In this Colony the use of ardent spirits induces the disease called delirium tremens, which frequently terminates in confirmed insanity" (Dax, 1975). Among the admissions to the lunatic asylum in 1848, almost as many women as men were alcoholics.

Other colonies in Australia and New Zealand did not suffer the same type of political and economic hardships engendered by a corrupt military administration, but naturally they endured the difficulties created by the other factors such as the strange environment, exile, and the scarcity of food and materials. The discovery of gold in the mid-nineteenth century attracted many immigrants and gave the colonies their first major impetus to rapid development. In 1859 Howitt wrote: "Drunkenness goes on in the diggings uncontrolled. It is carried on in the most open, palpable, public manner possible. You could not avoid running your head against crowds of drunken diggers, your nose against the fumes of vile rum, and your ears against the din and uproar of dozens of dens of debauch. . . . Grog shops abound, notwithstanding the professed severity of the police; and we hear the noisy set of roisterers at them night after night, singing, fighting and shouting, generally till the morning" (Holloway, 1967, p. 4).

As a measure of reform, the administration subsidized the brewing of beer to replace spirits in New South Wales. The first breweries failed commercially, but gradually Australians were induced to turn to this form of alcohol. Unfortunately, the consequences of alcohol use did not change in the hoped for direction. Today the majority of alcoholics in Australia do not drink spirits at all, only beer (Wilkinson et al., 1969).

In the 1850s a roisterous tavern life continued to flourish (Saint, 1970). Pearl (1965) described Sydney in 1880, with a population of 288,000 people and 3,167 hotels, as a place where drunkenness was common at all levels of society and accompanied by a gross public indifference to the scandalous behavior it caused. The increase in restrictions on sale introduced in the early 20th century produced much improvement, but in the past few decades these have been relaxed again to be followed in a short period by indications that the former scale of use may be returning. Encel and Kotowicz (1970) found that "for virtually every population sub-group heavy drinking is the characteristic pattern for males." Rankin (1971) summarized a review of Australian statistics to state that approximately 80 percent of men and 70 percent of women drink alcoholic beverages and that 10 percent of the men were either constant or intermittent excessive drinkers. This scale of use, massive as it is, continues to increase (Bell et al., 1975), most rapidly of all among young people. In 1976 Australians were the highest consumers of alcohol in the English-speaking world, with an annual intake of almost 13 liters per person over the age of 15 years. Each year this increases by 5 percent. If it continues, by 1990 Australia will have

> . . . outstripped France as the top drinking nation of the world, provided of course that in the world-wide trend of increasing alcohol consumption (de Lint, 1975) some other nation does not seize this dubious laurel first. As it is, the per capita consumption of beer in Australia is among the highest of any nation in the world (Sulkunen, 1976).

Associated with this high and increasing consumption of alcohol is a "high degree of approval for the drinking of alcohol in large quantities" (Hetzel, 1975). A leading trade unionist in Australia featured in the Guinness Book of World Records (1971) for many years because he held the OxfordUniversity "sconce" record of 12.0 seconds for downing two pints of beer in 1955. The same book of records noted that whereas the nation with the highest beer consumption per person was West Germany, with 29.9 gallons per person in 1969, in the Northern Territory of Australia the annual intake was estimated to be as high as 52 gallons per person. The figures gain significance when it is appreciated that the alcohol content of Australian beer is considerably higher than that in Germany.

The group with the highest consumption rate of all in Australia is the aboriginal adult male population, of whom in certain areas an estimated 53.2 percent are heavy drinkers and 31.4 percent problem drinkers (Kamien, 1975b). The fate of the aborigines has been determined by factors identical to those seen in many other countries colonized by Europeans; for that matter their susceptibility to alcohol is identical to   the vulnerability of any community or racial group to the introduction of a drug new to its culture and consequently not subject to long-standing cultural and social controls on its use (Bell, 1970). The disastrous effect of alcohol on the aborigines was observed from the first days of the colony. In 1824 Lesson, a visitor to the new colony, observed that the aborigines had "acquired from European civilisation only an inordinate taste for tobacco and strong drink. . . . These unfortunate savages, when drunk, often quarrel in the middle of the Sydney streets, where circles form to urge them to fight until one of their champions is forced to beg for mercy, for their combat consists of delivering, turn and turn about, blows of a club to the top of the skull; the one who collapses under the impact is defeated" (Royle, 1973).

After alcohol was introduced to the aborigines, the culture they developed around its use was based on the obvious European models they saw around them of drunken excess. Those few white men who drank in moderation usually did so in private, whereas the public model was the brawling drunken white man at the hotel bar (Beckett, 1964). The "rum riots" in the early days of old Sydney town set the pace. In the vast hinterland where the majority of aborigines lived, the pastoral workers spent long periods alone in the sparsely populated grazing stations, at intervals coming to town to squander their pay checks in a few days of heavy drinking.

The aboriginal male, bereft suddenly of his own culture and his traditional methods of entertainment in folk dancing, singing of ceremonial songs, and the performance of complicated sacred rites, was left with little else for passing his leisure hours beyond drinking; his use of alcohol, tobacco, other drugs, and gambling is a caricature of the European culture he saw around him. He did not regard drunkenness as an aberration or a crime. The partly inebriated aboriginal even tends to exaggerate the symptoms of drunkenness, ostentatiously staggering around and quarreling noisily to attract the esteem afforded a "man." For the adolescent male, drunkenness and arrest by the police could almost be regarded as a form of initiation rite. "Their parties are conducted with a maximum of noise and exhibitionism. They stagger about even more unsteadily than they need to and their endless brawls are accompanied by challenges and abuse which are audible from one end of the settlement to the other" (Beckett, 1964).

In many settlements practically all that remains of the original aboriginal culture is the group sharing of wealth. The community has ceased to expect of its members a strict observance of any moral code, but there remains the general assurance that neighbors and kinsfolk will extend food, clothing, and other help in times of adversity. This lack of organized sanctions or economic demands has reduced the mass to a severe degree of poverty and demoralization. The group pressure hinders the member who wishes to become economically self-reliant or adopt a higher standard of living. The policies adopted by the white man have failed to solve this dilemma.

Stringent restrictions of the aboriginal's right to drink were introduced in New South Wales through the Supply of Liquor to Aborigines Prevention Act of 1867 (repealed in 1962). In other states similar provisions persisted for longer or still remain. Unfortunately the act was more often breached than observed. The police were ineffective in preventing the supply of liquor to aborigines. Europeans were rarely charged with this offense, but the aborigines were commonly arrested for drunkenness. In consequence, the aborigines came into sharpest conflict with European society over drinking and the fines and prison sentences they suffered were disproportionately high in relation to the rest of the Australian society. Now that the restrictions have been repealed, the situation is possibly even worse, but promising moves are being initiated by the aborigines themselves through the Central Australian Aborigines Congress, which has developed a pickup service for drunks at Alice Springs and is planning to purchase a farm to serve as a night shelter and a halfway house (Perkins, 1975 and 1976).

New Zealand has in the main been subject to the same influences that affected Australia.The Maoris fared much better than the Australian aborigines mainly because they had a more advanced technology, were able to wage organized warfare, and they became better integrated with the white population, particularly after the Maori Wars that were fought between 1845 and 1865. Both countries experienced gold rushes at much the same time, suffered depressions, and the adverse effects of falls in the price of their main products, wool and wheat (Dax, 1975). Australia and New Zealand have shared a good record of pioneering moves in early social legislation, but this has not necessarily included an advanced approach to alcoholism or other forms of drug dependence.

Both communities inherited their drinking pattern from the English and Irish models of the last century. The public hotel has the structural characteristics of the English pub, with its long bar "analagous to similar linear processes ushered in by the mass production methods of the industrial revolution" (Csikszentmihalyi, 1968). This structural organization has the advantage that individuals can move about freely without inconvenience to each other and can even remain isolated in the interpersonal sense although in close proximity. Above all it permits rapid mass sale and drinking in limited time, for example, before the pub closed in the days not so long ago when this was strictly enforced for all at 6:00 p.m. The evening pub rush became infamous as the "six o'clock swill."

The Irish, the second largest migrant group in the first 100 years of settlement, brought with them the cultural attitude of tolerance for drunkenness, contributing to their high rate of alcoholism (Walsh, 1972). The recognition of this cultural influence in Australia is summarized in the saying, "You do not have to be Irish to be an alcoholic, but it helps," a trend also noted in the United States, Scotland, and England (Walsh, 1969).

In both nations the consumption of drugs follows the pattern of Western communities. Tobacco is used extensively, joining alcohol as the most widely used drugs of dependence. The use of sedatives and minor tranquilizers is considerable, pratically among females. Stimulants were used in large amounts until their prescription was prohibited for most purposes in the late 1960s. Perhaps the only distinctive national feature of the Australian scene is the exceptionally high consumption of nonnarcotic analgesics such as aspirin and compound preparations with phenacetin or paracetamol, being 50 times the rate of North America (Royal Australasian College of Physicians, 1969). The prevalence of complications such as analgesic nephropathy or gastric ulcer is correspondingly high.

No cause has been recognized for this exceptionally high consumption of analgesics. Possibly the skillful and aggressive merchandising of certain proprietary brands was the significant influence, particularly on women. One particular advertisement aimed particularly at women remained unchanged over decades, possibly a unique record for durability among messages of this type, promising that the drug could be taken with "confidence." What is more likely is that the drug is taken to achieve "confidence." Confidence is the word used most often by drug users to explain the desirable results they seek from drug use and possibly indicates the essence of what is sought in drug use and leads to psychological dependence (Bell, 1975).

The use of drugs by the aborigines of Australia follows the model of the Europeans for analgesics as well as alcohol; women have a much lower rate of alcoholism than men (Kamien, 1975b) and the reverse applies for analgesics (Kamien, 1975a).

The use of volatile inhalants has been known for many years in

Australia, but the practice has remained relatively uncommon and restricted to young people in early adolescence. A singular exception has been the practice of petrol sniffing, which has become a common practice among the aboriginal children in the Northern Territory and which bears close resemblance in its pattern to the problem among children in North America (Tomlinson, 1975). Deaths have been reported among the general population, once again in early adolescence, resulting from the inhalation of the inert propellant gas from pressure pack sprays, the aim being to produce anoxia, which is also the cause of death.

Stimulants enjoyed a vogue in Australia, beginning in Sydney in the 1950s with the activities of an eccentric Bohemian cult that practiced "black magic." Led by a "witch," the group practiced sadistic rites on cats and perverse sexuality on themselves, using amphetamines as an adjuvant. Although the group tended to be exclusive, the willing neophytes congregated at a coffee house run by a church body and from this focus began the friendship that spread among the disturbed and deviant of Sydney. In the 1960s amphetamine use became widespread throughout Australia. At a later stage visitors frequenting this unconventional drug referral center were offered aid by a "social worker," a man recruited with no better qualification than a notorious criminal career and an apparent desire to reform. Under cover of this disguise he organized a gang that committed many brutal armed holdups until it was apprehended. The fringe area of addiction attracts many fringe people, "helpers" as well as sufferers.

Narcotics use has a longer history in New Zealand than Australia. Before the discovery of gold the use of narcotics in New Zealand was confined to opium taken orally. Gold miners from California introduced a demand for American nostrums containing morphine and cocaine and the Chinese who followed them to the fields brought with them the habit of opium smoking (Ashforth, 1970). After these stormy times, narcotics misuse became almost entirely restricted to the small Chinese population. During the last few decades most of those affected had acquired their habit before immigrating to New Zealand.

In the 1940s drug use was not policed closely and the total heroin consumption rose almost threefold. New Zealand was "named" by the international control authority as one of the world's highest per capita users. Efforts for more strenuous control were begun in 1949. Importation of heroin was suspended in 1953 and as a result of restriction on the prescription of heroin, by 1955 its use was virtually eliminated from hospital practice. The next major outbreak occurred in the mid-1960s. In retrospect it is realized that it began with an outbreak of narcotic use around the area of Hastings in the 1950s (Ashforth, 1970). Up to 1963 the persons charged with offenses under the narcotics and poisons acts were mostly Chinese involved in opium smoking. In 1965 and 1966 special police squads made intensive efforts to stamp out the habit and finally closed the last of the city opium dens. Any pleasure at this success was quickly lost with the realization that a much larger problem was growing in the European population. The numbers charged with narcotics offenses increased from 10 in 1965 to 28 in 1966, 50 in 1967 and 153 in 1968. The numbers admitted to a hospital with a diagnosis of drug dependence increased from 43 in 1965 to 59 in 1966, 70 in 1967 and 110 in 1968. In 1969 of those seen at the Alcoholism and Drug Addiction Centers 85 percent were between the ages of 14 and 20 (Board of Health, 1970).

This outbreak of narcotics use was treated as energetically as in the past with strong police measures, and offenders were sent to a prison farm or compulsorily committed to a closed security ward at Oakley Psychiatric Hospital. One consequence was that many narcotics users fled New Zealand to the more tolerant shores of Australia, where they initiated the epidemic of narcotics use that was still extant and growing in 1976, a pattern of initiation and spread not unlike the experience witnessed in the United Kingdom when narcotics users fled authority in Canada and initiated the heroin epidemic in complacent Britain. Drug addicts are possibly the most mobile of all population groups in Australia, moving freely from city to city evading law enforcement officers. Their moves include a "hippie circuit" through Southeast Asia, from Malaysia through Thailand to India, where they can obtain heroin cheaply or even take part in the lucrative drug smuggling to Australia and New Zealand.

THE CURRENT SITUATION

Alcohol

Some idea of the current extent of alcohol use in the community has been given above. The data from recent surveys are summarized in table 2.1. The distribution pattern of alcohol consumption established for a sample of the population of Melbourne follows the long normal curve (Hetzel, 1975) characteristic of other countries (Smart and Whitehead, 1973). The increasing consumption of alcohol between 1949 and 1971 indicates that in this period the number of people consuming more than 100 cc absolute alcohol per day had almost doubled, in 1971 being 6.46 percent of the population (Hetzel, 1975).

These habits begin early. By age 16 years, only 9 percent of boys and 10 percent of girls attending school in New South Wales have never tasted alcohol and most were introduced to drinking in their homes (Egger et al., 1975). The data for the various states of Australia are so similar that most surveys can be considered representative of the nation as a whole. The young drink more with increasing age and the males start earlier and drink more heavily than the females. Schoolchildren in Canberra reach the average adult male consumption by about age 16 years and exceed the average by age 17 years (Irwin, 1975). Drinking for young males aged 18 to 21 years correlates with a "need for power" and validates their self-conception as adults and their claims to adult status (Critchley and Gardner, 1975).

Certain groups of young people reach higher levels still of alcohol consumption; for example, 53 percent of apprentices and 43 percent of school dropouts drink most days of the week (Graves, 1973), but even of those still attending school 11 percent consumed ten or more drinks a

Table 2.1. Rates of Alcohol Use

Year	Reference	Sample Number	Population	Age	Current Users %	Use Most Days %
1968	Rankin and Wilkinson, 1971	1,600	Melbourne suburb	20+	84.3 (M) 68.3 (F)	7.9 (M) 1.1 (F)
1968/69	Encel and Kotowicz, 1970	820	Sydney adults		91.0 (M) 82.0 (F)	—
1969	Connell et al., 1975	8,000	Sydney school students	15-16	28.0 (M)* 12.0 (F)*	
				17-18	42.0 (M)* 28.0 (F)*	
1970	Connell et al., 1975	2,000	Sydney youth, left school	15-16	45.0 (M)* 18.0 (F)*	
				17-18	70.0 (M)* 35.0 (F)*	
1971	Bell et al., 1975	7,000	N.S.W.;†	15-19	77.6	5.1
1971	Hennessy et al., 1973	135	Canberra	13-18	56.7	—
1971	Kamien, 1975 b	250	Aboriginals		90.3 (M) 29.0 (F)	— —

37

Table 2.1 (cont'd.)

Year	Reference	Sample Number	Population	Age	Current Users %	Use Most Days %
1971	George, 1972	650	Sydney suburb	14+	84.0 (M) 80.0 (F)	17.7 (total)
1972	Bell et al., 1975	7,500	N.S.W.†	15-19	77.6	6.1
1972	Graves, 1973	1,600	Melbourne	13-23	88.7	7.0
1973	Bell et al., 1975	7,500	N.S.W.†	15-19	80.2	6.2
1973	Healy, 1975	1,000	Sydney suburb	14+	81.0 (M) 65.0 (F)	10.1 (total)
1973	Irwin, 1975	5,000	Canberra high school students	12-17	49.8	
1974	Irwin, 1975	5,000	As above		49.5	
1974	Egger et al., 1975	2,700	N.S.W.† school students	15	90.0 (M) 82.0 (F)	
1974	Carrington-Smith, 1974	500	Hobart women	18-60	85.0	10.8
1974	Turner and McLure, 1975	3,300	Queensland high school students	11-17	61.6 (M) 48.8 (F)	8.0 (total)

*Use at least once a week   †New South Wales

Fig. 2.1. The young equate drinking with adult status.

day on drinking days. Egger et al. (1975) found that as many as 3.6 percent of male schoolchildren aged 16 years or more are "problem users" and 21.9 percent "potential problem users." This may be the reason for the exceedingly high rate of road accidents and deaths among males aged less than 25 years in Australia. In urban areas alcoholism in male adolescents equals that in the adult male population (Stoller and Krupinski, 1974) and alcoholism accounts for 88 percent of the total admission rates for drug dependence to psychiatric hospitals (Kraus, 1973). In general, parents seem to be aware that their children drink alcohol, but unaware that they are drinking so much (Turner and McClure, 1975).

The surveys by Bell et al. (1975) of drug use in New South Wales provide data for each of three years, 1971-1973, for comparable populations of young people, ranging along the continuum from low to high deviancy, that is, from a complete cross section of high school students to delinquent youth committed to institutions, and in the age range from 15 to 19 years. The surveys were designed to permit monitoring of drug use in the community on an annual basis and to establish trends in use and attitudes that may predict developments in the immediate future. This data will be referred to in the case of each group of drugs.

Using the trends in prevalence of use as a criterion of change was found to be misleading for alcohol, simply because these groups for practical purposes had reached saturation point. The majority of school students used alcohol, as many as 7 percent of males in sixth grade using it most days of the week. On the other hand, using as the criterion of change the prevalence of heavy use established a steady increase over the three-year period.

Tobacco

Tobacco smoking is also extensive among the adult and adolescent population (Table 2.2). Until recently males smoked more than females, but the trends (Bell et al., 1975) reveal that here as elsewhere in the world women are rapidly catching up and may soon smoke more than males. Tobacco use increases with age and those groups that consume alcohol at an earlier age and in large quantities also smoke more than the average (Graves, 1973). As with alcohol the prevalence of use did not increase, probably because it had reached saturation point, but heavy use did increase over the years 1971-1973 (Bell et al., 1975); in 1973 almost 20 percent of schoolchildren sampled used tobacco daily.

Sedatives, Hypnotics, and Minor Tranquillizers

Whereas alcoholism is more common among males, dependence on most other legally available drugs is more common among the females in this community (Whitlock and Lowrey, 1967). Sedatives and hypnotics, and more recently the so-called "minor tranquillizers," comprise the largest single group of drugs prescribed by medical practitioners in Australia (Rankin, 1971) and the use of self-prescribed drugs is probably even more extensive. In a household survey of one community in Victoria, Traralgon, nearly 60 percent of all medication was self-prescribed

Fig. 2.2. Women are rapidly catching up and may soon smoke more than males.

Table 2.2. Rates of Tobacco Use

Year	Reference	Sample Number	Population	Age	Current Users %	Heavy Users* %
1967/68	Edmondson et al., 1969	26,000	Australian school students	15	37.4 (M) 14.7 (F)	— —
1968	Rankin & Wilkinson, 1971	550	Melbourne	15-24	43.1 (M) 39.9 (F)	13.4 (M) 8.7 (F)
1969	Connell et al., 1975	8,000	Sydney school students	15-16	25.0 (M)** 12.0 (F)**	
				17-18	28.0 (M)** 10.0 (F)**	
1970	Connell et al., 1975	2,000	Sydney youth, left school	15-16	55.0 (M)** 35.0 (F)**	
				17-18	58.0 (M)** 33.0 (F)**	
1971	Bell et al., 1975	7,000	N.S.W.+	15-19	39.4	—
1971	Hennessy et al., 1973	136	Canberra	13-18	22.1	2.6
1971	George, 1972	650	Sydney suburb	14+	50.6 (M) 44.3 (F)	14.9 (M) 5.1 (F)

Table 2.2 (Cont'd.)

Year	Reference	Sample Number	Population	Age	Current Users %	Heavy Users* %
1972	Bell et al., 1975	7,500	N.S.W.†	15-19	42.1	2.0
1972	Graves, 1973	1,600	Melbourne	13-23	49.0 (M) 40.0 (F)	13.0 (M) 6.0 (F)
1973	Bell et al., 1975	7,500	N.S.W.†	15-19	41.4	2.0
1973	Healy, 1975	1,000	Sydney suburb		51.0 (M) 33.0 (F)	—
1973	Irwin, 1975	5,000	Canberra high school students	12-17	27.0	—
1974	Irwin, 1975	5,000	As above		28.1	—

*20 or more cigarettes daily
**Use at least once a week
†New South Wales

(Bridges-Webb, 1972). The incidence of dependence on these drugs is correspondingly high (Abrahams et al., 1970). The use of sedatives increases with age, the steady progression producing a rate of 46.3 percent users among females aged 50 59 years in the household survey conducted in a suburb of Sydney (George, 1972). Until 1971 bromides were available without prescription in most states of Australia. They were the most common nonprescription drugs sold by pharmacists (Ranking, 1971) and the finding of a serum bromide level above normal or of bromism was common in psychiatric patients (Andrews, 1965; Sainsbury, 1967), specifically in 12 percent of alcoholics (Wilkinson et al., 1971) and in 25 percent of middle-aged female admissions (Kessell, 1969).

The data of recent surveys are summarized in Table 2.3. Bell et al., (1975) found that sedative use had not altered from 1971 to 1973 in their population samples, with the one ominous exception of an increase in the group of nurses. Over this same period the specific drugs used did alter, the use of barbiturates declining largely as a result of progressively severe restrictions that commenced in 1967 on prescribing of prescriptions through the national Pharmaceutical Benefits Scheme. Over the same period the use of diazepam and other sedatives rose steeply. The fluctuations in consumption of barbiturates in Australia have shown a dramatic relationship to the suicide rates. Suicide rose steeply from 1960 to 1967, parallel with a steep rise in barbiturate use, largely as a consequence of the overgenerous provision made for their prescription through the Pharmaceutical Benefits Scheme, and since then both the suicide rates and barbiturate use have shown a parallel decline (Oliver and Hetzel, 1972).

Among the nonbarbiturate sedatives, methaqualone, particularly in the combination known as "Mandrax," (Quaaludes in America) has become recognized as producing a particularly pernicious form of chronic intoxication associated with involuntary muscular movements and hallucinatory and delirious effects. It seems to be particularly favored by heroin addicts.

Analgesics

The exceptionally high use in Australia of nonnarcotic analgesics has been noted above. Purnell and Burry (1967) estimated from the extent of analgesic consumption in a country town that 4 percent of its population had already suffered appreciable kidney damage. Use increases with age and is more extensive in the lowest social classes, regular daily consumption being as high as 21.7 percent for females in social grades six and seven (Gillies and Skyring, 1972). As in the case for alcohol and other drugs, among young people higher levels of use are more common in working youth (17 percent) than in children still in school and higher still (24 percent) for school dropouts (Graves, 1973). Use is also very high in the aboriginal population; in a household survey of a part-aboriginal community 45.1 percent of women had used analgesic powders on the day of interview (Kamien, 1975a). Analgesic

Table 2.3. Rates of Sedative, Hypnotic, and Tranquillizer Use

Year	Reference	Sample Number	Population	Age	Ever Used %	Current Users %
1968	Unisearch, 1968	5,600	Sydney & Brisbane	15+	21.8	15.3
1971	Bell et al., 1975	7,000	N.S.W.†	15-19	29.0	15.9
1971	George, 1972	650	Sydney suburb	14+	33.0	16.6
1971	Hennessy et al., 1973	136	Canberra	13-18	4.5	—
1972	Bell et al., 1975	7,500	N.S.W.†	15-19	30.7	15.3
1972	Graves, 1973	1,600	Melbourne	13-23	Sleeping tablets "Tables for nerves"	11.3 9.7
1973	Bell et al., 1975	7,500	N.S.W.†	15-19	31.6	16.0
1973	Healy, 1975	1,000	Sydney suburb	14+	32.0	13.0
1973	Irwin, 1975	5,000	Canberra high school students	12-17	5.3	—
1974	Irwin, 1975	5,000	As above		5.1	
1974	Carrington-Smith, 1974	500	Hobart women	18-60	55.0	17.6

†New South Wales

use is particularly extensive among female unskilled process workers in factories. Ferguson (1973) established in one nationwide organization that the use of alcohol, tobacco, and analgesics was highest in the branch with the most stressful environment. The data from recent surveys are summarized in Table 2.4.

Marijuana

All surveys in recent years (Table 2.5) indicate that the use of marijuana is increasing, current users in the school population of New South Wales reaching a prevalence of 15.3 percent in 1973 and in the same year over 26 percent of the deviant population used marijuana weekly (Bell et al., 1975). Users of marijuana were not only more likely to use other illicit drugs, but were also more likely than nonusers to use alcohol and tobacco heavily. The trends over the three years from 1971 to 1973 indicated that some groups had stabilized, the use reaching what would seem to have been a plateau stage, but other groups which tend to respond to change at a slower rate were still showing an upward trend. This suggests that given no further change in factors affecting use, the upward trend will flatten out within a few years.

Hallucinogens

Apart from the synthetic substances such as LSD, a variety of hallucinogenic fungi of the Psilocybe & Copelandia genera grow and are used in Australia (Hall, 1973). Nevertheless, the rates of hallucinogen use have remained relatively low in these communities (Table 2.6). Predictably the highest rate was obtained for the students in the creative arts, of whom over 15 percent used hallucinogens (Bell et al., 1975). An encouraging sign in the trends for 1971-1973 was that in those groups that responded most rapidly to change, the use of hallucinogens was dropping, but it was still rising in the groups that responded most slowly. The overall effect was that the use of hallucinogens increased marginally, but it does suggest that the rate will drop soon.

Stimulants

Before the sale of amphetamines was severely restricted in 1969 the usage of these drugs was extensive; in a survey of prisons, hospitals, and other institutions in Sydney, Briscoe and Hinterberger (1969) found that 6.6 percent of the urine specimens tested were positive for amphetamines and in a study of 100 drug-dependent clients of a drug referral center, Wheeler and Edmonds (1969) found that 80 had used stimulants. By 1970 most health authorities had restricted the prescription of amphetamines so severely that they virtually ceased to be used for medical purposes. The move was successful in that it resulted in an abrupt reduction in the availability of amphetamines to the illicit

Table 2.4. Rates of Analgesic Use

Year	Reference	Sample Number	Population	Age	Users %	Use Most Days %
1968	Unisearch, 1968	5,600	Sydney and Brisbane	15+	83.0	11.4
1968/70	Gillies and Skyring, 1972	2,900	Industrial and clerical workers and housewives			7.9 (M) 14.7 (F)
1970	Bridges-Webb, 1972	350	Provincial Victorian city, all ages		9.5 (children) 30.0 (elderly people) 19.3 (total)	
1971	Bell et al., 1975	7,000	N.S.W.†	15-19	91.2	2.1
1971	George, 1972	650	Sydney suburb	14+	72.4	11.6
1971	Hennessy et al., 1973	136	Canberra	13-18	68.4	0.7
1972	Bell et al., 1975	7,500	N.S.W.†	15-19	90.7	1.7
1972	Graves, 1973	1,600	Melbourne	13-23	73.4	4.6
1973	Bell et al., 1975	7,500	N.S.W.†	15-19	89.2	1.4
1973	Healy, 1975	1,000	Sydney suburb	14+	75.0	11.3

Table 2.4 (Cont'd.)

Year	Reference	Sample Number	Population	Age	Ever Used %	Current Users %
1973	Murrell and Moss, 1974	—	Adelaide infants	5-14 mos.	19.2	—
1973	Irwin, 1975	5,000	Canberra high school students	12-17	35.2	—
1974	Irwin, 1975	5,000	As above		30.8	—
1974	Carrington-Smith, 1974	500	Hobart women	18-60	85.0	11.7

†New South Wales

Table 2.5. Rates of Marijuana Use

Year	Reference	Sample Number	Population	Age	Ever Used %	Current Users %
1970	Hasleton, 1971	168	University students		17.9	12.5
1971	Bell et al., 1975	7,000	N.S.W.†	15-19	11.7	7.5
1971	George, 1972	650	Sydney suburb	14-29	20.4	12.4
1971	Hennessy et al., 1973	136	Canberra	13-18	3.7	—
1972	Bell et al., 1975	7,500	N.S.W.†	15-19	21.2	14.1
1972	Graves, 1973	1,600	Melbourne	13-23	16.2	11.2
1973	Bell et al., 1975	7,500	N.S.W.†	15-19	22.3	15.3
1973	Healy, 1975	1,000	Sydney suburb	14-29	10.6	4.9
1973	Irwin, 1975	5,000	Canberra high school students	12-17	4.0	—
1974	Irwin, 1975	5,000	As above	—	5.3	—

Table 2.5 (Cont'd.)

Year	Reference	Sample Number	Population	Age	Ever Used %	Current Users %
1974	Carrington-Smith, 1974	500	Hobart women	18-60	4.0	2.6
1974	Turner and McLure, 1975	3,300	Queensland school students	11-17	5.8 (M) 3.6 (F)	3.8 (M) 1.9 (F)

† New South Wales

49

Table 2.6. Rates of Hallucinogen Use

Year	Reference	Sample Number	Population	Age	Ever Used %	Current Users %
1971	Bell et al., 1975	7,000	N.S.W.†	15-19	4.2	2.6
1971	George, 1972	650	Sydney suburb	14-29	3.9	1.6
1972	Bell et al., 1975	7,500	N.S.W.†	15-19	7.6	4.8
1972	Graves, 1973	1,600	Melbourne	13-23	5.6	3.1
1973	Bell et al., 1975	7,500	N.S.W.†	15-19	8.2	4.5
1973	Healy, 1975	1,000	Sydney suburb	14-29	3.9	1.6
1973/74	Irwin, 1975	5,000	Canberra high school	12-17	1.7	–
1974	Carrington-Smith, 1974	500	Hobart women	18-60	1.2	0.4
1974	Turner and McLure, 1975	3,300	Queensland school students	11-17	2.8 (M) 1.8 (F)	2.0 (M) 1.0 (F)

† New South Wales

50

market and in its illicit use. Unfortunately, heroin use seemed to take its place.

The surveys summarized in Table 2.7 all follow this period and indicate that illicit use continued, but the prevailing trend being a gradual drop in use. In the three years from 1971 to 1973 the use of stimulants decreased significantly each year in the school population and among general nurses, in other groups changing little (Bell et al., 1975). The trends for the stimulants and hallucinogens revealed divergent changes. While stimulant use decreased, the perception of danger from the stimulants increased and the reverse applied to the hallucinogens. Bell et al. (1975) pointed out that health education programs may have been expected to have had a similar effect on the attitudes toward both groups of drugs, both having enjoyed similar treatment in the education material.   On the other hand, only the stimulants were subjected to adverse attitudes originating at the level of the drug user, an attitude exemplified in the underground message "speed kills." If this were indeed the significant influence that has affected both attitudes and use for the stimulants, it demonstrates that the information gained from users may in exceptional circumstances discourage use through increasing the perception of danger, an effectiveness which does not seem to have been matched by health education.

Narcotics

The rates of narcotic use in Australia have been relatively low (Table 2.8) and considerably less than the prevailing rates in North America. The survey of young people in New South Wales (Bell et al., 1975) indicated that the use of narcotics remained relatively stable over the three years from 1971 to 1973, but each year schoolchildren showed a more permissive attitude and a decreased perception of danger. The authors warned that the change in these attitudes said little for the effects of education on illicit drugs and could portend an increase in use. Perhaps this is occurring. In New South Wales at the end of 1974 a total of 437 patients were on narcotic management programs compared to 381 in July 1973; 70 percent were males and 80 percent aged between 18 and 26 years. The numbers have continued to increase steadily ever since, being in excess of 600 by the end of 1975.

Multiple Drug Use

As in similar communities the world over, multiple drug use has become an increasing problem and complicates the assessment of consumption patterns. The basic principle would seem to be that the user of any drug of dependence is more likely to use any other drug of dependence than is the nonuser (Whitehead, 1974). Multiple drug use is particularly common among users of illicit drugs, but is by no means restricted to illicit drugs. In the Traralgon community survey, six percent of the

Table 2.7. Rates of Stimulant Use

Year	Reference	Sample Number	Population	Age	Ever Used %	Current Users %
1971	Bell et al., 1975	7,000	N.S.W.†	15-19	17.0	9.0
1971	George, 1972	650	Sydney suburb	14+	12.9 (M) 14.0 (F)	3.9 (M) 6.1 (F)
1971	Hennessy et al., 1973	136	Canberra adults		1.7 (M) 0.9 (F)	— —
1972	Bell et al., 1975	7,500	N.S.W.†	15-19	17.0	8.7
1972	Graves, 1973	1,600	Melbourne	13-23	8.2	4.8
1973	Bell et al., 1975	7,500	N.S.W.†	15-19	12.3	6.7
1973	Healy, 1975	1,000	Sydney suburb	14+	10.9 (M) 18.9 (F)	5.6 (total)
1973	Irwin, 1975	5,000	Canberra high school students	12-17	2.9	—
1974	Irwin, 1975	5,000	As above		2.7	—

Table 2.7 (Cont'd.)

Year	Reference	Sample Number	Population	Age	Ever Used %	Current Users %
1974	Carrington-Smith, 1974	500	Hobart women	18-60	14.6	1.8
1975	Turner and McLure, 1975	3,300	Queensland school students	11-17	5.7 (M) 5.6 (F)	4.2 (M) 3.8 (F)

†New South Wales

Table 2.8. Rates of Narcotic Use

Year	Reference	Sample Number	Population	Age	Ever Used %	Current Users %
1971	Bell et al., 1975	7,000	N.S.W.†	15-19	2.8	1.3
1971	George, 1972	650	Sydney suburb	14+	0.9	0.5
1972	Bell et al., 1975	7,500	N.S.W.†	15-19	4.2	1.6
1972	Graves, 1973	1,600	Melbourne	13-23	1.5 (oral) 1.0 (intravenous)	0.9 (oral) 0.4 (intravenous)
1973	Bell et al., 1975	7,500	N.S.W.†	15-19	4.5	2.1
1973	Healy, 1975	1,000	Sydney suburb	14+	1.1	0.5
1973	Irwin, 1975	5,000	Canberra high school students	12-17	1.4	–
1974	Irwin, 1975	5,000	As above		1.7	
1974	Turner and McLure, 1975	3,300	Queensland school students	11-17	2.3 (M) 1.4 (F)	0.9 (M) 0.2 (F)

†New South Wales

respondents had used four or more licit drugs for medication in the previous two weeks (Bridges-Webb, 1972). In the survey of schoolchildren in Queensland, multiple drug users in comparison to those who used only one drug were more likely to be regular users (Turner and McClure, 1975). Among young people in New South Wales, the users of any drug, with the exception of analgesics, were more likely than nonusers of that drug to use other drugs; users of any illicit drug were particularly likely to use other illicit drugs (Bell et al., 1975). Delinquents and other deviants were more likely than the general population sample to use a combination of illicit drugs or to consume large quantities of licit drugs, in particular, alcohol and tobacco.

THE RESPONSE OF THE COMMUNITY

For much of their history, the communities of Australia and New Zealand have accepted the excessive use of alcohol and tobacco among males and of sedatives and analgesics among females with little concern. While heavy use is condoned and even encouraged, obvious pathological use is rejected, but it must be obvious. When the alcoholic reaches this extreme of his disorder, he is labelled as such by his peers and excluded from their company.

The provision of treatment facilities reflects this ambivalent attitude to alcohol use. The alcoholic who can still maintain a social front will find that the complications of alcoholism such as hepatic or neurological disorders are easily taken care of in well-equipped general hospitals, are fully covered by the national health provisions, and in the statistics he does not feature as an alcoholic, but as having a disease related to the affected organ such as the liver, brain, or peripheral nerves. Officially the hospital bed is not occupied by an alcoholic, but, bearing the misleading omissions in mind, probably not less than 10 percent of admissions to public hospitals are substantially due to alcohol (National Health and Medical Research Council, 1975). In one public teaching hospital serving central Sydney, 19 percent of inpatients surveyed on two separate occasions had a drinking problem (Hennessy, 1975).

Despite the massive problem alcoholism presented from the beginning of settlement, the first legislation for its treatment was not enacted in Australia until 1872. Ever since then this legislation has received scant and tardy attention, becoming anachronistic because of failure to review it, while other mental health legislation has been periodically modified and updated. An alcoholics' retreat was opened in Melbourne in 1873, but even to this day the facilities for the treatment of alcoholism are sparse and inadequate. In recent years a Royal Commission in Victoria exhaustively reviewed the problem and recommended legislation, which has been largely enacted, and extensive treatment facilities are now being established by a branch of the Mental Health Authority.

An abortive attempt was made in New South Wales to implement a comprehensive plan for the treatment of drug dependence (Bell and

Rowe, 1971), but the Inebriates Act, in force since the turn of the century, still remains unaltered and the few wards opened for alcoholics in psychiatric hospitals were closed within months. The first detoxification unit for alcoholics established by the government health services in New South Wales was not opened until 1975 and in 1976 still remained unique; the central prison cells in Sydney housed so many alcoholics on the popular drinking nights that it became known as the "drunk tank."

The relative absence of facilities is equally serious throughout all the major cities and towns of this community, in fact being virtually nonexistent in most capital cities of Australia before 1975 when as a result of public pressure a number of states began to develop programs specifically for alcoholism and other forms of drug dependence. The facilities extant up to 1970 have been described by Luby (1969) and Dax (1971). Since then the Health Commission of New South Wales has concentrated on an outpatient service, developing facilities in existing community care clinics and using ex-addict counsellors as well as interested professional staff for all forms of drug dependence including alcoholism. About 30 centers in metropolitan and country areas were functioning by the end of 1975. The services in Victoria have taken a different form, being based on four specialized centers with inpatient/outpatient day and evening programs, in all providing 200 beds with plans to extend to 300 in the near future. Queensland, South Australia, and Western Australia have also set up authorities that are using a similar approach based on centers in the large cities. In these states most of the population lives in the major metropolitan centers where these facilities are being developed. The development of halfway houses and hostels and farms in rural areas are also part of the programs in most states.

Unfortunately, some of this effort in certain states over the past three years depended upon nonrenewable grants from the Australian government and was not incorporated into the regular budget for funding. With the change of government at the end of 1975 a policy of reduced spending in the public sector was introduced to counter inflation, cutting off the funds for these facilities in 1976. In New South Wales many alcoholism clinics were shut down and their staff dispersed with only a few weeks' notice. The sense of makeshift approaches permeates other areas as well; in most states no provision has yet been made for adequate ongoing staff training.

The facilities for the forms of drug dependence other than alcoholism have been subject to an even greater degree of neglect. Until recently many organizations tried to maintain a clear distinction between alcoholism, which was regarded as relatively respectable, and "drug addiction." To some extent this reflects the conflict between the establishment and the nonestablishment, between the old and the young, between the conformists and the nonconformists. Since 1970 the distinctions have been allowed to lapse to some extent and facilities have been planned to cater for all forms of drug dependence. By 1975 most of the public health administrations in Australia and New Zealand had created some authority entrusted with developing programs for the treatment of all forms of drug dependence. The lead was taken by New

Zealand with the Alcoholism and Drug Addiction Act (1966), which provided for compulsory treatment in designated institutions. The committal order is made by a magistrate and can remain in force for two years. Six psychiatric hospitals are designated to receive patients, one in particular, Oakley, providing special security accommodation. Some dissatisfaction seems to have arisen because of the custodial, and perhaps even punitive, approach taken in these institutions. The Board of Health (1970) report commented on the inadequate training of nursing and other staff in the management of drug problems in many hospital settings where addicts were managed. In contrast, an adequate training course for law enforcement personnel was initiated in 1965.

In Australia the number of beds devoted to addicts remains small. In Sydney, a city with a population of about three million, possibly no more than 40 public hospital beds are occupied by addicts other than alcoholics and perhaps an equal amount are used in private hospitals. Voluntary and church bodies have only just begun to extend their aid to the addict, moving out of their traditional preoccupation with the alcoholic and the homeless man.

For narcotic dependence the major modality of treatment has been the use of methadone, associated with approaches such as counselling, social assistance, and group therapy. Methadone programs run on an outpatient basis now exist in all major centers. The emphasis on methadone, here as well as in other countries, reflects the paucity of resources devoted to the problem of drug dependence, requiring as it does the least change in the conventional medical approach and the least drain on staff. In practice patients only seek treatment when they fall foul of the law and become subject to some legal compulsion or the threat of conviction. The bulk of narcotic users who evade trouble with the law do not seek or receive any attention.

In theory methadone may be prescribed for addicts only by medical practitioners approved by the Department of Health. In practice some general practitioners prescribe methadone without seeking formal authority and addicts exploit their gullibility. In the approved clinics the criteria for acceptance are that an addict should be over 18 years of age, have a history of fairly continuous opiate dependence, and have failed to respond to other management procedures. In practice very few are younger than 18 years, all give the required history, but this is usually uncorroborated, and "other management procedures" are not even available to be tried. The clinics are staffed by a mixed range of medical, nursing, and paramedical staff and by ex-addict counsellors, usually self-selected by developing an interest in the problem. In general the aim is to return the patient to a crime-free, self-supporting existence and in this sense the program in New South Wales has been held to be a modest success (Reynolds and Magro, 1975) and in New Zealand a failure (McLeod and Priest, 1973).

In general facilities are not provided for other forms of drug dependence, but here as with alcoholism the complications are given adequate or even elaborate attention. Because of the high rate of analgesic use in Australia, the associated nephropathy is very common and specialized units receive enough practice in kidney transplant operations to have achieved an enviable standard of technical excellence. The causal dependence is largely ignored and the drug remains available without restriction.

Health education has of course been given much prominence. For many years temperance organizations have issued pamphlets, which do not seem to have had any impact. In the late 1960s illicit drugs such as LSD and the narcotics began to be used by young people and public concern was roused suddenly. The obvious answer seemed to be a program for educating the young. Government departments set up divisions of health education, sometimes based on the department of education, sometimes on the department of health, or even in both. Police and justice departments developed their own initiatives. Voluntary bodies, small and large, added to the frenzy of activity. The growth of educational activity and drug taking followed a parallel course. After a while some efforts were recognized as counterproductive and more sophistication was demanded of the counsellors and advisers. Voluntary workers were enlisted in various programs, but here as elsewhere in the world the volunteers were a highly selected group, in particular, having a remarkably high proportion of current users of marijuana. The commonwealth government of Australia entered the scene by voting a large sum of money to drug education. One prime minister authorized a popular bandleader to make a film, which on its first showing to the experts was condemned so firmly that it has still not been given a public showing, despite expensive efforts to improve it. Intensive efforts have been made in the schools to discourage smoking and these have possibly made some impact. Although the rate of smoking is still increasing among young people, and especially among females, at least the nonsmokers are increasingly determined in the belief that smoking should be prohibited. Of course such a polarization of viewpoints is not necessarily healthy or even a desirable result of education. It may be merely part of the worldwide trend among nonsmokers to stand up for their right to not smoke, that is, to breathe an atmosphere free of the pollution generated by smokers.

The impact of alcoholism has extended beyond health problems. Considerable numbers are imprisoned for offenses relating to drunkenness, especially in South Australia and the Northern Territory (National Health and Medical Research Council, 1975); 35 percent of those convicted for drunkenness have at least one previous conviction. The reconviction rates for drunken driving and other offenses are particularly high, especially so in those under the age of 20 years. A considerable proportion of those convicted of more serious crimes, perhaps 50 percent, are heavy drinkers or alcoholics or were under the influence of alcohol when they committed the offense. In a survey of homeless men in Sydney, 65 percent were diagnosed as alcoholics. About half of the highway accidents would seem to be associated with drunken driving or walking.

The contribution alcohol consumption has made to the road accident rate has aroused public concern and some action. The state of Victoria has pioneered many legislative acts which have since been adopted by other states as well; for example, the use of the breathalyser, the adoption of a standard blood alcohol concentration beyond which conviction is mandatory, compulsory blood alcohol determinations on all traffic casualties presented to casualty department of hospitals, and the compulsory use of seat belts. At present the Victorian government is contemplating the introduction of random breathalyser tests for drivers (Hetzel, 1975).

The voluntary bodies concerned with drug dependence have been reserved for last, but certainly not least, mention. In Australia a special impetus was developed by the first voluntary body devoted to these needs, the Foundation for Research and Treatment of Alcoholism of New South Wales, which was founded in 1956. It established the Langton Clinic, the first public hospital in Australia devoted exclusively to the care of the alcoholic and the first outside the United States of America. It also developed the first halfway house for alcoholics, a small self-supporting and self-regulating group of recovering alcoholics in New South Wales, and at present it is developing a chain of hostels based on the Cyrenian Community House program of the United Kingdom. It assisted interested individuals in other states to set up similar voluntary bodies, which now exist in most of the states of Australia, and which have now created a national body, the Australian Foundation on Alcoholism and Drug Dependence (AFADD).

The second voluntary body to be formed, the Victorian Foundation on Alcoholism and Drug Dependence (VFADD), was particularly active in the legislative moves pioneered in Victoria. Perhaps its most significant recent contribution has been the generation of interest in management programs for alcoholism in industry, which are now well established in Victoria and gaining impetus in the other states.

The Salvation Army has played a significant part in the provision of aid to the derelict alcoholic throughout Australia and New Zealand. Its latest initiative is "The Bridge," a program using counselling and education to channel suitable people into a residential rehabilitation course (Williams, 1974). For many years the army operated a detoxification center in Sydney, with a minimum of medical assistance, at a time when all the government agencies provided for the alcoholic were the police cells and the psychiatric hospitals. The Roman Catholic and Methodist churches also have operated hostels for skid row in various capital cities. Alcoholics Anonymous has of course been a major influence, developing a network throughout the community that extends assistance to all who approach it.

PERSPECTIVES FOR THE FUTURE

Prophecy is a pursuit for the godly or the foolhardy. Gazing into the crystal ball evokes fantasies that reveal more of the hopeful seer than of the future. Nevertheless, the editor has demanded this exercise and for that reason alone the following predictions are made.

Current trends extrapolated into the future indicate that drug use, licit and illicit, will increase. The drugs that will enjoy the most rapid escalation in consumption will be alcohol, marijuana, and pharmaceutical preparations belonging broadly to the sedative class. Narcotics use will also increase, but in the main will be kept in check by continued strict controls and law enforcement. Increasing use of drugs will produce ever-increasing problems until the community will be roused into reaction, the proverbial "backlash," which will initiate the next downward phase of the cyclical changes in drug consumption.

In the absence of evidence establishing some degree of effectiveness, therapeutic, educational, and social approaches will enjoy limited and fluctuating financial support and will pass through phases as each new idea enjoys temporary popularity. In time and probably as a result of public clamor, controls on availability, in particular excise tax and restrictions on sale, will be increased and will gradually decrease drug use and the associated problems. The social changes which are gaining momentum and on which much hope is pinned for the solution of all social disorder, are more likely to increase drug use in the near future, principally as a result of the increased spread of affluence. From the experience of other countries such as Sweden and the United Kingdom, which have adopted an increasing degree of socialistic policies, the parallel social reforms such as improvement of opportunity are not likely to produce a balancing discouragement of drug use. Perhaps in the distant future massive social pressures will be generated by a centralist government, concerned among other things by the increasing drain on the national revenue of the ever-increasing size of self-inflicted diseases treated in a National Health Service. Presumably these will be based on the current Chinese experience, generating social disapproval to control the deviant individual.

Maintenance drug therapy will continue for some time, but will probably be abandoned eventually, not necessarily because it is futile, misdirected, and ineffective, but as a result of the backlash that will reverse the current permissive phase of the cyclical fluctuation in drug use. And regardless of whether their methods have proven effective or not and despite challenges from other groups, the medical profession and its associated massive empire of health services will continue to exercise a treatment role that will survive and influence central policy decisions in humanitarian and compassionate directions.

ACKNOWLEDGMENTS

The tables were prepared by Mr. Ralph Champion, whose assistance I gratefully acknowledge. The cartoons were prepared for the Australian Journal on Alcoholism and Drug Dependence by Mr. John Hanna, who has kindly permitted their use for this paper.

REFERENCES

(1) Abrahams M.J., Armstrong J., Whitlock F.A. Drug Dependence in Brisbane, Med. J. Aust., 1970, 2: 397-404.

(2) Andrew S. Blood Bromide Levels in Psychiatric Patients Taking Bromureides, Med. J. Aust., 1965, 1: 646-652.

(3) Ashforth J.I. A Short History of Drugs of Abuse and Drug Abuse Control in New Zealand in "Drug Dependency and Drug Abuse in New Zealand" New Zealand Board of Health, Report Series No. 14, 1970, Appendix VIII.

(4) Bacon S.D. The Classic Temperance Movement of the U.S.A.: Impact Today on Attitudes, Action and Research, Brit. J. Addict., 1967, 62: 5-18.

(5) Beckett J. Aborigines, Alcohol, and Assimilation, in "Aborigines Now" ed. by M. Reay Angus & Robertson, Sydney, 1964, 32-47.

(6) Bell D.S. Drug Addiction Bull. Narcotics, 1970, 22/2: 21-32.

(7) Bell D.S. Man and His Mind Changers – Health, Illness and Deviancy, in "Proceedings of the 30th International Congress on Alcoholism and Drug Dependence, 1972" ed.by A. Tongue and E. Tongue International Council on Alcohol and Addiction, Lausanne, 1975, 24-28.

(8) Bell D.S., Champion R.A., Rowe A.J.E. Monitoring Drug Use in New South Wales 1971 to 1973, Health Commission of New South Wales, Sydney, 1975 (75/22).

(9) Bell D.S., Rowe A.J.E. Plan for a Drug-Dependence Service for New South Wales. II Management of the Problem. Med. J. Aust., 1971, 1: 569-573.

(10) Board of Health Drug Dependency and Drug Abuse in New Zealand, New Zealand Board of Health Report Series No. 14, 1970.

(11) Bridges-Webb C. Drug Medication in the Community, Med. J. Aust., 1972, 1: 675-679.

(12) Briscoe O.V., Hinterberger H. A Survey of the Usage of Amphetamines in Parts of the Sydney Community, Med. J. Aust., 1968, 1: 480-485.

(13) Carrington-Smith C. Survey of Drug Use Amongst 500 Women in Hobart, Tasmania. Health Services, Hobart, 1974.

(14) Connell W.F., Stroodrant R.E., Sinclair K.E., Connell R.W., Rogers K.W. 12 to 20; Studies of City Youth, Hicks Smith & Sons, Sydney 1975.

(15) Critchley C.H., Gardner J.M. A Pilot Study of the Relationship Between Need for Power and Drinking in 18 and 21 Year Old Males, Aust. J. Alcohol. Drug Depend., 1975, 2: 86-88. Australian Journal of Alcohol & Drug Dependence.

(16) Csikszentmihalyi M. A Cross-Cultural Comparison of Some Structural Characteristics of Group Drinking, Hum. Develop., 1968, 11: 201-216. Human Development.

(17) Dax E.C. Alcoholism and Drug Dependence Resources in Australia, in "Alcoholism and Drug Dependence" ed. by L.G. Kiloh & D.S. Bell Butterworths, Australia, 1971, 48-54.

(18) Dax E.C. Australia and New Zealand in "World History of Psychiatry" ed. J.G. Howells, Brunner/Mazel, New York, 1975, 704-728.

(19) Edmondson K.W., Brennan T., Clements F.W., Krister S.J. Report of a Survey into the Smoking Habits and Attitudes of Australian School Children by The ad hoc Smoking Survey Sub-Committee National Health and Medical Research Council, Sixty-eighth Session, Canberra, 1969.

(19a) Egger G.J., Parker R., Trebilco P. Adolescents and Alcohol in New South Wales N.S.W. Health Education Advisory Council, Sydney, 1975.

(20) Encel S., Kotowicz K. Heavy Drinking and Alcoholism. Preliminary Report, Med. J. Aust., 1970, 1: 607-612.

(21) Evatt H.V. Rum Rebellion Lloyd O'Neil, Hawthorn, Victoria, 1971.

(22) Ferguson D. Smoking, Drinking and Non-narcotic Analgesic Habits in an Occupational Group, Med. J. Aust., 1973, 1: 1271-1274.

(23) George A. Survey of Drug Use in a Sydney Suburb, Med. J. Aust., 1972, 2: 233-237.

(24) Gillies M.A., Skyring A.P. The Pattern and Prevalence of Aspirin Ingestion as Determined by Interview of 2,921 Inhabitants of Sydney, Med. J. Aust., 1972, 1: 974-979.

(25) Graves G. Epidemiology of Drug Use in Melbourne in "Drug Use by the Young Population of Melbourne" ed. by J. Krupinski and A. Stoller Special Publication 4, Mental Health Authority, Melbourne, 1973, 22-23.

(26) Hall M.C. Problems in Legislating Against Abuse of Hallucinogenic Fungi in Australia, Bull. Narcotics, 1973, 25/3: 27-36. Bulletin of Narcotics.

(26a) Hasleton S. The Incidence and Correlates of Marijuana Use in an Australian Undergraduate Population. Medical Journal of Australia, 1971, 2: 302-308.

(27) Healy P. Use of Psychotropic Drugs in Australia. Informed Opinion, No. 14, N.S.W. Health Commission, Sydney, 1975.

(28) Hennessy B.L., Bruen W.J., Cullen J. The Canberra Mental Health Survey. Preliminary Results, Med. J. Aust., 1973, 1: 721-728.

(29) Hennessy W.B. Alcoholism — A multifaceted Problem, Aust. J. Alcohol. Drug Depend., 1975, 2: 58-62.

(30) Hetzel B.S. The Prevention and Control of Alcoholism in Australia, Aust. J. Alcohol. Drug Depend., 1975, 2: 17-22.

(31) Holloway I. Some Psychological Concomitants of Addiction, Thesis for Doctorate of Philosophy in Psychology, Univ. Adelaide, 1967.

(32) Irwin R.P. The Australian National University Drug Education Project in "Alcohol and other Drug Dependencies in the Australian Capital Territory" ed. Pang H., Scully G., Stolz P. Council of Social Services, Canberra, 1975, 20-28.

(33) Kamien M. A Survey of Drug Use in a Part-Aboriginal Community, Med. J. Aust., 1975a, 1: 261-264.

(34) Kamien M. Aborigines and Alcohol, Med. J. Aust., 1975b,1: 291-298.

(35) Kessell A. Serum Bromide Levels in a Mental Health Unit, Med. J. Aust., 1969, 1: 1073-1075.

(36) Kraus J. Alcoholism and Drug Dependence as Factors in Psychiatric Hospital Admissions, Aust. N.Z.J. Psychiat., 1973, 7: 45-50.

(37) Luby B.F. Public Health Approaches to Alcohol Problems in Australia, Med. J. Aust., 1969, 1: 924-932.

(38) Lint J. de Current Trends in the Prevalence of Excessive Alcohol Use and Alcohol-Related Health Damage. Brit. J. Addiction, 1975, 70: 3-13.

(39) McLeod W.R., Priest P.N. Methadone Maintenance in Auckland. The Failure of a Programme. Brit. J. Addiction, 1973, 68: 45-50.

(39a) Murrell T.G.C., Moss J.R. Health Care for Infants and Mothers, An Adelaide Survey. Report to the Commission of Equiry into Poverty. Department of Comunity Medicine, University of Adelaide, 1974.

(40) National Health and Medical Research Council Report of the Standing Committee on the Health Problems of Alcohol, National Health and Medical Research Council, Canberra, 1975.

(41) Oliver R.G.,Hetzel B.S. Rise and Fall of Suicide Rates in Australia: Relation to Sedative Availability. Med. J. Aust., 1972, 2: 919-923.

(42) Pearl C. Wild Men of Sydney, W.H. Allen, London, 1965.

(43) Perkins N. Submission to Minister for Aboriginal Affairs Concerning Pick-up Service and Night Shelter at Alice Springs, Aust. J. Alcohol. Drug Depend., 1975, 2: 29-30.

(44) Perkins N. Central Australian Congress Pick-up Service for Problem Drinkers, Aust. J. Alcohol. Drug Depend., 1976, 3: 13-15.

(45) Pullen K.J. Mary Reibey, Ure Smith, Sydney, 1975.

(46) Purnell J. Burry A.F. Analgesic Consumption in a Country Town, Med. J. Aust., 1967, 2: 389-391.

(47) Rankin J.G. The Size and Nature of the Problem of the Misuse of Alcohol and Drugs in Australia, in "29th International Congress on Alcoholism and Drug Dependence." ed. by L.G. Kiloh and D.S. Bell Butterworths, Australia, 1971, 11-20.

(47a) Rankin J.G. Wilkinson P. Alcohol and Tobacco Consumption in The Health of a Metropolis, ed. by Krupinski J. & Stoller A. Heinemann, Melbourne, 1971, 61-67.

(48) Reynolds I., Magro D. The Use of Methadone as a Treatment Tool for Opiate Addicts. Health Commission of New South Wales, Sydney, 1975.

(49) Roueche B. Cultural Factors and Drinking Patterns. Ann. N.Y. Acad. Sci., 1966, 133: 846-855.

(50) Royal Australasian College of Physicians. Statement on Analgesic Nephropathy, Med. J. Aust., 1969, 1: 1388-1389.

(51) Royle H.G. The State of Health in New South Wales in the 1820's, Med. J. Aust., 1973, 1: 950-953.

(52) Sainsbury M.J. Drug Dependence in Admission Centre Patients, Med. J. Aust., 1967, 2: 18-20.

(53) Saint E.G. Bacchus Transported. Purporting to be an historical impression of alcoholism in Australia, Med. J. Aust., 1970, 2: 548-551.

(54) Smart R.G., Whitehead P.C. The Prevention of Drug Abuse by Lowering Per Capita Consumption: Distribution of Consumption in Samples of Canadian Adults and British University Students. Bull. Narcotics, 1973, 15/4: 49-55.

(55) Stoller A., Krupinski J. Aspects of Psychiatric Morbidity in Adolescents in Victoria, Australia, Aust. N.Z.J. Psychiat., 1974, 8: 61-69.

(56) Sulkunen P. Production Consumption and `Recent Changes of Consumption of Alcoholic Beverages. Brit. J. Addiction, 1976, 71: 3-11.

(57) Tomlinson J. Petrol Sniffing in the Northern Territory. Aust. J. Alcohol. Drug Depend., 1975, 2: 74-77.

(58) Turner T.J., McClure L. Alcohol and Drug Use by Queensland School Children, Department of Education, Brisbane, 1975, pp. 130.

(58a) Unisearch. A Survey of Analgesic and Sedative Consumption in Sydney and Brisbane. University of New South Wales, Sydney, 1968.

(59) Walsh D. Alcoholism in the Republic of Ireland, Brit. J. Psychiat., 1969, 115: 1021-1025.

(60) Walsh D. Alcoholism and the Irish. J. Alcoholism, 1972, 7: 40-47.

(61) Wheeler L., Edmonds C. A Profile of Drug Takers. Med. J. Aust., 1969, 2: 291-294.

(62) Whitehead P.C. Multidrug Use; Supplementary Perspectives, Internat. J. Addictions, 1974, 9: 185-204.

(63) Whitlock F.A., Lowrey J.M. Drug-Dependence in Psychiatric Patients, Med. J. Aust., 1967, 1: 1157-1166.

(64) Wilkinson P. Santamaria J.N., Rankin J.G., Martin D. Epidemiology of Alcoholism; Social Data and Drinking Patterns of a Sample of Australian Alcoholics, Med. J. Aust., 1969, 1: 1020-1025.

(65) Wilkinson P., Kornaczewski A., Rankin J.G., Santamaria J.N. Bromureide Dependence in Alcoholics, Med. J. Aust., 1971, 2: 479-482.

(66) Williams H.W. "The Bridge" – A Salvation Army Concept of Alcoholism Rehabilitation, Aust. J. Alcohol. Drug Depend., 1974, 1: 111-114.

3 Singapore and the Southeast Asian Region
L. Hon Koon

INTRODUCTION

General factors that should be kept in mind when considering drug use and misuse in Singapore are that Singapore lies within a region that includes:

1. "Yunnan," which is not a country but smuggler's jargon for the region comprising the Shan states of Burma, the northern borderlands of Thailand, the western limits of Laos, as well as the southwestern corner of China — the geographical Yunnan province. These make up a "no-man's-land" where "Yunnan" opium is grown, the main source of illicit opium in the Far East. More recently, this region, with Chinese Yunnan sometimes excluded, has become known as the Golden Triangle.

2. Countries where the old pattern of opium smoking still prevails, e.g., Malaysia, Singapore, Taiwan, Hong Kong, Macao, Burma, Thailand, Laos, Vietnam, Cambodia (Khmer).

3. Countries where heroin dependence has taken root and given rise to greater problems than opium smoking — Hong Kong, Macao, Thailand. Since the end of 1974 Malaysia and Singapore have begun to experience heroin dependence.

4. Countries that until recently had an American "presence." This added a new pattern of GI heroin dependence onto the age-old opium dependence. The effects were ultimately experienced by the local populations — Vietnam, Laos, Cambodia — countries that are now experiencing great changes because of political turmoil.

HISTORICAL OVERVIEW

The history of drug use and abuse in Singapore began with the founding of modern Singapore in 1819 by an Englishman, Sir Stamford Raffles.(1) The history of drug use, in particular of opiates, cannabis, and alcohol, in the area that embraced variously designated territories (i.e., the Malay Archipelago, the East Indies, the Far East, Southeast Asia) goes further back into history. Malacca, a seaport on the mainland of the Malay Peninsula was founded by the Portuguese in 1511. They took over the existing trade in commodities, including opium. Barbosa, a relative of Magellan, wrote in 1516: "The Chinese are also great navigators. . . . They travel with all their goods to Malacca. For the return voyage they ship drugs of Cambay, much afiam, which we call opium, wormwood, saffron, etc." (Goldsmith, 1939).

When the Dutch succeeded the Portuguese in the control of the high seas, they in turn controlled the distribution of opium. In the seventeenth century the English superseded the Dutch and opium played a key role in the English colonial policy. Opium as a medicine was known in China, originally introduced by the Arabs, as the name for opium, "afuyung," of Arabic origin, shows. It became more popular in the 17th century, and it is generally assumed that opium smoking began at that time in China.

It was not until the second half of the eighteenth century that opium addiction in our sense of the word, nonmedical use of a drug, developed to any noticeable extent in China. It is said that Dutch traders who imported raw Indian opium to Java and then exported considerable quantities to China first introduced the habit of opium smoking to the Chinese. Opium smoking was thought to have originated in Formosa, according to observations published in 1746 by a Peking official, Huang Yu-Pu, sent to investigate the matter (Edkins, 1898). The smoking of opium was related to the smoking of tobacco. Tobacco cultivation and tobacco smoking were introduced into China from the Philippines in the latter years of the Ming dynasty (Edkins, 1898).

History of Opium in Singapore

The first record of opium in modern Singapore occurred on the day of the official signing of the treaty by Sir Raffles and the Temmenggong of Johore, February 6, 1819, during the festivities that followed to celebrate the event. Captain Crawford gave the following description: "After the ceremony of signing and sealing was over, presents were given consisting of opium, arms and woolens of a scarlet colour" (Hartzburg, 1954).

At this time there were a few Chinese gambler planters on the island and also some 120 Malay followers of the Temmenggong. In a few months there was an influx of Chinese, Bugis, and Malays in a population said to have been 5,000.

The Chinese formed a large proportion of the inhabitants, a "great many of whom were addicted to the opium and gambling habits." To obtain revenue for police purposes, the government established opium, spirit (alcohol), and gambling farms, which were essentially rights to import and manufacture opium and produce arrack (toddy), and sell them retail to customers in return for paying a fixed sum to the government. The monthly rentals for the four opium shops, arrack (toddy) shops, and gambling tables were $395, $100, and $95 respectively. The first opium farm was established in Singapore in 1820 (Little, 1847).

The settlement thrived and the first 40 years saw a rapid increase in trade, which was essentially entrepot. No figures are available on the extent of opium use in these early years, but in 1847 we get two glimpses of this. An eminent Chinese merchant, Siah U Chin, wrote on the occupations and activities of his fellow Chinese. Siah U Chin (1848) said that many of these men had left their homes in China planning to come to the southern seas to seek their fortune by means of hard labor and then to return home. "Alas, for those who originally intended to return to their native country after three years and yet after the lapse of more than 19 years have not been able to fulfill their wish, but what is the reason of it? It is because they became addicted to the prevailing vice of opium smoking."

Dr. Robert Little, a physician from Edinburgh, had opportunities to observe the "drug scene" in 1847 in Singapore.

> They enter the opium shop by pushing aside a filthy mat and, in a small space they see many men crowded and crouching on a narrow board; dim lights faintly disclose their squalid appearances; the air is impregnated with a close suffocating odour; the heat is oppressive; a few questions are asked by the visitor, a pipe is shown, a human being gazed upon as he slowly and to all appearances, with much gusto inhales the sedative vapours – at last, unable to endure it any longer, a rush is made by the visitor to the door, and, according to the preconceived notion, what has been seen is either a blot as black as Erebus, a canker eating into the vitals of society, a moral curse attended with great and deep physical evils, which are slowly but surely extending or it may be looked upon as one way of spending money, not a bad plan for raising the revenue, a lighter curse than dram drinking and a far pleasanter, when young men dream dreams and the old men see visions. In Singapore . . . we have every Eastern nation indulging in this luxury . . . the native of India . . . swallows opium, . . . the Chinese inhales the smoke not only into his mouth, but into his lungs (Little, 1847).

He painted a vivid picture of the addict during withdrawal, ". . . the picture of misery his eyes sunk, gait slouched, step trembling and voice quivering"; he described the addict facies of chronic opiate addiction, though not the first to do so, "a sallow cast of countenance and dull unimpressive eye." Little R. (1847). He described the mounting effects of succeeding doses of the drug on the addicted individual ". . . not until a third or a fourth whiff does the positive pleasure arise (Little, 1847).

According to law the number of opium shops was limited to 45 in town and 6 in the country. They were scattered all over the island, "whenever a number of Chinese are congregated there you have one or more." The opium shops varied in appearance from an attap hovel to a two-story brick house. The distinguishing sign of the opium shop was a red board, or Papan Merah.(2) However, Little mentioned that he visited and counted 80 shops within Singapore Town. The sign for these was a mat, and illegal opium places were known only to the initiated.

Little also mentioned the congregation of certain trades in certain streets — carpenters, blacksmiths, boxmakers, barbers, boatmen — and their association with opium use. "These trades seem almost entirely to be devoted to the drug; 85 percent were opium smokers." He calculated that of an estimated 70,000 inhabitants (40,000 of whom were Chinese), Chinese smokers numbered 15,043. Based on these figures, whose accuracy cannot be verified, the prevalence of opium smoking in Singapore in 1847 was an estimated 21.49 percent.

From 1832, Malacca, Singapore, and Penang came to be known together as the Straits Settlements (Blythe 1947). The population of Singapore increased and by 1860 it was 81,734, with the Chinese numbering over 50,000. Rubber was introduced into Malaya in 1877, but its expansion on a commercial scale did not begin until about 1895, and only in 1905 did rapid increase in planting take place. Labor was brought into Malaya, mainly Chinese and Indian immigrants, to work in these rubber plantations. The Chinese were mainly from Swatow, Amoy, and Canton. A description of a Chinese "Kongsi" (company) in 1895 mentions the clerk or "choyfoo" who "dispenses opium, tobacco."

The system of the opium farm, established in 1820, lasted from its origin till midnight December 31, 1909. On January 1, 1910, the government established a Monopolies Department, which took over the farms and then reopened them for business as before.

Opium revenue was about half the total revenue of the colony for the period 1819-1906. Apparently the government did have qualms about the extent of opium smoking and thus created an Opium Commission in 1907. In 1929, the government legislated to register opium smokers. Each smoker was given a registration card; there was no rationing though each person was not allowed to buy more than five tahils(3) at a time.

As of December 31, 1929, the number of persons who had registered as purchasers of opium with the government was 40,956. At that time, the Straits Settlements consisted of Singapore Island, Panang, Malacca, Province Wellesley, Dindings, Cocos, Christmas Island, and Labuan, with a total area of 1,508 square miles and a total population of 1,059,968 (1927 figures). The following formula is based on relating the registered smokers to the general population:

$$\frac{\text{Registered addicts (1929)}}{\text{Total population (1927)}} = \frac{40,956}{1,059,968} = 3.86\%$$

Actually it was estimated that there were 120,000 to 150,000 licit and illicit smokers in the population, so that the prevalence is greater.

The actual smoking of opium was done in opium divans. Up to 1926 these were licensed establishments; subsequently the licensed establishments were replaced by government smoking establishments. These were not popular and in 1930 all government divans had to be closed, owing to a lack of patronage. People smoked in the privacy of their homes or in nongovernment places. Registration of smokers was closed on December 31, 1934. A person could still get onto the register with medical certification; registered addicts were thus buying opium from government chandu (prepared opium) retail shops, until the outbreak of war in December 1941. The last "official" report on December 31, 1940, before war broke out in Singapore, showed that there were 16,552 addicts on the registers, buying opium from 28 chandu retail shops. The estimated population of the island of Singapore for the year 1941 was just under 770,000. This gives a minimum prevalence of 2.15 percent.

Opium in Singapore in the postwar years

The war came to Singapore on December 8, 1941. Singapore fell to the Japanese on February 12, 1942, and remained under Japanese occupation until September 5, 1945.

When the British surrendered to the Japanese they left behind large stocks of opium. The Japanese carried on sales in the same government chandu retail shops, after an initial period of facesaving abolishment of opium smoking. A large proportion of the stock found its way onto the black market.

After the war, Britain recovered Singapore and the British military administration governed Singapore from September 5, 1945, till March 31, 1946. Civil government began April 1, 1946. On February 1, 1946, the British military administration by Proclamation number 45 entitled, "The Opium and Chandu Proclamation," made the possession of all opium, prepared or raw, and all apparatus for smoking an offense. In 1946, there were 1,571 known smoking saloons. People who were hitherto contributors to revenue became overnight lawbreakers as a result of this proclamation.

There was an estimated 25,000 to 30,000 addicts who required monthly about 3,000 or 4,000 pounds of opium. Opium traffickers seized upon this opportunity and formed syndicates to smuggle opium into Singapore. In the immediate postwar years, Singapore became the center and entrepot of the illicit traffic in opium in the Malayan area and catered to South Malaya, the Borneo territories, Christmas Island, and Indonesia, in addition to her own needs.

The traffic was largely in the hands of a few powerful syndicates dealing in consignments of as much as 3,000 pounds at a time. Their agents were crew members in oceangoing steamers on a regular run between Singapore and ports in the Persian Gulf, India, Burma, and Thailand where cheap and plentiful opium was available. Shipments were also made from Burma and Thailand by aircraft and motor fishing vessels. Most of the opium appeared to be of "Yunnan" origin, with smaller quantities from India and Persia.

Around 1953, with the reopening of the gulf oil ports, Persian opium was found in consignments of lots of 100 pounds in Singapore. From 1960 to 1963, Thailand appeared to be the main source of supply. The opium was smuggled in Thai fishing vessels and then transferred to Singapore vessels around the fishing grounds of the South China Seas; it was then taken up by fast-speed boats outside Singapore territorial waters. Landing was made on the Singapore coast under cover of darkness. After landing, consignments were broken into small lots and distributed to small operators and converted chandu. The chandu (prepared opium) was packaged into bamboo leaf packets containing two hoons (11.66 grains or 0.76 g) of prepared opium with about a ten percent morphine content. Each packet was sold to smokers at $1.20 (Singapore). Each packet sufficed for four "smokes" or "pipefuls"; an ordinary laborer took about an average of three packets of prepared opium per day.

Historical Overview: Ganja

In Singapore from the earliest times, ganja, the local name for marijuana (Cannabis sativa) has been associated with the Indians and Pakistanis who brought over the traditional use from their motherlands. Its use, until recently, was confined to a small number from these ethnic groups. As such it was a localized pattern, with a ghetto like character and did not give much cause for concern.

From 1819 to 1867, when Singapore was transferred to the jurisdiction of the Colonial Office, Indian convicts were sent to serve their term in Singapore and were used to work on every type of building in Singapore. When convict labor was withdrawn agents were employed to recruit laborers from India. These Indian laborers introduced the use of ganja. They also took to opiate use by swallowing prepared opium.

Ganja was smoked as a cigarette rolled in "rokok daun," the leaf of the young nipah palm (Nypa fruticans) which was dried and used as tobacco paper; it was also used in a cigarette mixed with "tembakau siam," red tobacco, (used also as chewing tobacco), and in ordinary cigarettes like Lucky Strikes which are preferred to other brands. Another method of smoking ganja is to use the "chillum," a funnel-shaped pipe made of clay.

Because the smoke from the lighted ganja is irritating, some smokers use the hookah. This device enables the smoke to be filtered through water before being inhaled. Since ganja smokers are generally poor, and perhaps because it is an illegal activity, they do not use the traditional Indian or Middle Eastern hookah. Local ganja smokers use an improvised hookah made from a coconut shell or a glass brandy bottle. One way of "cooling" the smoke without using the hookah is to cup the chillum with the hands over a drinking glass containing water and smoke from an opening between the fingers or palms of the hands. Another esoteric mode of cooling the smoke is to smoke the cigarette through a papaya leaf stem or other filter made from the core of the pineapple. Cannabis in the form of "charas" and "hashish," used in India in foods and ingested by mouth, is also known but not much practiced.

THE CONTEMPORARY DRUG USE AND MISUSE SCENE

After World War II, Hong Kong experienced a change in the major drug of misuse, tending toward heroin. In Malaysia and Singapore until around 1970 and in Singapore until late 1974) the pattern was still that of the older opium smoker, with a smaller number of morphine injectors. The average opium addict in Singapore was a male Chinese, aged 49 years, who had smoked opium regularly for about 18 years. He was a laborer, a hawker, a boatman, a clerical worker, or a craftsman. He took opium to relieve pain, for pleasure, to allay fatigue and other symptoms, and for its believed properties as an aphrodisiac, a medicine, a prophylactic against ill health, as good for the voice, and as a drug to allay the pangs of sex hunger (Leong, 1959, 1974).

The Coming of Morphine

In Singapore, along with opium addicts there also existed small coteries of morphine injection addicts. These initially were associated with certain areas in the city, slum areas where the poorer people who tended to belong to certain occupations like trishaw-pedalers, laborers, and seamen had settled. Thus pockets of morphine dependence were found among the Henghua, the Hockchia, and the Hockchew in the Muar Road, Ophir Road, and Johore Road areas. In this group one would find an occasional Indian or Pakistani who would have taken to morphine through associating with Chinese friends. The typical morphine addict was generally about 38 years of age. He would have first been an opium addict smoking three packets of opium (each packet containing two hoons or 0.76 g) costing $3.60 (Singapore) a day; as a laborer working as a lighterman in the dockyards he would be earning $8.00 a day.

Perhaps, one day he would come into contact with a morphine addict or a morphine den operator. He would be persuaded to switch to morphine because it was cheaper, and it would make him less liable to be arrested for possession of opium-smoking utensils or for being found in an opium den; also the effects were faster and more intense. He would be started with a subcutaneous dose of 20 cents an injection which would substitute for the smoking of about $1.00 worth of opium. Soon, however, he would be stepping up the dosage, and after a few months he would switch to intramuscular and later intravenous injections.

Morphine with its relatively short history of discovery by Seturner of Paderborn in 1803, coupled with the invention of the first hypodermic syringe by Alexander Wood of Endinburgh in 1853 had been introduced into Singapore between 1890 and 1900. In 1903 the activities of itinerant injectors were noted as people who served their clients in back lanes and on street corners.

Morphine, unlike chandu (prepared opium) was never legalized. In fact it was regarded as harmful to the opium monopoly and laws were enacted against it. During the 1930s, morphine seemed to be relatively less important. Around 1957, however, morphine dens began to sprout in the poorer sections of the city. The majority of the customers were opium addicts who considered that opium was too weak for their needs. Because it was initially cheaper, more effective, and involved less risk of detection, trishaw riders, seamen, and unskilled laborers took to morphine. Their association with certain streets, certain racial groups, and certain occupations were noted. In 1972, the author learned that very young persons began getting morphine at the dens, starting with injections worth 40 cents (Singapore). They seemed to have overcome the barriers of language, class, and age. The den operators were older Chinese who belonged to the laboring classes and were uneducated or had received a very elementary Chinese education. The new young recruits were English-speaking, from the three main ethnic groups in Singapore − Chinese, Malays, Indians − and also Eurasians and middle class. The first known death of a young drug user, 17 years old, who had started using cannabis and Mandrax pills (Quaaludes in America) when he was 15 years old, occurred on May 10, 1973. He was found dead of an overdose of morphine in the back seat of a car in a back lane in an area known to have morphine dens.

The Coming of Heroin

A pattern that has emerged is that in a number of countries in which the main dependence was opium smoking, when heroin became available, it replaced opium. This appeared to have occurred after intensified attempts at control of opium smoking. In Thailand after opium was banned in 1959, heroin came into general use. In Hong Kong and Macau, after World War II, efforts on the part of government to suppress opium smoking resulted in traffickers and addicts turning from opium to heroin. In Singapore and Malaysia in the early 1960s, there had been no mention of heroin dependence although Iran, Hong Kong, Macau, and Thailand had heroin dependence problems.

There had been few and isolated seizures of heroin in Singapore and Malaysia from 1946 to 1953 (three seizures in 1947, 1948, and 1952). There were no cases of heroin dependence in the prison hospitals or in volunteers to the Opium Treatment Center during those years, when the author worked as medical officer-in-charge.

According to information from patients, there was some knowledge of heroin among the younger generation of opium and morphine addicts. They knew of Chinese from Hong Kong taking heroin and of American soldiers and sailors from neighboring war zones looking for heroin. Lack of a market, owing to Singapore smokers not knowing of heroin and not demanding it, lack of a certain class of personnel who could set up heroin "factories," and the work of police and customs were held to be factors responsible for the absence of a heroin problem.

In 1964, heroin had been detected in samples sent to the government laboratory in Sabah. In 1969, more samples of heroin were found, increasing in 1970. In 1972, authorities knew that heroin was being manufactured in Malaysia and exported to other countries in the form of cubes. On October 13, 1973, the first clandestine heroin laboratory in Malaysia was found in Bukit Mertajam. In Sinapore, heroin was discovered for the first time in Chinatown following police and customs raids in 1971. Isolated reports were appearing in the press regarding arrests of individuals for possession of small amounts of heroin. Between 1972 and 1973 the author saw two clinical cases of heroin use, both Chinese adult males. One gave a history of having smoked cigarettes "spiked" with heroin. The cigarette used was Lucky Strike, and spiking was done with a toothpick; a metal spike was also used. The first "official" heroin addiction cases were disclosed by the Director of the Central Narcotics Bureau and reported in the press on May 2, 1972.

Statistics of arrests made under the Dangerous Drug Act between January 1970 and August 1971 released by the Minister for Home Affairs were as follows:

Opium addicts	3,261
Ganja addicts	672
Morphine addicts	412
MX (Mandrax or Quaaludes)	21
Heroin addicts	5

In Peninsular of Malaysia reports of heroin arrests and heroin use had appeared earlier, in 1970, than in Singapore. In February 1970, a young girl of 20 years of age was found with a tube of heroin concealed in her brassier. In 1971 and 1972 more cases were being reported, the majority in Penang. In Singapore, similar press(4) reports of heroin arrests were being made by the end of 1974. In November 1974 it was reported that a heroin processing plant was believed to be operating in the outskirts of Ipoh (Straits Times, November 20, 1974).

The laboratory was said to be supplying drugs to neighboring countries (including Singapore) as well as Europe and the United States. The plant was producing the No. 3 heroin "a powdery impure form of heroin which is added to cigarettes and smoked." Narcotics experts in Europe had analysed seizures made early in 1974 and found that the heroin was made in a different way from those processed in Europe or the United States. A phial containing 0.5 grams of heroin was being sold for $6.00 near Ipoh, in the Peninsular of Malaysia, but $30 in Singapore.

In November 1974, the director of the Central Narcotics Bureau in Singapore revealed that 70 persons had been arrested(5) for using, having, or trafficking in heroin in the first ten months of 1974. All were English-educated, aged between 16 and 25 years. All but two had started on the drug between January and March 1974. The heroin was the No. 3 heroin which is put into cigarettes and smoked. The drug was believed to have come to Singapore from Malaysia. When "hooked" some of the users smoked 25 heroin-tipped cigarettes a day from two or three phials. Since each phial of 0.5 g costs $30 in Singapore, an addict would be spending some $90 a day on the drug.

In Singapore, in less than a year, from January till November 24, 1974, there had been 2,636 arrests as follows:

1,203 opium arrests
  867 methaqualone arrests
  287 cannabis arrests
  206 morphine arrests
   70 heroin arrests
    3 amphetamine arrests

The wholesale prices pertaining in June/September 1974 were as follows (in Singapore dollars):

Heroin	$11,500 per kg
Morphine	7,000
Opium	600
Ganja (cannabis)	360

Methaqualone $1.60 per tablet.
(Sunday Straits Times, Nov. 24, 1974)

For the year 1974, the number of heroin addicts arrested by the bureau was 110 (New Nation, July 2, 1975).

Cannabis Use

The early association of cannabis use with immigrants from India and Pakistan has been noted. To this day the use of cannabis, especially the smoking of it with a pipe, the gosah and the chillum (a cone-shaped clay pipe), is generally confined to older Indians and Pakistanis. As such for many decades it was a localized practice with a "ghetto" character and, although illegal, was not much of a police or social problem.

Around 1964, owing to the confrontation between Malaysia and Indonesia, the smuggled supplies from Indonesia were cut off, and traffickers introduced the seeds to local farmers. The addicts, mostly unskilled laborers and seamen who had become unemployed, introduced the drug to young pleasure seekers who frequented "sarabat" stalls in certain districts in Singapore. "Sarabat" is a sweetened, boiled ginger soft drink. The stall is generally an itinerant one; the hawker has a favorite pitch, stools are available, and favorite sites are near open spaces. Besides serving drinks, cakes, and occasionally cigarettes to legitimate customers, the stall holder is often a contact man for cannabis, in the form of ganja. Around this period, Hill noted a very large Malay following. He observed that certain places in Singapore were popular rendezvous for Malay ganja users. He noted the tendency of the younger Malays to have a meeting place. Many came from other areas like Amber Road, Kaki Bukitt, and Bukit Timah.

The ideas held about cannabis by the Malay users were several.

1. stimulates appetite
2. gives a sense of well-being, a feeling described as "hayal"
3. enables them to imagine or experience whatever personality they wish to be

4. enables them to overcome a feeling of inferiority
5. enables them to put up a bold front
6. helps to overcome worry and fatigue
7. helps to overcome physical strain in work
8. gives a "stimulating" and intoxicating" effect sexually.

This is much the way alcohol is used, only ganja is used as a cheaper substitute. It is the poor man's alcohol.

Information about the association of cannabis use with criminal activity is difficult to obtain and to interpret. Hill noted that to the "criminal," ganja smoking could give "sedative" effects, before and after a crime, a sense of fortifying them, and the ability to endure fatigue, exposure to inclement weather, and extra exertion.

Pill Taking

The author has been trying to pinpoint when exactly pill taking, particulary Mandrax, methaqualone with diphenhydramine, known to the users as MX, was introduced to the young in Singapore. In September 1970 the newspapers gave great publicity to an incident where two schoolgirls were alleged to have collapsed in class after taking pills. Around that time, it was noted that there were increasing numbers of young people who were being brought by police into hospitals for medical examination after being found collapsed or wandering about or staggering and fallen into drains, as a result of having taken drugs.

In April 1971 a drug dependence clinic was set up on a pilot basis to follow up these cases. Later new patients were being referred directly to the clinic. It was found that the drug users showed a new pattern. They were mostly young, their ages ranging from 12 to 23 years. They came from the middle classes, their parents being executives, businessmen, clerks, and teachers, and representing the four main races in Singapore, Chinese, Malays, Indians, and Eurasians. Some were students, or had been working mostly in jobs less "professional" than their parents, or were in national service, waiters, or laborers. They were from the English-educated sections of the community rather than from the Chinese or vernacular (Malay and Indian) sections.

The drugs they were using included ganja, Mandrax, Melsedin (methaqualone), known as the M pill, and another methaqualone product which because it had no markings was known as the blank pill. A few had gone on to experimenting with the smoking of opium and the injection of morphine. This is a clear instance of drug users crossing a cultural barrier in their seeking of a new drug to use. These young English-speaking Malay, Indian, Chinese, or Eurasian users have to go to opium dens which are operated and mostly used by older Chinese, generally of a lower social class, or to a morphine injection "den," again to queue for 40 cent injections with Chinese morphine addicts. The situation, since late 1974, is that heroin is replacing morphine as the drug of abuse.

Southeast Asia

The pattern of drug use among the young in Singapore – adolescent and young persons experimenting with cannabis and methaqualone in the privacy of their homes, hostels, stairways, open spaces, football fields, and parks, first noted in 1970, and the beginning and increasing heroin use noted in 1973 and 1974 – seems to be found in other neighboring countries.

Because of geography, Indonesia, with an area of 1,491,564 sq. km. and a population of 116 million, was a transit area for drug traffic. Cannabis sativa grows wild there in a manner difficult to control and Indonesia is a source of supply to neighboring countries. A pattern of drug use among the young was recognized as a drug problem in 1970, especially in large cities of Djakarta, Surabaya, Semarang, and Medan. The drugs were cannabis and morphine, and the users came from all socioeconomic classes.

In the Philippines, with an area of 115,000 square miles over 7,100 islands and a population of 37 million situated near the source of supply and within the principal sea and air routes of the international illicit drug traffic, the last few years have seen a rapid increase of drug abuse by the young. This has been associated with "youth discontent," restlessness, eagerness for new experiences, "hippie" fad, pop music, and parental indifference. About 150,000 people were reported using drugs like heroin, morphine, demerol, Mandrax, and alcohol.

Hong Kong's drug dependence is heroin addiction. In 1966, according to official statistics, there were 12,267 known addicts, 11,825 (96.4 percent) of them heroin addicts, and only 547 opium users (4.46 percent). The methods of heroin use include "firing the ack-ack gun" (heroin placed in the tip of a cigarette and smoked), "chasing the dragon," and "blowing the mouth organ" (the fumes of a mixture of heroin and barbital, placed on tinfoil and heated by a taper are inhaled, with a straw, a paper cone, or the open ends of a matchbox acting as funnels).

Thailand's main problem of narcotic dependence is that of heroin addiction in Bangkok. There is also a minor problem of opium smoking among the hill tribes in the north.

TREATMENT INTERVENTION

The Opium Treatment Centers (Singapore)

Up to 1941, the smoking of opium was legal in Singapore. Addicts were registered and could buy opium from government chandu retail shops. After World War II the smoking of opium became illegal, and was punishable by fines or imprisonment. No adequate provision was available for the treatment of addicts who might have desired to give up opium, and many turned to illegal sources for their supplies of the drug. Those who were arrested and unable to pay the fines were imprisoned, usually for periods up to two months; they received no opium during this imprisonment.   Because of their poor physical condition and because of withdrawal distress they spent some time in the prison hospital, where they received a measure of medical care.

No other medical measures followed on release from prison. In general addicts did not go to doctors for treatment, and no government institution existed for the purpose. There were a number of philanthropic and semireligious "temples," in which anti-opium remedies, which included oath taking, tea drinking, exhortation, group callisthenics, and group interaction, covered the withdrawal period. The "cure" was effected within a fortnight and there were no follow-up measures.

In 1955, the government set up facilities for opium treatment. Legal provisions were made to enable persons who had been convicted to undergo treatment, the court sentence reading: "twelve months' treatment at the Opium Treatment Center." It was up to the prison and medical department jointly to carry this out in practice. Addicts were remanded and examined by the doctor while the rehabilitation officer investigated their social and family backgrounds. The advisory committee then submitted a report on each addict and advised the court on the individual's suitability for treatment. From August 1955 on, when the author was appointed Medical Officer, opium treatment centers, he daily examined addicts who had been committed and, in the course of daily discussions, became more and more interested in what he saw and in what they told him about their lives and their addiction problems. There were the questions as to why they took opium, what kind of persons they were, whether they could be "cured," and by what means.

Practically all these Singapore addicts were Chinese, coming from the main "tribal" groups: Hokkien, Teochow, and Cantonese. They were mainly unskilled laborers, semiskilled workmen, masons, boatmen, hawkers, and a few clerical and other sedentary workers. Most of them were illiterate, and those who were educated had only received elementary Chinese education. Their ages ranged from the twenties to the fifties, the greater number being in the 45 to 55 age group. Many had not become addicted until their late twenties. The average number of years of addiction (i.e., from the time they started smoking opium) was 18.

As to their mode of taking the drug, they were smokers by choice, and only through necessity did they resort to swallowing. After a pre-addiction stage which they well recognized (calling it "p'a p'oon," "knocking the pan") and which existed from a few months to one, two, or, as some of them averred, even more years, they became addicted. They smoked one or two packets several times a day (the average amount for a day was 3.4 packets). One packet contains 11 grains of prepared opium, costing $1.20 (Straits). When they became poorer, they resorted to taking dross (the residue obtained after the first smoking), either by remixing it with fresh opium or merely swallowing it. The poorest men took second dross (what remains when dross is smoked); this is swallowed, as it cannot be smoked.

The treatment and rehabilitation program at the Singapore Opium Treatment Center was based on two essential principles: 1) looking upon the addict as a patient to be treated and not as a wrongdoer, and 2) treating the whole person. Treatment was carried out in three phases.

1. The Withdrawal Phase. Withdrawal treatment was carried out in the hospital, and took two to four weeks. As soon as the addict was remanded, he was admitted to the prison hospital, where, at an initial medical examination, the doctor obtained a full history and established a physician-patient relationship. The first step in treatment was bringing about the individual's realization that he was a patient and in need of treatment. The doctor explained that, as a result of the withdrawal of opium (in the form in which the addict has been using it), a period of distress for seven to ten days would follow, relieved, however, by certain medicines. In practice, the method used was rapid withdrawal covered by tincture of opium   Supportive and symptomatic treatment was also given. During the treatment, the rehabilitation officer interviewed the addict, investigated his home and social conditions, arranged for the welfare of his family, and planned for the addict's future employment. His report was submitted to the advisory committee of the court.

2. The Rehabilitation and Reeducation Phase. This second phase of treatment was carried out in the Opium Treatment (Rehabilitation) Center, St. John's Island. It lasted from about five months to a year. After sentence and transfer to St. John's Island, the patients had a further medical checkup before assignment to a trade – carpentry, canework, tailoring, gardening, helping in the hospital, working in the cookhouse, etc. There was ample provision for recreation: basketball, badminton, swimming, music, and painting for those interested. Many addicts who had had no opportunities for recreational activities before took to them with great enthusiasm.
During their stay at the rehabilitation center, the patients were, thus, not merely kept away from opium, but they gradually regained their self-respect, their lost dignity. They were helped to deal with their personal problems. They were not alone, for they found others with similar problems. Yet they learned that success ultimately depended on their own efforts. While on the island they had to develop the desire for, and learn to accept the need for, a new existence in the future, a life without recourse to drugs.

3. The Follow-up Phase. The follow-up took place after discharge, in the patient's own social environment. It is in the community that the final phase of adjustment and adaptation must take place. The treatment center doctor ran a follow-up clinic in the outpatient department of the General Hospital to help to remove the stigma of the patient's association with a prison establishment. This follow-up clinic also acted as a center where the addict could meet other addicts or bring along his addicted friends to see the doctor.

The treatment centers were established on February 8, 1955: 1) a main rehabilitation center on an island off the main Singapore Island for male committed and volunteer patients, 2) a ward in a general hospital with security arrangements for male patients, and 3) a prison block in the female prison for female committed patients and female volunteers.

The main rehabilitation center was on an island, St. John's, five and a half miles from Singapore, a quarantine station whose facilities were taken over for drug rehabilitation. It had an administrative office, a 24 bed hospital, residential camps with dining hall, kitchen, hall, and facilities for games, together with workshops for carpentry, can work, and tailoring.

The medical officer and the superintendent (nonmedical) assisted by three trained male nurses and three rehabilitation officers/clerks, and 34 custodial staff ran the establishment. In the first year of its existence beginning February 14, 1955, 284 male patients had been admitted including five volunteers. The admitted patients had been screened from 976 committed male persons by a selection committee comprising the medical officer, the superintendent, and the rehabilitation officers, after full medical and social histories, and examinations had been completed. The reason for the careful selection was because the center had only facilities to house 240 persons, who were kept in the center for an average six month period, later shortened to three months, so that the total number treated in a year ranged from 480 to 960.

In the same year, 1955, the selection committee, called the Advisory Committee also examined 42 females, and accepted seven for treatment and rehabilitation in the female prison. There were five male volunteers and one female volunteer. It is interesting to note that as there were no separate facilities for the volunteers, both male and female, they accepted the condition of being treated in the same manner as committed addicts. Following is a table giving the admissions to the Opium Treatment Center, St. John's Island, for 1955-1966.

Admission to the Opium Treatment Center, 1955-1966

	Total Admission	Volunteers
1955	284	5
1956	374	7
1957	347	17
1958	399	42
1959	488	35
1960	646	48
1961	478	54
1962	179	54
1963	189	60
1964	285	214
1965	465	349
1966	592	258

The changing pattern of drug use and abuse and changing attitudes and responses have brought changes to the center. In 1963 the center ceased to be a prison and its administration became the responsibility entirely of the health services. In the 1970s new patterns of drug use and misuse among the young became more noticeable and received more attention and provoked more response from the enforcement agencies. The facilities were converted for the reception of younger drug users and with the passing of new legislation in 1973, it became a drug treatment and rehabilitation center for drug offenders. Recently this center was used to house Vietnamese war refugees and still more recently it has been converted to other uses and the treatment facility resited in another part of the state. A drug dependence clinic for the follow-up of drug dependents discharged from hospitals and to which volunteer drug users were referred or referred themselves was in operation from 1971.

Hong Kong

Other countries in Southeast Asia were also setting up treatment and rehabilitation facilities for opiate users. Singapore's Opium Treatment Center was established in 1955. In Hong Kong, in 1958, the Prisons Department opened a center at Tai Lam in the New Territories for the treatment and rehabilitation of male addicts sentenced to prison. From its opening to the end of 1966, more than 15,000 prisoners were treated. Follow-up care was also provided.

Following a pilot scheme in a drug addiction center at the Castle Peak Mental Hospital (1960-1963), a government subsidized center of the Society for the Aid and Rehabilitation of Drug Addicts (SARDA) was established at Shek Kwu Chau Island in 1963. During the period 1963-65, voluntary patients were treated for three weeks at Castle Peak Hospital and then transferred to Shek Kwu Chau. In 1965, the Castle Peak Drug Addiction Center was closed down and since that time SARDA's hospital at Shek Kwu Chau has provided treatment for all volunteers. Since 1965, registration and physical examination of addicts prior to admission has been carried out at SARDA's town center.

Thailand

The Thai government's first hospital for the treatment and rehabilitation of drug dependents was the Government Opium Treatment Center opened in 1959. In 1962, it was succeeded by the Government Narcotics Hospital, which in turn was replaced by the Thanyarak Hospital. Thanyarak Hospital, which opened on January 1, 1967, is at Rangsit Thanyaburi, 29 km south of Bangkok. Addict prisoners receive treatment at Rangsit and at Bangkok Central Prison.

Treatment facilities were also provided for drug-dependent persons by the army, navy, and air force. In addition facilities were provided for general practitioners to treat drug-dependent persons, the health authorities giving annual quotas of narcotics to private practitioners.

Opium smoking was abolished in Thailand on January 1, 1959. Poppy cultivation is carried on by hill tribes in northern Thailand. There is a program, with United Nations cooperation, to abolish production by the hill tribes.

It is of interest to note that in the early years of the setting up of treatment centers in Singapore, Thailand, and Hong Kong, the doctors in charge of these various centers were in close liaison and exchanged experiences. Dr. P.M. Yap was associated with Castle Peak, Dr. Prayoon Narakarnphadung with the Thai center and the author with the Singapore center. The World Health Organization also interested itself in these early rehabilitation efforts for drug users.

Indonesia

The beginning of 1970 saw the rise of drug use among the young, especially in big cities like Djakarta and Surabaya. In Djakarta there is a government unit for treatment of drug dependents. Private clinics at Dharma wangsa, Dharma sakti, Dharma paya, and Dharma Bhakti Hospitals. In 1971, Indonesia established a national bureau for narcotics to deal with the problem.

The Philippines

There are facilities for the treatment and rehabilitation of drug dependents at the General Hospital, the Mental Hospital, and the NBI Treatment and Rehabilitation Center at Tagaytay City; in private agencies' psychiatric units affiliated with medical schools such as the University of Santo Tomas, Ramon Magsaysay Memorial Center, Sison Hospital, St. Luke's Hospital, and the Makati Medical Center; the Rehabilitation Center of the Narcotics Foundation of the Philippines, Inc. at Patanaque Rizal, for male and female patients, the Bahay Pag-asa at Trece Martires City, and the Silahis Center in Quezon City for males under the DARE program. The DARE programs at Bahay Pag-asa and Silahis are nongovernmental programs, based on the therapeutic center concept, and use persons who have themselves experienced drug-related problems and achieved a degree of rehabilitation. This is a departure from the many other programs in Southeast Asia which are government run.

The author visited two centers in Manilla in December 1974 and met and spoke to a number of young persons in the programs and ex-user program directors, and also spoke with the founder of the DARE program, Fr. Bob Garon, and his associates. The author is of the opinion that this sort of community-based nongovernmental response to the problem of drug abuse answers a real need among drug dependents who generally do not seek entrance to government-run centers. Two measures of the meeting of needs of such programs are the continuance of these centers after the initial setting up, and the availability of persons who have passed through the programs to continue working in these programs.

CONTROL OF THE DRUG PROBLEM

Legal Sanctions

In the immediate postwar years in Singapore, opium was the only dangerous drug in widespread illicit use. The Customs Department from the early years of its creation had been responsible for the control of smuggling of the drug. In 1952, the Singapore Police Force assumed, from Customs, the responsibility for the suppression of the internal traffic in dangerous drugs; external traffic remained in Customs control. A special branch of the Customs Department was reorganized to enable staff to devote full-time attention to the activities of leading opium traffickers. A Central Narcotics Information Bureau was set up within the framework of the Customs Department and functioned as a clearinghouse for information on the drug traffic in the Malayan area. It liaised with enforcement authorities in more than 26 countries, exchanging information with them.

Before the war broke out in Malaya in 1951, the sale of opium was controlled as a government monopoly. It was the policy of the government to bring about a gradual reduction in the consumption of opium in accordance with the provisions of the Hague Convention of 1912, the Geneva Opium Agreement of 1925, the recommendations of the League of Nations Commission to the Straits Settlements, 1929, and the Bangkok Agreement of 1931.

The registers were closed, except for medical cases on December 31, 1934. At the time of the Japanese invasion, there were 61,552 addicts on the Singapore registers, while in the Federation of Malaya the figure was probably four times this number. During the Japanese occupation of Singapore from 1942 to 1945, the registers were ignored and anyone who could pay for it was allowed to smoke. From the liberation of Singapore in September 1945, no opium was sold by the government, and all opium shops were closed. In February 1946, an Opium and Chandu Proclamation declared a total prohibition of the use and sale of opium.

In 1951, this proclamation was superseded by the Dangerous Drugs Ordinance prohibiting the import, export, possession, manufacture, and sale of opium. As noted earlier, opium treatment centers were established under the Dangerous Drugs (Temporary Provisions) Ordinance, 1954, as an effort by the government to undertake the treatment and rehabilitation of drug addicts. These were mainly opium addicts. In 1969/70 the older patterns of drug dependence, opium and morphine and cannabis among the adults, were augmented by patterns of cannabis and pills among the younger persons. The 1969 Singapore Year Book reported an "enhanced marginal interest in 'pot' shown by the younger generation." On June 12, 1969, the government passed the Drugs (Prevention of Misuse) Act 1969, which came into force in August 1969. It penalized the unlawful possession of drugs such as amphetamines and hallucinogens.

In March 1971, the minister of health mentioned in a speech the fact that in many countries severe penalties were being imposed on people who drove under the influence of alcohol. He added, "Fortunately, alcohol is not yet a serious problem in Singapore but there is need to be vigilant." In 1973, on October 20, the minister for health and home affairs said, "The drug abuse problem continues to grow in spite of the measures government has taken so far." He gave figures of arrests for drug offenses in support of his statement. The emphasis was on young persons.

In 1971, 557 persons under the age of 30 were arrested for drug offenses. The number rose to 993 in 1972. During the first half of the year (1973) 559 young persons were arrested for involvement in drugs. In July 1973, a new act, the Misuse of Drugs Act was enacted. This act provided for heavy penalties, including minimum jail terms and canning for drug traffickers. The maximum penalties of the new act included 30 years jail or a $50,000 fine or both and 15 strokes of the rotan (cane).

An idea of the proportions of drug dependents can be gained from this table of the 1,737 persons arrested for drug offenses in the first half of 1973.

Type of drug

Opium offenses
Cannabis offenses
Morphine offenses
Mandrax

Under the act, certain dealings in the "controlled drugs" are prohibited and made punishable, the severity of punishment varying with the seriousness of the crimes. These dealings include unauthorized trafficking, manufacture, importation, exportation, possession of controlled drugs, and cultivation of cannabis, opium, and coca plants.

It is an offense to permit any place or premises to be used for smoking, administration, or consumption of a controlled drug. The penalties have been increased and canning has been imposed on the more serious offenses. Other provisions give protection to informers, powers of search and seizure, powers of arrest, and power to search persons arriving at or departing from Singapore.

The act also empowered the direction of the Central Narcotics Bureau, an independent department set up in 1971, to require any person whom he reasonably suspects to be a drug addict to be mandatorily examined by a medical officer or practitioner and if necessary to undergo treatment at an approved institution. An addict was defined as "a person who through the use of any controlled drug – a) has developed a desire or need to continue to take such controlled drug; b) has developed a psychological or physical dependence upon the effect of such controlled drug." The law also provided for treatment. To achieve this the Misuse of Drugs Regulations made it compulsory for a medical practitioner to report to the Central Narcotics Bureau or other authorities all cases of drug addiction. Provisions were also made for addicts to volunteer for treatment. For such volunteers, statements made by them would not be used as evidence against them for prosecution purposes.

Legal Controls and Drug Abuse

Many countries in Southeast Asia have enacted laws to prohibit the nonmedical use of psychotropic drugs and prescribed severe punishments for those found in possession, using, or trafficking in controlled drugs.

Why is the criminal law invoked to prohibit the use, possession, and trafficking in of such drugs? Koh (1973) has given the following two reasons for society's action. One is that the drugs are capable of causing harm to those taking them. The state has the responsibility to restrict the availability of harmful substances and to prevent in particular, the exposure of young people to them. The criminal law could properly be invoked for this purpose. He calls this reason "state paternalism." For the other reason, he gives cannabis as an example. It would appear that state paternalism is not enough to justify the criminalization of the use, possession and trafficking in of cannabis. What then is the rationale for its suppression? The rationale is that the psychotropic drugs, particularly marijuana (cannabis) and LSD and to some extent, pills (MX), have become symbols of the counterculture. By counterculture it is meant the values and attitudes propagated by some people who are disenchanted with the mores of existing societies in the West. The advocates of counterculture are against hard work, against competitiveness, against materialism, against marriage, and against other values and institutions of conventional society. It is believed, then, that the final justification for the suppression of experimentation of drugs in some countries is that psychotropic drugs have become a symbol of the counterculture, and the counterculture is seen by their leaders as being subversive of the national welfare.

Drug Abuse Programs

The Philippines

The Department of Education and the College of Education of the University of the Philippines, with the sponsorship of DDB (Dangerous Drugs Board) have jointly developed a curriculum on drug abuse. The curriculum has been tested in sample groups of students and teachers. They plan to prepare trainers who in turn will train others in the schools.

Silliman University in Dumaguete City has a Drug Education and Prevention Center to develop programs in preventive education and information, and also in treatment and rehabilitation.

A nongovernment agency, Drug Abuse Research Foundation (DARE) founded in July 1971 by Fr. Bob Garon has educational and informational activities. It launched a DARE generation movement in February 1972, when persons from educational and nonschool institutions pledged to live a drug-free life. DARE has a hot line and newspaper and a television program on drug abuse.

Indonesia

In Djakarta, a coordination body for overcoming the problems of drug use has been set up with participation of police, health, university departments of psychiatry and law, attorney general Criminology Institute and Social Welfare.

Singapore

A Central Narcotics Bureau was established in 1971, and an Anti-Narcotics Association was started in 1972. The latter has a speakers panel that provides a corps of speakers for schools and the public and also publishes a newsletter. Recently, 1976, the association opened a halfway house for residents with drug problems. The objectives of the Central Narcotics Bureau were to coordinate activities to deal with drug pushers, traffickers, abusers, and also to educate the public.

A Note on Drug Prevention Programs

Drug education should not be confused with drug propaganda. Perhaps the most difficult issue that drug educators are confronted with is to explain society's divergent attitudes toward the use of alcohol, on the one hand, and the use of other psychotropic drugs such as marijuana, on the other. It is believed the only explanation for society's apparently inconsistent attitude is a cultural one. Marijuana is frequently identified as a symbol of the counterculture, whereas alcohol is very much the establishment's vice.

At best marijuana is only one symbol of the counterculture; it is not the counterculture itself. Some who smoke marijuana, especially those from a community with a traditional use, may be smoking marijuana because it is fashionable and not because they subscribe to the counterculture. The importance of educating the public, especially the young, on the dangers of experimenting with drugs is recognized; it is the methods to use, and by whom these should be carried out that little is known about.

PERSPECTIVES FOR THE FUTURE

Drug abuse continues to be emotionally laden. There are varied public demands for strong action to deal with this problem. Drug misuse and its associated factors has been in the past a social problem. Drug abuse is not limited to the misuse of psychotropic drugs alone. The controlled drugs are not the only drugs used to alter sensation, consciousness, or other psychological or behavioral functions. Patients get prescriptions from their doctors for tranquillizers and sedatives and other psychoactive drugs. Alcoholic beverages, in terms of quantity and appeal, affect far more than all the prohibited drugs. The advertising in mass media connected with alcohol makes a conscious or subconscious appeal to mood change. This extends even to other things besides ingestants and inhalants: every sense is the target of these conscious and subconscious appeals.

It is perhaps not a coincidence that the euphoria-producing properties of Mandrax were discovered by the younger generation in many countries throughout Southeast Asia (particularly Singapore, Malaysia, and the Philippines) as well as in Europe and Africa. Members of the medical profession will at least remember the monthly reminders in the mail of beautifully photographed pictures of flowers, one drooping and faded, the other by contrast fresh and bright like the dew in the morning, with the implication that that's how you would feel after a night's sleep with the aid of the medicine advertised.

What can we learn from the present for the future, in Asia as well as elsewhere? What should be done? By whom? For whom? It is not easy, out of the multiplicity of the trees of individual experiences to look for the wood of integrated insight and seek paths of wisdom and right action.

We often forget that the person we are treating is a person, a total person, and putting him into any system of treatment, however organized and well planned, is not the answer. A person needs another person. The author has been asked by medical colleagues, "I have an opium addict, or a morphine addict, what should I give him, doctor?" The simple answer would have been, "If you want to give him something to get him out of his withdrawal distress, you can give him tincture opii, or methadone. But if you really want to relate with and to him, then talk to him and see what he wants and how he feels."

The most important thing is the first contact with the patient; whether one uses methadone as one's first contact, or whether one invites him from the street, or whether one starts in a counselling center. The most important thing is contact with the patient to find out what he needs. This sounds simpler than it is. Many of the countries we have mentioned have no facilities where the drug user can come into contact with another person. Yet, he can get into a hospital because of a drug overdose and get all the treatment for his medical state. He can get arrested and go through rehabilitation services offered by the prisons. He is told that he can volunteer.

This perhaps answers the for whom.

Then, by whom. This is harder to answer.

Just as the drug user has to confront a number of problems as a result of using drugs, the potential intervention agent must come to that situation as a result of certain situations and experiences. Within any therapeutic community, such helping personnel must be available. They have to be trained. The persons to be trained in the center should receive training and experience in treating drug users, in field studies in the epidemiologies of beginning drug use, continuing drug use, and chronic drug use, in clinical work, and in independent exploration of new modes of approaches and interactions with individuals and groups. This is a lot to ask for, but our century has perhaps not come up against a problem of such importance and of greater urgency.

Then we come to what is to be done? What lessons can be learned from the experiences gathered in the treatment centers that were set up in Singapore, in Thailand, in Hong Kong, and more recently in Manilla, and Ipoh Malaysia? It is perhaps an admission that has to be made, that the persons who have had these experiences have not had the opportunity to set down their experiences and compare notes. It is only in actual experience that one can formulate plans for present and future action.

The experiences in Singapore and elsewhere in Asia have taught that contact can be achieved. Even drug users of many years standing can learn to seek help, provided there is no criminality or vested interests involved. We have seen that a person needing help for difficulties arising out of his drug taking could seek and find another person, within a facility, who was willing to listen to him and help him. The nature of drug dependence, especially opiate dependence, was perhaps such that relapse was part of its natural history. The problem of relapse was perhaps another problem and needed different facilities. Perhaps the answer lay in assigning to each and every person who had been discharged from a treatment center one person, outside the center, to whom he could regularly come for support. From our experience, with three rehabilitation officers to serve about 900 discharged people a year, this was a very difficult path to follow. Such a plan could be followed with the younger heroin addicts.

The experience with therapeutic communities in the Philippines (the DARE program) has shown that drug users can be treated outside a government program.

The author has addressed himself primarily to the reader who already has or soon will become involved in the management of persons who have presented themselves before him with problems related to the nonmedical use of dependence-producing drugs. The problems of discovering those who have just begun drug use, and who may not be aware of actual or potential problems, though touched upon, have not been discussed at length.

The area of drug abuse prevention has hardly been focused on in this chapter. The printed page, impersonal and cold, cannot take the place of personal contact. The author would like to invite his readers to share their experiences.

NOTES

(1) A diamond-shaped island, Singapore, about 41.8 km long and 22.4 km broad, together with 54 other smaller islands make up the Republic of Singapore, giving it a total area of 584.3 sq. km. Located approximately 136.8 km north of the Equator, Singapore is bounded by Peninsular Malaysia on the north, the Philippines on the northeast, and Indonesia on the south. A total of 2,074,507 persons were enumerated at the 1970 census of population, comprising Chinese (76 percent), Malaysa (15 percent), Indians and Pakistanis (7 percent), and others (2 percent). The gross domestic product in 1969 was $4,807 million. The per capita G.N.P. in 1969 was $2,443.

A forecast by city planners projects a 21st century Singapore with a population of 4 million. It is expected that before 1979, 80 percent of the propulation will live in urban high-rise flats. At present, 700,000 or one-third of the population live in public housing (1973).

(2) Papan Merah is Malay for "red board."

(3) Tahil is a Chinese measure of weight. 1 tahil = 1 1/3 ounce = 37.8 grams = 583 grains.
Prepared opium or chandu used to be sold in packets made of bamboo leaf. One hundredth of a tahil is called a hoon. A two hoon packet is the usual size sold. It thus contains 11.66 grains or .756 gram. It is the amount sufficient for four pipefuls of opium (smoked). The dried juice obtained when the unripe but fully grown capsules of the poppy plant (Papaver Somniferum) are incised is opium. This is raw opium the marketable merchandise, but it cannot be smoked. To be smoked, it is prepared by cooking in copper vessels. It is then called prepared opium, or smokeable extract, or chandu.

(4) Daily English language newspapers in Singapore are The Straits Times and New Nation.

(5) Laws in Singapore:
a. The Misuse of Drugs Act 1973 (No. 5 of 1973)
b. The Misuse of Drugs Regulations 1973
c. The Misuse of Drugs (Armed Forces) (Exemption) Regulations 1974

REFERENCES

Annual Reports, Opium Treatment Centre, Singapore 1955-1970.
Blythe W.L. Historical Sketch of Chinese Labour in Malaya Journal of the Malayan Branch Royal Asiatic Society, Vol. 20, 1947.
Edkins J. Opium: Historical Notes or the Poppy in China American Presbyterian Mission Press, Shanghai 1898.
Glatt M.M and Leong H.K. Alcohol Addiction in England and Opium Addiction in Singapore: some differences and similarities, Psychiatric Quarterly 85.1. 1961.
Goldsmith, M. The Trail of Opium The Eleventh Plague Robert Hale Ltd. London 1939.
Hill, H. The Ganja Problem in Singapore. International Criminal Police Review No. 221, Oct. 1968, 210-221.
Khoo, O.T., Fernandez P., Leong H.K. and Chan Y.F. One Year's Experience of a Drug Dependence Clinic in Singapore Proceedings of the 7th Malaysian-Singapore Congress of Medicine 1972.
Leong H.K. Opium Addiction in Singapore, Dissertation for Diploma in Public Health, London University 1959.
Leong H.K. (1973); Patterns of Drug Dependence in Singapore Singapore National Academy of Science Proceedings of the Second Congress 1971. Journ. S.N.A.S. Vol. 3 (1973) Supplement.
Leong Hon Koon WHO Working Group on measures for the Prevention

and Control of Drug Abuse and Dependence, Manila 1974: Working
Paper: Heroin Use in Singapore and Malaysia.

Little R. On the Habitual Use of Opium, Journal of the Indian
Archipelago and East Asia Vol. 2 Singapore 1848. Now defunct.

Report of the Opium Commission, Straits Settlements and Federated
Malay States, 1908.

Report on Drug Dependence Clinic, Medical Unit II, Outram Road
General Hospital, 1974.

Seah U. Chin General Sketch of the Numbers Tribes and Avocations of
the Chinese in Singapore, J.I.A. Vol. 2, Singapore 1848 (now defunct)

Society for the Aid and Rehabilitation of Drug Addicts Annual Reports.

Wurtzburg, C.E. Raffles of the Eastern Isles Hodder and Stoughton,
London 1954.

Canada

P.G. Erickson,
R.G. Smart

INTRODUCTION

A nation's response to drug use problems may take several forms dependent upon historical and sociocultural forces. This chapter reviews some of the reactions made by Canadian society, particularly in the last decade. Long-range historical developments will be touched upon briefly and general trends in narcotic legislation in Canada, compared to those elsewhere, will be summarized.(1) Some mention will be made of Canadian participation in international control measures. Key approaches to drug research, treatment, and education in Canada will be noted, but neither extensive reviews of these efforts, nor detailed descriptions of how agencies presently function, will be attempted.

With this background in mind, the major part of this chapter will be devoted to three topics which reflect the explosion of interest in drugs during the 1965-74 period. This decade marked the beginning of what has come to be called "the drug problem" in Western nations. Since an obvious development has been that some segments of the community, principally the younger members, have experimented with, used, and distributed various licit and illicit drugs for recreational, nonmedical purposes, the first area of interest is to review studies of the nature and extent of drug consumption in Canada. The second theme is the formation of public policy in the drug field as exemplified by a prominent government commission on the nonmedical use of drugs, the Le Dain Commission. Official response patterns as reflected in changes in the laws governing "narcotics" (chiefly cannabis) and their enforcement comprise the third major section of the chapter. Some discussion of the possible future outlook of Canada's response to drug use concludes this presentation.

In the early twentieth century the initial narcotic drug legislation was aimed at suppressing opium smoking among immigrant Chinese laborers (Cook, 1969). The first anti-opium statutes were enacted in 1908; subsequent debates, concerned also with cocaine and morphine, led to the Opium and Drug Act of 1911 and the Opium and Narcotic Drug Act of 1920. The addition of cannabis to the schedule of prohibited drugs in 1923 neither was preceded by nor provoked any discussion in Parliament. These earlier statues did not separate the offenses of importation, manufacture, and sale from that of unauthorized possession, in terms of the sentences provided. A series of amendments in the twenties stipulated progressively more severe penalties for these offenses. For example, the original maximum of three years imprisonment was raised to seven years in 1921; a minimum of six months in jail was passed in 1922; appeals for convicted traffickers were disallowed in 1923. Whipping was approved for conviction of sale to minors in 1922 and extended to possession and distribution offenses in 1929. In the same decade, peace officers received the right to search, without a warrant, any place except a dwelling house in which they suspected illicit drugs were concealed (1922). Police power was expanded further in 1929 through a measure called a Writ of Assistance which authorized a named constable "at any time to enter any dwelling house and search for narcotics" along with any assistants he requires to "break open any door, window, lock, fastener, floor, wall, ceiling, compartment, plumbing fixture, box, container, or any other thing." Thus, severe penalties and unusually broad police powers pertaining to both sale and possession of "narcotics" set the stage for defining the addict as a criminal.

This pattern, which was to dominate for over half the century, has been attributed to two principal factors (Cook, 1970). The first was that narcotic use was associated with a negatively stereotyped racial group (the Asiatics, and to a lesser extent, unconventional low-status whites) which made it possible to approach addiction as a moral crusade, demanding harshly punitive measures. The second factor was that law enforcement agencies in conjunction with the Division of Narcotic Control in the Department of Health gained a virtual monopoly over narcotics policies during the crucial early legislative period, at a time when the Canadian medical profession was only weakly organized. Historically, the predominant Canadian response to drug use has been enforcement rather than health-centered. This trend was similar to that displayed in the United States, where a more developed medical association acquiesced to the enforcement model. It contrasts with the British experience in which physicians, after some struggle with enforcement officials for control of the realm, gained nearly exclusive authority over the right to define who needed legal access to narcotics and under what circumstances these might be provided.(2)

The early 1950s saw a growing concern, both on the national and international level, with the problem of heroin addiction. In Canada this era was marked by the increasing influence of the illness model of addiction in opposition to the traditional law enforcement monopoly. A 1954 amendment to the Opium and Drug Act defined a new offense, "possession for the purpose of trafficking," and penalties for trafficking in narcotics were increased to 14 years. A special Senate committee, formed in 1955, heard conflicting testimony from law enforcement officials, members of the medical profession, and social service agencies on effective responses to opiate addiction. Its recommendations culminated in the Narcotic Control Act of 1961 which gave official recognition to the view that both enforcement and medical treatment should be involved in the control of addiction. At this time the penalty of whipping was eliminated for all narcotic offenses. Although minimum penalties for most offenses (except seven years for importation) were removed, the legislation had the effect of increasing maximum sentences for all offenses. Life imprisonment was possible for those convicted of trafficking or importing; seven years remained the maximum for possession and cultivation, but the summary option was removed. However, the act also returned more authority to the medical profession with respect to the distribution of narcotic drugs, and provided that "criminal addicts" were entitled to "custody for treatment . . . in lieu of any other sentence."(3) At about the same time, Canada became a party to the Single Convention on Narcotic Drugs, adopted by the United Nations in 1961.(4) These developments in response to heroin addiction paralleled those in the United States, while in Britain a counterreaction was occurring. By the mid-1960s, the situation in these countries was contrasted in this way:

> Thus, a convergence in response to illegal opiate use has begun to develop in three countries. In Canada and the United States, the illness definition of addiction has come to have a greater influence and new treatment modalities have developed in this sphere. On the other hand, in Great Britain, there has developed a more active and controlled treatment program for addicts and a greater use of legal sanctions as the previous laisser-faire approach became untenable in the face of an increase in drug addiction. (Cook, 1970: 132)

What, then, was the Canadian situation with regard to remedial or corrective approaches to various drug problems? Although criminal law powers with respect to drugs clearly fall within the federal preserve (as the foregoing discussion has illustrated), direct jurisdiction over public health services rests with the provinces.(5) Federal intervention is only permissible on the basis of its general power to deal with emergencies of national concern. That is not to say the federal government is prevented from providing financial assistance for treatment facilities. However, the constitutional division of powers means that the authority to initiate such facilities resides in provincial legislatures. Accordingly, programs for the study and treatment of alcohol and drug problems have evolved largely in provincial agencies or government branches. Numerous provincial responses to the need have developed. The Addiction Research Foundation of Ontario, which began operating in 1951 to deal with issues in treatment, education, and research regarding alcoholism, has become increasingly involved in activities pertaining to the nonmedical use of drugs in general. The Narcotic Addiction Foundation of British Columbia came into existence in 1956 largely in response to the problems of heroin addiction in that province. It has been superseded by the Alcohol and Drug Commission of British Columbia.

Most other provinces and districts support either foundations (Manitoba, Quebec, Newfoundland, Prince Edward Island) or commissions (Nova Scotia, Saskatchewan, Alberta); some approach drug treatment and education programs directly through government departments (New Brunswick, Northwest Territories, Yukon). Sustained communication and exchange between provincial bodies in the area of drug problems seems to have been minimal. This may be due in part to the lack of a strong central authority.

The federal government has been more active in supporting research activities than health services. The Non-Medical Use of Drugs Directorate (NMUD), formed in 1971 and responsible to the Health Protection Branch of the federal Department of Health and Welfare, has two principal functions. The first is to provide financial assistance for drug research through grants and contracts, and the second is to authorize and make available standard drug samples for research purposes. A related responsibility for NMUD is that of coordinating and setting standards for the federal effort in research, information, treatment, and prevention of problems associated with nonmedical drug use. The emphasis to date in NMUD programs has been nonalcoholic drugs although this has recently been changing. In brief, the usual noncoercive response to drug use in Canada has been the establishment of fledgling provincial agencies which combine treatment, research, and education efforts with respect to a wide array of problem drugs.

The foregoing overview of legal and health-oriented approaches to drug use in Canada has been of necessity, brief. We will now turn to a more detailed examination of the period of greatest interest in this chapter, that of the period 1965-74. The national setting at the beginning of this decade had several characteristics to be borne in mind. First, the heroin addict population had apparently stabilized and was not a matter of much public concern. Secondly, a concern was developing over rapidly escalating, principally youthful, middle-class drug use. Thirdly, drugs of particular attention in the media at this time were marijuana and LSD. No law existed to prohibit the use, possession, or sale of the latter, while cannabis was governed by severe penalties tailored expressly for the opiate narcotics. Fourthly, no local empirical studies had been done and very little was known about the actual extent of the use of illicit substances. This situation, coupled with the explosion of interest in drugs in the mid-1960s, lent importance to the three areas of major concern in this chapter.

STUDIES OF THE NATURE AND EXTENT
OF DRUG USE IN CANADA

The aims of this section are to indicate some major themes about drug use, to show how they fit into the general response, and what the effects have been.

Prior to 1965, epidemiologic interest in Canadian drug use was aimed at alcohol and the opiates alone. The specialized provincial organizations were mainly concerned with alcoholism, although those of

British Columbia and Ontario had small treatment and research programs for opiate addiction. Surveys of drug epidemiology in Canada have been made at several points in time, but since it is impossible to cover all studies and detailed reviews are available (Mercer and Smart, 1974; Smart and Whitehead, 1974) the emphasis here will be placed on studies done in Ontario.

In particular, we wish to look at studies of illicit drug use among young people in school, but mention will also be made of alcohol use as it is again becoming prominent as a drug of concern. The use of prescription drugs has received attention recently (Cooperstock, 1971) as has the use of drugs of all classes among adults (Smart and Fejer, 1973; Fejer and Smart, 1973; Leon, 1974) and specialized drug-using populations (Smart and Fejer, 1969; Smart and Jones, 1970; Smart and Cox, 1972; Whitehead and Brook, 1973).

Studies of Drug Use Among Young Persons

In 1966 and 1967 growing concern developed over the use of LSD, marijuana, and solvents by young people. This was reflected by school officials and parents in concern for how the use of such drugs might affect school performance and attendance. Some of the first drug use studies were made by a Toronto Parent-Teachers Association and by the Addiction Research Foundation (ARF) of Ontario in response to requests by school officials. In 1967 ARF established a study of self-reported drug use in Toronto that has been repeated every two years since 1968. This created a methodology that has been replicated in a variety of studies in other Canadian cities.

A number of studies of students have contributed to the development of drug education programs by providing an ongoing account of the extent of use in young persons (cf. Whitehead, 1971; Campbell, 1970; LaForest, 1969; Russell, 1970; Hagashi, 1968). Most of this research has been conducted in the larger urban centers, though some studies have examined drug use patterns in more rural settings (cf. Annis et al., 1971; Fejer and Smart, 1971; Fejer, 1971; Smart et al., 1970). These studies led to the tentative conclusion that, while the drug use rates among students were quite consistent across the country in metropolitan areas, larger communities displayed higher levels of use than more rural ones (Mercer and Smart, 1974:312-313).

Three studies of drug use among students that have been conducted at more than one point in time will be reviewed. These allow some assessment of changes in patterns of use, but they are of minimal predictive value. The studies of high school and university students conducted for the Le Dain Commission are the first and only systematic national surveys on drug use (Lanphier and Phillips, 1971). This research was carried out at one point in time only, in 1970, and as such provides valuable baseline data. A retrospective method was used to gain some approximation of cannabis use trends from 1966-70 (see Cannabis Report, 1972:202-204). The findings as to the extent of use of some drugs in 1970 will be reported briefly.

Campbell (1970), in his study of nonmedical drug use by students at a Quebec university between 1965 and 1970, found that LSD and marijuana use tripled during that period. A study of adolescent drug use conducted in Halifax, Nova Scotia, in 1969 was repeated one year later in 1970 (Whitehead, 1971). Marked increases in the use of some drugs were found, e.g., marijuana – 162 percent, LSD – 238 percent, and other hallucinogens – 168 percent, while only small increases characterized such drugs as tobacco, alcohol, stimulants, and tranquillizers.

A large scale cross-sectional study of Canadian drug use was begun in Toronto by Smart and his colleagues at the height of the "drug panic" of the late 1960s. The first wave of high school students was studied in 1968 and subsequent samplings were repeated at two year intervals until 1974 (see Table 4.1). Data from the earlier phases indicated a dramatic increase in the use of alcohol, marijuana, opiates, LSD, and other hallucinogens between 1968 and 1970. At this time references to a "chemical revolution," "the drug age," and "the turned-on" generation were common. However, between 1970 and 1972 the use of many drugs, especially the illicit ones (marijuana, LSD, opiates, and other hallucinogens) appeared to stabilize; increases were small or little change was found. During the 1972-74 period, the use of opiates, speed, stimulants, barbiturates, and solvents (other than glue) remained relatively unchanged (Smart and Fejer, 1974).

The use of alcohol and marijuana has continued to increase since 1968. Alcohol use, in particular, in 1974 involved almost 73 percent of the students in all grades. The finding that about 42 percent of the students do all or almost all of their drinking at the dinner table with their families suggests that heavy consumption would be rare for them. However, it also illustrates a widespread permissiveness in parents regarding alcohol consumption by their children, many of whom would be under the legal drinking age. Not all of the increase in the proportion of drinkers can be accounted for on the basis of a change in the legal drinking age in Ontario in 1971. The lowering of the drinking age may have had a rippling effect, increasing use among progressively younger age groups.

The use of many drugs appears to have reached a plateau over the past four years and, at least for high school students, the chemical revolution of the late 1960s seems to be waning. There are clear indications, as shown in Table 4.1, that usage has declined for the most dangerous illicit drugs after the peak was reached in 1970. However, alcohol and marijuana use continue to show small but steady increases.

Of the national high school sample (n=1213) studied in 1970, 2.5 percent reported using LSD in the last six months, and 3.3 percent in the preceding period (Lanphier and Phillips, 1971). Regarding marijuana, 84.1 percent said they had never used it, and 6.7 percent admitted use in the past six months. Frequencies of use in the national university sample were somewhat higher. Four percent reported the use of LSD in the last six months. While 74 percent of this group had never used marijuana, 7 percent had terminated use at least six months earlier and 18 percent were current users (i.e., in the last six months). Alcohol was the most used drug, with 80 percent of the university sample and 25.4

Table 4.1. Drug Use by Toronto Students in
Grades 7, 9, 11, and 13, 1968-1974

	Percentage Using Drugs at Least Once in Past Six Months			
	1968	1970	1972	1974
Alcohol	46.3	60.2	70.6	72.9
Tobacco	37.6	35.5	38.3	33.7
Marijuana	6.7	18.3	20.9	22.9
Glue	5.7	3.8	2.9	3.8
Other solvents	a	6.3	6.5	7.4
Barbiturates/sleeping pills	3.3	4.3	18.2	18.0
Opiates	1.9	4.0	4.0	3.6
Speed	a	4.5	3.3	2.7
Stimulants	7.3	6.7	6.4	5.8
Tranquillizers	9.5	8.8	10.2	9.0
LSD	2.6	8.5	6.4	4.1
Other hallucinogens	2.0	6.7	7.2	5.7
Total Students	6,447	6,890	6,641	3,479

Source: Smart and Fejer, 1974.
[a]Data not collected 1968.

percent of the high school sample reporting some use in the last six months.

At present, the current concern is that alcohol use is becoming more and more frequent among young persons and adults. All ten provinces have recently (since 1970) decreased the legal drinking age. There are clear indications both that drinking among young people is increasing and that alcohol-related traffic accidents among those under 21 are increasing (Schmidt and Kornazcewski, 1973). In 1970 only 4.4 percent of drivers under 19 involved in collisions were drinking, but by 1973 nearly 10 percent were drinking at the time of their accident. A variety of studies of youthful alcohol use have been made lately (e.g., Cutler and Storm, 1973) and more public interest in youthful alcohol problems exists than ever before. There is some tendency, in Ontario at least, for schools to have fewer drug education programs and to be more interested in alcohol education. A large-scale public information campaign concerning the hazards of drinking has begun in Ontario. There is considerable interest among federal agencies in research on alcohol problems and in social policy changes such as banning alcohol advertisements.

Studies of Drug Use Among Adults

The vital concern with drugs developing in the late 1960s derived from illicit use by young persons. The problems posed by prescription drug use and adult recreational use of drugs such as marijuana was scarcely mentioned at that time. However, some studies were made of adult (i.e., not in school) drug users in the early 1970s (Fejer and Smart, 1973a,b; Cooperstock, 1971; Leon, 1974).

An interview study by Fejer and Smart (1973) was made of 1,200 adults in Toronto. The results indicated that 23.8 percent of the sample had at least one prescription for psychoactive drugs in the past year. By far the majority of those receiving prescriptions were females (73.1 percent). This overrepresentation of females among psychoactive drug users has been found in a number of other studies (i.e., Parry, 1968; Manheimer et al., 1969; Cooperstock, 1971). Young persons (aged 18-19) had fewer prescriptions and those over 60 years had more prescriptions than others. The average number of prescriptions for those reporting having a prescription was 3.2 prescriptions or refills in the past year. When projected to the entire sample the rate of prescription was 76 per 100 adults.

The same study also investigated the frequency of marijuana use among these Toronto adults (Smart and Fejer, 1973). It found that in 1971 12.2 percent of male and 5.5 percent of female adults reported trying marijuana in the past year. However 41.5 percent of males and 20 percent of females under 25 reported some usage. In this younger adult group, marijuana use was most common among males, single or divorced persons, the better educated, drinkers of alcohol, and users of other psychoactive drugs. The study was repeated in 1974 and male use increased to 18.3 percent and female use to 7.4 percent. The increase was greatest among males and persons under 24. Nearly half of those under 25 had used marijuana during the past year in 1974.

A study by Leon (1974), utilizing a self-report questionnaire, examined the frequencies of drug use among three population groups — two student and one adult — in Oshawa, Ontario. The adult group, a sample of 978 industrial employees aged 26 years of age and under, were asked about their use of a variety of drugs. It was found that 2.5 percent reported using LSD or other hallucinogens in the last six months. While 9.6 percent had tried but discontinued the use of speed, only 0.8 percent had used it in the last six months. Not quite half the sample (47.4 percent) reported never trying cannabis; 25.6 percent had consumed this drug in the last half a year. Higher users of cannabis tended to be also heavier users of alcohol, and the highest levels of use of LSD and other hallucinogens were positively associated with high levels of cannabis use. Sedatives, tranquillizers, and sleeping pills were used by 5.1 percent, 4.6 percent and 3.1 percent of the sample, respectively, in the past six months.

These studies indicate that marijuana and other psychoactive drug use is not exclusively an adolescent activity, but involves young adults as well. Prescription drug use especially involves large proportions of older adults. These realizations put youthful drug use in a larger context and indicated the need for general educational and legal postures. One of the Le Dain commissioners (Bertrand) was moved to recommend the establishment of a new commission to investigate the problems raised by prescription drug use; however, this has not occurred as yet and no plans are being made for such a commission. Concern with such issues is reflected in the educational programs and printed materials of several provincial agencies, although they are considered less important than alcoholism or youthful illicit drug use.

Studies of Special User Populations

As indicated earlier, only opiate addicts and alcoholics had received much study in Canada prior to 1965. However, in the late 1960s numerous heavy drug-using groups of young persons were being identified in major Canadian cities, e.g., Toronto, Vancouver, and Montreal. At first these were "flower-children" or "hippie" groups using primarily LSD, marijuana, and other "soft" drugs. In 1969 and 1970 there was a trend toward fewer LSD users and more speed-using young persons. Some studies have been made of a variety of heavy using populations, i.e., LSD users (Smart and Fejer, 1969; Smart and Jones, 1970), speed users (Smart and Cox, 1972), and heroin addicts (Whitehead and Brook, 1973). Generally, these studies showed that speed and LSD users were young multidrug-using males who often had preexisting psychological problems such as psychoses of a schizoid or paranoid sort, and anxiety states. Heroin addicts tended to be older, more often have criminal records, and less often be users of a variety of nonopiates. However, it was difficult to achieve any reliable estimates of the numbers of speed abusers, heavy LSD users, or heroin addicts in a given area.

The Le Dain Commission national surveys indicated extremely low levels of "hard drug" use in the general populations studied (Lanphier and Phillips, 1971). Only 3 of the more than 1,200 individuals sampled in the high school population and 13 of the 1,213 students contained in the university sample reported ever using opium, heroin, or cocaine. These findings highlight the special nature of the relatively very small opiate or cocaine-using populations; studies of these user groups obviously require different sampling techniques.

Heroin addicts in Canada have been counted by the Division of Narcotic Control, now the Bureau of Dangerous Drugs, chiefly from police, court, and pharmacy records. The validity and reliability of these records for establishing accurate counts of numbers of addicts has never been established, and given the closed nature of many of the data sources such reliability and validity may never be known. These data showed 10,250 illicit narcotic drug users in 1973; this is an increase of 248 percent from the 2,947 known in 1964. Prior to 1964 the number of criminal addicts was stable or decreasing, and from 1964 to 1969 increases were small. Most of the rise in the past decade occurred in the 1969-73 period (from 3,733 to 10,250). This increase resulted in the development of many therapeutic community and methadone programs for addicts in the years 1970-73. Since that time some programs (at least those in Ontario) have had problems in attracting new cases and several have closed down. Also, 1973 marked the first year in a decade in which the official figures showed a decline in the number of new cases compared to the previous year.

During 1968-70 a large increase in services for hallucinogen and stimulant abusers occurred. Nearly all large cities saw the development of indigenously run day centers, drop-in facilities, referral services, or free clinics. This was in addition to an expansion of regular hospital, outpatient, and emergency care for young drug abusers. However, by 1973 almost all indigenously run services had closed or changed their clientele and many regular services also were contracted or closed, chiefly because of a shortage of clients.

The special user populations of greatest interest in 1975 were alcoholics (especially youthful alcoholics), barbiturate users, and, to some extent, young polydrug users. It appears from a variety of data, (i.e., hospital admissions, surveys, and street intelligence) that much of the heavy drug-using population has retired or moved on to other activities. Treatment concerns are now more with the traditional drug abuse problems rather than the exotica of the late 1960s.

THE LE DAIN COMMISSION

The Le Dain Commission is formerly entitled the Commission of Inquiry into the Non-Medical Use of Drugs. During its more than four years of existence, commencing in mid-1969, the commission produced four reports. These were the Interim Report (1970), Treatment (1972), Cannabis (1972), and the Final Report (1973). This chapter will not deal with the material and issues covered at length in these four volumes. Rather it will concentrate on the genesis and modus operandi of the commission, its recommendations regarding the legal status of certain drugs, and official reactions to these proposals.

Origin and Functioning of the Commission

The buildup of conflicting pressures on the federal government with regard to its drug control policies in the late 1960s, which is extensively documented in Cook (1970: 153-180), culminated in the formation of the Le Dain Commission. (A nearly simultaneous second response, arising from the same pressures, was the passage of the Narcotic Control Act Amendment, which will be dealt with in the third section.) The concerns that gave rise to the commission, as set out by the minister of health and welfare, were described in these terms:

The Committee of the Privy Council have had before them a report from the Minister of National Health and Welfare, representing:

That there is growing concern in Canada about the non-medical use of certain drugs and substances, particularly, those having sedative, stimulant, tranquillizing or hallucinogenic properties, and the effect of such use on the individual and the social implications thereof;

That within recent years, there has developed also the practice of inhaling the fumes of certain solvents having an hallucinogenic effect, and resulting in serious physical damage and a number of deaths, such solvents being found in certain household substances. Despite warnings and considerable publicity, this practice had developed among young people and can be said to be related to the use of drugs for other than medical purposes;

That certain of these drugs and substances, including lysergic acid diethylamide, LSD, methamphetamines, commonly referred to as "Speed", and certain others, have been made the subject of controlling or prohibiting legislation under the Food and Drugs Act, and cannabis, marijuana, has been a substance, the possession of or trafficking in which has been prohibited under the Narcotic Control Act;

That notwithstanding these measures and the competent enforcement thereof by the R.C.M. Police and other enforcement bodies, the incidence of possession and use of these substances for non-medical purposes, has increased and the need for an investigation as to the cause of such increasing use has become imperative.(6)

The appointment of the commission on May 29, 1969, was authorized by the Order in Council which set the following terms of reference:

That inquiry be made into and concerning the factors underlying or relating to the nonmedical use of the drugs and substances above described and that for this purpose a Commission of Inquiry be established, constituted and with authority as hereinafter provided,

a) to marshal from available sources, both in Canada and abroad, data and information comprising the present fund of knowledge concerning the non-medical use of sedative, stimulant, tranquillizing, hallucinogenic and other psychotropic drugs or substances;

b) to report on the current state of medical knowledge respecting the effect of the drugs and substances referred to in a);

c) to inquire into and report on the motivation underlying the non-medical use referred to in a);

d) to inquire into and report on the social, economic, educational and philosophical factors relating to the use for non-medical purposes of the drugs and substances referred to in a) and in particular, on the extent of the phenomenon, the social factors that have led to it, the age groups involved, and problems of communication; and

e) to inquire into and recommend with respect to the ways or means by which the Federal Government can act, alone or in its relations with Government at other levels, in the reduction of the dimensions of the problems involved in such use.

The five commissioners, all university educated, occupied academic or professional positions at the time of appointment. They were drawn from the fields of law, criminology, political science, sociology, psychiatry, and social work.(7) The lack of direct representation from the law enforcement field is itself noteworthy, in view of the strong enforcement bias in traditional Canadian drug control policy. The first task of the commissioners was to interpret their terms of reference. They did so first by defining non-medical drug use very broadly to cover a wide range of psychotropic substances, including tobacco and alcohol, and secondly by attempting to draw a line between medical and non-medical drug use. This definition was presented in the Interim Report and was applied throughout the inquiry:

Medical use of drugs is taken by the Commission to be use which is indicated for generally accepted medical reasons, whether under medical supervision or not; all drug use which is not indicated on generally accepted medical grounds is considered to be non-medical use. (1970:3)

The commission functioned in a variety of ways. It conducted two sets of public hearings, spanning 27 cities, many educational institutions, 46 days, and 50,000 miles traveled in all. These hearings provided an opportunity for members of the public to express their views anonomously in diverse settings that varied in informality. Although tape recordings and stenographic records were kept, no audiovisual record nor photographs by the press were allowed. In addition, the commission gave assurance that the hearings would not be exploited for law enforcement purposes (Interim Report, 1970: 7-8). Written and oral submissions to the commission, from individuals and organizations, numbered 639. The commission's research program encompassed 120 projects and a reference collection of 14,600 pieces of literature. The cost of the commission, by the time the last report was issued, was $3.5 million.

Legal Recommendations

Although the commissioners were in general accord regarding recommendations in the areas of treatment and rehabilitation, and the noncoercive influences of research and education, there was considerably less agreement displayed in their recommendations on the role of legal restraints. Both Cannabis and the Final Report contained a majority report and two minority reports on the subject of appropriate legal controls. These three contrasting positions have been labelled variously by media commentators as "conservative, liberal and radical," and "hard-line, middle-of-the-road, and soft-line." Whatever the label applied, it does seem that the differing points of view of the Le Dain commissioners reflect unresolved conflicts in Canadian society at large as to the proper control of non-medical, and particularly illicit, drug use.(8)

The recommendations on legal controls may be grouped according to type of offense and type of drug. First, with regard to the offense of simple possession, the commission recommended against any further extention of the criminal sanction, stating: "We believe that we should gradually withdraw from the use of the criminal law against the non-medical user of drugs rather than extend its application" (Final Report, 1973:129). Thus, they were not in favor of creating an offense of simple possession for amphetamines (i.e., "controlled drugs" under the Food and Drug Act (FDA)). However, the majority were opposed to removing the offense at this time for opiate narcotics and cocaine (in the Narcotic Control Act) and the strong hallucinogens (i.e., those classified as "restricted drugs" under the FDA). One minority report favored the elimination of the criminal offense of simple possession for all these latter substances. In contrast, the majority supported the abolition of the offense for cannabis only, but the other minority report favored its retention.

Regarding penalties for simple possession, when this offense would be retained the general recommendations were toward greater leniency. The commissioners would abolish imprisonment for possession of the restricted drugs and reduce it to a maximum of two years for the simple possession of opiate narcotics and cocaine. The maximum penalties suggested for possession of cannabis were $25 for a first offense and $100 for a subsequent one.

The recommendation in the Final Report that has generated a great deal of controversy was the majority view favoring short-term compulsory confinement for opiate dependent persons.(9) This approach would be distinguished from creating a crime of use (favored in one minority report, to be detected by analysis of bodily fluids) in that it would represent a form of diversion from the criminal process to a treatment facility. The time suggested was for not less than one month and not more than three months. One minority report was opposed to compulsory confinement for opiate addicts.

Regarding the offenses related to availability and distribution — trafficking, possession for the purpose of trafficking, importation, and manufacture — the commissioners were in general agreement that present Canadian laws and penalties concerning the opiates, cocaine, and controlled and restricted drugs were adequate and need not be changed.(10) They would shift the burden of proof for the possession for purpose of trafficking offense from the accused to the prosecutor, for all illicit drugs. The recommendation that minor exchange of cannabis between users be excluded from the definition of trafficking was not extended to the other drugs listed above. One commissioner was in favor of the controlled, legalized sale of opiates to drug-dependent persons, but the majority opposed this view, and favored instead the treatment approach of methadone maintenance over heroin maintenance in most cases.

With regard to cannabis, the majority recommended that the offense of importation be included in the definition of trafficking, with no mandatory minimum penalty. The majority also favored awarding the courts greater flexibility in dealing with the two types of trafficking offenses (by providing the option of summary or indictable proceedings) and reducing maximum penalties. It was proposed that cultivation of cannabis for the purpose of trafficking, but not for one's own use, remain an offense subject to the same penalties as trafficking. A minority report supported the removal of all cannabis offenses from the Narcotic Control Act, and favored the legal sale and regulation of cannabis under government control. The commission's recommendations for legal controls are summarized in Table 4.2.

Reactions to the Commission's Recommendations

One area of reaction to the commission might have been creation of new drug laws. Although the Cannabis Report was tabled in May 1972 and the Final Report in December 1973, no legislative proposals to alter drug laws were put forward by the government until late 1974, and then only regarding cannabis. However, in May 1972, the minister of health announced that the government would not remove the criminal penalty against simple possession of cannabis (as the Le Dain majority had recommended in its Cannabis Report), but would introduce legislation to move cannabis to the Food and Drug Act.(11) This government proposal resembled that contained in the Interim Report, tabled in April 1970. At that time, the commissioners were not willing to recommend the repeal of the prohibition against simple possession (1970:242), but did favor classifying cannabis with the restricted drugs in the Food and

Table 4.2. Le Dain Commission Recommendations for Legal Controls, by Type of Offense and Drug

	Recommended Legal Control								
	Cannabis			Opiates and Cocaine			Strong Hallucinogens (Restricted Drugs)		
Type of Offense	Le Dain Majority	Bertrand Minority	Campbell Minority	Le Dain Majority	Bertrand Minority	Campbell Minority	Le Dain Majority	Bertrand Minority	Campbell Minority
Simple possession.	No offense.	No offense.	First offense: A fine of $25. Subsequent offense: a fine of $100.	Maximum penalty: 2 years.	No offense. Confiscation if unjustified possession.	Offense of use for opiates. Move cocaine to FDA.	No imprisonment.	No offense. Confiscation if unjustified possession.	Same as majority.
Trafficking	Summary: Maximum penalty 18 months. Fine in lieu of imprisonment. Indictment: Maximum penalty 5 years. Fine in lieu of imprisonment. Exclude exchange of small amount between users.	All stages of production and marketing should be conducted by the federal and/or provincial governments. Penalties for illicit production and distribution not specified.	Same as majority.	No change.	Controlled, legalized sale of opiates to drug-dependent persons.	Same as majority.	No change.	No change.	No change.
Possession for the purpose of trafficking	Same as trafficking, but it should be sufficient for accused to raise a reasonable doubt as to his intention to traffic.		Same as majority.	No change.	Same as trafficking.	Same as majority.	No change, except shift of burden of proof.	No change.	No change.

105

Table 4.2 (Cont.)

Type of Offense	Recommended Legal Control								
	Cannabis			Opiates and Cocaine			Strong Hallucinogens (Restricted Drugs)		
	Le Dain Majority	Bertrand Minority	Campbell Minority	Le Dain Majority	Bertrand Minority	Campbell Minority	Le Dain Majority	Bertrand Minority	Campbell Minority
Importing or Exporting	Importing and exporting should be included in definition of trafficking but subject to higher maximum penalties. No mandatory minimum penalty.		Same as majority.	No change.	Retention and reorganization of criminal penalties.	Same as majority.	No change.	Same as for opiates.	No change.
Cultivation	Not a punishable offense unless it is cultivation for the purpose of trafficking. If for the purpose of trafficking, same punishment as for trafficking.	All stages of production and marketing should be conducted by the federal and/or provincial governments. Penalties for illicit production and distribution not specified.	If not for trafficking, same as simple possession. If for trafficking, same punishment as for trafficking.	No change.		Same as majority.			

Drug Act (1970:249). Other interim measures favored by the commission were the abolition of imprisonment for the simple possession of any psychotropic drugs and the provision of a maximum fine of $100 (1970:243).

When the government finally did introduce its cannabis bill in November 1974, the proposed amendments, particularly regarding simple possession, were more similar to those contained in the minister's statement of 1972 and in the Interim Report (1970) than they were to those found in the Cannabis Report (1972). This recent bill would move cannabis to its own special section of the FDA, reduce the maximum penalty for a first possession offense to $500 with jail only in default of payment, and provide greater flexibility and lower maximum penalties for the distribution offenses. (The specifics of this proposed bill will be discussed in greater detail and more appropriately in the following section on legal controls.) Thus, it is evident that in terms of specific legislative proposals, the commission's final recommendations on cannabis have not been implemented for possession, but have to some extent for the distribution offenses.

In a second area, that of bringing relevant information before the lawmakers as a basis for their decision, the commission's impact again appears limited. When the cannabis bill was introduced into the Senate in November 1974, its committee on legal and constitutional affairs initiated a set of hearings on the amendment. The hearings, which began in February 1975, involved submissions from organizations and individuals, a number of which had contributed to the Le Dain deliberations. At the time of this writing (April 1975) the proposed amendment has not yet gone to a vote in either the Senate or the House of Commons.

In a third area related to the formation of public policy, the commission's impact is difficult to assess. This is the area of knowledge, beliefs, and attitudes to non-medical drug use held by the general public, and by significant subgroups such as members of the judiciary and drug users themselves. The commission's work, particularly the public hearings, may have performed a significant educational role. One commissioner has suggested that the commission contributed to increasing the information level on drugs and debunking the stereotypes of drug users.(12) It has been suggested that the commission may have seen itself as functioning to decrease the alienation of Canadian youth, especially over the illegality of marijuana (Cook, 1970:178), but such an outcome is difficult to gauge.

In summary, the formal reaction to the commission's legal recommendations, in terms of legislation and policy making, appears negligible; however, the informal impact, in terms of more elusive changes in social attitudes, is a result that is impossible to calculate. It should be remembered that the constitutional framework of Canada disallows any change in current criminal drug laws at other than the federal level. Thus a small-scale experimental change in the law, such as the one in Oregon making simple possession of one ounce or less of marijuana a civil offense,(13) is not permitted under Canadian law. This constitutional situation would seem to reinforce the traditional enforcement approach to drug control, and contribute to very slow changes in the direction of liberalization of drug laws – the subject of our next section.

LEGAL RESPONSES TO DRUG USE

The Canadian constitution specifies that only the federal government is empowered to enact or change criminal law. Drug violations under the Narcotic Control Act (NCA) and two sections of the Food and Drug Act (FDA) have been defined as intrinsically "criminal." This means that no provincial government may act unilaterally to revise laws pertaining to the illicit drugs covered by these statutes. A certain degree of consistency is inherent in the structure of Canada's drug laws, as compared to, for instance, the United States where a state or even a city directive may supersede a federal one. In Canada, the pressure toward uniformity has been enhanced by assigning the primary responsibility for enforcement and prosecution of drug laws to the Royal Canadian Mounted Police (where it has rested since 1920) and the federal crown prosecutors from the office of the Department of Justice, respectively.(14) Judges, by custom members of the legal profession who are appointed until retirement by provincial cabinets, exercise their discretion within the limits set by the federal laws. These various components of the criminal justice system were mobilized in the mid-1960s to deal with the newly defined "drug problem."

The official response pattern of the last decade, in continuance of historical precedent, has been to rely primarily on the criminal sanction to deter drug use. As was discussed briefly in the introduction, law enforcement has been the traditional response to various forms of drug use throughout this century. The treatment approach, which gained some momentum in the fifties in response to problems of heroin addiction, was not extended to the emerging category of youthful users of marijuana and other hallucinogenic substances. For several reasons, this section will concentrate on official reactions to cannabis rather than other drugs that also gained popularity in the mid-1960s. As Table 4.3 shows, in terms of sheer volume, convictions for cannabis offenses have affected far more persons directly than any other illicit drug. This indicates that a large proportion of resources for the detection and processing of drug offenders have been absorbed by this particular drug. In addition, convictions for cannabis have risen sharply and steadily from 1965 up to the present, while those for heroin have increased more gradually and those for LSD have actually declined. Lastly, response to cannabis has been controversial, and has precipitated several changes in laws directly and indirectly related to drugs.

Our interest will be largely confined to legislative and enforcement responses to cannabis use, which is translated into legal terms as the crime of simple possession. Other offenses (i.e., trafficking, possession for the purpose of trafficking, importing, and cultivation) will receive less attention. Table 4.4 indicates that for any given year, at least 80 percent of all convictions are for simple possession. Although these figures show that 1965-74 was a decade of increased enforcement for cannabis use, this period was also marked by a lessening in severity of

Table 4.3. Total Convictions for Various Drugs, Canada, 1965-1975

Year	Heroin	Methadone	Cocaine	LSD[a]	MDA[a]	Cannabis
1965	266	6	3			60
1966	221	3	1			144
1967	348	19	—			586
1968	279	23	2			1,429
1969	310	15	1			2,964
1970	383	14	12	1,558	72	6,292[c]
1971	502	82	19	1,644[b]	325	9,478
1972	923	81	44	1,161	534	11,713
1973	1,290	43	123	970	792	19,929
1974	798	24	237	1,482	501	29,067
1975	511	26	289	1,570	318	27,367

Source: Bureau of Dangerous Drugs, Health Protection Branch, Department of National Health and Welfare.
[a]Not prohibited until 1970 under Part IV of the Food and Drugs Act (Revised Statutes of Canada, 1970).
[b]Corrected from Bureau of Dangerous Drugs summary table to correspond to Table E.55 of Final Report (1973:891).
[c]Corrected from Bureau of Dangerous Drugs summary table on the basis of data presented in Table A.1 of Cannabis Report (1972:322).

dispositions for simple possession (see Table 4.5). Phases in the response to cannabis use can be discerned, and these may be characterized as the "Get Tough Period" (1965-68), the "Initial Softening" (1969-71), and "Selective Decriminalization" (1972-74). Each of these three periods will be examined around the subheadings of the law, sentencing trends, enforcement practices, and official arrest and conviction statistics.

"GetTough Period" (1965-68)

The legislation governing illegal behavior with respect to cannabis during the period 1965-68 was the Narcotic Control Act (NCA). Cannabis had been added to its schedule of prescribed drugs in 1923. From that time, all the changes in the NCA that incorporated progressively more severe penalties automatically applied to cannabis. When the first influx of persons charged with simple possession of marijuana began to appear on court dockets, the prosecutor had no choice under the NCA but to treat the charge as an indictable offense. The term "indictable" refers to offenses that are viewed as "more serious" in law and carry a maximum penalty of more than two years incarceration. The "less serious" summary proceeding (carrying lesser penalties) was not allowable at this time.(15) If the defendant was found guilty of simple possession, the NCA provided for a term of imprisonment up to seven years. The only option open to the judge, other than incarceration, was to suspend sentence and impose probation. The monetary sanction was prevented by a related provision in the Canadian Criminal Code (Section 646 (2)) which prohibits a "fine only" penalty for any indictable offense that carries the potential for more than five years in prison.(16) At this time, the penalty for cultivation was the same as for simple possession, and conviction for trafficking, possession for the purpose of trafficking, and importing could result in life imprisonment.

Total convictions for cannabis offenses in Canada rose from 60 in 1965 to 1,429 in 1968 (see Table 4.3). It is indicative of belated official concern that a breakdown of total convictions by offense was not retrievable until 1968. In this year, 96 percent of total convictions were for simple possession (see Table 4.4). During this interval the chances of going to prison for simple possession were about 50-50. Table 4.5 shows that the odds were slightly in favor of getting a suspended sentence rather than jail. In addition to the factor of a prior record, sentencing variation has been held to be related to regional discrepancies in judicial behavior (Cook, 1970:138; Whealy, 1970:276). Ontario magistrates' and Appeal Court decisions at this time tended to be generally more lenient than their western or eastern counterparts. In 1967, the Alberta Court of Appeal took the position that imprisonment for three months in the case of a first offender for possession of marijuana was appropriate, and invalidated the original one day sentence. A year later, in British Columbia, the Court of Appeal quashed a suspended sentence for simple possession and imposed six months' imprisonment.(17) Similarly, courts in Manitoba and New Brunswick were also

Table 4.4. Charges and Convictions Involving Cannabis Under
the Narcotic Control Act, Canada, 1968-1975

Year	Total Persons Charged[a]	Total Convicted	Persons Convicted[b]				
			Simple Possession	Trafficking	Possession for the Purpose of Trafficking	Importing	Cultivating
1968		1,429	1,378	211	131	2	7
1969	4,756	2,964	2,313	454	179	6	12
1970	9,977	6,292[c]	5,419	448	356	26	43
1971	12,543	9,478	8,389	476	533	22	58
1972	17,153	11,713	10,695	290	620	33	75
1973	37,668	19,929	18,603	299	914	27	86
1974	49,676	29,067	27,202	429	1,281	24	131
1975	47,157	27,367	25,056	649	1,523	34	105

[a]Source: Crime Statistics, Police, Catalogue 85-205, Statistics Canada. Cannabis was not separated from other narcotics under the NCA in this source until 1969.

[b]Source: Bureau of Dangerous Drugs, Health Protection Branch, Department of National Health and Welfare; and Cannabis Report (1972:322-323).

[c]Figures for 1970 have been corrected on the basis of data presented in Table A.1 of Cannabis Report (1972:322).

Table 4.5. Sentences Awarded in Convictions[a] for Simple Possession
of Cannabis, 1967-1975, Canada

	1967[b] %	1968[b] %	1969[b] %	1970[c] %	1971[c] %	1972[d] %	1973[d] %	1974[d] %	1975[d] %
Imprisonment	46	46.3	33.9	10.1	6.8	5.3	4.7	3.7	4.4
Fine only[e]	1	1.0	17.6	68.2	77.3	70.4	70.8	68.6	66.1
Suspended sentence/ Probation	53	52.7	48.5	21.6	15.9	11.5	8.5	7.6	6.9
Discharge[f]						12.8	16.0	20.1	22.6
Total	100	100.0	100.0	99.9	100.0	100.0	100.0	100.0	100.0
n	(431)[g]	(1,378)	(2,313)	(5,419)	(8,389)	(10,695)	(18,603)	(27,202)	(25,056)

aIncludes discharges, as presented in BDD tables.
bPresented in Cannabis (1972):249.
cTable A.3, A.4 in Cannabis (1972):324-325.
dBureau of Dangerous Drugs, Health Protection Branch, Health and Welfare, Canada.
eBefore August 1969, not technically a legitimate exercise of judicial discretion.
fNot an option until July 1972.
gCannabis (1970):290.

reported to be favoring a jail term for possession. Meanwhile, Ontario judges were generally choosing the option of suspended sentence and probation for this offense unless a prior conviction existed (Cook, 1970:139-140). The more punitive decisions above referred to the intent of Parliament to treat the matter of simple possession as serious by permitting a maximum seven-year sentence. The judicial reasoning appeared to be that the increase in marijuana use required the imposition of severe punishment in the interests of deterrence (Cannabis, 1972: 247-249).

The ever-increasing numbers of accused who were being channelled into the courts during the "Get Tough Period" were the product mainly of the enforcement efforts of the R.C.M. Police. This agency had a 43-year history of close cooperation in the drug field with national enforcement agencies in other countries, Interpol, municipal and provincial forces in Canada, and the Division of Narcotic Control in the federal Department of Health. Most police departments in larger cities already had a drug squad, sometimes as part of the morality squad, and these were expanded to deal with the upsurge in availability of cannabis and other drugs. The procedure at this time was for local forces to turn over evidence of drug crimes to the R.C.M. Police for further action.

The NCA provides all police with unusually broad powers of search with respect to drugs. The police may enter and search any premises except a dwelling house, and search any person found therein, when they reasonably believe an offense regarding a prohibited drug is being committed, without the necessity of an arrest. The R.C.M. Police have an additional power, granted under a general warrant called a writ of assistance, to enter and search a dwelling house under the same conditions. A writ of assistance is not limited to time or place and is valid during the entire career of the particular officer to whom it is issued. This has meant in practice that a raid can be conducted on a dwelling with the assistance of local police, as long as one RCMP officer present has a writ.

In summary, then, during this period, judges, prosecutors, and police personnel had inherited a NCA that provided severe penalties, few sentencing options, and broad powers for apprehending and punishing cannabis offenders. The application of a criminal justice apparatus designed for opiate control to the ever-increasing availability and use of cannabis resulted in a rapid increase in convictions for simple possession of marijuana. Imprisonment was a common outcome. During this "Get Tough Period," however, the public awareness and debate over drug use that had contributed to the formation of the Le Dain Commission also focused attention on the growing criminalization of young persons for marijuana.(18) Questions and criticisms were raised in Parliament concerning the severity of sentences being given by the courts (Cook, 1970:145). In late 1968 the new minister of health and welfare made the following comments on the law against "pot":

Nor does it seem to me that giving criminal records to several thousand curious kids each year serves any worthwhile purpose.(19)

The climate was beginning to change.

"Initial Softening" (1969-71)

Although statements by the minister of health and welfare in late 1968 suggested that marijuana might soon be added to the schedule of restricted drugs, along with LSD, in the Food and Drug Act (Cook, 1970: 153), this was not the legal change that did occur during this period. Instead, an amendment to the NCA in August 1969 permitted summary proceedings in cases of simple possession of any narcotic.   The discretion of crown prosecutors to choose this option was limited by the federal Department of Justice which issued "general rules" to guide the application of the new amendment. For cannabis, summary conviction was recommended for a first or second offense, indictment was directed for a third or subsequent offense and after a conviction relating to hard drugs (Cannabis, 1972:246). Sentences under the summary election were limited to a six-month jail term and/or a fine of up to $1,000 for a first offense and one year's imprisonment and/or a $2,000 fine for subsequent ones.

During 1969-71, the figures representing total arrests and convictions for cannabis offenses continued to swell. As Table 4.4 indicates, convictions for simple possession numbered 2,313 in 1969 and 8,389 in 1971 – more than a threefold increase. Convictions for offenses other than simple possession also rose, but numerically represented far fewer persons. It is evident that the NCA was being enforced mainly against possession of the drug rather than distribution.

Trends in sentencing for simple possession shifted abruptly in 1969. Judges evidently began making use of the "fine only" option that was made possible in mid-1969. The imposition of imprisonment or a suspended sentence were reduced from 33.9 percent and 48.5 percent of all cases in 1969 to only 10.1 percent and 21.6 percent in 1970. By the end of 1971, just over three-quarters of all convictions resulted in only a fine. Data which was not available until 1970 on sentencing for the two types of trafficking offences shows a fairly stable trend toward imprisonment in about 80 percent of convictions.(20)

The beginning of an important change in enforcement patterns occurred in this period. The R.C.M. Police enlarged its own drug squad from about 185 men in 1969 to nearly 300 in 1971 to respond to the increase in trafficking.(21) The R.C.M. Police began to prepare municipal forces to recognize and deal with drug offenses and started to turn over responsibility for the laying of charges in possession cases to regular police officers. It is not possible to pinpoint just when this changeover began or at what rate it occurred. The Le Dain Commission, writing in 1972, was not able to be more specific than "the last year or two" (Cannabis, 1972:244). In light of the transformation of drug enforcement from a highly specialized R.C.M. Police task to a more routine police activity, local forces instigated or enlarged their own drug squads and trained police constables in related procedures. The shift appears to have been a gradual process of the early seventies, and was given official public recognition by 1973.(22) The resulting infusion of manpower into the drug enforcement field has been widely assumed to be at least partly the cause of the continued rapid rise in arrests and convictions for simple possession in the seventies. The position has received some empirical support in the work of McDonald (1969) which showed that the strength of police forces had a strong positive association with the crime rate for summary (less serious) offenses over time.

In review, then, the "Initial Softening" response, 1969-71, was characterized by a legislative change that led to more lenient dispositions for the offense of simple possession of cannabis. However, this period was also marked by a large upswing in arrests and convictions, and by an increase in the police resources for enforcement. "Softening" in our discussion was meant to apply only to possession, since the law remained unchanged and penalties severe for all other NCA offenses. Although the summary option applied in theory to other "narcotics," in practice it apparently did not (Whealy, 1970: 257). Nor does greater leniency describe the response to other hallucinogens, since during this period possession of substances including LSD and MDA was declared illegal,(23) and persons charged with those offenses began to appear in court (see Table 4.3).

"Selective Decriminalization" (1972-74)

Decriminalization refers to measures that reduce the overall amount of criminalization. For the purposes of this discussion, criminalization is itself defined as the process that results in a finding of guilt with respect to a criminal offense, and the resulting consequences that follow the official designation of a criminal label. Another view of criminalization holds that the term applies only to the first part of our definition, i.e., the registering of a conviction. In this latter conceptualization, the consequences in the form of a criminal record are assumed to be constant. However, in the definition adopted here, it is argued that the consequences will vary according to sentence. "Consequences" is used in a broad sense, beyond that associated with a criminal record, to include the sociopsychological notion of stigmatizing responses from both self and others to the "criminal" status. Implicit in this definition is the assumption that incarceration is more criminalizing than a nonpenal disposition. Thus, an index of criminalization for any offense would be a function of both the number of criminals produced and the type of consequences associated with the sentence imposed by the court. We might call the first dimension "official" criminalization and the second dimension "social" criminalization. This conceptualization, incorporating two aspects of the criminalization process, provides a framework for more rigorous assessment of any efforts to alter the "criminalization" associated with a particular offense in the society.

Decriminalization, then, can be seen as having two components: first, measures that decrease the flow of individuals charged, preceding the point of the finding of guilt; and secondly, steps which reduce the severity of penalties meted out to those found guilty. The 1969 amendment to the NCA allowing for summary proceedings for possession of cannabis is an example of the latter type of decriminalization. The abolition of a law, or a policy decision to enforce it less frequently, would be an example of the former type in which the overall volume of charges is reduced.

During the 1972-74 period the federal government took two steps aimed at mitigating the severity of penalties for cannabis offenses. The first was the passing of the discharge provision in 1972, and the second was the introduction in 1974 of a bill to move cannabis from the NCA into the FDA. This most recent development will be discussed later in this section.

A discharge is generally intended to relieve the first offender of some consequences of a conviction and lifelong criminal record, in circumstances in which this course is in the best interests of the accused and not adverse to the interests of society. The Canadian lawmakers had this model before them in English jurisprudence since 1948,(24) and indeed had constituted a parliamentary committee in the mid-1960s to consider the matter. Submissions in support of a move to reduce the impact of a criminal record were made by the Provincial Judges Association of Ontario (Criminal Division), and the Canadian Committee on Corrections.(25) The first publication of the Le Dain Commission recommended absolute discharge for first offenders in cases of simple possession of psychotropic drugs (Interim Report, 1970:252). Although this type of provision had been under consideration for some time, there is a likelihood that concern with the growing number of young drug offenders hastened its passage into law sooner than might otherwise have been the case.

In July 1972, the discharge provision came into effect. The court was given the option, when an accused pleaded or was found guilty, to grant an absolute discharge or a conditional discharge (in which a term of probation is imposed).(26) A key section reads that an accused who is discharged "shall be deemed not to have been convicted of the offence." However, an amendment to the Criminal Records Act, which entered law at the same time as the discharge provision, stated that, "This act applies to a person who has been granted an absolute or conditional discharge . . . as if he had been convicted.(27) Since the Criminal Records Act(28) provided terms by which someone could receive a pardon and "removal" of a criminal record attained through conventional conviction for a criminal offense, this amendment seemed to contradict the intention of the original change creating the discharge option. Not surprisingly, confusion resulted surrounding the discharge provision; however, the correct interpretation is held to be that a discharge avoids a conviction but creates a criminal record (Swabey, 1973). In practice, then, the effect of the discharge provision was to reduce the waiting period before an offender became eligible to apply for a pardon. This meant, with respect to the summary offense of simple possession, that a person awarded an absolute discharge had to wait one year, while a person who was convicted had to wait two years before applying for a pardon and "removal" of his criminal record.

Although the new law did not relate the discharge option to any offense specifically, when it came into effect federal drug prosecutors received a policy directive from the Department of Justice in Ottawa. This directive instructed prosecutors to recommend absolute or conditional discharge in all cases of first offense of simple possession of cannabis where there was not a previous criminal record or a concurrent conviction for another offense (Final Report, 1973:955). There has been some question, however, as to whether the onus is on the prosecutor or defense counsel to initiate the submission for a discharge, or whether the prosecutor fulfills the intent of the directive simply by not opposing such a petition (Sommerfeld, 1974:7). The Le Dain commissioners also noted that initial reaction from the courts was not favorable toward applying discharge automatically in a particular type of case unless legislation clearly required it (Final Report, 1973:955). As a provincial judge commented:

> It is my opinion that the discharge . . . should never be applied routinely to any criminal offense, in effect labelling the enactment violable. It should be used frugally, selectively and judiciously, as Parliament obviously intended. If it is considered that an absolute or conditional discharge is the appropriate penalty for a first offence under this section, then Parliament should do so declare. The courts should not compromise or circumvent the law.(29)

That the discharge provision did not become a popular exercise of judicial discretion in cases of simple possession of cannabis is evident in Table 4.5. While 12.8 percent received a discharge in 1972 when it was in force for the last six months, the proportion increased to only 16 percent in 1973. In comparison to 1971, the figures indicate a slight tendency for discharges to replace fines and suspended sentences. It is of interest that this trend should be so mild compared to the dramatic shift from imprisonment and suspended sentences to fines in 1970 (see Fig. 1). If the statistics that show a proportion of discharges are an accurate reflection of judicial behavior (rather than a result of recording errors), it is evident that a decriminalizing measure in law – the discharge provision – has had a minor impact in practice, that is in terms of reducing severity of penalties actually awarded.

Between 1972 and 1973 (the last year for which data is available) arrests for cannabis offenses more than doubled and convictions for possession increased by 78 percent (see table 4.4). Since a proportion of charges for a given year are not disposed of in that year (due to the interval between arrest and trial), it seems likely that convictions will continue to increase in 1974. By 1973 the assumption of responsibility by local police, rather than R.C.M. Police, for possession cases was generally established.(30) The strength of the RCMP drug squad had risen to 530 by the end of 1974.(31)

The second major step taken by lawmakers during this period of "selective decriminalization" was to introduce, in late 1974, a bill that would place cannabis in its own special section of the Food and Drug Act. If the new bill becomes law, the changes that would affect the official response to simple possession are the following. First, prosecutors would have no option but to proceed by way of summary conviction. Secondly, no jail sentences would be permitted except in default of payment of a fine, and these would be limited to three months for a first and six months for a subsequent offense. Thirdly, the maximum penalties would be reduced to a fine of up to $500 for a first offense and $1,000 for a subsequent one.

The more comprehensive shifts in legal definition are with regard to the other types of cannabis offenses. The proposed new section of the FDA would permit the summary alternative for trafficking and possession for the purpose of trafficking (similar to the change in 1969 for simple possession). This would mean that a "fine only" penalty could be applied to these trafficking offenses. Conviction by the summary proceeding would result in a fine up to $1,000 and/or a term of imprisonment up to 18 months. Conviction upon indictment would reduce the maximum from life imprisonment, as it is at present, to ten years. These reductions in the maximum sentence would also make absolute or conditional discharge technically possible for either form of trafficking offense. The law presently governing discharge does not permit it for an offense that provides a minimum prison term, 14 years or more, life, or death. While the new bill would also provide the choice between summary and indictable proceedings for both importing and cultivating offenses, it would reduce the maximum penalty for importing (from life to 14 years) and increase it for cultivation (from 7 to 10 years).

In general, then, the proposed legislation would provide the criminal justice system with greater flexibility in dealing with cannabis offenses, and reduce maximum penalties. It would still provide the same range of criminal sanctions for simple possession as does the Narcotic Control Act, as well as the same broad powers of search. The bill's significance, perhaps, lies in it being the first piece of legislation in Canada framed specifically for cannabis. Since cannabis was added to the schedule of the NCA in 1923 virtually without parliamentary comment, it has been subject to all the same legal constraints as the opiates and cocaine. Conversely, although efforts at "decriminalization" in this decade seemed to be principally in response to cannabis use (as indicated by federal Department of Justice directives concerning prosecution of marijuana cases), these changes applied equally, in law, to the possession of other illicit drugs as well. If this new bill is passed in Parliament, cannabis will have its legal "home" in the FDA with such drugs as LSD and amphetamines, but with its own section. A summary of Canada's drug laws is provided in Table 4.6.

This third section has explored official response patterns in the 1965-74 decade as they have been manifested in both formal laws and the law in action. Changes in the law, enforcement practices, arrest and conviction statistics, and sentencing trends have been combined to provide a developmental picture of response to drug use. The emphasis has been primarily on the drug whose prohibition has affected the most

Table 4.6. Summary of Canada's Drug Laws, by Year, Act, and Substance

Year	Legislation	Substance
1908	Opium Act	Opium
1911	Opium and Drug Act	Cocaine, morphine, and its compounds
1920	Opium and Narcotic Drug Act	Au:?
1923	Amendment	Cannabis
1961	Narcotic Control Act	All of above, plus numerous opium derivatives and synthetic analgesics
1970	Food and Drug Act	
	Part III	Controlled drugs (amphetamines, etc.)
	Part IV	Restricted drugs (LSD, MDA, etc.)
1974	Proposed Amendment to Food and Drug Act Part V	Cannabis

persons, has absorbed many resources, and generated the greatest controversy — cannabis.

This decade has been marked by a continuous and rapid increase in arrests and convictions for the simple possession of cannabis. Undoubtedly the first upsurge of arrests in the mid-1960s was a function of the number of users, and level of use in the population likely continued to be a major factor in the growing cannabis crime rate throughout the decade.(32) There are at least two other likely major contributing factors to the climb in official cannabis offenses, although it is not possible to determine their relative effects. One probable factor has been the growing strength of the police in this field. From having the main responsibility for all NCA prohibited drug enforcement in the sixties, the R.C.M. Police had transferred this role with respect to possession offenses to municipal forces by early 1973. Thus the actual numbers of police officers who were empowered to investigate and lay charges for simple possession of marijuana were expanded from a squad of a few hundred persons to include virtually the entire patrol roster of all municipal forces. As McDonald (1969) has demonstrated, the crime rate for summary offenses (as cannabis has been since 1969) bears a strong direct relationship to police manpower.

The other factor likely to be of some importance in explaining the increase relates to the type of decriminalization measures instigated. It will be recalled that except for the "Get Tough Period" prior to 1969, sentences for simple possession of cannabis have become progressively more lenient, in response to legal changes enacted in 1969 and 1972.

Research summarized elsewhere (Lettieri, 1974) has suggested that a secondary consequence of changes in drug control laws has been a shift in discretionary decision making. In this interpretation, reducing the severity of drug control laws that have been considered too harsh has led to an increase in the willingness of the police to charge, the prosecutor to prosecute, and the judge to convict. This has an overall impact of increasing the number of convictions. The Canadian data (see Table 4.3) that shows the largest increase in convictions for simple possession in 1970 and 1973 (the years following the two "softening" measures in the law) offers some tentative support for this explanation. Thus, paradoxically, measures that have reduced the severity of penalties for those found guilty may have contributed to an increase in the flow of individuals into the various steps of the criminal justice system — one dimension of decriminalization at the expense of the other.

The most recent indicator of official efforts at "decriminalizing" this crime, the proposal to place cannabis under the FDA, would in a sense recognize and formalize the practices and types of sentences that are already generally evident. If judges interpret the bill to mean that Parliament now considers the possession of cannabis "less serious," sentencing trends may be in the direction of greater leniency. However, even if enforcement resources and practices and levels of consumption of cannabis remain relatively stable, the forthgoing discussion has suggested that the number of arrests and convictions will continue to increase, due to greater willingness to exercise positive discretion at all levels of the criminal justice system.

ADDENDUM

Malign Neglect (1975-1977)

When this period opened, it appeared that Canada might be on the verge of enacting "new" cannabis legislation. As established in the previous discussion, a possible amendment to place cannabis in the FDA had been raised in government statements as early as 1968, and such a proposal also resembled the interim Le Dain Commission recommendation of 1970. However, from the time the FDA amendment (Bill S-19) was introduced into the Senate in November 1974 up to the time of the present writing (March 1977) the law governing cannabis has continued to be the Narcotic Control Act. The NCA has been unchanged since the 1969 summary provision for simple possession was enacted.

The sequence of events surrounding Bill S-19 has been as follows. After several months of hearings and debates in the Senate on the proposed legislation in 1975, the bill was passed with several modifications. The first was a provision for automatic pardon to accompany the awarding of a discharge for a first offense of simple possession. The discretion to impose a discharge or some other sentence would remain with the presiding judge. The granting of the pardon would occur immediately in the case of an absolute discharge and upon satisfactory completion of probation in the instance of a conditional discharge. Since under the present terms of the Criminal Records Act any person with a record must take the initiative to apply for a pardon, which is granted only after a police investigation, the Senate proposal appears to create a unique category of "instantly pardoned offender" for this particular crime. It seems doubtful whether the criminal sanction could be stretched any further in the direction of leniency while still retaining the offense.

How this provision for automatic pardon would operate in relation to repeated offenders is unclear. Under present law, it is possible for an accused to receive more than one discharge, and in practice this is known to occur.(33) If the new amendment was in effect, would the judge lose his discretion to award a second or even third discharge? The proposed change could be interpreted as requiring an automatic conviction of second offenders, who would then be receiving harsher penalties than they might now under the present system.

Other amendments introduced by the Senate were to raise the maximum penalty for trafficking from 10 to 14 years less a day, and to modify the maximum jail term for importing by subtracting one day from the fourteen year term in the original bill. The significance of the "fourteen years minus one day" clause is that it makes discharges technically available for these offenses. For the same reason, apparently, the Senate also recommended that the three-year minimum sentence for importing be eliminated. One other change affected the "burden of proof" clause in the "possession for the purpose of trafficking" offense, and shifted the onus more equitably to both prosecutor and accused.

With these amendments, Bill S-19 moved on to the House of Commons where it received first reading. It remained on the order paper of Parliament and died there when the session ended in late 1976. The bill has not been reintroduced in the current session of Parliament, and recent indications are that it will likely not reappear before the fall of 1977 at the earliest.(34)

What then has been happening with regard to arrests and convictions since the FDA amendment was introduced? The most recent statistics available are for 1975. They indicate that for the first time since such data has been recorded, the total number of charges and convictions for cannabis has declined (see Table 4.4). The decrease in total convictions is attributable to the possession offense for which 2,146 fewer convictions were recorded than in 1974, a decline of 8 percent. Increases were recorded for 1975 in the number of both types of trafficking offenses. This overall pattern of decline for possession was not displayed uniformly across the country. In three provinces (Nova Scotia, New Brunswick, and Manitoba) convictions for possession actually increased over 1974 figures.

Sentences for simple possession in 1975 did not display any marked departure from trends exhibited in 1973 and 1974 (see Table 4.5). There was a slight decrease of 2.5 percent in the proportion of fines and an increase by the same small percentage in the proportion of discharges between 1974 and 1975. Fines remained the most common sentence, as they have since the dramatic shift in 1969-1970 (see Fig. 1), being given out in two-thirds of all cases. It does not appear that sentencing practices were being unduly affected by the existence of the new cannabis bill at this time, but as was pointed out earlier, the proposed FDA amendment was more a recognition of existing sentencing patterns than a departure from them. The one sentencing alternative that Bill S-19 might have influenced de facto was imprisonment, which it disallowed; however, since 4.4 percent of all possession offenders (1,094 individuals) were jailed in 1975, it apparently did not. It should be noted that this was the largest actual number of persons sent to jail in any one year since cannabis offenders begin appearing before the courts.

Within the frame of reference of our decriminalization model, the total amount of criminalization for possession may be seen to have leveled off in 1975, rather than declined, since the small reduction in number was not accompanied by a major shift in sentencing patterns. Moreover, despite the 8 percent drop in convictions over 1974, the figure of 25,056 remains higher than any of the years prior to 1974. This represents a tenfold increase since 1968 (see Table 4.5).(35) Possession offenses still account for more than 90 percent of total cannabis convictions. Even if we assume no change in convictions for possession in 1976, this would still provide a volume of approximately 50,000 criminalized individuals (minus repeaters) in the two years since Bill S-19 was introduced. Thus our title for this period, "Malign Neglect," is in reference to the inactivity of the legislative body while the police and courts continued to generate a high level of criminalization.

No evidence is available as to whether enforcement practices altered in 1975-1977. It was hypothesized that increased police manpower might have contributed to the rapid and large rise in cannabis possession cases up to the peak figure in 1974. Conversely, the small decline in cases for 1975 may represent a stabilizing trend in police personnel and policy in this enforcement area. It could also reflect an increased reluctance to lay charges, assuming levels of use and detection remained constant.

Other illicit drugs were not neglected in this period either. As Table 4.3 shows, offenses involving various other drugs continued to be prosecuted. In 1975, the total number of convictions recorded for heroin and MDA declined, while an increase was shown for methadone, cocaine, and LSD. No new laws affecting these other prohibited drugs were proposed or considered during this interval.

In conclusion, the official response to drug use in the phase of "Malign Neglect" has been a continuation of the enforcement-centered approach displayed in the preceding decade. While legal changes aimed at reducing penalties are currently under consideration for cannabis, official reliance on the criminal sanction to control use and distribution appears likely to persist. The current minister of health, who first introduced Bill S-19 in 1974, stated publicly that "the government of Canada is not prepared to give legal sanction to the use of cannabis. . . . Bill S-19 does not propose the legalization or decriminalization of cannabis."(36) However, two years have passed since that statement was made, and recent reports have suggested that further reduction of penalties for possession might be proposed jointly by the ministers of health and justice.(37)

The lull before reintroducing a cannabis bill may simply reflect the conservative nature of Canada's drug control policies, inherent in the constitutional framework, as noted earlier.(38) It is also possible that the hiatus in cannabis legislation may provide the opportunity to consider measures that depart from the FDA proposal (first voiced in 1968) and move closer to removal of the criminal penalty for small amounts of cannabis (as recommended by the Le Dain majority in 1972 and as implemented recently in some U.S. jurisdictions). Within our model, both types of measures represent a form of decriminalization, but the second, by reducing the numbers charged, would likely have the more significant and immediate effect on the total amount of criminalization for possession of cannabis.

SUMMARY

This chapter has attempted to provide an overview of responses to drug use in Canada. A historical background has been introduced in order to set contemporary events in perspective, but emphasis has been replaced on reactions made in the 1965-74 decade. The first section reviewed selected studies in the epidemiology of drug consumption that indicate that except for marijuana most forms of illicit drug use appear to have peaked around 1970. In contrast to the attention given in the sixties to the use of speed, solvents, LSD, and other hallucinogens, treatment and research concerns of the mid-1970s have been directed toward the use of alcohol, prescription drugs, and to some extent cannabis and heroin. The Le Dain Commission, itself part of the official response to issues arising out of drug use, was the topic of the second section. The impact of the commission on public policy, with regard to its recommendations for legal changes, has been minimal. A review of legislative, enforcement, and sentencing responses to illicit drug use comprised the section on legal controls. These factors in combination suggest four discernible trends in cannabis control in the past several years. These eras can be characterized as the "Get Tough Period," "Initial Softening," "Selective Decriminalization," and "Malign Neglect." The future outlook of Canada's response to drugs seems likely to continue to be enforcement rather than health-centered. Although the treatment model has gained some ground with respect to opiate-dependent persons, the criminal sanction is still the predominant reaction to users of recreational illicit drugs.

NOTES

(1) The authors are grateful to Shirley J. (Cook) Small and P.J. Griffen for permission to draw on largely unpublished work, which will appear in their forthcoming book, Politics of Canadian Narcotic Drug Control: A Study in the Sociology of the Law.

(2) See Cook (1970) for an analysis of the structural differences producing the patterns in these different countries.

(3) Statutes Canada, 1961, Chapter 35, page 218. This section was never proclaimed, however.

(4) In contrast, Canada has reserved its decision as to whether to become a party to the Convention on Psychotropic Substances, 1971.

(5) The exceptions being in areas of federal concern, such as the armed forces, the indigenous Indian population, and the federal prison inmates.

(6) Order in Council P.C. 1969-1112.

(7) This composition is in interesting contrast to that of the American National Commission on Marijuana and Drug Abuse. Its membership consisted of four active and one former politician, four representatives from the medical and two from the legal professions, and one academic.
   The names of the Canadian commissioners and their affiliations were as follows: Gerald Le Dain, dean of law; Marie-Andrée Bertrand, criminology professor; Ian L. Campbell, dean of arts; Heinz E. Lehman, psychiatrist; J. Peter Stein, community worker.

(8) The emphasis in this section, and indeed in this chapter, on legal responses should not lead the reader to suppose that the issues surrounding licit, medical and nonmedical, use of drugs in Canada have been resolved, and no longer present problems. The Le Dain Commission represented alcohol as Canada's most serious drug problem, and also expressed concern over the use of tobacco, barbiturates, and other sedativelike drugs, stimulants, and solvents. However, the origins of internal discussion, and external reactions to the Le Dain Commission have been marked by controversy about legal control of illicit substances. The law is a major instrument of social policy. In Canada, the official response of the community at large to drug use has been primarily tolerance of "acceptable" (licit) drugs and enforcement against illicit ones. Hence the emphasis throughout.

(9) This is the significant exception to the commission's unanimity on treatment matters. Since the primary enforcers of this recommendation are designated as the police, it is included in this section on legal recommendations.   The boundaries between coercive treatment and criminal sanction approaches are not easily distinguished.

(10) Under the Narcotic Control Act (covering opiates and cocaine) the maximum penalty for the two trafficking offenses and importation is life imprisonment. The Food and Drug Act, which applies to controlled and restricted drugs, includes importation within the definition of trafficking. The maximum penalty upon summary conviction is imprisonment for 18 months, and upon indictment for ten years.
   The commissioners were also in favor of Canada becoming a party to the Convention on Psychotropic Substances, 1971.

(11) Reported in The Journal, Vol. 1, No. 4, September, 1972.

(12) The Journal, Vol. 3, No. 2, February, 1974 (Bertrand).

(13) This occurred in October 1973, only 18 months after the United States National Commission on Marijuana and Drug Abuse completed its own report on cannabis, including a recommendation favoring decriminalization of marijuana for personal use.

(14) The Division of Narcotic Control, within the federal Department of Health, occupied a powerful central role in the communications network between government, RCMP, and drug prosecutors. Small and Giffen (forthcoming) have documented how de facto power over the enforcement and administration of narcotic laws was centralized in the Division of Narcotic control from its inception in 1919 to shortly after World War II. Its power was gradually diffused, and by 1972, when the division became the Bureau of dangerous drugs, it functioned primarily as a record-keeping agency within the Health Protection Branch.

(15) The indictable-summary distinction is similar to that between felony and misdemeanor in the United States and indictable and nonindictable in Britain.

(16) However, the official data collected by the Bureau of Dangerous Drugs shows that some fines were apparently imposed even when this option was not provided in law (see Table 4.5).

(17) Both cases reported in Whealy (1970:277):
R. v. Lehrmann (1968) 2 C.C.C. 198, 61 W.W.R. 625 (Alta.C.A.)
R v. Adelman (1968) 3 C.C.C. 311, 63 W.W.R. 249 (B.C.C.A.)

(18) A bill making the possession of LSD a crime was first introduced in the Senate in 1967, was reintroduced in the next session, and finally died when an election was called in 1968, without ever coming into effect (Cook, 1970:145). It was not until 1970 that a new section of the FDA, creating the category of restricted drugs, which included LSD, was enacted. The NCA was paralleled in every way, including the special police powers, except that penalties were somewhat less severe.

(19) House of Commons Debates, p. 1,464, 1968; from a newspaper account read to the House by P. Reynard, October 17, 1968.

(20) Data presented in Cannabis Report (1972:250) also indicates that approximately 90 percent of the sentences were for less than two years.

(21) The Journal, Vol. 1, No. 4, October, 1972.

(22) By Inspec. G. Tomalty, officer in charge of RCMP drug enforcement, in an interview quoted in The Journal, Vol. 1, No. 4, October, 1972; and by Crime Statistics, 1972-73, p. xii.

(23) Also DET, DMT, STP, MMDA, LBJ, in Schedule H, Part IV, defining "restricted drugs" under the Food and Drug Act.

(24) English Criminal Justice Act, 1948.

(25) Personal communications, Judge T.R. Swabey, March 14 and April 15, 1974; and Canadian Committee on Corrections, Report, Ottawa, Queen's Printer, 1969.

(26) Section 662.1 of the Criminal Code.

(27) The Criminal Law Amendment Act (1972 Stat. Can. c. 13 s. 72).

(28) R.S.C., 1st Supp. c. 12.

(29) R. v. Derksun, 9 C.C.C. (2d) 97 (B.C. Prov. Ct.).

(30) The Journal, Vol. 4, No. 5, May, 1974.

(31) Reported by Inspector G. Tomalty, Criminal Lawyers Association "Drug Law Seminar," November 30, 1974.

(32) Although studies that attempt to show changes in consumption of illicit substances must be interpreted cautiously, consistent support for an increase in cannabis use was provided in research by the Le Dain Commission (Cannabis, 1972:202), and by Smart and Fejer (1974) and Leon (1974:12).

(33) P.G. Erickson (1975), "Research Note, Parts I and II: Sentencing for the simple possession of cannabis." Criminal Lawyers' Association Newsletter 1 (Feb.): 15-18 and 1 (April): 20-23.

(34) The Journal (1977) 6 (March): 1. ARF publication.

(35) If an estimated 3,000,000 Canadians have used cannabis by 1975, and given that total convictions for simple possession from 1967 to 1975 number almost 100,000 (see Table 4.5), the chance of conviction is one in 30 for this period. The Le Dain Commission (1972:290) estimated that by 1971 less than one percent of those who had used cannabis had been convicted; thus this proportion had risen to more than three percent by 1975.

(36) Toronto Star (1975) Letter to the Editor, February 22.

(37) The Journal (1977). Supra note 2.

(38) Some readers in an international audience may be puzzled as to why Bill S-19, when passed by the Senate, did not become law. In Canada, the House of Commons with its elected representatives (as opposed to the Senate whose members are appointed) is the law-enacting body.

Normally, new pieces of federal legislation are introduced directly in the House, but the Senate has occupied historically a special role with respect to drafting drug control policy. For example, the Special Senate Committee of 1955 recommended several provisions that were introduced into the Narcotic Control Act of 1961. Neither the Senate nor the provincial governments are empowered to change or enact drug laws; that responsibility rests with the elected Members of Parliament.

REFERENCES

Annis, H.M., Klug, R. and Blackwell, D. Drug use among high school students in Timmins. addiction Research Foundation, Toronto, 1971.

Campbell, I.L. Non-medical psychoactive drug use at Bishop's University: 1965-70. Unpublished paper, Sir George Williams University, Montreal, 1970.

Commission of Inquiry into the Non-Medical Use of Drugs (Le Dain Commission). Information Canada, Ottawa. Interim Report, 1970. Treatment, 1972, Cannabis,1972. Final Report, 1973.

Cook, Shirley, J. Canadian narcotics legislation, 1908-1923: A conflict model interpretation. Canadian Review of Sociology & Anthropology, 6, 34-46, 1969.

Cook, Shirley, J. Variations in response to illegal drug use. Addiction Research Foundation, Toronto, 1970.

Cooperstock, R. Sex differences in the use of mood-modifying drugs: An explanatory model. Journal of Health and Social Behaviour, 12, 238-244, 1971.

Cutler, R. and Storm T. Drinking practices in three British Columbia Cities. Alcoholism Foundation of British Columbia, Vancouver, 1973.

Fejer, D. Drug use among high school students in North Bay, Ontario. Addiction Research Foundation, Toronto, 1971.

Fejer, D. and Smart, R.G. Drug use and psychological problems among adolescents in a semi-rural area of Ontario: Haldimand County. Addiction Research Foundation, Toronto, 1971.

Fejer, D. and Smart, R.G. The use of psychoactive drugs by adults. Canadian Psychiatric Association Journal, 18, 313-320, 1973.

Hayashi, T. The nature and prevalence of drug and alcohol usage in the Fort William Schools. Addiction Research Foundation, Fort William, 1968.

The Journal. A publication of the Addiction Research Foundation, Toronto Ontario, Canada.

LaForest, L. The incidence of drug use among high school and college students of the Montreal Island area. Office de la Prevention et du Traitement de l'Alcoohisme et des Toxicomanies, Quebec, 1969.

Lanphier, C.M. and Phillips, S.B. Secondary School students and non-medical drug use: A study of students enrolled in grades 7 through 13. University students and non-medical drug use. Attitudes and Behaviours regarding the non-medical use of drugs: A survey of Canadian adults. Unpublished reports, Survey Research Center, York University, Toronto, 1971.

Leon, Jeffrey S.   The Oshawa drug study: Frequency and patterns of drug use among the young people of Oshawa. Addiction Research Foundation, Toronto, 1974.

Lettieri, D.J. The impact of drug control legislation on drug users and drug use. Paper presented at the North American Congress on Alcohol and Drug Problems, San Francisco, December, 1974.

Manheimer, D.I., Mellinger, G.D., and Balter, M.B. Marijuana use among urban adults. Science, 1966, 1544-1545, 1969.

McDonald, Lynn. Crime and punishment in Canada: A statistical test of the "conventional wisdom". Canadian Review of Sociology and Anthropology, 6, 212-236, 1969.

Mercer, G.W. and Smart, R.G. The epidemiology of psychoactive and hallucinogenic drug use. Pp. 303-354 in Research Advances in Alcohol and Drug Problems, Vol. 1, R.J. Gibbins et al. (Eds.), Wiley, New York, 1974.

Parry, H.J. Use of psychotropic drugs by U.S. adults. Public Health Reports, 83, 799-810, 1968.

Russell, J. Survey of drug use in selected British Columbia Schools. Narcotic Addiction Foundation of British Columbia, Vancouver, 1970.

Schmidt, W. and Kornaczewski, A. A note on the effect of lowering the drinking age on alcohol related motor vehicle accidents. Addiction Research Foundation, Toronto, 1973.

Smart, R.G. and Cox, C. Personality and psychopathological traits of speed users: A study of MMPI results. International Journal of the Addictions, 7, 201-217, 1972.

Smart, R.G. and Fejer, D. Illicit LSD users: Their social backgrounds, drug use, and psychopathology. Journal of Health and Social Behaviour, 10, 297-308, 1969.

Smart, R.G. and Fejer, D. Marihuana use among adults in Toronto. British Journal of Addictions, 68, 117-128, 1973.

Smart, R.G. and Fejer, D. Changes in drug use in Toronto High School Students Between 1972 and 1974. Addiction Research Foundation, Toronto, 1974.

Smart, R.G., Fejer, D., and Alexander, E. Drug use among high school students and their parents in Lincoln & Welland Counties, Addiction Research Foundation, Toronto, 1970.

Smart, R.G. and Jones, D. Illicit LSD users: their personality characteristics and psychopathology. Journal of Abnormal Psychology, 75, 286-292, 1970.

Smart, R.G. and Whitehead, P.C. The uses of an epidemiology of drug use: The Canadian scene. International Journal of the Addictions, 9, 373-388, 1974.

Sommerfield, S.F. Prosecution and law amendment program. Criminal Lawyers Association "Drug Law Seminar". Toronto, November, 1974. 1974.

Swabey, T.R. Absolute and conditional discharges under the criminal code. Criminal Reports, 20, 132, 1973.

Whealy, Arthur C. Drugs and the criminal law. Criminal Law Quarterly, 12, 254-278, 1970.

Whitehead, Paul C. The epidemiology of drug use in a Canadian city at two points in time: Halifax, 1969-1970. British Journal of Addictions, 66, 301-314, 1971.

Whitehead, Paul C. and Brook, R. Social and drug using backgrounds of drug users seeking help: Some implications for treatment. International Journal of the Addictions, 8, 75-85, 1973.

5 United States
R. King

Almost certainly, no one would be writing essays and publishing volumes like these about the so-called drug problem today if King George III had held the American colonists in line two centuries ago, or if for some other reason the United States had not grown into an international heavyweight in the modern community of nations. For along with other exports and exploits good and bad, the Yankees have almost single-handedly pushed the notion that nontherapeutic use of medicines is a horrendous threat to the welfare of nations. Even today, in most of the world there is simply not much interest in what an American president recently characterized as a threat to Americans that if not met heroically "will surely in time destroy us."

Apart from the legitimate and reasonably effective controls over purity, strength, labelling, and now to some extent efficacy and price, which have been developing in the United States since the Food and Drug Act of 1906,(1) the community response to drug use (abuse) in this country has been directed in three areas: promoting global repression by concerted international action, attempting to impose absolute prohibition by harsh criminal sanctions, and manipulating individual addicts and drug abusers in "treatment" programs and rehabilitation efforts.

The broader history of international controls is detailed elsewhere in these volumes.(2) But it is noteworthy here for our forebears in western Europe, and particularly the English (with more than a few American partners), actually played the role of dope peddler in the exploitation of China in the eighteenth and nineteenth centuries, and fought two shameful wars to protect their profits from the one-way flow of opium into the Celestial Kingdom.(3) Some of America's great fortunes were founded on China-clipper trading in this drug.

Nevertheless, occasional efforts were made in Washington even before the Civil War to restrict American participation in the opium traffic, and in the latter part of the nineteenth century, influenced by the army of American missionaries then invading heathen lands, Congress began reflecting a growing public sentiment against this and other predatory exploitations of "natives."

But what changed the American role from that of critical spectator to active participant was Admiral Dewey's seizure of the Philippines in 1898. Civil governor, later president, W.H. Taft found the Philippines saturated with opium which had long been distributed under the Spaniards through a system of auctioned private monopolies. Taft first proposed to reinstate the Spanish distribution system, but this aroused such a storm of protest at home that he appointed an Investigating Committee to study the matter, with the result that in 1905, probably misunderstanding what the Investigating Committee had concluded, Congress decreed prohibition of all nonmedical opium use in the Philippines, to be imposed gradually over a three-year period and to become absolute on March 1, 1908. When that deadline was reached, the Philippine opium traffic went entirely underground, and Americans thus had the world's first direct experience – apart from the victimized Chinese – with large-scale clandestine drug operations.

President Theodore Roosevelt took the initiative in organizing the first International Opium Conference, which met in Shanghai in 1909. From the outset, American spokesmen pressed for international action to prohibit opium smoking in the Philippine pattern, but among the other twelve delegations (Austria, China, France, Germany, Great Britain, Hungary, Italy, Japan, Netherlands, Persia, Portugal, Russia) only the Chinese concurred. Nevertheless, three years later, again as a result of pressures emanating mainly from the United States, a second conference was convened at The Hague, and this time a special protocol (The Hague Convention of 1912) was approved, calling upon participating nations to cooperate in International control measures and also to take steps to curb nonmedical use of drugs in their own territories.(4)

But obtaining ratifications for this unusual treaty, which purported to preempt the freedom of sovereign nations to deal with their own citizens, was another matter. By 1915, despite two further American-sponsored conferences to push for action, only China and the Netherlands had signed, and the whole undertaking might have ended there had not the convention, again principally at American insistence, been made part of the Paris Peace Treaties so that all signatories to the latter automatically became party to the former.

Although the United States eschewed participation in other League of Nations activities, from the outset an American spokesman sat as a special observer on the League Advisory Committee on the Traffic in Opium and Other Dangerous Drugs. At the Second International Opium Conference, convened by the league in Geneva in 1924 (the first conference was attended by representatives of China, France, Great Britain, India, Japan, Netherlands, Portugal, and Spain, and the second by 41 nations), the U.S. representatives, accompanied by the Chinese, walked out after unsuccessfully trying to persuade other delegates to impose a world ban on heroin and to outlaw all drug production for nonmedical purposes. Nevertheless, the United States continued to play an active role in the new control agency (Permanent Central Board) created by the Geneva Convention of 1925, which resulted from this conference. Americans were again in the forefront at the Geneva Limitation Conference of 1981, which established a new Supervisory

Body to police opium production, and in the drafting of another convention in 1936 aimed at forcing participants to strengthen criminal penalties imposed for narcotics offenses within their jurisdictions and facilitating the extradition of drug traffickers.(5)

Early in 1941, while other league agencies were disappearing in Geneva, the U.S. Commissioner of Narcotics rescued the entire league machinery for international drug control by inviting key officials from the League Secretariat, the Supervisory Body, and the Permanent Central Board to move to branch offices in Washington. During World War II, when ordinary sources of medical opium were cut off, half a dozen previously resisting nations were forced to sign the opium conventions because the U.S. Congress specified that no drugs could be exported from U.S. sources to any nation which was not a party to these treaties. Then as World War II progressed and American forces began to tip the scales as liberators of occupied areas all over the world, spokesmen in Washington let it be known that they would be loathe to send American boys into regions where America's allies had formerly tolerated opium smoking, and officially extracted a promise from all of them to put an end to "the troublesome opium-smoking problem" when hostilities ceased.(6)

In the postwar structuring of United Nations drug agencies – a new Commission on Narcotic Drugs under the Economic and Social Council and a new narcotics division in the Secretariat at Lake Success – American spokesmen once more played an overbearing role from the outset. Pressures for tighter controls on opium production were relentlessly continued; other new protocols were promoted; and in 1961, culminating an effort that had been launched by the U.S. Commissioner of Narcotic Drugs in 1948, the UN adopted a comprehensive Single Convention which incorporated and strengthened all the old control machinery and for the first time brought coca products and cannabis into the same category with opium poppies as raw crops subject to control. Some 80 nations are now parties to this Single Convention, and the present 24-member Commission on Narcotic Drugs and 11-seat International Narcotics Control Board flourish as exhortatory bodies, continually studying the world drug situation and convening frequently to hear harangues from American officials about how the international community should be doing more. The latest U.S. project is an elaborate Convention on Psychotropic Substances, bringing a whole catalogue of new drug items, natural and manufactured, under international controls.(7)

All of these efforts, more than six decades of pressure to encourage meaningful cooperation in joint activities for international control, have amounted to little more than wishful posturing. The league and UN bureaucracies which have flourished over the years never had power to do more than observe and exhort. Occasionally spokesmen for other nations have sounded off, echoing the American theme or seeking to magnify problems of their own (the Egyptians, for instance, have sometimes tried to stir up enthusiasm for a genuinely repressive campaign against hashish), but mostly the agitation and pressure has come from Washington. Countries like Turkey and the Burma-Laos-

Thailand "Golden Triangle," whose drug-crop growers and drug pro-
cessors profit from the fabulously lucrative American black market,
acknowledge no significant drug abuse problems within their own
borders. Opium poppies can be grown in many parts of the world, and
both opium and cocaine are ecnomically significant in remote mountain
areas of South America and the Middle and Far East. American
policymakers themselves have allegedly faced this realistically when
obliged to do so.(8)

Nonetheless, commencing in 1969 when the Nixon administration
began whipping up new hysteria about the threat of drugs to the
American electorate,(9) this country has gone further than ever before
in its futile pursuit, expanding the force of U.S. drug agents posted
abroad from a handful to 200, prodding and bribing allegedly offending
states like Mexico and Turkey with threats (to cut off U.S. aid
programs), loans and gifts (to recruit and arm drug police and to develop
other crops to replace opium and coco), and putting pressure on U.S.
ambassadors to become more aggressive about drug abuse with the
governments to which they are accredited. The president has power to
cut off foreign aid to any nation that in his judgment is not doing its
best to curb illicit drug activities among its own people, and the United
States has handed over more than $10 million to seed a UN "special
fund" for drug abuse control (a gesture that has generated responses of
only a few million from all other sources).

In short, the first method of control pursued by the United States
(pressuring the world community to concern itself with our problem) is
pathetically misguided, and except for serving as an attractive political
issue at home, it has never had significant effects or results. Perhaps
the best way to put this aspect in perspective is to consider two
analogies: one is actual, the perennial effort of sovereign states to curb
the dangers of war by mutual disarmament, never effectively pursued
much beyond hypocritical posturing; the other is hypothetical, an
imagined reversal of roles in which the Turks, suddenly frightened about
the menace of Yankee cigarettes, might come swarming into Virginia
and Kentucky to compel the good people of those states to mend their
tobacco-growing ways.

The second American approach to controlling drug abuse – harsh
criminal sanctions – grew indirectly out of the first. Though Americans
like to view themselves as uniquely endowed with generosity, wisdom,
and mercy by comparison with most of the rest of the Western world,
the record of our forebears in dealing with unpopular minorities has
sometimes been cruel to the point of savagery. Remember New England
witch-hunts, the virtual annihilation of North American Indians, the
fierce record of "gringoes" in Mexico in the nineteenth century, Yankee
liberators in the Philippines at the turn of the twentieth, and
contemporary American bullying in Southeast Asia for most of two
decades. Other "civilized" communities abandoned slavery centuries ago
and have largely forsaken the death penalty which today still seems to
enchant American politicians, and to enlightened penologists in other
lands our propensity to mete out penitentiary sentences in decades and
lifetimes is incomprehensible.

So, not surprisingly, Byzantine cruelty remains a prominent element in America's attitudes toward her drug addicts, in a pattern that has been fairly consistent – and quite relentless – for half a century.(10) To encapsulate the story of how we shifted from a calm order in which no one had ever dreamed of associating drug abuse with criminality to the all-out "war on dope" of the 1920s: Congress passed the Harrison Act in 1914 purportedly as America's acceptance of its obligation to impose controls under The Hague Convention; World War I propagandists linked drug abuse with spy scares and anti-German propaganda; America embarked on her remarkable prohibition debauch at the same time; and the federal Treasury agents who set out to arrest everyone connected with bootlegging (assigned enforcement of both the Volstead and Harrison Acts because both were tax measures) enlarged their efforts to include a similar assault on abusers of opium and cocaine. Addicts of the nineteenth century (mostly female, middle-aged, white, and rural-southern) became "fiends" (portrayed as criminal types, sinister Orientals, and maniacal blacks) in the early twentieth.(11)

The chief thrust of the federal drug campaign at the outset was to close down the so-called "clinics" which had been established by doctors and public health authorities in many cities to minister to the needs of addicts,(12) and then to drive the doctors themselves entirely out of the field.(13) In 1923 the Supreme Court interpreted the Harrison Act to mean that any administering of a narcotic substance to an addict as treatment for the symptoms of addiction was a crime. With this ruling in hand, the federal narcotics authorities bullied and threatened doctors and sometimes packed them off to prison, until the American addict had nowhere to turn but the illicit trafficker who moved in to fill the void by catering to his needs.(14)

In that era there emerged what might almost be called a de facto partnership between drug-law enforcers, who keep addicts helplessly cut off from all legitimate sources of relief while simultaneously insuring scarcity in underworld supply channels, and pushers, who reap great profits exploiting their helpless victims – and who have been exposed with surprising frequency actually sharing the bonanza in "arrangements" with their law enforcement counterparts.(15)

In the mid-1920s, in the very heyday of Prohibition, there were more prisoners serving time for federal drug offenses than for bootlegging.(16) The Treasury Narcotics Bureau, supposedly merely enforcing collection of a federal tax, so dominated the scene in the four decades between World War I and the Kennedy era that virtually no one in America was permitted to study phenomena associated with addiction or so much as suggest alternative approaches to the problem, let alone experiment with any disapproved ministrations to addicts.

In 1937 the Narcotics Bureau obtained passage of the Marijuana Tax Act(17) of that year by a crude propaganda campaign(18) that has left its effects – exaggerated misunderstanding and witless fears about this near-harmless garden weed – even today.(19)

Before turning to the details of U.S. control efforts via punishment, two general features of the picture are noteworthy. In the first place, the Harrison Act, as has been noted, was only a mild federal tax measure, designed and intended at the time merely to bring distribution channels for opium and coca products into the open by means of a system of registration and required record keeping.

From 1914 to 1970, when the constitutional underpinnings of drug repression were at last changed by Congress, the entire federal attack on drug abusers rested on no more than their failure in one way or another to pay applicable taxes or to use forms and procedures supposedly required merely to facilitate tax collection. So within the federal structure, America's drug repression campaign owed its very existence to an unparalleled distortion. (In contrast, when the simultaneous campaign against alcohol was launched, it was accepted without question by all concerned that this could only be accomplished by a full-blown constitutional amendment, the Eighteenth; it was then abandoned in 1933 by another, the Twenty-first.)

Secondly, there has always been a serious overshadowing question as to why the federal government should have any place in this field at all. The Ninth Amendment, which may one day be recognized as a sleeping giant in the Bill of Rights, says that the enumeration of certain rights conferred on branches of government by the Constitution "shall not be construed to deny or disparage others retained by the people." If one's personal choice among toxic substances to be inhaled, ingested, or injected into one's own body is not among rights thus "retained by the people," and hence protected from federal interference, what could the Founding fathers conceivably have had in mind when they specified that reservation? And what, in any event, could imaginably be further than this from any area of legitimate federal concern?

So it might be reasonably argued, at least in the abstract, that public attitudes and policies toward drug abuse, and the enactment of measures to deal with it if any be thought necessary, should be left to local communities, like other so-called "victimless" crimes – e.g., drunkenness, prostitution, gambling, pornography, and deviant sex practices. And for that matter it may also be suggested, as a number of responsible commentators are now doing,(20) that these areas should be "decriminalized" altogether in order to free our force of narks, vice cops, and drunk-busters to redirect their efforts to deal with crimes that truly threaten the common welfare.

When Messrs. Nixon and Mitchell came to Washington waving their Law and Order banner, the nation had already had a full two decades' experience with exaggerated penalties for drug offenses. Soon after World War II (during which drug abuse was greatly curtailed because of disrupted supply channels), Commissioner Anslinger and the Federal Bureau began issuing alarmed reports of new drug epidemics and – as always – increased involvement of youngsters, which they blamed on "soft" judges who were loath to hand out sufficiently harsh sentences for drug violations. In 1950 and 1951 this campaign focused on new legislation, passed in the latter year on the wave of excitement generated by the Kefauver hearings, specifying mandatory minimum sentences in all principal federal narcotics laws. Under this (Boggs Act(21) judges were required to give sentences of not less than two, five, and ten years respectively for first, second, and subsequent violations of the federal laws, and for all but first offenders the sentence could not be suspended nor probation granted.

Five years later, after a series of Senate hearings that again whipped up near-hysteria about the drug problem and the way courts continued to deal mildly with drug offenders, Congress passed another measure (Narcotic Control Act of 1956)(22) increasing the mandatory minimums to five years for first offenders and ten years for all subsequent convictions (maximums of 20 and 40 years), and wiping out even parole eligibility for anyone receiving one of these sentences. This undermining of the federal parole program, which had been available for virtually all federal prisoners since 1910, soon began to have adverse effects in federal penal institutions. Hapless victims of these savage, mandatory no-parole penalties, some serving sentences as long as their natural life expectancies for insignificant violations such as repeated possession of marijuana cigarettes, saw everyone around them, rapists, murderer's, and traitors alike, eligible sooner or later for parole release which they alone could never hope for or work toward; their hopeless presence wrecked prison morale, created custodial problems, and derailed rehabilitation programs.(23)

Simultaneously, Congress had decreed life imprisonment, or death if the jury so recommended, for anyone over 18 caught selling heroin to a minor, ten years to life for such a sale where other drugs – morphine, cocaine, marijuana, etc. – were involved), and though no one ever lost his life to this heroic sanction, the federal enforcers achieved some remarkable results with it. In one case in 1957, a 21-year-old Mexican-American epileptic with an IQ of 71 was committed for life, with no parole eligibility, after he had been tricked into selling heroin to his 17-year-old shooting partner who turned out to be a bureau informer.(24)

State legislatures followed the lead of Congress, many enacting even tougher penalties than the federal pattern. Ohio prescribed not less than 20 years minimum for any first offense involving a sale. Maximums were often increased to life (for repeaters), and death sanctions were added in Alabama, Georgia, Louisiana, Missouri, Oklahoma, and Texas.(25)

The situation created by these oppressive measures has never been much alleviated by lawmakers. In 1966 Congress relented slightly by reestablishing parole eligibility for marijuana offenders only, but it was executive intervention, pardons, and commutations in the regimes of Presidents Kennedy and Johnson that eventually released many of the hopeless federal longtermers. (This stopped when the Nixon administration took over; in his first year, President Nixon granted zero pardons and zero commutations.)

Notwithstanding timid (and illogical) steps here and there to "decriminalize," pot smoking, current American attitudes and present U.S. leadership seem almost as hostile and punitive toward drug abusers as ever. When Attorney General Mitchell succeeded Ramsey Clark in 1969, official estimates of the nation's addict population had ranged steadily around 60,000 for many years. The federal enforcement agency of that day, a newly created Bureau of Narcotics and Dangerous Drugs in the Department of Justice, had a budget of only $16.8 million, and operated with 742 agents. Since then federal officials have puffed the claimed addict population to as many as 1,000,000, and the latest federal drug agency, the Drug Enforcement Administration, has a budget of over $100 million and has over 2,000 agents deployed in offices in 40 states. The total federal commitment for special offices, agencies, and programs in the drug field has reached almost $800 million. In 1973, according to FBI Crime Report figures, the total of all arrests for drug offenses reached a high of 628,900. Of these, 420,700 involved only marijuana, and 92,109 arrested offenders were under 18 years of age.

In 1970 the Nixon administration pressed for a complete revision and consolidation of all federal drug laws to make them tougher and tighter and to transfer all enforcement powers from the Treasury Department and other agencies to the attorney general. Penalties with mandatory minimums ranging from 5-20 to 20-80 years were sought, together with arbitrary new classifications to retain marijuana as a major prohibiton target and bring in additional stimulant, depressant, and hallucinogenic categories.

In the resulting act (Comprehensive Drug Abuse Prevention and Control Act of 1970)(26), Congress at last shifted the basis of federal jurisdiction from the narrow constitutional power of taxation to sweeping reliance upon congressional powers over interstate commerce. Controlled drugs are classified in five schedules,(27) graded by their degree of abuse potential and whether or not they have "currently accepted medical use" and "accepted safety." Responsibility for classifying reclassifying substances in these schedules rests, illogically, with the attorney general.

Penalties and control measures are graded in relation to the schedules. Mandatory minimums were largely removed, but excessive maximums remain: 15 years and a $25,000 fine for first offenses involving "narcotics" (which still, illogically, include cocaine); 5 years and $15,000 for marijuana and other stimulants and depressants, though with a reduced penalty, 1 year and $5,000 for simple possession without attempt to distribute, and a special probationary disposition for first offenders guilty of mere possession.

The foregoing penalties double for second and subsequent offenses, and judges are required to impose a mandatory "special parole term," which commences after completion of any term of imprisonment, and which has the effect of keeping drug offenders in jeopardy for much longer periods than is usual among other kinds of offenders. Death sentences were deleted, but for any distribution of drugs by an adult (over 17) to a minor (under 21) the otherwise applicable maximums double upon first conviction and treble for second and subsequent repetitions.

Two extraordinary new offenses were created by this act: participating in a "continuing criminal enterprise," or merely being a "dangerous special drug offender." The continuing enterprise offense requires conviction of a felony that is part of a continuing series of similar activities, shared by at least five persons under the supervision or management of the defendant, and that provides the latter with "substantial income or resources." For this, a mandatory minimum – ten years – has been retained, with a maximum up to life, plus a fine of not more than $100,000 and forfeiture of all "profits obtained" and interest "affording a source of influence" over the activity.

Punishment for being a dangerous special drug offender, which involves two prior felony convictions for drug offenses, or proof that the instant offense was "part of a pattern" involving "special skill or expertise," or participating in a multiple-party conspiracy in which the defendant was a leader, is a discretionary maximum of 25 years.

Though the attorney general is, of course, already the nation's chief law enforcer, commanding the formidable power and resources of the FBI, this 1970 act conferred a whole bouquet of special additional powers on him, designed to assure maximum toughness in his pursuit and prosecution of drug offenders. Agents of the Drug Enforcement Administration (formerly the Bureau of Narcotics and Dangerous Drugs) are specially authorized to carry weapons, to serve warrants and make warrantless arrests, to seize evidence and contraband, and, with the approval of a judge, to make "no knock" entries by force without the usual warning and identification.(28) DEA personnel are empowered to inspect any premises where drug records are required to be kept or where drugs are stored or processed on mere notice, and to copy documents and take samples in the course of such inspections.

Prosecutors may use civil restraining orders and injunctions to enforce the act if they elect to proceed that way. Conferring immunity to wipe out Fifth Amendment rights of witnesses is specifically authorized, as are rewards and payoffs to informers – in any amount the attorney general may "deem appropriate." The act also contains an extraordinary section making it an offense under the laws of the United States to manufacture or distribute prohibited substances outside this country, with knowledge or intention that they are to be unlawfully imported here.

While it was pushing the 1970 federal act through Congress, the Department of Justice also prepared and promoted a new Uniform Control Substances Act(29) for adoption by the states. This Uniform Act, already docilely enacted in 40 jurisdictions, contains a system of classification that follows the federal pattern of schedules and sets up duplicate offenses in all categories. The Uniform Act does not itself specify penalties, but state lawmakers have generally followed the federal pattern, or in some instances prescribed more severe terms.

The overall result is that anyone involved in activities related to proscribed drugs, unlike perpetrators of crimes in most other areas, is subject to at least double overlapping laws, enforced by federal and state authorities, and, in the case of many larger cities, to municipal ordinances and the jurisdiction of local police forces as well. This sometimes results in collusion among enforcing agencies to bring a drug offender to trial in whichever of several courts he will be most disadvantage and likely to receive severest punishment.

In 1973 Governor Nelson Rockefeller, who had long postured as a leading proponent of education and rehabilitative efforts to cope with the drug problem, did a cynical turnabout to pose as a "tough" enforcer and promoted legislation in New York which has reestablished mandatory minimums and possible life sentences for drug offenses in some categories. President Nixon's parting utterance on the subject was a message to Congress characterizing the nation's courts as "frequently little more than an escape hatch" in dealing too leniently with drug offenders:

> Sometimes it seems that as fast as we bail water out of the boat through law enforcement and rehabilitation, it runs right back in through the holes in our judicial system. I intend to plug those holes.

The third line of approach which characterizes U.S. attempts to control drug abuse is "treatment" or "rehabilitation." This has been pursued with mixed motives. Ever since the clinics of the early 1920s and the 1929 Porter Act,(30) which created two "narcotic farms" (eventually the U.S. Public Health Service hospitals at Lexington, Kentucky and Fort Worth, Texas), there has been a genuine effort on the part of responsible physicians and public health officials to deal with addiction by means of noncriminal, therapeutic measures.(31) But such efforts have often been intertwined with, and sometimes over-shadowed by, what are in effect no more than penal sanctions with the sugar-coating of a different name.

Even in President Harding's day there were those who urged isolation or life-quarantine for addicts who were unable to give up their compulsion to use drugs. The original thrust behind the Porter Act narcotic farms was partly to create separate institutions where addicted convicts could simply be isolated from the general prison population. And after World War II, as lawmakers vied with one another in calling for longer prison terms and tougher enforcement policies, there was also heightened interest in taking the addict out of circulation through enforced "rehabilitation" or "treatment."

A number of states had long provided that addicts might be processed and institutionalized under their statutes for dealing with insane persons or chronic drunkards, but these sanctions were little used. So-called civil commitment remained unimportant because, excepting the federal facilities at Lexington, and Fort Worth, there were no suitable institutions or programs seriously oriented toward dealing with the problems of drug addiction per se. Typical of attitudes in this era (the forties and fifties) was the 1956 report of the Daniel (U.S. Senate) subcommittee concluding its marathon hearings on the illicit narcotics traffic:

> Despite this knowledge – that chronic addicts are not amenable to cure, that they infect others with drug addiction, that they habitually engage in crime, and that, thus, they are a menace to society – neither the federal nor state governments has met the threat with special facilities for the isolation, or quarantine, of these individuals. . . .

The pattern is endless, and so is the cost in terms of crime, taxpayer dollars, and human havoc. These incurable addicts who have in reality lost their power of self-control and who are dangerous to the health and welfare of the community not only are habitual criminals but also spread their addiction to others, much on the same order as persons with contagious diseases. Experts agree, therefore, that both in his interest and in the interest of community protection, the chronic drug addict must be "quarantined" or otherwise confined for long periods of time or permanently if relapses continue after releases from isolation or confinement.(32)

In the early 1960s more serious attention commenced to be paid to programs actually aimed at therapy, rehabilitation, and compulsory aftercare for drug abusers. California innovated a pioneering civil commitment statute, providing for treatment of addicts and persons "in imminent danger of becoming addicted," in special facilities, in 1961. In 1963 the so-called Metcalf-Volker Act was passed in New York, authorizing commitment of addicts to the custody of the New York State Department of Mental Health, with initial hospitalization and follow-up supervision for a maximum period of three years.

In 1963 a special Advisory Commission appointed by President Kennedy(33) recommended a federal program of civil commitment as an alternative way to handle federally convicted drug offenders (including, curiously, not only narcotic addicts but marijuana users as well), and three years later, in the Narcotic Addict Rehabilitation Act of 1966(34) (NARA) Congress responded with the federal law which is still substantially the framework of federal rehabilitative efforts. This act begins with a congressional declaration of policy specifying that some persons charged with federal crimes, "who are determined to be addicted to narcotic drugs, and likely to be rehabilitated through treatment," should be diverted into programs "designed to effect their restoration to health, and return to society as useful members," and further, that addicted persons not charged with crime should also be afforded an opportunity, through civil commitment, to be similarly rehabilitated "in order that society may be protected more effectively from crime and delinquency which results from narcotic addiction."

The act established three categories: persons charged with federal offenses (but not including violent crimes or drug peddling); persons convicted of federal offenses (again, not including violent crimes or drug sales or smuggling); and addicts applying voluntarily for admission to the treatment program. Marijuana users are, happily, excluded, though the NARA provisions may be applied to users of nonnarcotic substances like cocaine, and the act does not reach abusers of fearfully addicting barbiturates. Admissions to the programs are severely restricted, depending on approval by a federal judge, limited by a requirement that the surgeon general or the attorney general must certify the availability of facilities and personnel to provide appropriate treatment, and depending also on a finding in each case that the individual applicant will be likely to benefit.

NARA participants admitted at the preconviction stage are subject to control in the program for a total period of 36 months, no less than 6 of which must be spent in some kind of incarceration; those who enter after conviction of a crime are subject to control for a maximum of 10 years (or the longest sentence that could have been imposed for the subject offense, if that is less); while persons applying voluntarily (or being involuntarily committed on the petition of a relative) also must serve in incarceration or under supervision for a total of 36 months.

The result of all the foregoing restrictions has been that NARA programs are not widely used. Few prospective candidates are certified likely to benefit from treatment, and many have been turned aside on the ground that no facilities are available to take them in. Since 1968 the Lexington hospital has been directed primarily into research and demonstration project activities, restricting its intake of addicts to those who happen to meet the particular current needs of its staff. Recently the Federal Bureau of Prisons established special treatment units for convicted NARA participants in its own institutions, at Danbury, Connecticut, Alderson, West Virginia, Terminal Island, California, and Milan, Michigan, and at the former U.S.P.H.S. hospital at Fort Worth, Texas, which the bureau took over. But all these new facilities together can handle less than a thousand inmate-addicts at a time. Aftercare is provided through federal probation officers and by contract with local public and private agencies, of which there are currently 30; altogether these have provided supervision for approximately 10,000 patients. It is noteworthy that with even these limited current capacities the facilities of NARA are mostly underenrolled.

Private organizations have to some extent also undertaken to deal with the problem of drug abuse, through religion-oriented endeavors like Addicts Anonymous, and through a variety of self-help groups and so-called therapeutic communities. The latter, commencing in 1958 with Synanon and Daytop, have developed programs based on mutual efforts among highly motivated addicts who work intensively together, usually insisting on a drug-free environment and characterized by group or "encounter" therapy.(35) The importance of Synanon, irrespective of its current focus legal problems is that it opened up another model of care – mutual help.

Often staffed by ex-addicts, these centers provide continuing support for persons who have graduated from their program, and they are generally credited with a high rate of success in preventing relapses. Therapeutic communities are currently in operation in all major cities where drug abuse problems are acute. Many of them are funded by federal grants, and frequently they coordinate their efforts with local courts and welfare agencies by accepting referrals from the latter on a regular quota basis. All these private treatment programs and addict communities taken together, however, deal with no more than a few thousand persons per year, generally believed to be only a small fraction of the U.S. addict population.

By far the most interesting and promising development in the addiction-control field, dealing with treatment of users of heroin and related opiates only (which is also where the chief problems have always been encountered), was the appearance of methadone on the scene, and its gradual acceptance by U.S. enforcement authorities. Methadone, isolated as a substitute for morphine by German chemists when Germany's access to opium was cut off during World War II, was released in the United States in the late 1940s, and soon came to be used at Lexington and other hospitals as the preferred drug for easing the symptoms of withdrawal from opiates. Very like heroin and morphine, it is nonetheless slightly slower acting, and is believed less likely to produce euphorific "highs." For this reason it was selected by Doctors Dole and Nyswander for their pioneering experiments, commencing in 1964, in which they administered methadone in large and steady dosages to heroin addicts to achieve either gradual long-term withdrawal or stabilized maintenance on a controlled basis. Dole and Nyswander found that many of their experimental patients, unable to give up drugs, were nevertheless capable of functioning normally and achieving adequate readjustment while being treated with methadone.

At the outset the Dole-Nyswander project operated in defiance of federal and local authorities, and when other public agencies and private practitioners began also experimenting with methadone they were threatened, harassed, and sometimes prosecuted. But by 1970 the value of this approach was so thoroughly established that methadone programs had been instituted all over the nation.(36) In cities like New York, the District of Columbia, and Los Angeles methadone patients numbered in the thousands. Inevitably there were mistakes, failures, and abuses in some of these programs. Since methadone is so nearly an equivalent of heroin and morphine, black market trafficking in the drug began to be encountered. An occasional "O.D." (overdose) death was attributed to methadone; some dispensaries were very loosely run, and private practitioners were sometimes accused of profiteering acting as mere peddlers of the substance to all who wanted it.

In June 1970 the Bureau of Narcotics and Dangerous Drugs and the Food and Drug Administration made a joint finding that methadone when used for "maintenance" was legally "experimental,"(37) thereby automatically bringing it under the tight restrictions and controls developed to prevent dangerous experimenting on human subjects with potentially injurious new substances such as thalidomide. The result, as intended, was that all organizations and programs relying on methadone were suddenly obliged to apply to the federal authorities for permission to continue, and had to meet elaborate standards and protocol requirements – so complicated that in fact no one could comply if the administering bureaucrats wished to keep raising technical objections. Thus in practical effect, although permission to carry on was generally given at the outset, all dispensers of methadone found themselves operating at the pleasure of the Washington hierarchy, and some have since been arbitrarily restricted or shut down.

Thereafter, a new set of regulations were adopted to set forth obligatory methadone procedures and dosages, with the aim of entirely withdrawing methadone from all private practitioners and ordinary distribution sources.(38) Now the drug may be dispensed only through "approved" dispensaries and public agencies. Since all-important federal funding is rigidly controlled in Washington, the practical result has been that politically oriented officials and patronage-minded advisory groups in state capitals are able to exert virtually total control over the methadone approach to addiction.

So this account ends as it began: controlling drug abuse in America is still a major preoccupation of politicians at all levels, and particularly of federal lawmakers and bureaucrats; the United States is still obsessed with the unrealistic notion that we can bully or wheedle the rest of the world into sharing our obsessions and enforcing our domestic prohibition by restrictions in their own lands; drug abuse is still generally associated with criminality and still fought in idioms of war with penalties of mindless savagery, and efforts to treat drug abusers as "patients," entitled to "treatment" for their supposed affliction, are still having minor impact because they are in large part misdirected and also because they remain unpopular with politically ascendant law-and-order prohibitionists.

NOTES

(1) Act of June 30, 1906, P.L. 59-384. This pioneering act was completely revised in 1938 (Act of June 25, 1938, P.L. 75-717), and tightened by the Kefauver-Harris Amendments of 1962 (Act of October 10, 1962, P.L. 87-781). The most convenient library reference to this law is Title 21, United States Code, SS01ff. For a general account of the so-called legitimate drug marketers in the U.S., see, Silverman, M. and Lee.

(2) (Insert appropriate cross reference.)

(3) Collins, M., Foreign Mud (1946). Knopf, NY.

(4) Taylor, A.H., American Diplomacy and the Narcotics Traffic, 1900-1939 (1969). Duke Univ. Press, Durham, NC.

(5) Renborg, B., International Drug Control (1947), Carnegie Endowment, New York, N.Y.

(6) U.S. Treasury Department, Bureau of Narcotics, Traffic in Opium and Other Dangerous Drugs (Annual Reports, 1944 et passim.). Government Printing Office, Washington, D.C.

(7) United Nations Social Defence Research Institute, Psychoactive Drug Control: Issue and Recommendations (Rome, 1973).

(8) McCoy, A.W., The Politics of Heroin in Southeast Asia (1973). Harper & Row, NY.

(9) Epstein, Edward J., Agency of Fear (1977), Putnam, NY.

(10) Musto, D., The American Disease: Origins of Narcotic Control (1973). Yale, New Haven.

(11) King, R., The Drug Hang-Up: America's Fifty-Year Folly (1973). Thomas, Springfield, Illinois.

(12) Lindesmith, A.R., The Addict and the Law, Indiana 103 U. Press, (1965).

(13) Terry, C.E., and Pellens, M., The Opium Problem (1928; reprinted, 1970). Haddon Craftsmen, Camden, NJ.

(14) King, R., "The Narcotics Bureau and the Harrison Act," 62 Yale Law Journal 736 (1953).

(15) In 1968 when the Department of Justice took over the federal narcotics forces from the Treasury Department, nearly half the veteran agents resigned, and some 40 were prosecuted for bribery, trafficking, and similar crimes.

(16) In 1928, of 7,738 prisoners in federal custody, 2,529 were there on drug counts, and 1,156 for liquor violations. Schmeckebier, L.F., The Bureau of Prohibition (1929). Brookings Inst., DC.

(17) Act of August 2, 1937, P.L. 75-238.

(18) See, e.g., Anslinger, H.J. and Cooper, C.R., "Marijuana Assassin of Youth," American Magazine, July 1937.

(19) Solomon, B., Ed., The Marijuana Papers (1969), Bobbs-Merrill, NY; Kaplan, J., Marijuana – The New Prohibition (1970), World, NY.

(20) Packer, H.L., The Limits of the Criminal Sanction (1968), Stanford U. Press; Schur, E.M., Crimes Without Victims (1965), Prentice Hall, Englewood, NJ; Kittrie, N., The Right To Be Different (1973), Johns Hopkins, Balto.

(21) Act of November 2, 1951, P.L. 82-255.

(22) Act of July 24, 1956, P.L. 84-728.

(23) See, e.g., Federal Prisons, 1956, Report of the Federal Bureau of Prisons, U.S. Dept. of Justice, 1956, pp. 38-9.

(24) See, Congressional Record, March 13, 1969, S. 2583.

(25) Eldridge, W.B., Narcotics and the Law, App. B (2d Ed., 1967). Amer. Bar Ass'n., Chicago.

(26) Act of October 27, 1970, P.L. 91-513. The most convenient library reference to the main parts of this law is Title 21, United States Code, SS801ff.

(27) Sched. I (most dangerous) includes heroin, LSD, and marijuana; Sched. II (dangerous, but useful as medicine) includes morphine and other opiates, and cocaine.

(28) In November 1974, after disastrous episodes involving raids on wrong addresses and unnecessary violence, Congress repealed the "no knock" provision.

(29) The National Conference of Commissioners on Uniform State Laws adopted its first Uniform Narcotic Drug Act in 1932; this was modified in 1956 by the Model State Drug Abuse Control Act; and besides the Uniform Controlled Substances Act of 1970, the commissioners are now also sponsoring a Uniform Drug Dependence Treatment and Rehabilitation Act (1972).

(30) Act of January 19, 1929, P.L. 70-672.

(31) Livingston, R.B., ed., Narcotic Drug Addiction Problems (U.S.P.H.S. Pub. No. 1050, 1963), G.P.O., DC; Lindesmith, A.R., ed., Drug Addiction: Crime or Disease? (1961), Indiana U. Press, Bloomington, Ind.; Kolb, L., Drug Addiction (1962), Thomas, Springfield, Ill.

(32) U.S. Senate Report 84-1850 (1956).

(33) President's Advisory Commission on Narcotic and Drug Abuse, Final Report (1963).

(34) Act of November 8, 1966, P.L. 89-793. The main provisions of this act may be found in three Titles of the United States Code, 18 U.S. C. SS4251ff., 28 U.S.C. SS2901ff., and 42 U.S.C. SS411.

(35) Meyer, R.E., Guide to Drug Rehabilitation (1972); Yablonsky, L., The Tunnel Back: Synanon (1965). Macmillan, NY.

(36) Proceedings of the Fourth National Conference on Methadone Treatment (San Francisco, 1972); Wikler, A., ed., The Addictive Status (1968).

(37) 35 Federal Register 9014 (June 11, 1970).

(38) 36 Federal Register 6075 (April 2, 1971).

6 United Kingdom
M.M. Glatt

INTRODUCTION

As will be discussed in the final section of this paper in greater detail it is important to keep in mind that the above title is in all its aspects one that invites generalizations – but undue generalizations should be avoided as far as possible. For example, within the national community attitudes toward drug use vary considerably between various sections of the populations – i.e., between the middle-aged and the young, the "establishment" and the various "subcultures," between those who take drugs illicitly and those who condemn such illicit use. Again, "response" is impossible to measure apart from the legal response, but how far such legal response reflects the view of the whole, or even the majority of society, or merely that of certain influential sections of the community (for instance, doctors, lawyers) is another open question. The term "drug," of course, has been employed in many different ways. A recent W.H.O. Study Group (1973). For example, defined it as "Any substance, that, when taken into the living organism, may modify one or more of its functions." This would clearly include such wisely accepted substances as tea, coffee, and certainly alcohol and tobacco; and as regards alcohol one only has to think of the long-standing bitter arguments between the "dry" and "wet," between the temperance organizations and their opponents, raging since the early twentieth century, and among temperance itself between the "moral suasionists" and the prohibitionists (Glatt, 1958), to note once more that it is impossible to speak of a or the response of the British community. Again, the average middle-aged man having his usual double whisky in the evening and smoking his cigarette, while holding forth about today's drug-taking youngsters, is offended if the latter point out to him that he is in fact as much of a drug taker with his alcohol and nicotine as they with their cannabis and LSD. Finally, what constitutes "use" and "misuse" (the latter term is preferred by the author as it is less judgmental than "abuse"; see Keller, Glatt, 1974) again depends on who does the "labelling": for example, in view of the dangerous long-term consequences of regular tobacco smoking, the latter activity might well be regarded as misuse, as should be habitual heavy drinking so common in business and among the professions.

However, it seems likely that what the editor had in mind when suggesting the above title was in the main a discussion of the prevailing attitude in Britain toward the modern use by a minority of the population of drug dependence-producing agents. Although if one wants to speak of a British "drug problem," it was for hundreds of centuries an alcohol problem (Glatt, 1958), and it is at present an alcohol and "soft drug" rather than a "hard drug" problem; abroad and particularly in the U.S. it is the British approach to narcotic drugs that has for years aroused the main interest. Under the circumstances, the present paper, therefore, will in the main discuss the history (as well as the present situation) of the use in Great Britain of the opiates and the development of the so-called "British System" of their control — although passing references will be made to cocaine and the "soft drugs."

OPIATES: USE AND CONTROL MEASURES OVER THE YEARS

Throughout recorded history, crude opium was used for a great many indications. European doctors certainly administered opium from the beginning of the sixteenth century; the famous German doctor, Paracelsus, for example, talked of Laudanum as his secret therapeutic weapon (Lewin) and Germany had its quota of opium addicts from the sixteenth century onward. It seems likely that Britain, too, must have had its share of addicts (at least of "therapeutic addicts") at the same time, since by the seventeenth century opium had become a well-known and long used drug. "Among remedies," wrote the famous English physician, Thomas Sydenham, in the late seventeenth century, "which it has pleased Almighty God to give to man to relieve his sufferings, none is so universal and so efficacious as opium . . . without opium there would be no medicine." Wide popularity among doctors of such a potent addiction-producing drug must have produced a certain number of "therapeutic addicts"; the isolation of morphine in 1805, the invention in 1843 of the hypodermic needle, and to a minor extent the production of opium from poppies by the Edinburgh surgeon, Young, are known landmarks in the history of addiction. But there have always been doctors who were aware of the risks accompanying injudicious medication of the opiates and warned both the general public and their medical colleagues against their misuse. De Quincey and his fellow writers of the nineteenth century are widely blamed for popularizing the drug; but its misuse both by doctors and without medical recommendation seems to have been widespread for some time before De Quincey, at least in certain parts of the country.

This is clear from the description given by Dr. Thomas Trotter (famous as being one of the first physicians to call alcoholism a disease) of conditions at the turn of the nineteenth century. Although opium was "the noblest attribute of Medicine," Trotter called it a, ". . . misfortune when ... dispensed by injudicious hands; for it is often prescribed by the most ignorant, in diseases when it is forbidden." Clearly, then as now, iatrogenic illnesses and complications were not unknown, but similarly there was pressure exerted on doctors by patients to give them certain drugs, popular because of contemporary fashion. Some patients claimed that "opium alone gives relief," though in Trotter's judgment "it must feed the disease. Such persons seem to compound with their physician for sound nights, and days of ease. . . ." As in modern times, the doctor was often in a dilemma: if he did not comply with the patient's demands ". . . he must be changed. Hard is the task imposed on the medical attendant; he must obey or starve. The night draught thus becomes familiar in the family: the servant goes to the apothecary for it with as little ceremony as he buys kitchen salt. He sees the shop boy count the drops into the phial, and when he gets home, narrates the composition of the placebo to the cook. Not a domestic in the house but soon learns what a fine thing laudanum is, and master swears he can get no rest without it."

Trotter was well aware that there were many women who "feel such horror at taking opium, as nothing can equal," so that whatever the illness they warn the doctor against giving it to them. But in weak-nerved people ... it is apt to be the more craved for, and converted into habit. . . . The languor and dejection which follow its operation pave the way for the repetition of the dose, till general debility succeeds." Trotter warns strongly against giving opium to individuals "with such constitution ... on slight occasions. Midwives, nurses, and other persons out of the medical profession, who dispense laudanum at random, ought to be solemnly warned against it." At any rate laudanum was then "daily getting more into use as a cordial, and privately consumed by a number of persons. As a tincture it is easily carried about and drunk at pleasure. . . . It . . . has grown . . . general in high life and fashionable circles. . . ."

Thus laudanum (an alcoholic opium tincture) was used freely at the time in various social circles. But there were also those who were strongly opposed to taking drugs. Nowadays, too, it is not too uncommon to meet long-standing alcoholics who proudly proclaim that they would not dream of taking any "drug": Many middle-aged women – in Trotter's time – were apparently using laudanum as freely as aspirin and the tranquillizers are taken today. A few years ago the same type of person may have regularly taken barbiturates and nowadays the benzodiaz-epines. Such people would often be mortally afraid of the opiates and horrified at youngsters smoking cannabis and "tripping out" on LSD. Yet, early in the nineteenth century, encouraged by the day's fashion, many people did not regard opium as a dangerous drug and pestered their doctors into prescribing it for them. Among doctors then, some, like Trotter, were cautious, but others (at a time when there was no National Health Service:) had to think of their finances and may have thought it prudent to fall in with their patients' wishes. The general public was apparently informed by a "grapevine" method of the beneficial and pleasurable qualities of laudanum, and (as in the late 1950s and 1960s) the names of medical practitioners prepared to prescribe the drug must soon have become well known. Already in Trotter's time it would seem that there were addicts who had started their opium-taking career for "therapeutic" reasons after initial introduction by a doctor, and others who, at least for a period, took it for "pleasure."

Trotter was obviously fully aware of the addictive properties of opium but there are reports indicating the possibility of "stabilized addiction" long before the First Brain Committee (1961) wrote about it in some detail. Thus, Clive of India (who returned to England in 1767 and died in 1774) took opium for the last 20 years of his life, and William Wilberforce reputedly took opium day after day for 45 years before his death in 1833. That a man like Wilberforce — leader of a great humanitarian crusade, the antislavery movement — continually in the public eye, could go on taking opium without attracting too much public criticism, indicates that its use was either widespread and widely accepted, or alternatively that its dangers were less generally known than assumed by Trotter. Regarding the phenomenon of the "stabilized addict," the examples given by the First Interdepartmental (Brain) Committee in 1961 all referred to middle-aged, "therapeutic addicts," whereas such occurrence among the young, often more unstable and immature, "non-therapeutic addicts" of the 1960s and 1970s must be rare. It is, therefore, of some interest to note that both Clive and Wilberforce were apparently aged 30 or over when they started to take opium, and that Trotter warned against its dangers mainly when used in the emotionally unstable and "on slight occasions." It would thus seem that he made a difference between prescribing the drug for its "proper" indications, and otherwise, and between prescribing the drug for the essentially stable personality (where by implication it seemed that Trotter felt there was not much risk of the development of dependence) and the unstable individual with a definite risk of addiction.

Opium consumption was thus well known and practiced in Britain long before De Quincey and his fellow writers and intellectuals publicized it. Many youngsters in the present-day drug-taking era tend to ascribe the onset of their habit to "curiosity," after having heard or seen in the mass media that other young people have taken drugs. Because of such occurrences and risks of glamorizing drugs the Pharmaceutical Society has repeatedly requested press and TV not to mention the names of drugs which lend themselves to abuse. It is interesting that as long as 200 years ago — i.e., quite a few years before De Quincey, who in fact quoted him — another eighteenth century writer had been deliberately vague on the properties of opium as he "thought the subject of too delicate a nature to be made common; and as many people might then indiscriminately use it, it would take from them that necessary fear and caution, which should prevent their experiencing the extensive power of this drug: for there are many properties in it, if universally known, that would habituate the use, and make it more in request with us than the Turks themselves ... the results of which knowledge must prove a general misfortune. . . ." In declaring the moratorium on news about the drug, this early writer was thus much more cautious than some more famous authors in the twentieth century who did not share his inhibitions. Aldous Huxley, the best known among them, certainly was no friend of opium. But in the knowledge that humanity would never dispense with "Artificial Paradise" and would for ever remain in need of frequent "chemical vacations" from intolerable selfhood and repulsive environment, Huxley wrote in glowing terms of his own glorious experiences one year earlier with mescalin. That was in 1954, and his influence in encouraging youngsters in the 1960s toward a realization of "the universal and ever-present urge to self-transcendence" by use of psychedelic "doors in the wall" seems to have been much greater than the "Confessions" of De Quincey on his contemporaries in 1821.

De Quincey, like Huxley, did not believe that there was much danger attached to writing about drugs. It has also been stated that – again resembling Huxley's arguments one and a half centuries later – "Romantic writers like Coleridge and De Quincey deliberately experimented with opium and other drugs "to drive out reason and let imagination take sway" (Gombrich). But certainly at some stage both these writers had become definitely addicted, although at other times they may have been "experimenters." De Quincey estimated his intake in 1813 as 8,000 drops of laudanum per day (he reckoned 25 drops as equivalent to one grain, 0.06 mg of opium). Coleridge had started his opium intake in Cambridge in 1791, perhaps because like many of his contemporaries, he was influenced by a hypothesis put forward a few years earlier by Dr. John Brown, i.e., that possibly the best way of obtaining receptivity to stimulation – the most important feature in life – was by taking laudanum (R. Lewis, 1968). On at least one occasion he also took Bhang, though writing against the consumption of drugs. By 1801 he was said to have been "addicted" and "under fearful slavery" (Drinkwater, 1957).

In De Quincey's time, and later in the nineteenth century, the list of opium users among intellectuals was lengthy: Byron, Crabbe, Keats, Shelly, Scott, and in the second half of the nineteenth century, Wilkie Collins and Francis Thompson. In general they were reported to have taken laudanum for some illness or other; De Quincey, too, began his opium-taking career because of rheumatic pains. Coleridge claimed that he had become seduced into the taking of narcotics. This may possibly be true in a rather wide sense of the term in that the intellectual climate of his time may have been a contributory factor (R. Lewis, 1968). To a certain degree this reminds one of today's discussions as to the similarity or otherwise of the spread of drug misuse to the infectious diseases (Bejerot, 1970, Glatt, 1964). There are obvious similarities, but unlike the infectious diseases, the "victim" in drug misuse is not in general a passive recipient but goes out of his way to obtain drugs. This is, of course, a matter of some controversy. Most drug addicts who admit to the occasional or regular selling of drugs in order to ensure their own supplies usually go out of their way to stress that they only sell to people who have already used such drugs in the past, and that they would never sell drugs to newcomers to the scene. To what extent this is so, it is impossible to say. The Misuse of Drugs Act (1971) attempts to differentiate clearly between "pushing" and mere possession. In the U.K. professional pushers must be rare and there is no evidence of a real organized trade; in the case of "Chinese Heroin," however, it seems that it has often been sold by people who themselves were not "mainliners," and who often recruited young adults, often girls, to sell the stuff on their behalf. The addicts, in lieu of their fee, could retain some of the stuff for their own use. There seem to be all kinds of intermediate stages between the activities of the addict who sells drugs exclusively to ensure his own supplies (a very common occurrence), those of the "dealer," and of the "pusher." Pushing implies a positive attempt to foist drugs onto other people whether they want them or not (Morris, 1972). Dealers have been described as being in it for the money, either full-time or part-time, but they may think of themselves as fulfilling a necessary public service, and as being conscientious about dosage and the quality of the stuff they distribute (Morris, 1972).

However, the very great majority of young drug takers in this country (i.e., using cannabis, amphetamines) were introduced to drugs not by dealers or pushers but by friends, casual acquaintances, etc., at parties or similar occasions. The general climate of this drug age, the regular presentations by the mass media, the efforts of the "legalize cannabis" lobby, the widespread interest in "mind-bending" and "consciousness-extending" drugs must all have exerted a very important background influence. In many cases the presence of various forms of subcultures must have played an important role, as, e.g., in the case of young students enrolling in a university and wishing to "belong" to a circle in which the smoking of cannabis may have been a common, though not a predominant, exercise. Incidentally, "junkie-subcultures" emerged in London in the early 1960s   (Glatt et al., 1969) despite Schur's pronouncements at the time to the contrary (and although heroin could then be obtained quite legally from certain London doctors) (Schur, 1963). This is of some interest in connection with the nineteenth century drug-taking fashion when, in R. Lewis' view, the lack of prohibition of the use of drugs made the development of a junkie-subculture unnecessary. The same writer likens the intellectual interest in stimulation at the turn of the nineteenth century to the cannabis lobby and the general fascination with hallucinogenic drugs in Britain in the late 1960s; Coleridge could be seen as possibly "as much the victim of his age as the burned out acidhead is of ours." (Lewis, 1972)

It would seem that the taking of opium in the nineteenth century was not restricted to a special social class. De Quincey (1821) noted it among Manchester cotton factory workers as well as among his intellectual friends; Trotter saw it among women of all social classes; mothers (at the time of the industrial revolution) quieted their crying infants with a few drops of the drug. (Trotter, 1807) As regards its prevalence throughout the various social classes, drug-taking habits in the 1960s do not appear to have been very different from those prevailing in the previous century. In the United Kingdom, unlike the United States, one always saw heroin-cocaine misuse and dependence among the middle classes as well as working-class youngsters; and while by and large amphetamines seemed always to have been much more popular among the latter and cannabis and LSD more among the middle class and students, the psychedelic drugs in the late 1960s were quite commonly used by members of all social classes (Glatt, 1967). As regards the amphetamines it must not be forgotten, either, that long before they were "discovered" by youngsters in the early 1960s, they were consumed by many middle-class women in the quest, initially, for slimming and subsequently, for euphoria (Glatt, 1974). Similarly long before youngsters in the late 1970s took to the "mainlining" of barbiturates – largely because after the exit of the readily prescribing "junkie doctors" in 1968 the official treatment centers were much less forthcoming in prescribing narcotics – middle-class women had been regularly taking barbiturates as prescribed by their G.P.'s, and quite a proportion of them must have become psychologically and physically dependent (Glatt 1962, Brooke and Glatt). At present, too, the drug-taking habit – of course including alcohol (Glatt, 1972) – is prevalent throughout all strata of British society. However, one important difference between the opium consumption in the nineteenth and twentieth centuries is the lack of official and social sanction in the past. There can, therefore, have been no question then of any possible criminalization, of any labelling as "deviants" by the establishment, of secondary "self-fulfilment of prophecy" behavior of addicts, all of which in the views of radical sociologists (Young, S. Cohen) are claimed to play such an important role nowadays. Nevertheless, whether because of easy accessibility and lack of restrictions and sanctions, or in spite of it, the English apparently consumed opium freely in the nineteenth century; by mid-century the average Englishman took over one-quarter oz. per year, and between 1830 and 1850 opium consumption had tripled. Doctors prescribed it for many organic and functional illnesses, and among the noblesse it was apparently popular as a cure for hangovers (Hughes) – which certainly must have contributed greatly to pushing up its consumption. Though probably being a poor second in this respect to alcohol, opium also was employed widely by the new urban proletariat for physical and mental pain and distress. At the time of the beginning of the Opium Wars against China in 1840 there were probably, in the view of Hughes, "few Englishmen who had not taken opium for relief or stimulus." (Hughes, 1972)

The Opium Wars started because the Chinese, worried about the growing social problem as a consequence of its import from the West, tried to put a stop to it. However, following the two wars the Treaty of Tientsin in 1858 forced China to legalize the opium trade. Afterward import of the drug (mainly from India) rose rapidly as did the cultivation of poppies in China itself. Voices were raised in Britain from time to time throughout the nineteenth century against the opium trade. In 1893, commissions were set up to investigate the cannabis and opium situation in India. China had become increasingly worried about the opium problem and decided to stop its cultivation, signing an agreement with Britain to that effect in 1907. Britain, in turn, was gradually to reduce imports into China within the next ten years.

Nevertheless, toward the turn of the twentieth century there seemed to be a curious "ambivalence" (A. Lewis) or "dissociation" in many people's minds when comparing the effects of drugs such as the opiates at home and far afield. Thus a London doctor in 1909 referred to the findings of various commissions saying that the opium habit "amongst some races, in certain districts, is not utterly to be condemned" (Hillier). Indeed, under certain conditions of native life, he felt that its effects rather than being harmful might probably be even beneficial, perhaps because people like the Indians might have a "higher tolerance" (Hiller, 1909).

Similarly, two prominent British doctors in 1906 condemned the familiar use of opium in any form in Britain as tantamount to playing with fire and catching fire. Yet, they felt that as far as the Orient was concerned the situation might be quite different; there the drug is often used, "rightly or wrongly . . . not as an idle or vicious indulgence but as a reasonable aid to life." These doctors – Clifford Albutt and W.E. Dixon – then posed the question (to some extent anticipating the later writings of Huxley, Leary, and some contemporary sociologists in regard to the modern psychedelics): 'wherein lies the harm of stimulants and narcotics? If they are short cuts to happiness, why not use paths so pleasant? . . . It may not be true to say that opium and other agents cannot do anything for the higher life . . ." (Lewis, 1968).

Half a century later Aldous Huxley to a certain extent echoed these remarks although he ruled out opium: the new drugs needed to relieve and console suffering mankind; had to be potent in minute amounts and synthesizable so that, unlike alcoholic beverages and tobacco, its production would not interfere with the raising of foodstuff and fibers; it had to be less toxic than opium and cocaine, less harmful socially than alcohol and the barbiturates, less dangerous to heart and lungs than nicotine; and it should produce more interesting and valuable changes in consciousness than mere sedation, omnipotent delusions, or freedom from inhibitions. In short, Huxley thought of a substance like mescalin: '. . . almost completely innocuous to most people." But although peyote had been well known to American Indians for hundreds of years and although Louis Lewin had published a study of the cactus, later named after him, in 1886, early in the twentieth century the psychedelics were among Albutt and Dixon's "other agents" which were to acquire popularity and become controversial in the distant future. At the turn of the twentieth century laudanum was going out of fashion but the number of people addicted to some drug or other was said to have increased. Again anticipating statements to be heard frequently in the 1960s, one doctor wrote in 1909: 'whilst . . . avoiding the alarmist attitude . . . we admit the grave peril' (Hillier). Some opium smoking was then still taking place in the opium dens of East London's Chinese quarter. This was apparently greatly frowned upon, since the London Country Council at the time acquired the right to suspend or revoke the licensing of lodging houses in which opium was smoked. But the Chinese in London kept the opium to themselves – unlike the situation in the late 1960s and 1970s when "Chinese heroin" peddled in London's West End was sold directly or by European intermediaries to British addicts.

Morphia, which had been isolated in 1805, was at the beginning of the twentieth century becoming more popular than opium. Some doctors apparently regarded it then as a safe substitute for opium, putting forth the surprising claim that if it was taken by hypodermic or intravenous injection it would not excite appetite for it (i.e., psychological dependence), unlike oral medication. However this statement, diametrically opposite to present-day views, already ran counter to the experience of other doctors at the time. Thus Hillier in 1909 claimed that it was the frequent adoption in medical practice of hypodermic injections that was responsible for the "considerable increase in the (morphine) habit . . . the dangers of contracting the habit is . . . serious' and fully recognized by doctors: '. . . scrupulous care and discrimination in this form of medication is one of the canons of orthodox medical practice. . . . It should be a golden rule that a patient never be allowed to use the hypodermic syringe on himself or herself, and much discrimination and judgment must be exercised, in deciding whether the constitution and moral temperament in each particular case justifies its use." Half a century later, however, it was the lack of such "care and discrimination" in prescribing heroin and cocaine by a handful of London doctors that, in the view of the Second Brain Committee, greatly contributed to the emergence of the London heroin and cocaine epidemic. Moreover, the newly established out-patient treatment centers from 1968 onward, after much soul-searching debate, adopted a method of prescribing heroin, cocaine, and later methadone, in such a way that the addicts themselves carried out the injections on themselves; and in order to diminish the risks of local and generalized septicaemia and of syringe hepatitis, treatment centers in recent years have even adopted the custom of providing the addict with sterile plastic syringes and with needles.

Cocaine was a drug reported to be habitually taken in England at the beginning of the twentieth century by many people of either sex, by doctors, writers, and politicians (Lewin). Doctors often combined its use with that of morphia (others took it with alcohol). This simultaneous ingestion of a stimulant with a narcotic or sedative drug thus antedated by more than half a century the popular habit of young addicts in the 1960s of counteracting the effects of excessive heroin dosage by also taking cocaine (or in 1967 methylamphetamine) and also the similar custom in the 1950s of combining the stimulating amphetamines or phenmetrazine with barbiturates or carbromal (Glatt, 1959).

A clear indication that at the time at least a certain number of doctors regarded drug misuse as a problem deserving attention is evident from the foundation, in 1884, of the Society for the Study of Inebriety by Dr. Norman Kerr. He described the opium habit as a "true inebriety" and stated that "there is some risk inseparable from the social use of all intoxicants." In a similar vein, in 1903, Sir William Collins suggested that "addiction to drugs might be dealt with along that to alcohol." This recommendation has a very modern ring, since it was not until 1966 that a World Health Organization Committee suggested a "combined" approach to alcohol and "other drugs" (W.H.O. 1966).

Another topic once again very much in the public eye — the "disease concept" of alcohol and drug dependence — was often debated at meetings of the Society for the Study of Inebriety in those early days. Kerr and others described it as a disease, whereas in the view of Collins, "A disease it may be called, but a disease of the will . . . and assuredly a disease in which the individual possessed has in many instances a most essential cooperative influence in his own worsement or betterment." and reminding the student of the 1970s drug scene of the polarization between the followers of psychosocial and of chemical methods of treatment and rehabilitation, Collins, passing on from his own psychological views to those who believe in chemical methods, claimed that the latter ". . . will continue to search in vain for something out of a bottle or, maybe, a hypodermic injection, wherewith to redeem the sot and rehabilitate the will."

Another theme of topical interest nowadays which was discussed by Collins 60 years ago was the role of legislation and of compulsory treatment in the addictions. In the U.K., dependence on alcohol or on "other drugs" is in itself not sufficient reason for a compulsory treatment order. Indeed the only one of the Second Interdepartmental (Brain) Committee's recommendations (1965) not to be implemented by the government was the suggestion referring to the possibility of keeping narcotic addicts compulsorily in hospital for treatment of withdrawal symptoms. Official policy in regard to inebriety – as described by Collins at the time, and essentially still in force today – was of taking action only "when obvious and serious annoyance, danger or wrong would result to others." Collins, however, felt that a principle of "the suppression of slavery from within as well as from without" was applicable to addiction, so that a certain restraint of liberty may sometimes be indicated "to secure a larger and truer liberty."

Britain, though not suffering from a serious narcotic problem at the time – played an active role in the international control system (Glatt, 1969) that started with the Shanghai Conference in 1909. Throughout the years the U.K. in general faithfully implemented the recommendations of the International Convention – including those referring to drugs which did not pose any problems in this country at the time, as for example the inclusion in the list of narcotics and prohibition of cannabis at the Second Opium Conference in 1925. In the 1950s and in particular since the 1960s there was increasing use or "misuse" (the label depends, of course, on one's personal view) of cannabis in this country, and as anywhere else controversy about its dangers and the possibility of its use being legalized (Wootton Report). While there is considerable divergence of views in regard to other aspects of the cannabis question, there is probably widespread agreement that it is factually wrong to include cannabis under the term "narcotics" and, moreover, unwise to apply to it the same laws as those pertaining to the undoubtedly dangerous drugs heroin and cocaine. In any event, as described by Bean, out of Britain's eight major Dangerous Drug Acts four directly followed international agreements; it is only since 1964 that Britain enacted regulations not arising out of international control recommendations.

Before the 1960s drug misuse never caused public concern in the U.K. apart from a minor episode of cocaine use and trafficking during and after the First World War (Jeffrey). Special regulations brought in to deal with the cocaine problem during the war were extended in 1920 to include all the drugs affected by the 1912 International Convention. There was in the 1920s a gradual fall in prosecutions for cocaine and morphine offenses. This improvement was, in a Commons debate at the time, attributed to the deterrent effect of increased penalties (Bean).

How did the medical profession, or that small minority of doctors taking an active interest in the problem at the time (even in the 1960s it was always only a small proportion of medical men who were concerned with the treatment of drug addicts), view drug misuse in the 1920s? Dixon stated in 1925 that when cocaine occurred as a single condition – not associated with morphine use – it usually resulted from imitation and opportunity: cocaine users were thus a menace to others as well as to themselves. The people affected were "neurotics." Dixon did not see the drug habit as a disease but "rather as a symptom of a preexisting mental condition." He took strong issue with the New York police commissioner's statement in 1924 that addiction comes within the province of the police. This, in Dixon's view, was "suggestive of the medieval," reminding him of the old days when lunatics were punished and subjected to every indignity. "In truth, addicts make poor criminals."

By and large cocaine misuse was thought by doctors to be less common in the early 1920s than one might have assumed from reports published in the lay press. Even at that time it was believed that the mass media did not always report drug issues in an objectively correct way. Cocaine snuff addiction was, however, held to be common among "pleasure seekers." Morphine addiction, in 1923, was thought to be more common than generally assumed; many users were probably not recognized and obtained drugs surreptitiously, the legal restrictions being evaded" (Willcox, 1923). At any rate, it seems that the combined opiate-cocaine habit, which was to become so prevalent among youngsters in the 1960s, was not uncommon during and after the First World War. Cocaine was used by pleasure seekers as a snuff but only rarely in hypodermic forms, except when secondary to the morphine or heroin habit. In the 1960s, on the other hand, youngsters often had started with "sniffing" cocaine but usually proceeded quickly to "skinpopping" and "mainlining" (Glatt et al.). At the time of World War II drug addicts were already classified into two groups: a smaller section who had originally started to take drugs for pain relief or treatment of disease (today's "therapeutic addicts"), and a larger group in whom addiction was seen as a feature of "neurosis." However, environmental factors were recognized as important, as for instance imitation and opportunity in those taking cocaine by itself. Cocaine, described in the twenties as a "menace," was widely prescribed by the "junkie doctors" in the 1960s, a custom that virtually come to an end soon after the advent of the treatment centers in 1968. Then, as now, the outlook was regarded as better in those addicts who had contracted the drug habit as a result of illness; and the importance of aftercare was recognized, such as the necessity of providing "an entirely new environment" for those claimed to have been "cured" of cocainism (Scharlieb).

Compared to the U.S., the drug problem in the U.K. has always been relatively small. This is how a British doctor keeping an eye on the American drug scene saw the position in 1923 (Campbell):

> In the U.S.A. a drug habitue is regarded as a malefactor. . . . The Harrison Narcotic Law . . . passed severe restrictions upon the sale of narcotics and upon the medical profession, and necessitated the appointment of a whole army of officials. In consequence of this stringent law a vast clandestine commerce in narcotics has grown up in this country. The small bulk of these drugs renders the evasion of the law comparatively easy, and the country is overrun by an army of pedlars who extort exorbitant prices from their hapless victims. . . . The Harrison Law . . . far from bettering the lot of the opiate addict, it has actually worsened it . . . sent up the price tenfold. . . .

If this was the view of the American approach as seen by British doctors, it is no wonder that the Rolleston Committee, composed of medical men only, in 1926 stuck clearly to a medically oriented approach. Under certain circumstances heroin or morphine could be prescribed to addicts: i.e., for prolonged withdrawal treatment with a view to cure; where prolonged attempts at cure had led to severe withdrawal symptoms; and where it had been demonstrated that addicts could not lead a useful and relatively normal life when deprived of the drug but could do so on regular administration of "a certain minimum dose." Such drugs should not be prescribed merely for the "gratification of addiction," and "the primary object of the treatment is the cure of the addiction, if practicable."

The Rolleston Committee, as the <u>British Medical Journal</u> commented in 1926, recognized addiction as manifestation of a disease frequently requiring treatment, and not as a vice demanding punishment. However, it warned against too ready an acceptance of a patient's claim for continued supplies. Nevertheless, as related by Jeffrey, there were occasionally "script doctors" prepared to ignore the Rolleston Committee's warnings, without it leading to any major problems before the 1960s. The reason was probably that the number of addicts at the time was small (Jeffrey) and that the type of addict was in many ways different from the younger, often more unstable, "nontherapeutic" one emerging in the 1960s (Glatt et al.). In retrospect it is clear that the "British System" – a system that never really was, but consisted of practices gradually developing from the Rolleston recommendations – did not prevent the emergence of a heroin-cocaine epidemic in the 1960s (although, as in preceding years, only a few doctors were involved in the prescribing of these drugs, the great majority keeping aloof). It is interesting that Rolleston (1934) and Willcox (1923) (who nine years earlier had both been members of the Rolleston Committee) in 1934 ascribed the "warning" of morphine and heroin to the "addicts" difficulty in getting hold of them because of the "judicious legislation." Adherents of the "British System" abroad, voiced the opposite view; i.e., that its success was due to the ability of addicts to obtain supplies legitimately. Thus they did not have to "hustle" for drugs on the black market with all the dangers inherent in this practice.

Between the 1930s and the early 1960s the number of narcotic addicts known to the Home Office averaged about 500 per year. Most of them were "therapeutic" in origin, middle-aged or older; about ten percent were "professional addicts." A small number (about five percent according to Jeffrey), in a slightly younger age group (35-50 years), had originally obtained their drugs illicitly. But the only illicit traffic between the war years concerned opium and was largely limited to resident Chinese and visiting seamen. There was no heroin problem in the 1950s so that a governmental proposal in the mid-fifties to follow UN recommendations and to ban heroin production and prescribing aroused strong opposition in certain medical quarters. For example, Dr. J.Y. Dent, the editor of the British Journal of Addiction, in an editorial in 1955 called the proposal a retrograde step which might lead to a black market on American lines. On the other hand, strong diametrically opposite views were expressed in other quarters. For example, A. Agnew, the author of a book published in 1956 and describing the London's West End drug (mainly Indian hemp) scene in the early 1950s declares that "the authorities are treating the problem too lightly. Not the detectives of the Vice Squad or the men on the bench, but the politicians and civil servants of Whitehall. It has taken years of pressure by the United Nations to get Britain to agree to a ban on the manufacture of heroin. The ban finally came into force at the end of 1955. Until then the international smuggling rings had been able to get supplies from this country which they could not find in a single nation of size and responsibility anywhere in the world. Now at last, thank God, we have fallen into line with the rest of the world." There is no evidence presented in the book to buttress these claims.

In 1957, Dr. Dent (who incidentally strongly denied that this country was a base for the smuggling of heroin) in an editorial jubilantly announced that "the medical profession has beaten the Government's proposed ban on the legal production of heroin." He went on to say that it was "now . . . the turn for government . . . to beat the profession and induce it to prescribe less of the addictive drugs, especially the barbiturates." Already in the 1920s and 1930s Willcox had warned repeatedly of the dangers attached to the use of barbiturates, which he described as being "foremost . . . among the drugs of addiction." On the other hand, there were men such as Willcox's Home Office colleague Luff (1934) who thought of barbiturates as "one of the great gifts . . . offered to suffering humanity." By the mid-fifties the misuse of the barbiturates, and to a lesser extent of the amphetamines (Connell, Glatt, 1957), had certainly become obvious to doctors interested in the addiction problem (Lancet 1954, Glatt 1954). But neither the state, the medical profession, the general public, nor the mass media paid any attention to the addiction problem until in the early sixties youngsters started to take cannabis, amphetamines, heroin, and cocaine. Over the years until today for some reason or other the existence of an oral barbiturate problem among middle-aged women has been largely ignored, although it must be numerically much larger than that of youngsters "mainlining" these drugs. Certain sociologists ascribe the general preoccupation with the drug use of youngsters to the exclusion of the more prevalent drug taking of the middle-aged (including that of alcohol and tobacco) to the projection of guilt feelings of the adult community and the resulting "scapegoating" of youth. However, many would prefer the alternative explanation of the lack of newsworthiness of adults' drug-taking habits due to long-standing social acceptance of alcohol and tobacco (Smart and Krakowski) and the much greater popular interest in youngsters' activities.

In the 1950s the cannabis traffic began to supersede the traffic in opium, and in 1951 there was for the first time evidence of the peddling of narcotic drugs in London (Jeffrey, Spear). The Home Office at the time looked for a way of revising the provisions of the Rolleston Committee (which had lain dormant) to stop the "script doctors" from overprescribing. This intention, however, got bogged down in administrative problems. Arising out of the prescribing habits of a few doctors, the number of heroin and cocaine addicts rose gradually in the 1950s to a figure of 68 by 1959, before its marked, rapid increase in the 1960s.

However, these changes were not obvious at the time when the Interdepartmental Committee on Drug Addiction (the First Brain Committee) was appointed in 1958, although they gave rise to a somewhat heated discussion at a meeting of the Society for the Study of Addiction in 1961 when Lord Brain talked on the forthcoming committee report. Rather, the committee was intrigued by two other developments in the 34 years since the Rolleston Report, i.e., the production of newer analgesics capable of producing addiction, and the development of newer methods of treating addiction. The findings of the First Brain Committee are nowadays of historical interest only; at any rate their view that there was little to worry about regarding the drug situation, and no need for any radical changes, already seemed out of date in 1961 when the report was published. Of much more interest from the aspect of our theme of attitude and response of the British community to drug use and misuse are certain comments made by the Brain Committee at the time pertaining to the greatly increased use of sedative and stimulating drugs in the preceding decade. The committee ascribed the rise in the number of such prescriptions to various factors: the advertising campaign of the pharmaceutical industry, directed both at doctors and the general public; possibly the accelerated tempo and heightened anxieties of modern life; and "perhaps of considerable consequence . . . the materialistic attitude adopted nowadays to therapeutics in general, . . . one feature of an age which owes much to science. For every deviation from health, great or small, a specific chemical corrective is sought and, if possible, applied, and it is also widely believed that health may be positively enhanced by the use of these drugs. . . . Often . . . a prescription is given for a drug when the patient's real need is a discussion of his psychological difficulties with the doctor. . . ."

The committee had no "definite information about the volume of purchases (of drugs) without prescription," but it had already recommended in an interim report in 1959 that "any drug or pharmaceutical preparation acting on the CNS, and liable to produce physical or psychological deterioration, should be supplied on prescription only." Corresponding action had subsequently been taken by the government. That such purchases without prescription were not uncommon was clear from statements of many patients at the Warlingham Park Alcoholic Unit in the 1950s, who had frequently or habitually taken all kinds of sedatives and hypnotics with or without prescription, although as a rule the imposing of restrictions on a given drug practically always led to a greater demand for, and misuse of, alternative drugs not so restricted (Glatt, 1962, 1974). Before 1960 there was no evidence of such misuse of drugs by youngsters. The Brain Committee's remarks, thus, refer to the active interest in CNS affecting drugs (and this quite apart from alcohol and tobacco) shown by adults, long before the same phenomenon emerged among youngsters.

Two further comments made by the Brain Committee are of interest in view of similar, though often farther reaching, statements occasionally heard nowadays. The committee felt that "it was not for us to decide whether (the) occasional or even regular use (of CNS affecting drugs) is justified if it enables a person to lead a happier and more useful life." This pronouncement coming from an "establishment" body is interesting in view of statements made by radical sociologists that it is the reason why a drug is taken that determines social reaction: where it aids productivity the drug is socially approved of: where it is taken for purely hedonistic motives it is condemned (Young). The committee was also aware of the need, in some cases, to treat recourse to drugs as a symptom and to look for its cause "perhaps as much in social conditions as in the mind of the individuals." It should be noted that the committee was composed of medical men only and had no sociologists as members.

Within a few years the Brain Committee had to be reconvened. It acknowledged in its report of 1965 that there had been a disturbing rise of heroin and cocaine addiction especially among the young. The proportion of professional and "therapeutic" addicts had fallen, that of "nontherapeutic" addicts increased. The recommendations of the Second Interdepartmental (Brain) Committee Report aimed at stemming the rising tide of heroin and cocaine abuse (an American report estimated that at the same rate of increase Britain within a few years would have 11,000 narcotic addicts), included the introduction of a notification system for addicts, the provision of treatment centers, and the restriction of supplies to addicts of heroin and cocaine. In the future only doctors working in the treatment centers were to be allowed to prescribe heroin and cocaine to addicts, though G.P.'s could continue to prescribe methadone. The first two treatment centers began to operate in 1967, though more started under official encouragement and pressure in 1968, almost all initially in the London area which contained the great majority of addicts. This probably is still true today but gradually drug taking also affected the provinces. A list published in December 1973 (Drugs and Society) named 17 clinics in the London area and 20 in the provinces, although the latter look after a much smaller proportion of the officially known total of about 1,600 narcotic addicts. In 1967 an amending Dangerous Drugs Act empowered the Home Secretary to make the regulations relating to the limitation of heroin and cocaine prescribing and the notification of addicts.

Though attempting to keep the approach of the various treatment centers fairly uniform there are of course quite a few differences between them. Some are known among addicts to be more generous in their prescribing habits than others but it is difficult for addicts to switch from one center to another. Within the time, and with the staff available, the medical, nursing, and social staff attempt to build up a positive relationship with their patients, to motivate them toward reduction and possibly giving up of their drugs and to introduce them to (often voluntary) organizations that could support them in the long-term rehabilitation process. In general the treatment centers prefer methadone to heroin; according to the latest available figures (relating to December 31, 1972), out of 1,619 known addicts, 1,280 received methadone (of whom 201 were also prescribed heroin) and only 138 received heroin (either alone or in combination with drugs other than methadone). Two hundred one (mainly "therapeutic") addicts received narcotics other than heroin and methadone, mainly morphine and pethidine. The treatment centers in general seem to accept that in a proportion of addicts one has to be satisfied with realistic, limited goals. However, insofar as the narcotic problem has been contained (and the prescribing of cocaine virtually stopped) it may perhaps be said that in this respect the centers have achieved some measure of success.

This relative success, however, has been achieved at certain cost, in terms of a rise in illicit drug taking. Even before the advent of the centers there was, in the 1960s, a gradual rise of consumption among youngsters not only of heroin and cocaine but also of cannabis, LSD, and amphetamines (Glatt et al.). Illicit drug taking subsequent to the establishment of the centers in the main related to six drugs: cannabis, LSD, amphetamines, barbiturates, "Chinese heroin," and methadone. The increasing use of cannabis is reflected in the rise of convictions for cannabis-related offenses (9,219 in 1971, 12,611 in 1972), although it would seem that in general the police are not too anxious to bring people to court for mere possession.

Convictions for drugs controlled under the Drugs (Prevention of Misuse) Act (1964) — which was concerned with ampetamines and hallucinogens such as LSD — numbered 5,515 in 1971 (1,601 were for LSD offenses) and 5,284 in 1972 (1,457 were for LSD offenses). In contrast to the increase of cannabis offenses there was thus a slight drop in LSD offenses, and a considerable decrease in offenses related to amphetamines — from 2,388 in 1971 to 1,955 in 1972. The amphetamines drop is thought to be related to the gradual acceptance by doctors of the lead given by the British Medical Association in a memorandum a few years ago and by strenuous efforts of certain branches of the B.M.A. in greatly cutting down the number of prescriptions; this in turn makes it unnecessary for pharmacies to stock large supplies. On the whole, however, the total number of persons convicted for offenses controlled under the Drug Acts increased from 11,712 in 1971 to 13,998 in 1972. The Chinese heroin problem has already been touched upon. Methadone is often prescribed by the treatment centers in injectable form and thus lends itself to misuse and the risk of dependence to a much higher degree than when prescribed in the oral form. It has become a widely misused drug on the London Black Market; however, in order to keep contact with such drug users the treatment center doctors often feel that they should agree to the addicts' demands for the prescribing of methadone ampoules. This is only one of many problems facing the doctor working in such treatment centers (Glatt, 1972). He is a member of a multidisciplinary therapeutic team (comprising social workers, nurses, voluntary workers) that, in association with local authorities and a great number of voluntary bodies, aims at helping the addict to find his place toward full functioning in the community and, if at all possible, to give up drug taking altogether. But all too often the addict is neither willing, nor often seemingly in a condition, to cooperate in this aim; and if his supply of drugs is cut down too drastically he easily obtains more dangerous drugs, such as Chinese heroin or barbiturates, on the black market. In fact, nowadays the average British young drug taker is a polydrug misuser who takes any drug he can get hold of.

Barbiturates, when taken intravenously, are probably the most dangerous ones, with the risk of local and systemic septicaemia, viral hepatitis, psychological and physical dependence, and accidental and intentional overdosage. It is interesting that until the late 1960s British youngsters looked down on the drinking and taking of hypnotics by their elders. Their claim was that what they, the young, wanted from drugs was to obtain a lift or an expansion of consciousness. However, following the greater difficulties of obtaining addictive drugs since the advent of the treatment centers, youngsters adopted the habit of injecting barbiturates and of taking the nonbarbiturate "Mandrax" (diphenhydramine plus methaqualone known as Quaaludes in America) by mouth (Glatt, 1969). Reliable figures are not available but it would seem that — since G.P.'s in the past few years have gradually become aware of this new habit of youngsters and have become more cautious in their prescribing habits — such barbiturate misuse among the young is gradually receding. It seems remarkable that the barbiturates, which in spite of their usefulness for certain conditions are probably the most dangerous drugs to be misused, are not subject to control under the Misuse of Drugs Act (1971) which came into force in July 1973. This act has replaced the previous acts, and controls, in various schedules, the opiates, cocaine, cannabis, LSD, the amphetamines, etc. The wide powers given to the police to search came in for some criticism, and there was a long debate in February 1971 in the House of Lords when the provisions in the bill relating to cannabis were discussed. The act gives the Home Secretary powers to deal with offenders (including doctors) much more rapidly than in the past, by the much greater flexibility of its provisions. It also clearly recognizes that by itself legislation cannot prevent and curb the drug problem, nor fill the vital need for education and research in this field.

RESPONSES, REACTIONS, ATTITUDES TO DRUG USE AND MISUSE

As indicated at the start of this paper, and as is obvious from the brief review of the history of drug use in the U.K., it is impossible to talk of a response of the British community to drug use. Throughout the known history of the use of drugs, various sections of the community varied in their responses and reactions to what they regarded as beneficial or harmful, as "good" or "bad" drugs. Foremost among the "good" drugs (Camps), throughout the centuries, in the eyes of most sections of society including the majority of doctors who prescribed it for all types of illnesses, was alcohol. But, on the other hand, there were always those who regarded alcohol as "evil," and since the nineteenth century there has always been a more or less influential temperance movement. Similarly, the great majority of the population, despite a royal "counterblast" against the use of tobacco near the start of its British history, always accepted tobacco as a "good" drug, still now paying £1,000 million a year in taxes (Norton) even though medical sciences has clearly shown it to be a danger to health and life. Barbiturates were always regarded by doctors and the general public as "good" drugs, and Willcox's lonely attempts to induce doctors to curtail their prescribing of barbiturates led to bitter emotional attacks on him by other doctors (Glatt, 1962). Barbiturates became so generally accepted by the population that women who would not dream of ever using an opium type of drug had no qualms in habitually taking barbiturate tablets. The influence of different social attitudes to drug taking by the sexes is clearly indicated in the predominance of heavy drinking among men and of barbiturate dependence among women; it would seem that in many cases where a frustrated, anxious, or harrassed man would take to alcoholic drink, the woman under similar circumstances would take barbiturate tablets (Glatt, 1962). On the other hand, a drug regarded as "good" and acceptable by wide sections of the community at an earlier time in history may later become unacceptable and "bad." As we have seen, in the nineteenth century laudanum was fashionable and popular among wide sections of the British public and among at least a section of doctors (though others, like Trotter, disagreed). Nowadays opiates, like cannabis and LSD are condemned by medical and general public opinion alike as "bad" drugs, although a minority (e.g., subcultures mainly among the young) protest against such "labelling" by "establish-ment" and adults as unjust and unfair. This minority feels that if an often aggression-producing drug is legal, it is quite arbitrary and unfair for cannabis – not known in this country to induce aggression and violence – to be condemned and outlawed.

Among doctors themselves, too, opinion in regard to certain drugs has often been bitterly divided. It was (probably) an influential minority of doctors who in the mid-1950s, felt passionately that heroin was an indispensable drug in certain conditions and brought about a reversal of a governmental decision which had aimed at stopping its production and prescribing. Also, throughout the years following the Rolleston Report, although it was quite legitimate under certain conditions to prescribe opiates and cocaine to addicts, the great majority of doctors fought and involved in the treatment of, and prescribing to, addicts; yet a very small minority not only prescribed such drugs but habitually over-prescribed without regard to the legal restrictions. In one case known to the present writer, one of the "prescribing doctors" – who was passionately convinced that his method of regularly prescribing heroin and cocaine to youngsters was vastly preferable to their obtaining them on the black market – in a letter to a London court (in about 1964) declared that this method of prescribing large doses of heroin and cocaine to young addicts constituted "good medical practice." Thus, what is a 'good' or 'bad' medical practice, legitimate use or misuse or willful abuse is not only a matter of fashion of the times or of subcultures, of age or sex of the drug consumer, but varies even among medical men – at times evoking bitter controversies such as the "Battle of the Barbiturates" in the 1930s and the emotionally highly charged discussion between the "junkie doctors" and their opponents in the early and mid-1960s (Glatt et al.).

The changing responses among youngsters to alcohol and "sleepers" are another illustration of changing fashions. Until the late 1960s such drugs were definitely "bad" ones in the eyes of many young drug takers who regarded them as "good" only for their elders but quite unsuitable for young people who desired a "lift" by stimulants. However, since the late sixties, barbiturates have become acceptable to the young – although probably mainly as a consequence of treatment centers cutting down on opiates – and alcohol once again is making an ever-increasing and dangerous comeback in popularity among youngsters.   Amphetamines, once popular as a slimming and energy providing drug among middle-aged housewives in the 1950s, have since become some of the most widely misused drugs among the young. Moreover, while the great majority of doctors regard amphetamines as useless and often dangerous drugs, a small minority of doctors continue to prescribe them. But by and large, today's 'good' drugs, beloved by the general public as well as by doctors, and gradually ousting the older favorites (barbiturates and amphetamines) are the tranquillizers and the modern antidepressants; in recent years their prescriptions have been rising steadily (Glatt, 1974). In fairness, it would seem that as yet these newer drugs as a group seem less dangerous than their predecessors. But then it takes time before all the dangers attached to recently introduced drugs become known. Tobacco was regarded as practically free from risks for centuries, and heroin and pethidine were introduced as substitutes for the older opiates with the claim that they would not lead to dependence. But it is interesting that among tranquillizers, meprobamate – for long so popular in the U.S. – never rivalled the benzodiazepines' popularity in Britain. Again, doctors in this country by and large seem to prescribe the benzodiazepines widely but in smaller dosage than in the U.S. and certain parts of the European continent. This may perhaps explain why reports of physical dependence on benzodiazepines following in the wake of the regular medication in Britain are very rare (Glatt, 1974).

One prevalent attitude throughout British drug history is the dislike of extremist prohibitionistic approaches. Throughout many centuries of heavy alcohol use in Britain there was only one very short-lived attempt in the eighteenth century amounting to something like prohibition (Glatt, 1958). An attempt by the Liberal government in 1906 to introduce a very restrictive alcohol licensing legislation led to bitter public protests and was immediately thrown out by the House of Lords, it needed the mortal danger of the 1914-18 war to produce a strong liquor-restricting legislation. The recommendations of the 1912 International Committees in time led to the stringent Harrison Act in the U.S. (strongly condemned soon afterward by leading British doctors), but to the nonprohibitionist Dangerous Drugs Act of 1920 in Great Britain. Some British doctors objected strongly to heroin prohibition in the mid-fifties. Even following the emergence of the heroin-cocaine epidemic among the young in the 1960s, and the loss by G.P.'s of the right to prescribe heroin and cocaine to addicts, treatment centers did not adopt a prohibition approach, but in the main substituted methadone in place of heroin. Nevertheless, there still remains, naturally enough, a wide gulf between the treatment centers' and the addicts' views as to what constitutes "use" and "misuse." In particular, in the earlier days when the treatment centers began their work there often was a battle of wits between addicts who claimed that they needed a certain, and often very high, amount of heroin and cocaine and the doctors who frequently felt that the amount claimed was what the addicts wanted but did not really need. At any rate, at the present time most treatment centers probably have a proportion of addicted patients who are maintained on a certain dosage; this by implication is thus probably regarded as "use" and not "misuse," although it may be hoped that in time a certain number among such patients may be motivated to come off drugs, possibly helped by a process of emotional "maturation" from within, and by support from community agencies, from without.

It is often held that addicts are so unreliable and untrustworthy that any statements coming from them must be accepted with great skepticism (Goulding, Paton, Wade). This, of course, is true to a certain extent but in the present author's experience statements by addicts whom one has known and treated over a certain period, and with whom one has built up some relationship, are often very reliable, whether such patients have been seen in the hospital, in a treatment center, or in a special prison unit (Glatt, 1974). Rightly or wrongly, at present members of a small group of "stabilized" addicts seen by the author over a period of six years at a treatment center claim that they need drugs in order to be able to function "normally."

This consideration brings us back to a question posed at the start of this paper, i.e, which section of the population can be regarded as most representative in talking about community attitudes to drug use. After all, drug addicts, too, are members of the community. But the Brain Committee, for example, made their recommendations without speaking to addicts. One might perhaps have thought that in contrast to widely varying moral and social reactions the legal response might possibly be the best indicator of a community's response to drug use and misuse. Does the law reflect the attitudes of the "silent majority" better than, for example, all the pronouncements by vociferous psychiatrists and sociologists? After all, the two latter groups are often in conflict. Certain sociologists think of the hospital psychiatrists, who in the mid-sixties clamored for action to stop the increasing heroin-cocaine misuse, as "moral entrepreneurs" (Bean) whose motivations they suspected. Allegedly, these psychiatrists became concerned only after it was the young who took to drugs, having formerly remained strangely silent as regards the drug use of the middle-aged. It may seem difficult to explain, under these circumstances, why some of these psychiatrists accepted such young drug addicts into existing units for middle-aged alcoholics and addicts and attempted to treat them in exactly the same way as middle-aged drug takers (Glatt et al.). Most psychiatrists would probably also disagree with the views of certain sociologists who ascribe the main reason for society's attitude to young drug addicts to such mechanisms as "scapegoating" because of unconscious guilt feelings (Wiener) – though to a certain extent this mechanism may often be at work – and to society's envy of the young's hedonism (Young), and who describe psychiatrists as instruments of social control under the guise of treatment (S. Cohen, Young). Moreover, radical sociologists attack psychiatrists for allegedly seeing psychological factors as the only ones of importance in causing drug misuse and for neglecting the social factors (Young); though writing as a psychiatrist one may find it difficult to think of examples of psychiatrists interested in this issue who ever proclaimed psychiatry to be the only, or perhaps even the main, answer to the problem of drug misuse. In general psychiatrists have always regarded drug use as an interdisciplinary problem in which "agent," society, and "host" are all involved (Glatt, 1974). In turn, psychiatrists fail to understand how sociologists, rightly attacking an exclusively psychologically oriented approach to drug misuse, prescribe social changes as "the" solution (Young). Surely it would seem that, just as one cannot talk of "the" response of "the" British community to drug use, so also no one discipline has on its own "the" best answer to the problem.

On the other hand, undoubtedly moral reactions play a great role in determining people's attitudes and reactions to drug misusers and in the labelling of certain minority activities as "deviant" which, in time, may cause many drug users to react in a way that confirms the initial labelling. But "amplification of deviance" is not necessarily the outcome of measures of interference by establishment organs (such as the police) with activities of drug users (Wilkins, Young), e.g., those smoking cannabis. Not taking any steps, of course, also means embarking on a certain course, so that amplification of deviance may also arise from "sins of omission" (Glatt, 1974) as well as from those "sins of commission" usually condemned by radical sociologists. For example, as de Alarcon has pointed out, "prompt action to stop the uncontrolled availability of the drug during the early phase of consolidation would have prevented the exponential progression to the explosive stage of the (British heroin) epidemic" in the 1960s. There was, over a period of several years, clear evidence of ready availability of heroin and cocaine leading to the spread of misuse of the drugs by youngsters (Bewley, Glatt 1964, Glatt et al.). Instead of taking preventive action there was warning against premature "panic measures," and nothing was done for several years even after the Second Brain Committee had clearly described, in 1965, the great dangers of the situation. Similarly, a few years later nothing was done to stop the overprescribing of methylamphetamine by a London doctor who was permitted to continue his well-publicized activities for a further period of several months while appealing against having been struck-off by the General Medical Council.

Yet, as we have seen in our brief historical review, moral reactions and ambivalent attitudes have often been at work in determining the responses by society and leading doctors to problems of drug use and misuse. Moreover, in the past, the committees advising governments on how the law should deal with drug misuse problems have been completely or almost exclusively composed of medical men, although clearly such problems are complex in nature with wide social and personal implications and should be discussed by a multidisciplinary team. In the shaping of the law value judgments of various sections of the community should be considered and not only those of a few groups. Sociologists have attacked the mass media for fanning indignation over drug use by youngsters; this may lead to a demand on police to adopt sterner measures, with "amplification of deviance" as a result of greater police activities. Such increased "deviant behavior" is then regarded as confirming, and in turn reinforces, the initial bias against drug users (Bean, Young). It is claimed that mass media by creating unfair "stereotypes" may so affect public opinion that in time law changes may be the consequence. In turn, the law may influence and shape the "deviant" drug user's behavior (Bean). As in other countries, the criminalization of a great many youngsters is a main argument used by those who clamor for marked changes in the cannabis laws. On the other hand, a survey carried out in 1973 (Drugs and Society) found that no more than 15 percent were in favor of free availability of cannabis.

At any rate, clearly there are widely divergent views held by different sections of British society on the subject of drug use and misuse. Doctors as a group have often been accused of a general tendency to overprescribe (quite apart form the few "junkie doctors" in the sixties). Dunlop has given three reasons for doctors' overprescribing: the doctor cannot keep pace with the incessant flow of new drugs; he is exposed to the advertising campaign of pharmaceutical manufacturers; and as many as 50 percent of patients are disappointed if they have to leave the doctor's office without a drug prescription. As we have seen, already nearly two centuries ago Dr. Thomas Trotter complained of the influence exerted on doctor's prescribing habits by his patients' expectations. In a recent survey of the drug use of a large representative sample of the general population in England, Wales, and Scotland as many as 91 percent reported that they had experienced at least one "symptom" during the preceding fortnight, and during this period 80 percent had taken some form of medication (Dunnell and Cartwright). These drugs came to a certain extent from doctors' prescriptions but self-medication with drugs obtained from pharmacists was twice as common as prescribed drugs. Forty of those interviewed had taken aspirin or other analgesics. Ten had taken sedatives, hypnotics, or tranquillizers. These figures may seem surprisingly high, but so were the results of a survey commissioned by the BBC and published in August 1973 (Drugs and Society, Sept. 1973). Approximately four million people in Britain had used cannabis, over 650,000 had used LSD at least on one occasion, 1,286,000 had used amphetamines, and over 580,000 had used barbiturates without a doctor's prescription.

It would thus seem that today's society, in spite of all attempts at education and appeals for moderation, is becoming more and more a drinking and pill-taking society (and moreover shows little inclination despite all warnings to give up the long ingrained habit of also being a tobacco-smoking one).

SUMMARY

Use of opiates, and later of other drugs, has occurred in the U.K. with some frequency at least since the eighteenth century. However, throughout the years, in the past as now, it seems impossible to speak of a fairly uniform response of the community to drug use and misuse. What was regarded, for example, as normal prescribing by certain doctors at the turn of the nineteenth century was criticized by others – a divergence of view that was much more pronounced in the 1960s. Correspondingly, a form of drug taking that is regarded as grossly "deviant" behavior by possibly the great majority of the population, may be considered quite "normal" among other sections and certain subcultures. While by and large throughout the years the medical profession and the general population were fairly tolerant of drug-taking habits of individuals not corresponding to majority views, there was often evidence of an ambivalent attitude; for example, the use of opiates at the turn of the twentieth century by Oriental people was often considered to be not harmful, whereas the same form of drug taking in this country was regarded by the same doctors as harmful and was greatly frowned upon. Nevertheless, there is no evidence that (alcohol apart) drugs were ever seen in this country as constituting a "problem" before the onset of the heroin-cocaine epidemic among the young in the 1960s. Three minor pieces of legislation apart (in the nineteenth and early in the twentieth century, and again during the First World War), the Dangerous Drug Acts did not come into being until the 1920s. Such legislation never aimed at prohibition but was restrictive in nature and, up to the present time, has always acknowledged the right of at least certain licensed doctors to prescribe narcotics to certain addicts.

In the past it was for the most part doctors whose views determined subsequent drug legislation. Whether the present drug laws reflect the views of the essentially silent majority any more than the pronouncements of professionals such as psychiatrists and sociologists (who often seem to contradict each other), does not seem certain. There has never been a "British System" of narcotic control but a number of practices gradually developed out of the Rolleston Committee recommendations in 1926. They worked fairly well for over three decades but failed when subjected to the test by a spread of drug use in the 1960s. The responses of doctors and other sections of the population to the changing situation at the time reflected widely different views, but, as in the past, the law, professional opinion, and probably the great majority of popular opinion have continued to regard the habitual drug user and addict as a person in need of understanding and help, and not as a criminal deserving punishment.

REFERENCES

Advisory Committee on Drug Dependence (Wootton Committee) (1958). Cannabis, H.M.S.O., London.
Agnew, D. (1956) in R. Thorp: Viper. p. 188. Robert Hale, London.
Albutt, C. and Dixon, W.E. (1909). Quoted by Lewis, Sir A.
Bean, P. (1974) The Social Control of Drugs. Martin Robertson, London.
Bejerot, N. (1970) Addiction and Society. Charles C. Thomas, Illinois.
Bewley, T. (1966) Bull. Narcot. (U.N.) 18, (4), 1. Bulletin of Narcotics (U.N.)
Brit. Med. J. (1926) Edirot. 1, 998.
Brooke, E.M. and Glatt, M.M. (1964) Medicine, Science and the Law, 4, 277.
Campbell, H. (1925) Brit. J. Inebr. 20, 47. British Journal of Inebriation.
Camps, F.E. (1968) in: Adolescent Drug Dependence (ed. C.W.M. Wilson) Pergamon, London. p. xv.
Cohen, S. (1971) Images of Deviance, Penguin, London.
Collins, Sir W.J. (1916) Brit. J. Inebr., 13, 132.
Connell, P.H. (1958) Amphetamine Psychosis, Maudsley Monograph No. 5, Oxford Univ. Press, London.
De Alarcon, R. (1971) Milroy Lectures. Royal College of Physicians, London.
Dent, J.Y. (1955) Brit. J. Addict. 52, 1 (Editor.) British Journal of Addiction.
_____ (1957) ibid. 53, 71 (Editor.)
De Quincey, T. (1821) Confessions of an Opium Eater, Walter Scott, London.
Dixon, W.E. (1925) Brit. J. Inebr., 22, 103.
Drinkwater, J. (1957) The Outline of Literature. George Newnes, London.
Drugs and Society (1973) Sept. 2 (No. 12), 3.
_____ (1973) Dec. 3 (No. 3), 5.
Dunlop, Sir D. (1970) Proc. Royal Soc. Med. 63, 1279.
Dunnell, K. and Cartwright, A. (1972). Quoted by G. Stimson. Drugs and Society Dec. 1972, 2, 25.
Glatt, M.M. (1954) Lancet, ii, 143.
_____ (1958) Brit. J. Addict. 55, 51.
_____ (1959) Lancet i, 887.
_____ (1962) Bull. Narcot. (U.N.) 14 (2), 19.
_____ (1964) Brit. Med. J. 1, 1116.
_____ (1967) Lancet ii, 1203.
_____ (1969a) Pharmaceut. J., Oct. 4, p. 393. Pharmaceutical Journal.
_____ (1969b) Lancet ii. 429.
_____ (1972) The Alcoholic and the Help He Needs. Second Ed. Priory Press, London.
_____ (1974) A Guide to Addiction and its Treatment (Drugs, Society and Man). Med. & Techn. Publ., Lancaster.

Glatt, M.M. Pittman, D.J., Gillespie, D.G., Hills, D.R. (1969) The Drug Scene in Great Britain. Revised Reprint. E. Arnold, London.

Gombrich, E.H. (1952) The Story of Art, 5th Ed. Phaidon Press, London.

Goulding, R. (1968) in: Adolescent Drug Dependence (ed. C.M.W. Wilson) P. 507. Pergamon, London, New York.

Hillier, S. (1909) Popular Drugs, T. Werner Laurie, London.

Hughes, R. (1972) B.B.C., Time, Life Books, P. 561.

Huxley, A. (1959) The Doors of Perception, and Heaven and Hell. Penguin Books, London.

Interdepartmental (Brain) Committee on Drug Addiction (1961). First Report. H.M.S.O., London.

_____ (1965) Second Report. H.M.S.O., London.

Jeffrey, C.G. (1970). In: Modern Trends in Drug Dependence and Alcoholism, ed. R.V. Phillipson. Butterworth, London.

Keller, M. Quoted from Glatt, M.M. (1974)

Kerr, N. Quoted from Sir W. Collins.

Lancet (1954) Editorial ii, 75.

Lewin, L. (1964) Phantastica. Rutledge & Kegan Paul, London.

Lewis, Sir A. (1968) Brit. J. Addict. 63, 241.

Lewis, R. (1972) Drugs and Society (Jan.) 1, 11.

Lord Brain (1961) Brit. J. Addict. 57, 81.

Luff, A.P. (1934) Lancet 1, 423.

Morris, A. (1972) Drugs and Society (March) 1 (No. 6), p. 6.

Norton, A. (1973) Collins, Fontana, London.

Paton, W.D.M. (1968) in: Adolescent Drug Dependence. ed. C.W.M. Wilson p. 244.

Pharmaceutical Society (1973). Quoted from Drugs and Society (Oct.) 3 (1), p. 4.

Rolleston, Sir Humphrey (1934) Brit. J. Inebr. 31, 138.

Scharlieb, M. (1925) ibid. 22, 115.

Schur, E.M. (1963) Narcotic Addiction in Britain and America. Tavistock, London.

Spear, H.B. (1969) Brit. J. Addict. 64, 245.

Trotter, T. (1807) A View of the Nervous Temperament. Longman, Hurst, Rees & Orme, London.

Wade, O.L. (1968) Adolescent Drug Dependence, ed. C.M.W. Wilson. Pergamon, London, New York, P. 244.

Wiener, R.S.P. (1970) Drugs and Schoolchildren. Longman, London.

Willcox, Sir W.H. (1923) Brit. J. Inebr. 20, 162.

_____ (1925) ibid. 22, 112.

_____ (1934) ibid. 31, 131.

World Health Organization Expert Comm. on Mental Health (1967) Fourteenth Report. Wld. Hlth. Org. Techn. Rep. Ser: 363.

World Health Organization (study Group (1973) Youth and Drugs ibid. 516, 8.

Young, J. (1971) The Drugtakers, MacGibbon & Kee, London.

7 Israel

M. Amir

INTRODUCTION

Recently, Israeli society underwent national scandals over the issue of nonmedical drug use. The newspapers repeated the discovery of hashish use in high schools and the formation of Israeli drug-smuggling rings. It culminated in the "Attorney General's Report on Drug Abuse." (Barak Report, 1976).

Such scandals have been recurrent since 1967. It is accepted that until 1967, drug abuse, almost exclusively hashish smoking, was concentrated either among Arabs where it is accepted and indigenous, marginal groups in the Jewish sector of the population – mainly adult offenders, pimps, and prostitutes (Friedman and Peer, 1968), and juveniles from families who came from Moslem culture countries (Bein, et al., 1974; Berman, 1970; Drapkin and Landau, 1966; Geva, 1971). There were a few hundred addicts, mainly among survivors of the Holocaust and army veterans who were "hooked" on morphine after medical treatment. The problems of nonmedical drug use became dramatically serious in the public mind after the Six-Day War in June 1967. The change since 1967 has mainly been on four levels: that of the spread and scope, the demographic and social characteristics of drug abusers, the type of drugs used, and developments of the concomitants of a drug abuse culture.

The seriousness of Israel's drug problem is related to the following trends:

a. The conception of a transition from endemic to an epidemic phenomenon. This is because of changes in the scope of the problem, i.e., the alarming increase in confiscation of drugs; of arrests of drug offenders (police statistics did not differentiate until 1972 between using, abusing, selling, and "pushing" of drugs, and does not differentiate between "experimenters" and chronic users). More alarming to the public was the Ministry of Health report that those addicted to "hard" drugs number about 2,000 with a yearly increase of 150 to 200 new cases (Barak, 1976).

b. Changes in the social characteristics of drug abusers. The use of drugs (again mainly hashish) is said to be spreading to the middle class, including high school and university students as well as the army (Barak Report 1976; Berman, 1969).

c. Changes in the types of drug used – encompassing hashish, various kinds of amphetamines, LSD, raw opium, and even heroin (Barak Report, 1976).

d. The appearance of offenses connected with addiction, e.g., burglaries, robberies, theft from the army (including weapons), etc. (Barak, 1976 and various newspaper reports).

e. The development of a specialized underworld and organized crime connected with drugs. In the last few years it was reported in newspapers and by informers that an organized network of drug smugglers, who use violence and corruption, had been formed. These new networks cooperating with Arabs led to the argument that the enemy is using drugs as a weapon to undermine the morale and health of Israel. Gang fights and gang killings over the monopolization of the distribution over certain areas were recorded.

f. Drugs became a security problem with the discovery that: hashish is prevalent in the army (regular and reserve), drug smugglers cross military zones and fortified borders with the neighboring enemy countries, and church personnel and United Nations officers abused their immunity from search to smuggle drugs in and out of Israel (Newspaper Reports).

g. Drug smuggling, as it appears, put Israel on the map of international smuggling networks with all the associated characteristics of violence, huge amounts of money, corruption, and the watching eyes of Interpol and U.S. narcotic agents (who came to Israel in order to train the Israelis in drug control).

h. Changes in the public and government perception of the drug abuse problem such as: that it "got out of hand," that it became a security problem, or that it is a serious crime problem. It is no longer considered just an educational problem to be relieved or ameliorated by "talks" in class. It became a social, medical, and normative national issue. Because of Israel's special security situation, drugs also became a security problem. Thus, the government and the public, through the media, became aware that the existing policy (or lack of policy) toward drugs and their misuse could not cope with these new trends, and that a new policy of prevention, maintenance rehabilitation, education, and law-enforcement was needed.

Geopolitical Note

Israel is in the middle of the hashish route, and in the midst of countries where hashish is indigenous to their societies. Historically, the drug grown in Lebanon and Syria traveled from these countries through Israel either via the sea from Lebanon to Egypt, or (mainly) by land to Egypt and from there to Sudan and other African countries (Even-Zohar, 1973). Caravans of camels brought the drug to the Negev, the desert bordering between Israel, Egypt, and Jordan, and from there to Sinai – the Egyptian desert. With the establishment of the State of Israel, and the continuous state of war between Israel and her neighbors, new smuggling routes were developed; from Lebanon, hashish went to Egypt via the sea and some via Jordan to Egypt crossing in some points the Israeli southern desert. It meant security problems for Israel who understood that this same smuggling route is, and was, used for the traffic of spies, marauders, and weapons. Thus, the availability and the price of hashish and opium in Egypt and in Israel (before 1967, but especially after that) was dependent upon the operations of the Israeli security forces.

Change, also in geographical terms, came after the Six-Day War in 1967. The Sinai peninsula was brought under Israeli administration. It interrupted the traffic route and large quantities of drugs have remained within the Israeli borders. In the first months after the war it led to the availability of drugs (almost only hashish) for the growing market within Israel (Police Internal Report).

HISTORY

Until 1967, nonprescription drug abuse was not considered a social problem. Neither was alcoholism. "Alcoholics" were only known to welfare authorities who supported the alcoholics' families, and to some mental hospitals, which nationally had no more than 20 beds to accommodate alcoholics referred for treatment.(1)

Until 1967, nonprescription drug abuse was mainly conceived of as being a law enforcement problem, involving the police, the judicial system, and the authorities who dealt with delinquents and adult offenders who used, distributed, or smuggled drugs – mostly hashish (Bein, et al., 1974; Berman, 1967, 1969). It should be remembered that close to 50 percent of the new immigrants to Israel came from Middle East Moslem culture countries, where the use of drugs was both accepted and widespread. But in the Diaspora, very few Jews used hashish. Many developed resistance toward the diffusion of the use of drugs from the Arab-Moslem cultures into the Jewish ghettos. The resistance stems from the traditional effort to maintain their separate identity and a defense against loss of control. Those who used hashish were considered deviant – especially the women (Palgi, 1976).

The newcomers formed the demographic basis of a drug culture. They were composed of large families, and were ill-equipped educationally, socially, and economically for the modern technologically developing Israeli society (Jermulowitz and Turnau, 1962; Miller, 1971). Also, for some groups, mainly Moroccan Jews, their patterns of immigration at times resulted in their exposure to and use of hashish. Many young came without their families. They were sent by their poor, often deteriorated families alone to Israel. They were without the traditional community protection. They associated with the Arab culture and part of their alienation and delinquency made them the main and known consumers of hashish. Thus, hashish became, in the dominant culture, associated with marginality, criminality, and prostitution. For the drug users, it meant a "medicine" against depression arising out of failure and loss of self-esteem (Palgi, 1975).

A medical definition of the problem of drug abuse pertained for the few hundreds of "addicts" who mainly used morphine and amphetamines. There were few beds in mental hospitals to accommodate those who were willing to be treated. Until 1966, there was a kind of maintenance program, whereby those addicted could get their daily ration from the public health clinics of the Ministry of Health (Barak Report, Chesler Gampel, 1971). However, this group, too, was defined or condemned by the public as deviant and marginal, actually belonging to the criminal sector of our society.

Until 1967, the number of drug abusers can only be conjectured. Estimates run as high as some thousands. There were a few arrests, mostly among marginal, often criminal groups, who also used drugs. Drug-related arrests never exceeded 0.7 percent of all criminal offenses and 70 percent of the offenders were either born in Arab countries or were Israeli Arabs (Drapkin and Landau, 1966).

Nonprescription drug abuse, considered as endemic to certain groups, was viewed as neither an educational nor a security problem. This was a social problem which needed special attention besides that given by the law enforcement agencies and the medical authorities. The assumption was that Israeli society, especially the youth and the middle-class sectors, were immune from the attraction of drugs which represented a deviation from the assumed mainstream of the Israeli value system and style of life, collectivism, service, and middle-class ethics (Chigier, 1972; Cohen, 1970; Davidson, 1970; Peled, 1972; Shoham, et al., 1974).

There is growing evidence that drug misuse related violations became a combined health, security, and educational problem since the end of the 1967 Six-Day War (Bein, et al., 1974; Berman, 1970; Landau, 1970). There are several reasons given for this. The connection that was formed, and the resulting exposure, of the Israeli society to the Arab culture where hashish smoking is indigenous. With the unification of Jerusalem and the occupation of the West Bank and the Gaza Strip, it became relatively easy to transfer hashish (as well as other drugs) to the Israeli sector.

The continuous attempt by smugglers to resupply the market, and their cooperation with terrorists from the neighboring countries who were ready to risk their lives, led to the argument that the terrorists purposely aimed to spread drugs among Israelis (Karti, 1970). Drugs became, then, a political-security problem.

The ability of Arabs to freely travel in and out of the Jewish sectors resulted in hashish becoming more available and cheap to those who wanted to use it. Paralleling this was an increased demand for the drug by two new groups in the Israeli society:

a. The thousands (about ten thousand) of American and European young tourists, students and volunteers who came to help the country immediately after the June 1967 war. They brought with them the ideology and practice of drug abuse; mainly of marijuana and amphetamines.   Hashish, a relatively potent derivative of cannabis was discovered most coveted and welcomed by this group.

The importance of this group must also be understood in terms of their effect on Israeli youth. Until 1967, hashish was rare in the Jewish segment of the population. Hashish meant deviation. The outsiders introduced the idea that hashish meant association with the modern Western world. They also introduced the drug by the most favorable learning technique, i.e., interpersonal contact contiguous with the development of a youth culture. The learning of smoking techniques, the knowledge of various drug effects, and acquiring a favorable attitude toward recreational drugs were made more easy for the middle-class youth culture. The contact between Arab and lower-class Jewish youths developed the drug culture among marginal youth before 1967, and with some middle-class youth (mainly from Jerusalem) after 1967.   But generally speaking, the lack of contact between Jews and Arabs prevented development of a drug culture until the arrival of volunteers, tourists, and students from the West.

b. The Israeli youth, first students and the Bohemia, and then high school students and other middle-class youth were exposed to and gradually accepted the ideology and symbolism of hashish smoking. It generally symbolized participating in Western and especially the youth culture; it furnished a sense of independence, maturity, protest, or rebellion against the establishment. The open debates about drug abuse and its meanings which were waged at the universities, high schools, in the mass media, and public forums (including the Parliament) may have added incentive to many to experiment with hashish (Lehman, 1973; Jermelowitz, 1970).

Thus there developed a youth subculture emphasizing hedonism and concepts of self-enrichment among Israeli middle-class youth.   They pursued their experience with drugs as part of curiosity, adventure, risk taking, and the obedience to primary group pressures (Peled, 1972). The involvement with drugs, or being against it, was found to be related to value judgments in other spheres of life (Shoham, 1974).

The fact that the drug was available and relatively inexpensive made it easy, for many, to experiment with it. However, until 1970, morphine, heroin, and other "hard" drugs were almost unknown.

We see, then, a combination and interrelationship among some factors which may explain the spread of drugs in Israel after 1967: the availability of good quality drugs, and the demand and expanding market (the volunteers, tourists, and students from the West, and the ensuing development of a hedonistic youth culture among middle-class and college youths). Indeed, the first new centers of drug abuse were in the universities or other centers where the "outsiders" were concentrated. Thus, drug abuse, as a moral problem (i.e., an expression of values opposed to those officially proclaimed), joined to political, security, and health facets of this problem. These processes led to the acceleration of other developments in research, government policies, and public reaction.

Before 1967, no studies on drug abuse or on violation of drug-related law were conducted. Only the "Police Annual Reports" contained some statistics about the violation of drug laws. When the scare of the "epidemic" of drug abuse started, because of the infiltration of drugs to the middle-class sectors, special studies of the prevalence of hashish use, mainly among high school students were made (Peled, 1972; Shoham, 1974). Various authoritative persons gave their often conflicting estimation as to the scope of the problem. Police arrest statistics showed an increase but still stayed in the range of hundreds (see Table 7.1), while other estimates ranged between 5 and 120,000 hashish users (Shamgar, 1973), without differentiating between "experimenters" and chronic users. These estimations caused alarm among the authorities, mainly educators and the police. Educational programs (for high schools and universities) were hastily developed, mainly using scare techniques and appeals for patriotism. The police increased surveillance of dealers and users. Volunteers, tourists, and foreign students were harassed, and when found in possession or use of hashish, they were most often deported. Arrests of middle-class students and even some V.I.P.'s from the Bohemia were more often made. The police, the special border police, and the army stepped up their control over the smuggling of drugs from the neighboring countries and over the nomads within the country.

Gradually, partly because of lack of hashish, new kinds of drugs appeared on the scene: LSD, amphetamines, raw opium, and lately heroin. Networks of pushers and smugglers were discovered, and marked increases were noted in the confiscation of drugs, with increased quantities of "hard" drugs confiscated each year since 1970. Moreover, the number of junveniles arrested and charged with drug offenses rose gradually (see Table 7.1). The same is true of tourists who came to Israel to consume and buy drugs more freely and cheaply (e.g., hashish) in hippie centers, and in some places in the main cities, especially the Arab sector of Jerusalem. An increased number of arrests were also made of tourists who attempted to smuggle drugs out of the country, for their own use as well as for selling ventures.

As a result of all these developments, drug offenses received a new definition as part of the value and social crisis that afflicted the Israeli society, especially after the October war of 1973. A new drug "scare," the second after the 1968-69 scare, arose after the presentation of these developments to the public and to the Parliament in early 1976. The scare had two aspects: once centered around the discovery that high school students were using hashish, the other around the fact that there were hundreds addicted to "hard" drugs who were left with no source for their ration but one private physician who sold them drugs. After the Ministry of Health cancelled his license, there was an increase of theft and burglaries from pharmacies and dispensaries. The public became aware that there was no maintenance program, and that other programs for the control and treatment of drug addicts were not sufficient.

A special cabinet session was devoted to the drug problem, where the attorney general who is the head of the Inter-Ministerial Committee on drugs surveyed the drug problem. Recommendations to step up information campaigns, police activities, maintenance and community

Table 7.1. Files Opened, Persons Charged, Drugs Confiscated

	1966	1967	1968	1969	1970	1971	1972	1973	1974	1975
Use of illegal drugs							827	915	1,129	
Distributional selling							2		158	
Production and selling							8	5	19	
Total: illegal[1] drug abuse files	399	599	811	1,029	1,744	1,315	920	868	1,228	1,691
Total: no. of persons[2] arrested	511	879	1,187	1,535	23,553	1,869	1,275	1,385	1,928	28,112
No. of persons arrested: noncitizens, tourists[3], volunteers, etc.		69	123	345	1,178	372	223	126	167	
No. of youths arrested (up to age 10)	53	109	120	361	657	499	120	217	8,115	
Hashish confiscated[4]			3,894	3,179	4,304	614	213	96	671	271
Opium confiscated			813	813	56	176	29	45		

[1] Only from 1972 police statistics differentiate among cases of use, distribution, import and export.
[2] Only from 1972 police statistics differentiate among arrests for use, distribution, import, and export.
[3] Only from 1968 police statistics include tourists among those arrested for drug abuse.
[4] Quantities of drugs confiscated include those found by the army patroling the sea or land

programs were made and put on the planning phase. Five weeks later a new drug-related concern was noted. There were police reports to the newspapers about the discovery that large quantities of heroin were found smuggled by a well-organized smuggling ring. Drugs became again more a police problem than a social or a health problem. Currently, Israel is prepared for more comprehensive and serious programs designed to deal with drug problems in all their aspects.

THE SCOPE AND SOCIAL CHARACTERISTICS OF THE PROBLEM

The debate continues among Israeli officials about the scope of the drug abuse problem. All agree that: (a) the main problem is that of hashish smoking, (b) the number of those involved in nonmedical drug use is unknown, (c) official statistics are inaccurate and unreliable and, therefore, only estimations can be made, and (d) the official statistics do not reflect the real extent of the problem. The authorities admit that the extent of the problem is greater than the statistics show, and that these unreliable statistics cannot be used as indicators of trends nor as a basis for policies.

The different estimates given by various sources are to be used with caution. Overlapping does exist in these sources. Similarly, wide discrepancies exist between private and government assessments of the prevalence of drug abuse in Israel. Since police statistics until 1972 did not differentiate between types of drug-related arrests, these statistics represent just those files opened on offenders arrested for violation of the dangerous drug act.

As with other types of offenses, police statistics reflect the extent and intensity of police work in the area of drug abuse in general and in special areas of these offenses, e.g., against users in certain sectors or dealers.

Table 7.1 represents the number of charges and arrests statistics taken from the "Police Annual Reports," 1966-1975.

One can see clearly that from 1966 to 1969 there was a sharp increase in the number of police files opened for investigation. From 1970 we see fluctuation with a decrease in 1972 and 1973. We could explain it by the decline in the experimentation with hashish and this drug's use being stabilized on certain groups while each year new people tended to experiment. It may also reflect the less ardent police activities emphasizing the control of dealers and smugglers rather than users.

The number of persons arrested also fluctuated with marked increases from 1966 to 1970 and a slight decrease from 1971 to 1974. However, there is no way except by a special study to know the characteristics of violators of drug laws, the kind of violation, and the type of drugs involved. The argument that official statistics mainly reflect the extent and kind of efforts of the police is evidenced by the observation that while the case files for use of illegal drugs increased, those for illegal distribution and selling only increased from 2 in 1972 to 158 in 1974, with no case in 1973. This was an unbelievable situation given the fact that Israeli newspapers and numerous community and street workers knew the identity of drug dealers and pushers.

From 1967 we see, with fluctuation, a not so gradual increase of those arrested for offenses connected with drugs. But, again, the number of those arrested does not reflect the number who were involved in drug offenses; especially those consuming drugs. Of those arrested, we observe an increase since 1966 of noncitizens. The peak year is 1970 and since then a decrease is observed. It reflects the attention given by authorities to this group. The number of volunteers, foreign students, and tourists declined since 1970 and especially since 1973. Also, since 1972 police emphasized in their activities the apprehension of dealers and pushers.

The number of youths, aged 9-20, arrested for drug abuse (almost only for use of hashish), has been increasing since 1966, reaching almost a 40 percent proportion in 1976. The amount of hashish confiscated fluctuates and actually reflects police efforts with informers or other activities (the statistics do not include the tons of hashish caught on the boats and Bedouin caravans on their route to Egypt or other countries). The same can be said about opium. The other types of drugs (barbiturates, amphetamines, LSD) are not recorded, but to our knowledge they increased during the surveyed years. During 1975, heroin appeared in Israel. It was smuggled from Amsterdam by an Israeli smuggling ring operating in Europe.

Another drug use information source, although not empirically based is the prison service which reports that about 20 percent of the prison population (i.e., 500 or 2,500) are consuming illegal drugs, mainly hashish, smuggled into the prison. Government street workers (also not an empirically based source) report that of 2,700 juveniles under their supervision, about 500 use different kinds of drugs in various frequency.(2) Of the 1,400 delinquent girls about 10 percent are drug abusers. The Ministry of Welfare reported to the attorney general that of the 750 who were placed in delinquent institutions in 1975, about 50 percent had consumed illegal drugs and about 10 percent used opiates and amphetamines. The Adult Probation Service in the Ministry of Welfare reported that 120 were sentenced to probation for drug offenses. According to the estimation of the service about 40 percent of the 3,500 who have been sentenced by the court to probation have used illegal drugs at least once.

All of these resources may report an overlapping of drug misusers. But this population has some characteristics in common: they are mainly (about 75-80 percent) from lower classes and from Asian-African backgrounds; i.e., either they or their parents came from Moslem culture countries.

The Ministry of Health reports that while there were about 300 "hard" drug addicts in 1966 (Jermulowitz and Turnau), the number had increased to about 2,000 cases in 1974. The estimate is that the number increases every year by about 200 cases. Ironically, or sadly, the number of those hospitalized in 1971 reached 96 cases only (Chesler-Gamble, 1971).

Special studies designed to explore drug offenses and offenders found the same characteristics: lower class and oriental (Asian/African) background, poor adjustment to school, employment, and the army. They are marginal to Israeli society and have a history of wayward behavior, delinquency, and criminality (Drapkin and Landau, 1966; Landau, 1970; Berman, 1967, 1971; Miller, 1971).

The studies on the middle-class youth (Peled, 1972; Shoham, 1974) show that the favorable attitudes toward, and experimentation with drugs (mainly hashish) accompanied the acceptance of hedonistic values and personal contact with peers who have experimented with drugs; only health-related fears and lack of opportunities to experiment with hashish prevented them from experimenting with the drug.

It should be remembered that the studies on middle-class youth were self-reported studies and there is no way to estimate from them the numer of those who experimented with, or chronically misused, drugs. The lack of adequate, empirically based data has resulted in a continuous debate among the country's officials about the scope of the problem. All agree that Israel's main current drug problem concerns the smoking of hashish. The estimations in 1968 and 1969 varied between 5 and 9 thousand, and from 15 to more than 100,000 in 1975. These estimations do not differentiate between drug user types (i.e., experimenters, chronic users) and are based on "inside knowledge" of those who make these assessments (Barak Report, 1976).

The median age of hashish users is about 18, and for users of other drugs, particularly opiates, 23. Since 1966 the median age of arrested drug offenders was lowered from 32 percent, age 20 and under, to 23 percent. Although most of Israel's drug users are from Moslem culture countries (or their families emigrated from these places) (Berman, 1967, 1969; Landau, 1970), the number born to parents from Europe and the West has been increasing gradually. The major chronic or regular users of hashish or "hard" drugs, have a history of sociomaladjustment and delinquency. A proportion of hashish smokers (with the real number of proportion being unknown), are middle-class youth in high school or universities. The sex ratio of hashish smokers is 1:12, male to female. Girls who smoke hashish, and also use other drugs (mainly amphetamines), are mostly delinquents – and more specifically prostitutes.

A final note should be made about medical drug abuse by clients of outpatient clinics. Off and on newspapers report that the free prescription drugs given to members of Israel's medical insurance organizations cause hoarding and consumption of large quantities of all kinds of pain killers, cough medicine, and other drugs. Recently, a new policy was introduced, whereby the patient must pay a small sum for every medicine prescribed.

After reviewing the historical development of the nonmedical drug problem in Israel, together with the social perspective, we turn now to three other interconnected aspects of the problem: the legal-judicial, the treatment-rehabilitation, and the preventive aspects.

LEGAL CONTROL

Israel is involved in various efforts concerned with control of production and traffic of drugs, which are grounded on international agreements. On the regional level the contemporary drug situation in Israel must be understood within the context of the Israeli-Arab conflict, resulting in a situation of noncooperation. Although Israel is a key state in the middle of a known drug traffic region, she is excluded from regional cooperation with the neighboring Arab states where drugs and their distribution are indigenous phenomenon (Even-Zohor, 1973).

One must remember that throughout history the legal basis for drug control, or degrees of permissiveness about specific types of drug use, have been and continue to be based on value judgments. In Israel, where drug abuse has been defined more as a political and security problem, and less as a health problem, the control is naturally relegated mainly to law enforcement and judicial agencies. They concentrate on prevention of smuggling, the arrest of dealers, merchants, and lastly of users. The law of Israel underlying the activities of police, the prosecutors, and the courts is defined under the Dangerous Drug Ordinance of the Mandatory period, 1936, and the amendments (New Formulations, 1973; 1974). This ordinance is based on the various international treaties about dangerous drugs.

The following prohibitions exist, according to the Dangerous Drug Ordinance: (a) exporting, importing, local commercial distribution; (b) moving dangerous drugs from any vehicles that arrive in Israel; (c) changing its pharmaceutical function; and (d) the holding and keeping of dangerous drugs and instruments for its use. All these are prohibited without the permission and the licensing of the director-general of the Ministry of Health (thus, medical doctors, pharmacists, or special drug importers or distributors are allowed, upon being licensed, to do some of the things prohibited to other persons).

As far as punishment provided by the law, the violation of the Dangerous Drug Ordinance is a crime, to be prosecuted in district court: (a) maximum conviction for sale can be 10 years of imprisonment or a fine of 50,000 IL., or both; (b) charges of possession and use of dangerous drugs can be made in law courts, and then the maximum penalty can be 3 years of imprisonment or a fine of 10,000 IL., or both. These ordinances apply also to the army where violators are additionally court-martialed; (c) conviction for enabling a minor to possess drugs and/or enticing him to use drugs unlawfully (e.g., a physician), incurs a mandatory imprisonment of 10 years. It should be mentioned that the prosecution tends to charge drug offenders in district courts, except in rare cases when the offense is minor or a first one. Also, a noncitizen involved in drug offenses can be penalized by imprisonment or fine, or both, by deportation, as well as prohibition from entering Israel. If an Israeli citizen is convicted for drug offenses outside of Israel, this conviction will be registered as part of his Israeli criminal record.

Within the ordinances that permit the practice of medicine or the licensing as a pharmacist, there are regulations about the possession and use of drugs. A physician can and is permitted to prescribe drugs only if he is specially licensed and if the drug is needed for treatment. However, the unlicensed physician is not allowed to maintain addicts. The director-general of the Ministry of Health can revoke the license of the physician who does so.

Given that each drug influences its user differently, a legal control mechanism relating to one type of drug may not necessarily apply to another type. Within this context it is meaningful to dwell upon drug-related offenses, other than drug possession and use. The following distinctions can be made: (a) In the most frequent situation, an offense, most often against property, is committed in order to acquire the means to purchase drugs. In this situation, the offender, it is assumed, usually operates clearheadedly and rationally, although his motive and immediate urge is to acquire drugs. (b) In the second situation, an offense is committed while the offender is under the influence of the drug he has consumed.

In the first instance, there is no legal order that allows release from or diminishing of criminal responsibility. However, there is a legal directive that allows the court, upon conviction, to order the offender to be sent to prison or to an institution for treatment – which actually is only drug detoxification. In the second situation, the very fact of addiction, or drug-affected behavior, even if it caused an offense, is not recognized as a mental aberration or illness. In this situation, if being an addict is accepted as a defense, the court can order hospitalization for detoxification for a period specified by the court, or that he be sent to a prison for up to three years. If sent to a hospital for detoxification, he will continue to serve his sentence in a prison after the treatment to the end of that sentence. In Israel criminals who are addicted or who are drug users are not provided with special treatment.

Three conditions are to be distinguished as the legal basis for committing an addict to an institution for detoxification vs. "treatment:"

a. Whoever voluntarily commits himself for such treatment is considered by the law as a mentally ill person who voluntarily enters a hospital, and is permitted, whenever he wants, to terminate the "treatment."

b. According to Probation Ordinance (1969) the court can compel an addict to submit himself both to probation supervision and to treatment, and if necessary to stay in the institution where he receives treatment. In this case, the institution is not considered a "closed" one, although for others the same place can be considered a "closed institution." Such a patient, under a probation order, cannot be held involuntarily, although leaving the place or terminating the treatment is considered a violation of probation order. The probation officer must be notified by the institution upon such a situation, and in turn must notify the court.

c. A person imprisoned for six months or more for a drug-related offense and who, it is felt may continue to commit more offenses, can be placed by the court in a closed institution for "treatment." This court order remains in effect even if the physician thinks that the prisoner patient has no chance of recovery.

Any institutionalization order can only be given for three years (or less). If the sentence of imprisonment is for a longer period, then the institutionalization order can be concurrent with the imprisonment sentence or part of it. Also, it should be mentioned that release from a closed institution does not mean a release from imprisonment which the person has to serve from a former period. It seems that the law operates only in the framework of a judicial-penal procedure.(3) Therefore no hospitalization order can be given involuntarily, and outside the process of legal charges for an offense committed.

The Police

The police and the border patrol expend much effort in detecting drug smugglers, dealers, and users, and bringing them to trial. Being very legalistic and due to the nature of the drug crime phenomena, the police are facing difficulties in detection and providing evidence for the court. They recently developed a special unit to deal with drugs, drawing on the help provided by special agents from the U.S. Customs Service, who train Israeli police in various aspects of drug control police work. Police spend much time, together with national intelligence agencies, mainly intervening in the area of drug smuggling. The police keep close contact with Interpol and police forces in other countries. Public pressures, such as when drug use was discovered in the high schools, cause the police to start special periodic campaigns against consumers and dealers, besides the continuous operations of the police in this area. It should be mentioned that there is differential treatment of Arabs and Jews by the police. Arabs tend to be arrested less than Jews for using drugs (Cohen, 1968).

Prosecution

The general policy of the prosecution is to bring a juvenile before the junvenile court only after a probation officer's social report is brought before the district prosecutor. Adults who are charged with taking drugs are usually prosecuted in the lower (criminal) court. Others, for more serious charges, are prosecuted in the district court. For drug dealers and distributors the policy of the prosecutor is to ask for the maximum penalty. The tendency is to ask the court for a more lenient sentence (mainly probation or fine) for those charged for the first time with taking drugs.

Until 1975, the Israel Defense Forces' policy was to bring soldiers before disciplinary court for violating army regulations. Yet until 1970, the I.D.F. officially denied the existence of drug use. Now, the general policy is that soldiers caught possessing or using drugs are brought before a military district court.

The Court

The courts, under the penal policy, distinguish between consumption and possession of drugs. Special attention is given to those who possess more drugs than would be needed for their own use. Drug dealers and merchants usually receive a sentence of imprisonment, the length of which depends on the seriousness of the offense. Generally the court does not take into consideration personal factors as extenuating or mitigating circumstances.

Such is not the case for consumers; personal factors and the fact of addiction are considered by the court. Minors who consume drugs usually are not sentenced to imprisonment but receive probation orders. In the army, those who consume drugs for the first time, or in small quantities, may and usually are imprisoned up to two months.

Tourists and foreigners after serving their sentences, or paying fines, are deported. Volunteers working on a kibbutz, if found using drugs, are usually asked to leave without resorting to the police. One should be aware that there are no reliable statistics of the magnitude of drug abuse among this group, although they are blamed as the major source of the spread of drugs among Israeli youth (Berman, 1969; Even-Zohar, 1973).

Generally speaking, the judicial system did not have a special policy vis-a-vis the drug problem, probably because, until 1967, the scope of the problem was not considered serious enough to merit special attention. Thus, fines were small and deterred neither users nor dealers and merchants. Imprisonment sentences were quite rare and generally for short periods. The situation changed after 1967 – the legal ordinances made the penalties for possession, dealing, and using drugs more severe (Landau, 1970).

Only one-quarter to one-third of those charged for violation of the drug laws are brought to trial. This is because of difficulties in providing the court with convincing evidence (Landau, 1970). For juveniles (aged 9 to 17), about 30 percent of the files opened against them are closed at the police level. Educational considerations and the recommendations of probation officers lead to these decisions.

Only one study is available comparing court policies toward drug offenders before and after 1967 (Landau, 1970). The study shows that:

a. Since 1967 police tend to close less files, bringing more drug offenders to trial, especially dealers, distributors, and merchants, even if no fullproof evidence is at hand.

b. Penalties are becoming more severe, that is, more frequent, longer conditional sentences, higher fines, and the combination of both.

c. From 1967 till 1970 there were fewer prison sentences, and these generally were for a shorter period of time (Geva, 1971), with the tendency again for conditional sentences, fines, or both.

Since 1970 there has been a policy to sentence more drug offenders to imprisonment, although conditional sentences and fines, or both, are more frequent (Barak Report, 1976).

TREATMENT

Similar to the drug control issue, the treatment aspects of drug abuse depend upon the public and the authorities' drug-related conceptions, philosophy, and political considerations. Treatment, as well as the control aspect still operates under the, as yet, unresolvable basic dilemma: not knowing which is the best policy or treatment technique to control the spread of, and to rehabilitate, drug addicts. While there is some evidence of relative success in alleviating the physical dependence on drugs, the psychological dependence is far from being successfully overcome by the most used chemical, psychological, or sociological therapeutic techniques.

Israel takes the position that treatment and rehabilitation must be comprehensive (including the medical, social, family, self-help, and community factors to be supported by back-up services, early case-finding procedures, and using the best known techniques). But very little has been done to date. While the control aspect is relegated to law enforcement and the legal-judicial authorities, the treatment aspect is in the hands of the health authorities. In some cases the treatment aspects in Israel are operated on two levels: treatment and rehabilita-tion in the framework of criminal procedure for an offense committed and treatment in other noncompulsory agencies or institutions. Regard-ing the former, the law allows the court to issue a nonvoluntary treatment order. The treatment – detoxification – is given in government mental hospitals which allocate 20 beds (Amir & Eldor, 1975) for the involuntary court order treatment of addicts, including alcoholics (Barak Report, 1976). Such procedures have met severe criticism by treatment personnel, hospital administrators, judges, and prosecutors. The procedure has shown no success. Cases keep reopening in court. During hospitalization, these patients disrupt activities, and continue to use drugs, even to deal and entice others to consume dangerous drugs. The reluctance of the health authorities to allocate more beds for addicts has meant that they must stay in prison instead.

As mentioned above, the prison population contains a sizeable proportion of drug addicts. The prisons' physicians do not conduct treatment or rehabilitation programs, but a kind of a maintenance program in which addicts get the drugs in order to calm them down. Sometimes there are attempts at a physical detoxification program. Most of the addicts who are released from prison resort back to their addiction patterns (Barak Report, 1976). Some who were not addicts when entering the prison come out addicts; drugs are available illegally in prison in large quantities (Karti, 1970).

As for detoxification and treatment programs which partially use judicial procedures, the following are available:

a. beds in mental hospitals, in addition to the 16 beds allocated for those sent by the court;

b. two outpatient clinics, part of the Ministry of Health's clinics. One center in Jaffa combines detoxification (a methadone treatment program), with psychological and social work treatment. To date, the program has some 70 patients while hundreds are on a waiting list. The center also started group treatment with some of the patients. The second center, in Acre, has a methadone program with some rudiments of psychological treatment. The program treats approximately 40 people. Again many are on the waiting list. Because of the public concern, and given the lack of facilities to treat addicts the government is planning to open three more centers: in Jerusalem for 200 patients (even though the number of addicts are unknown in the city) in Ramle-Lod, and in Haifa. Jerusalem's program, governmentally funded but under the auspices of a private psychiatric hospital, is being modeled as a small verbal therapy clinic which will also serve to train intervention agents in other agencies. In Ramle-Lod the future program is to emulate the Jaffa center which has no system for built-in evaluation. Agreement has already been reached to use the facilities of mental hospitals in the area. In Haifa, the medical supervision will be provided by union-fund-socialized-medical services.

c. The municipal departments working with street corner groups, especially with Jerusalem's juveniles, offer social work guidance to those served by them and refer willing boys and girls to psychological and physical detoxification programs in the government's mental health clinics.

A special problem is that of maintenance programs for those who refuse or cannot benefit from detoxification programs. Until a few years ago there was a maintenance program where opiate addicts got their daily ration from the public health centers of the Ministry of Health. This program was cancelled because the center could not control the abuses and violence which were daily occurrences. As a result, some physicians developed their own maintenance programs and gave prescriptions to multitudes of addicts who flocked to them.(4) Again abuses of dealings with drugs and violence occurred in the physicians' offices, and the Ministry of Health removed the physicians' licenses to issue prescriptions. In Tel Aviv, the city public clinic also started a maintenance program with the same negative results. When all these maintenance programs were phased out, there was an increase of thefts of drugs and blank prescriptions from hospitals, pharmacies, and physicians' offices.(5) The result was the planning of new kinds of maintenance programs, centered around detoxification and treatment centers of the Ministry of Health, Union Medical services or city public medical outpatient clinics.

In short, what can currently be observed in Israel is the lack of: maintenance programs, early case-finding programs, self-help programs, and necessary back-up services. The programs are mainly the traditional, unevaluated chemotherapy with some psychiatric or psychological services models. Furthermore, there are neither detoxification treatment programs, which experiment with new – at least to the Israeli scene – ideas and programs and which are evaluatable. Nor are there the necessary teaching and training programs for treatment and prevention personnel for the positions that will be open when the various current plans are actualized.

PREVENTION

The pessimism related to the outcome of treatment of drug addicts has encouraged current thinking about drug use prevention. Two kinds of preventive efforts can be distinguished in Israel: (a) education, information, and propaganda, and (b) preventive social action. The Inter-Ministerial Committee for the Prevention and Treatment of Drug Abuse, headed by the attorney general, initiated the former. The information service of the Prime Minister's Office is responsible for its planning and execution. The main attempt was to educate, to inform, and actually to scare youth, mainly in high school, by using policemen from the Juvenile Squad, physicians, and school personnel. The mass media presented information and special programs on drugs, and public meetings and lectures were given on the subject.

A movie – Jimmy the Beautiful was shown about a nice-looking army officer in an elite unit who deteriorated because of his "fall" into drugs. Also, information material about types of drugs and their impairing effects were prepared for teachers and for the army. Recently, a more cleverly made movie was prepared – the String Manipulators. It portrayed a situation where youths are influenced by the pressure of their peers to follow a certain course of action. It only touched upon drugs lightly. It was designed to show that group pressure and "weak personality" bring youths to experiment with drugs, to take risks with drugs. The argument was raised by the attorney general (Barak Report, 1976) that information and propaganda may backfire and induce or entice youths to experiment with the forbidden. It cited a study (Peled, 1972) which shows that some youths decided to experiment with drugs (hashish) after they had been exposed to information and propaganda campaigns against drugs.

In the area of preventive social action the main activities involve street corner groups among whom the use of drugs was found to be prevalent. The program contains lectures, group discussions, and referring individual youngsters to medical and psychological treatment. It should be mentioned that none of the staff of these programs had special training in the area of drug abuse. Nor were the various programs of prevention and treatment ever evaluated.

AGENCIES THAT DEAL WITH DRUG ABUSE

In Israel there continue to be various bodies and agencies that deal with various aspects of the drug problem, often without cooperation and coordination. These include for example:

1. A psychiatric subcommittee in the Ministry of Health, part of the permanent psychiatric committee at the ministry.

2. A special committee in the army, headed by the army surgeon general, which plans and directs the drug control activities in the army.

3. A special committee at the Ministry of Education.

4. A special three-member committee in the Ministry of Justice, headed by a judge and including a psychiatrist and a physician. This committee's task is to recommend the release of addicts sent to treatment institutions.

5. A research committee within the National Council for Research and Development.

6. The Inter-Ministerial Committee. This body, established in 1970 by the attorney general, is supposed to coordinate the activities – preventive, treatment, control, legislative, and resources – in the areas of drug abuse, which are conducted within the various government ministries. It also has the mandate to initiate legislation, research, and the planning of action programs. The committee has a parallel district subcommittee. The main Inter-Ministerial Committee had decided to establish three subcommittees whose areas are: education, treatment, and research.

Outside the government there are other local committees such as the Municipality Committee of Tel Aviv, or local committees in other parts of the country (rural and urban). There is also a voluntary association "Al-Sam" (no drugs), which provides help to addicts and advises families whose members have "deteriorated" into drugs. The association operates in close contact with the Ministry of Health which provides resources (money and trained personnel). The association operates a center in the Tel Aviv area and plans to open others in other parts of the country.

It should be obvious from this brief overview that drug abuse intervention in Israel, whatever its focus, is limited by the lack of clear role and goal definitions for the institutions that are operating in this area.   A growing number of governmental and public groups are undertaking various activities in an uncoordinated manner for an as yet undetermined number of drug abusers.

PUBLIC OPINION AND CONCEPTIONS

As said, until 1967 public awareness and the opinion of the authorities about nonmedical drug abuse had been associated mainly with social minorities or marginal groups. Therefore it was possible to confine the drug problem to a limited place on the agenda of public action; it belonged only to the law enforcement and judicial level. The narrowness in conceptions and action made it also possible to avoid viewing drug abuse as a threat to official, mainstream norms. The moral order, especially for youth, was upheld by the fact of publicized legislative pressure and court actions against drug offenders. Since 1967, public awareness, conception and attitudes about drugs and drug abuse has changed. While this chapter is being written, drug abuse has received another apex of public attention and concern.

The background of this change has been discussed above: the spread of drugs, the new types of drugs used, the new groups experimenting with and using drugs – the middle class, the army and other dominant groups in society – and the development of a criminal drug culture. The discovery of drug abuse among middle-class youth brought a new sensitivity to the dangers of drugs and their abuse. They are beginning to be viewed as both causes and reflections of contradictory norms and oppositional styles of life to the official and traditional ethos of the State which specify: voluntarism, pioneering, hard labor, cooperation, egalitarianism, and social justice. Hashish, which was considered part of the Arab culture, is now feared as causing, and reflecting, the Levantanism of values, the transition toward hedonism, and the emphasis on the improvement of personality and style of life – all norms and orientations taken from Western youth culture (Reifen, 1972). New types of sensitivity and concern arose from the belief that Arab terrorist organizations were aiming to spread drugs among Israeli youth. Drug use became a sign of a nonpatriotic style of life bordering on treason (Cohen, 1970). It was conceived as a security problem because of its spread to the army.

The negative significance of drug abuse as a normative deviation and a security problem centered mainly around middle-class youth. This perception has diverted the attention from the traditional conception of drug abuse as a health problem and as being related to marginal groups. This transition was occurring from the results of the surveys and studies conducted on drug abuse, mainly in high schools (Peled, 1972; Shoham, 1974). Thus, a general survey of public opinion which was carried out in 1970 (Institute of Applied Social Sciences, 1970), revealed that 89 percent of the respondents were opposed to the nonmedical use of drugs. However, this opposition was directly related to age and inversely related to education. The survey also disclosed that drug abuse is mainly conceived of as a health problem and that of an oppositional style of life exemplified by early cigarette smoking. This study, as well as others, was used by the mass media, which made drug abuse a national issue, to call for initiating intervention by the authorities mainly for middle-class educated youth.

The scare that the media created and spread brought a new phase into the area of drugs and the public – the search for explanation, the analyses of why it happened. The answers given were invariably: export from abroad of new norms; the multitude of foreigners – particularly as students and volunteers – entering the country after 1967 bringing the demand for drugs as well as the ideologies for its use; the failure of Israel's education, mainly ideological cultivation of the youth; the result and reflection of social ideologies and poverty subculture beginning to develop in Israel (Even-Zohar, 1973).

While some explanations emphasized the generational conflict argument (Gal, 1976; Lehman, 1973; Shoham, 1974), this interpretation was dropped with the discovery that adults, too, were attracted to drugs. All these explanations were couched in a general assumption that the "new" phenomenon of drug abuse was part of the rejection of social pressures to conform and the general revolt against the establishment and its normative demands (Cohen, 1970). What was almost always absent in all these explanations was the psychopathological approach, the idea of criminality – at least not for the middle-class youth who became the center of concern. One of the reasons for this is that until 1974 very little crime, at least as reported to the public, was committed by drug addicts. Thus, instead of psychopathological and criminal explanations, the deviation was explained as that of lifestyle and norms: hedonism, permissiveness, and nonpatriotic attitudes, especially because of new-left ideologies.

However, Israel saw no development of an extreme counterculture of an antiestablishment stance. Thus, while the public was exposed to the new symbolistic nature of drug abuse and abusers, no repressive mechanisms were erected against drug users. But they were erected against drug merchants and dealers. Also very little political tension developed between youth and the regulative agencies except for some rare instances in high schools. One of the reasons for this situation may be the fact that there has been no movement for the legalization of hashish, except for some unorganized voices from the Bohemia and university people who endorse experimentation with hashish and LSD. Part of their argument was that Israeli authorities are influenced by the nondefinitive results of U.S. studies that emphasize the harmful results of drug abuse. They also argued that a gap exists between the reality of the situation vis-a-vis the scope and nature of drug abuse and abusers, and the "unrealness" of public awareness of the drug problem.(6)

Policy

The perception in Israel of drug-related problems being less a pathological type of deviance and more a value deviation and sometimes a criminal deviation, has led to an emphasis on legal efforts, on education or propaganda, and less on treatment. Since the drug problem involves all kinds of specific issues – criminal, health, education, welfare, etc. − various agencies representing government ministries are involved in reacting or pro-acting to the drug problem. The decision or activities of each ministry impinge on other agencies. Thus, for instance, the decision of the court regarding drug detoxification and treatment is related to the facilities existing or provided by the Ministry of Health. The police action to eradicate the sources of drug supply in the market directly influence the amount of pressure on the clinics of the Ministry of Health to provide drugs to opiate-using addicts.

The police in Israel are in charge of controlling the importing, exporting, sale, and distribution of nonmedical drugs. The police, especially in cases of minors, are responsible for the prosecution of drug offenders in the lower courts. The juvenile division of the police is also actively involved in education and propaganda of youth. Adult groups also receive information from the police.

There is an assumption of the existence of a generally accepted moral system involving collective-national elements which allows the viewing of drug abusers as nonpatriotic, social and moral deviants.

The main emphasis in Israel's propaganda and educational programs is the use of the scare orientation: on the harmful effects on health and drug use as symbolizing personal weakness, value deviation, marginality and criminality. The same emphasis is made by professionals − psychologists, teachers, physicians − who are engaged in drug education and propaganda. The tools of education are mainly lectures, sometimes small group talks, written material and films from the U.S., and films produced in Israel. There is still a debate about the negative effects of propaganda and education in alluring some youngsters to experiment with the forbidden and dare the dangers and risks that drug use is assumed to bring about. Educationally, it is still unclear how best to approach a heterogeneous audience.

Thus the emphases oscillate between public-society interests in controlling drug abuse and its spread and between individual harmful consequences. However, as suggested above, in both orientations there is the common element of the negative symbolic nature of drug use, and the negative connotation for abusers vis-a-vis nonusers of drugs.

Treatment policy is mainly psychiatrically oriented with periods when the State allowed a maintenance program for addicts to "hard drugs." First offenders are exposed, willingly or because of court decisions, to psychological treatment in the form of clinics or private psychologists in the first case, and probation officer's guidance and treatment in the case of unwillingness and court sanction. As mentioned above, almost none of the staff in these programs are specially trained in treating drug addicts and their problems.

Prognosis and Suggested Changes in Policy

The drug problem in Israel calls for a review and renewal of current policies, not only due to the existing situation described above but because of the prognosis of the problem. It can be assumed that the crest of the experimentation with hashish is over. The scare technique, the hardening of the punitive approach may have deterred many. We can expect each year new groups of high school graduates who will experiment with hashish or "pills." The main problem, however, is that of the continued development of a drug culture based on both "illegal" drugs and social pharmacology. It will not only involve lower-class youth and adults, but also middle-class youth. Since 1970, each year there are about 150-200 new cases of drug addicts.(7) Furthermore, with growing tourism and especially vacationing U.S. soldiers from Europe, the drug culture will have better opportunity to develop.

The new and forecasted development calls for a planned comprehensive policy on all levels and aspects of the drug problem. It involves the assumption about the trends in the drug phenomenon. It also assumes that priorities, usable criteria, and achievable goals must be set up for the content of the policy plan as well as for the agencies that will execute the various programs of the policy. This policy must take into consideration and make priorities in terms of:

a. Defining the scope and nature of the variety of drug-related problems, as well as the number and types of users and misusers.

b. The modes of potential usable intervention in Israel, and their direct or indirect consequences for all who are concerned (prevention, treatment, law enforcement, and education).

c. Evaluation and research of the programs and the changing nature of the drug scene.

d. Israel's special problems and need for special programs to meet the changing nature of the drug scene (Barak, 1976; Doube, 1973).

Specifically, the following was suggested by various scholars and committees (Barak, 1976; Doube, 1973; Lehemann, 1973) as part of a comprehensive policy: strengthening needed regional cooperation, controlling smuggling of and trafficking with dangerous drugs, and prevention of a repressive policy such as that of the U.S. with the adverse effects of such policy.

On the prevention level:

a. Efforts should be directed toward eradicating or minimizing the causes of drug abuse, and toward providing meaningful alternatives to drug use such as alleviating feelings of marginality and of negative and low self-worth.

b. Education and general information-dissemination should be differentially employed in terms of methods, content, and audience specificity.

c. In the education sphere, the main orientation should be toward strengthening the conformist attitudes of the majority rather than spending the main energy against a minority of the population.

d. Prevention (as well as other intervention programs) should also include the army.

On the judicial level:

a. First offenders, especially youth, should receive special attention with the aim toward experiments with treatment rather than strict penal measures.

b. The sentencing policy must be reevaluated; some forms of drug offenses must be more severely punished.

c. The prosecuting machinery must be strengthened with changes that will make it easier and speedier to prosecute drug offenders.

d. The detoxification and rehabilitation policy, as related to the court and penal policy, should also be evaluated in terms of the results of the existing arrangements.

On the treatment level:

a. Methadone – maintenance programs, both in the prisons as well as in the community, should be instituted and become part of Israel's intervention lifestyle. Consideration must be given to whether the treatment of addicts will be voluntary or enforced by the courts (Barak, 1976).

b. Prevention and treatment programs necessitate: 1) the development of back-up services, e.g., beds in major hospitals, regional outpatient, and local services; 2) the training of educational and treatment personnel for all kinds of programs; 3) experimentation with new ideas (i.e., self-help groups, agricultural colonies, etc.).

c. A comprehensive research policy on the various aspects of drug use and misuse in Israel: background causes, epidemiology, typologies, drug culture, drugs and crime, etc. Such research must include the evaluation of the various drug programs. No such policy is yet existent in Israel. In view of the country's more pressing problems – e.g., defense, economics, and absorption of immigration – a sufficient and appropriate budget is unlikely to be obtained for research as well as action programs. At the present time in Israel, one fears a troubleshooting kind of policy rather than a comprehensive one. One potentially usable approach could be instituted by transferring the overseeing of

Israel's drug problem from the interministerial committee to a special expert committee that would receive and budget personnel and have authoritization to plan and execute a national drug policy program.

On the research level.

This chapter is based on some empirical evidence on the scope, patterns, and processes of the drug abuse problem in Israel. However, much is based on inside knowledge gathered by interviewing policemen and other officials who are involved in the control of drug abuse. Also inside knowledge in the hands of newspapermen who divulge their information only in newspaper reports was gained.

Scientific studies of drug abuse are scarce and do not follow the developments in the phenomenon of drug abuse. Thus, almost every aspect of this phenomenon needs research. In Israel, however, such research has special merits: (a) the drug abuse problem is fairly recent and can be relatively easy to study, e.g., the formation of drug culture or of organized crime in the area of drugs: (b) the fact of ethnic pluralism allows the study of the acceptance or rejection of drug abuse in certain ethnic groups; (c) the special situation of Israel – a society at war, undergoing rapid social changes – allows the study of the relationship between these facts and various aspects of the drug abuse problems in Israel.

PERSPECTIVE INTO THE FUTURE

The drug problem in Israel is a relatively new phenomenon, but many factors suggest that, sadly, it is here to stay. One gets the impression that it will get worse.

First, the level of hashish smoking will remain in scope and nature, but there is a beginning of the invasion of "harder" drugs, mainly opiates and especially heroin. This, in turn, is connected with better organized drug smuggling and distribution, with all the known criminal and other negative social concomitants, e.g., corruption and violence because of competition of smuggling, trafficking, and distribution.

Second the social reaction to these developments was, in essence, police activities, public alarm, the formation of official and civil organizations to ameliorate, prevent, treat, and punish drug abusers or drug dealers. However, the impression is gained that the existing lack of coordination of trained personnel with basic knowledge about the processes of drug abuse is interfering with effective, efficient, and adequate programs to combat the drug problem.

Third, there will be changes in the legal, judicial, prevention, and treatment efforts concerning drug abuse. In the legal sphere we envisage a more punitive approach. In prevention and treatment, there will be a proliferation of agencies and programs. But economic considerations will put obstacles in the way of imaginative programs. In short, the author is very pessimistic, unless the initial, still small developments in these efforts gain strength due to the growing awareness that drug abuse is a serious social problem.

APPENDIX

Since this chapter was written some important changes have occurred in the Israeli drug scene.

During the last two years heroin and opium have infiltrated the country: opium, mainly from Iran, heroin from Europe (mainly Amsterdam and Frankfurt) and also from Thailand. The smuggling and the distribution of these drugs has been accompanied by the development of organized crime, specializing in this (economic) activity, i.e., smuggling corruption, "gang land" killing, etc. As reported in the Knesset, since 1976 approximately a thousand people have been considered to be addicted to heroin and about two thousand more to opium. Although the general view remains that the population of addicts to "hard" drugs are lower class youth, there seems to be an increase in the proportion of middle-class youth addicted to these drugs. Hashish is still the main drug used in Israel. A new source for hashish has developed – a direct supply from Lebanon. This is becuase of the opening of direct contact with Lebanon in 1976.

The police, to date, are worried about the increase in crime due to drug addiction, (i.e., the increase in burglaries, robberies, purse snatching) by addicts – users who need money for their daily supply. Also there is an apparent increase in police reporting of deaths from overdose – but it has not been carefully documented.

These facts led to new interacting developments:

a. Police reinforced their activities in the area of drug control; more policemen were allocated to surveillance, undercover activities, international connections with police forces abroad, etc.

b. More resources were allocated for studying drug related topics. For example, epidemiological studies, especially among youth, and drug use in the army (where mainly hashish has become a serious problem). Life styles and career patterns of addict and drug users. Misuse of medical drugs among various subgroups of the population.

c. In the Knesset (the Parliament) various committees have spent much time on drug problems: Drug use among youth, drug educational and prevention aspects, legal control efforts, etc.

New treatment programs have been developed since 1975: (a) four methadone programs in Acco, Haifa, Jaffa-Tel-Aviv, Lod-Ramle. (b) Once center for consultation and guidance for youth in north Tel-Aviv. (c) One outpatient treatment center with a more comprehensive approach in which only a few drug users receive methadone daily, as part of their treatment.

The Ministry of Health plans to develop 6 more treatment centers over the next few years, The Ministry of Welfare has taken on the responsibility for treating alcoholism.

The Ministry of Education has undertaken the responsibility for developing drug prevention curricula and staff training toward this goal. As of the writing of this chapter no active programs have been initiated.

Finally, due to the concern of the public and officials in this area, drug abuse and addiction have become daily news items.

Two major reports on Crime in Israel, by special government commissions, dealt with the problem of drug addiction, and portrayed an alarming picture of the present and future of the drug scene in Israel.

BIBLIOGRAPHY

Amir, M., Eldar, P. 1975. Alcoholism and its Treatment in Israel. Ministry of Social Welfare, Jerusalem.

Barak, A. (Attorney-General) 1976. Report on Drug Abuse in Israel. Jerusalem.

Bein, D. 1970. Legal aspects of the drug problem in Israel. Symposium on Drug Addiction in Israel. Hebrew University (in Hebrew).

Bein, D. Amir, M., Landau, S., Sebba, L. 1974. Nature and trends of drug use and abuse in Israel. Israel National Report, submitted to the International Association of Penol, Budapest (September).

Berman, Y. 1967. Survey of Drug Offenders. Ministry of Social Welfare (mimeo).

Berman, Y. 1969. Drug-Use Among Youth in Israel. Ministry of Social Welfare (mimeo).

Chesler-Gampel, J. 1971. Increase in the Numbers of Drug Dependent Patients Admitted to Israeli Mental Hospitals from 1966-1971. Jerusalem Mental Health Services, Ministry of Health.

Chigier, M. 1972. Drug abuse among juveniles. Criminology, Criminal Law, and Police Science, 1 (2), 146-65. Institute of Criminology, Tel Aviv University (in Hebrew).

Cohen, E. 1968. Hashish and hashish users in Acre. Delinquency and Society 3 (1), 34-39 (in Hebrew).

Cohen, E. 1970. Social Patterns of Drug-Taking. Paper delivered at the Symposium of Drug Addiction in Israel. Hebrew University (in Hebrew).

Davidson, S. 1970. Drug taking as a manifestation of adolescent rebellion in Israel: Clinical experience with Cannabis. International Symposium on Drug Abuse. Jerusalem: Ministry of Health.

Doube, E. 1973. Developing a drug policy for Israel. In S. Shoham. (Ed.) Israel Studies in Criminology, 2: 153-170.

Drapkin, I., Landau, S. 1966. Drug Offenders in Israel. British Journal of Criminology, 6, 376-90.

Even-Zohar, I. 1973. Drugs in Israel: A study of political implications for society and foreign policy. In L.P. Simmons and A.A. Said. (Eds.) Drugs, Politics and Diplomacy, 2, 178-212.

Friedman, I., & Peer, I. 1968. Drug addiction among pimps and prostitutes in Israel. International Journal of Drug Addiction, 3 (2).

Gal, S. 1976. Dangerous Drugs. Israel Police. Jerusalem.

Geva, H. et al., 1971. Patterns of Cannabis users in Israel. In Drug Abuse: Non-Medical Use of Dependence Producing Drugs. Proceedings of Sixth Round Table Conference, Geneva.

Institute of Applied Social Science. Public Opinion Survey. June-July, 1970. Jerusalem.

Jermulowitz, Z.W., & Turnau, A. 1962. Control and treatment of drug addicts in Israel. U.N. Bulletin on Narcotics, 2, 11-18.

Karti, Y. 1970. Israel police experience of the drug problem. Symposium on Drug Addiction in Israel. Jerusalem: Hebrew University (in Hebrew).

Landau, S. 1970. Comparative research on drug involvement in Israel before and after 1967. Symposium on Drug Addiction in Israel. Jerusalem: Hebrew University (in Hebrew).

Lehemann, H.E. 1973. Some aspects of non-medical use of drugs in Israel. Prime Minister's Office: National Council for Research and Development.

Miller, L. 1971. The epidemiology of drug abuse in Israel. Israel Annals of Psychiatry, 9 (1), 3-10.

Ministry of Police, 1966-1975. Annual Reports, Jerusalem.

Palgi, P. 1975. The traditional role and symbolism of hashish among Moroccan Jews in Israel and the effect of acculturation. In U. Rubin (Ed.), Cannabis and Culture. The Hague: Mouton Press.

Peled, A., & Schimmerling, H. 1972. The drug culture among the youth of Israel. In S. Shoham (Ed.), Israeli Studies of Criminology, 2, 125-53. Jerusalem: Academic Press.

Reifen, D. 1972. The Juvenile Court in a Changing Society. London: Weidenfeld and Nicholson.

Sebba, L. 1974. Some Legal Aspects of Drug Abuse in Israel. Paper submitted to the 24th International Course of Criminology, and 4th Symposium of L.I.C.L. Teheran, May 22.

Shamgar, M. (Attorney-General) 1973. Report of Inter-Ministerial Committee on Drug Abuse. Jerusalem: Ministry of Justice.

Shoham, S. et al. 1974. Drug abuse among Israeli youth: A pilot study. Bulletin on Narcotics, 27 (2), 9-28.

NOTES

(1) On the problem of alcoholism in Israel, see M. Amir, and P. Elder, 1975.

(2) Internal Report to the Attorney General, Ministry of Welfare Report (mimeo), Jerusalem, Israel, 1976.

(3) On some of the legal issues involved in the Israeli law pertaining to drug addiction, see Bein, 1970; Bein, et al., 1974; and Sebba, 1974.

(4) Taken from newspaper reports of the last six years, which periodically portray the problems of drug addicts.

(5) Ibid.

(6) Pi-Aton. Hebrew University student weekly, June 19, 1968.

(7) Various inside reports by street corner groups of workers and by police reveal that hashish is often given free to novices together with opium, which makes the transition to addiction quicker. Also, heroin was introduced to Israel in 1975 and from one or two cases, the number is now about 15-20 cases.

II

Drug Education

8 Drug Abuse Prevention: Issues, Problems, and Alternatives

S. Einstein

INTRODUCTION

Preventing the misuse of certain drugs, reinforcing the appropriate or socially-medically approved use of others, and doing little about substances such as alcohol and tobacco products has become an area of increasing concern and importance for all segments of society, particularly in industrialized nations. The logic of this relatively recent concern and its associated efforts is quite simple. Increasingly we have given up on drug misusers, involving them in what euphemistically passes for treatment. Instead the contemporary effort is to save the nondrug misuser (who is often a drug user), and more specifically so-called populations at risk (Einstein, 1975; Lennard & Assoc., 1971; Marin & Cohen, 1971; Middlemiss, 1926).

The logic underlying this is no doubt commendable. Its historical antecedents are many. Indeed, historically we might tag the logic as the Moses 40-year desert trip. The results of this type of logic have to date bordered on disaster. A major reason for this is that we have all too often made the illogical leap of translating drug prevention into drug education and/or training without ever questioning whether prevention efforts automatically lock us only into educational processes or training techniques (Barnes & Messdonghites, 1972; Cohen, 1971; Edwards, 1972; Nowlis, 1970; Segal, 1972). Prevention is an area of intervention, whereas education and training are only two of the possible subunits in the area. Secondly, education and training are not equivalent, and until they are sharply delineated their potentials can only suffer (17).

Drug abuse-misuse training and education, both past and present, have been many things in the U.S. as well as in many other countries: a misnomer, an anachronism, a form of political expediency, a format for hustling, a focus of religiosity, etc. Such efforts have rarely ever been defined in terms of content, goals, or who is to be responsible for their development, maintenance, and evaluation. Because of the confusion, both of these approaches, education and training, have tended to grow arithmetically as the use of drugs for recreation has seemingly grown geometrically. Within this context many of society's formal institutions (family, school, religious institutions, corporations, unions, etc.) are now being asked, as well as pushed, to intervene effectively.

This paper will attempt to explore those issues that relate to:

1. why a given institutional structure seeks to establish a drug prevention, training or educational program (Aubrey, 1971; Barber, 1967; NCC DAGI, 1971; Einstein, 1971; Fort, 1969; Lennard & Assoc., 1971; Nowlis, 1967; Smart & Whitehead, 1972, Szasz, 1972; Weil, 1972; Zinberg & Robertson, 1972).

2. the consequences of our definitions of drugs, drug addicts, and drug addiction on such efforts (Einstein, 1975; Nowlis, 1970; Szasz, 1972; Weil, 1972).

3. what the content of these programs has been and what it should be (Edwards, 1972; Einstein, 1971; Erikson, 1963; Johnson, 1968; Kitzinger, 1969; Kolodny, 1972; Lennard & Associates, 1971; Marin & Cohen, 1971; Middlemiss, 1926; N.Y. Times, 1972; Nowalk, 1968; Richards, 1971; Segal, 1972; Stuart, 1973; Teaching About Drugs, 1971; Zinberg & Robertson, 1972.

4. the possible roles available to institutional and noninstitutional efforts in drug abuse intervention (Delone, 1972; Einstein, 1975; Lawler, 1971, Nowalk, 1968; Virgilio, 1971; Weil, 1972).

5. the possible and appropriate use of the media in drug misuse intervention efforts

CRITICAL DEFINITIONS

All drug abuse training and education programs are contingent upon a series of definitions that a society makes concerning the following:

1. What is a drug?

2. What is a dangerous drug?

3. What drugs, taken in what way, by themselves or in combination with other drugs, and for what conscious or unconscious reasons, are to be condemned or condoned?

4. Is the nonmedical use of drugs a disease predictor and/or an indication of criminality, a societal symptom, or a condition?

5. Who is a drug user, a drug abuser, or a drug addict?

6. What is the format of prevention and what are its goals?

7. What is the format of training and what are its goals?

8. What is the format of education and what are its goals?

9. What are the roles and responsibilities of all those involved in a prevention, an educational, or training program – the student, the prevention and educational representative, and the general community?

10. What are the roles and responsibilities of all those involved in a prevention, drug educational, or training program – the abstainer, the nonabstainer, the nondangerous, drug-using educational representative and/or information disseminator, and the abstinent and nonabstinent general community?

11. Who is to define this process and who is to be responsible for its success as well as its failure?

12. What are the agreed upon techniques for attempting to change man's appetites – medical, legal, social, religious, educational, etc.?

13. What are the appropriate roles for the various media in drug misuse intervention?

Drug-Related Definitions

Drugs have traditionally been defined in terms of four sources – social-religious, medical, legal, and scientific (see Table 8.1).

Social religious definitions

The oldest source of definition has been the social-religious. This source has historically taught us that a variety of substances, irrespective of their medical, psychiatric, or social consequences are permitted for use if they fit into the social value structure or religious ritual structure of a given community at a given time (Einstein, 1975; Fort, 1969; Nowlis, 1967). As long as the user of the substance adhered to the social and religious rituals of his group he was not given a deviant status. As a consequence, there was no problem – just behavior that may and may not have given rise to various issues.

From this perspective drugs were not considered dangerous or not dangerous. The critical definition became, and indeed still is, approved social or religious use or disapproved social or religious use. Thus, whereas alcohol has traditionally had sacramental value, as has peyote for members of the Native American church, LSD is not given this status, notwithstanding its association with the League for Spiritual Discovery (Clark, 1969; Leech & Jordan, 1967). Thus, in spite of alcohol's toxic effects, its devastation of an estimated 9,000,000

Table 8.1. Definitions and Sources of Definitions of Drugs

Source of Definition:	Medical	Legal	Scientific
Socioreligious Definition: Imputed status: aid to ritualization	Medicine	Dangerous substance for individual and/or community	Any substance that by its chemical nature alters the structure or functioning of a living organism.
Consequence of Definition:			
Social Rituals		Control of:	
Holidays Festivals Birthdays Special occasions Rites of passage	Prevent illness Maintain health Treat illness Relieve Pain	Growth Manufacture Distribution Importation Use Possession	
Religious Rituals			
The mass Greeting of sabbath Mescaline rites			

Americans (130,000 American servicemen) we still honor it as a social beverage. As for the various forms of tobacco products, none of them are generally perceived as being, or reacted to, as drugs. They are simply catagorized as tobacco products.

The most immediate consequence of social-religious definitions is that decisions to reinforce or inhibit the use of particular drugs are not related to the imputed dangers of drug effects but to the arbitrariness of human decision making (Clark, 1969; Einstein, 1975; Fort, 1969; Leech & Jordan, 1967).

One immediate consequence of this semantic delineation in any prevention effort is the increasing difficulty of educating individuals, young or old, to the following:

1. Certain substances are not to be used, or used in certain ways for certain reasons, simply because we want it so. The arbitrariness of this is a normal part of societal functioning because all individual and community decisions are basically arbitrary ones.

2. Our concern about the nonmedical use of drugs goes beyond disease and health concepts and embraces the notion of maximizing human adaptation and functioning. It is assumed that this maximizing process is interfered with by the nonmedical or nonsocially approved use of drugs.

Medical definitions

The medical field has by definition suggested that drug use is a problem when a substance is generally used for nonmedical reasons, outside of the authority of the physician and other specific health professionals (I.e., nurse and pharmacist), and specifically when the goal of such use in recreation, pleasure, and imputed self-exploration (Fort, 1969; Lindesmith, 1967; Richards, 1970). By ambiguity and specious reasoning the medical world has foisted upon the community the notion that nonmedical drug use is a medical problem, rather than being an issue with possible medical facets. It is these medical facets which need intervention by the medical profession. It is only a short step to also conclude currently that any type of intervention, be it treatment, education, or whatever, is the province of the physician.

A number of immediate consequences arise from this:

1. By training, most physicians perceive behavior in terms of pathology and disease concepts which may limit them in being able to explore the varied meanings and ramifications of drug use or in being able to introduce a new concept – social pharmacology.

2. By training, many, if not most, physicians assume that treatment and/or education should continue in the traditional medical model or pyramidal structure for lines of authority and decision making. Given this type of structure, the biggest constituency for drug education, the community, is given only a passive role for integration of information and decision making and an active role for funding.

3. By status and imputed knowledge the physician is asked, or takes it upon himself, to become active in a variety of drug educational roles that are often not commensurate with his training or interest. These include developing school drug abuse curricula, serving on the now traditional school program panel of physician, pharmacist, teacher, religious leader, policeman, ex-addict, and politician, talking to the PTA, allaying the anxiety of parents concerned about their children's possible drug use, developing and supervising student drug surveys, defining for the general community who is the drug abuser and therein what is drug abuse, both in the school and the business world, defining what the content and process of treatment programs should be, as well as what should go into legal control.

It becomes patently clear that the various consequences of the medical definition of drugs go far beyond the boundaries of the medical world.

Legal definitions

Legal definitions of drugs and drug use are perhaps the most ambiguous because of their apparent clarity. Legally, at any point in time anywhere in the world, drugs are generally defined as substances that are considered to be dangerous either to the individual or to the community. This apparently simple definition leads to intervention through controlling growth, manufacture, distribution, sale, possession as well as use (Barber, 1967; Cazalas, 1971-72; Dawtry, 1968; Einstein, 1975; Fort, 1969; Hills, 1970; Jeffee, 1970; Szasz, 1972).

This type of definition results in a number of immediate serious consequences.

1. By training, most law enforcement representatives perceive changing or controlling man's appetites in terms of legal controls – notwithstanding the lack of sufficient data to substantiate that this is at all possible. Indeed, at no time or place in history have laws in and of themselves ever adequately controlled man's appetites.

2. Drug-related laws have resulted in determining who a drug addict or alcoholic is. But drug addict and alcoholic at best connote something about a person's drug behavior and not who he is (Einstein, 1975; Fort 1969; Lindesmith, 1967).

3. One of the consequences of legal definitions of drugs and drug use is the perception of drug-related behavior in limited terms – deviant-criminal concepts. We all too often forget that in legally designating someone as a "deviant," he is or becomes the deviant that we say he is because he meets the criteria that we created and not because he is a deviant (Einstein, 1975). This may make it difficult, if not impossible, to reach this person. For example, the associated harrassment that physicians have experienced or anticipated in treating the drug addict and user may have served to limit them in being able to explore the valid, achievable roles that they may and/or should play in contemporary social pharmacology as well as recreational drug use (Einstein, 1975; Lindesmith, 1967).

4. Given the relative absence of meaningful involvement by representatives of most of society's intervention institutions in drug education in the U.S., as well as elsewhere, in the past, law enforcement on many levels has been able to reinforce as facts a number of dangerous myths –

   a. Dangerous drugs should be the focus of our intervention efforts. By implication certain drugs are not dangerous, and thus do not deserve being covered in prevention efforts. But the reality is that there are no undangerous drugs!

b. Drugs can be categorized as <u>soft</u> and <u>hard</u>. By implication prevention efforts should focus on preventing participants in such programs from going on, or moving on to, "hard drugs." The soft-hard drug typology is scientifically meaningless. On a very simplistic level it may put an intervention program in the awkward position of attacking heroin use and saying little about barbiturates, amphetamines, alcohol, etc., when our concern, if not our mandate, should be the development of nondrug options to the problems and pleasures of living and not to the relative toxicity of chemicals. There are no soft drugs or hard drugs. There are just "drugs."

c. Drug misuse is a critical, if not <u>the</u> critical, factor in determining and/or escalating criminal behavior in a given community. By implication, were drug misuse to disappear, crime, by type, incidence, and prevalence should be dramatically lowered. Thus, drug prevention is given the additional imputed task of changing the criminal nature-status of a given community. There is little hard data to substantiate this contention. Surely one would not want to rely upon soft data for an assertion as serious as this one.

If defining drugs legally has consequences that go beyond the legal system, and often impinge upon the delivery of health services and the continuing education of many suspected and actual drug misusing youth, what roles are there for any of us, as professionals, citizens, and as concerned human beings in effecting these consequences?

Clearly, we could and should use the necessary knowledge and status we may have in our different roles, and gain the knowledge we still need to see to it that effective drug-related intervention is based on facts and not fantasies, that policy making for prevention programs is based on maximizing the functioning of both individuals and the community-at-large and not based on expediency or the vested interests of parochial groups, and that we become a source of hope rather than one of harrassment.

It should be clear by now that drug definitions are not simply semantic games. From a scientific perspective <u>a drug is any substance which, through its chemical activity, alters the structure and/or functioning of a living organism</u> (Nowlis, 1967). What does this mean for our current or even past prevention efforts? As valid as this definition is, it is presently almost meaningless for our society. Nations and their policy makers have decided not to be concerned about such chemical substances as coffee, tea, tobacco, food, etc. This has apparently resulted in problems and confusion for everyone. "Hypocrisy" has become the newest shibboleth tossed at prevention programs. In their response, those responsible for the programs have wasted energy and time in trying to explain and defend their stand instead of noting the reality — to be alive is to be a hypocrite.

But this scientific definition does raise an important issue for our consideration. Prevention programs can help communities acknowledge that they have a drug problem not when certain people are using certain drugs, but when an increasing part of the population turns to things — to substances — to meet their legitimate and illegitimate needs rather than to people.

Pragmatically this is so because social institutions cannot continue for long if individuals isolate themselves from others, are involved in parallel play, or relate to others as objects rather than sources of humanness. Should this occur, the role of prevention, the meaning of normal functioning, and the roles and responsibilities of society's institutions will significantly change.

All of this is a long way of saying that 1) drug prevention efforts should utilize the broader more encompassing scientific definitions of drugs in order to help define what entails a drug problem, and 2) no single group or institution can and should play the significant role in this process. There is more than enough work for everyone.

DRUG ABUSE-MISUSE

Drug abuse-misuse has come to be one of those terms that everyone understands but no one apparently knows what to do with or about. One of the most frequently asked questions these days is: what are the alternatives to drug abuse, drug misuse, drug dependency, habituation, drug addiction? The specific term seems to matter very little in terms of the response. While the most immediate answers are inevitably treatment and education, or changing the laws, the most immediate sensation is that of being overwhelmed. This is understandable when we acknowledge that the question is huge in terms of what it actually and potentially encompasses. From an intervention point of view, possible alternatives to drug abuse and the roles that we can play in these alternatives become more obvious when we begin to pinpoint what drug abuse is or may be.

Drug abuse is not a single entity, nor a unitary concept. Indeed, there are at least three sources of definitions for drug abuse (Einstein, 1975; Nowlis, 1967). These are:

1. Abusing drug laws and rituals. This encompasses the breaking of drug-related laws, mores, and rituals by particular people, using particular drugs in particular ways at a particular time and for particular reasons.

2. Self-abuse. The direct or indirect consequences resulting from the use of drugs for other than medically and/or socially approved reasons to the person taking them — irrespective of the consequences occurring to others.

3. Abuse of others. The direct or indirect consequences of the use

of drugs for other than medically and/or socially approved reasons to people other than the drug user – irrespective of the consequences to the actual drug abuser.

Developing meaningful and workable alternatives to drug abuse, and delineating our roles and their associated responsibilities and consequences in this process, begins to be possible only if we note the type of drug abuse that we are considering at a given point in time. This has perhaps been one of the major failings in contemporary prevention efforts. We rarely spell out the type of drug abuse that is to be prevented. Most often we pinpoint a specific drug or drug family instead. Rather than delineating issues we focus on the chemical and in doing so often imbue it with even more magic. The aforementioned differentiation helps us understand what viable roles and actions are possible for each of us for each type of drug abuse. This is not simply a semantic issue.

DRUG ABUSE EDUCATION

At the present time there are a limited number of techniques being used in drug education for either the general population or specific target groups such as adolescents (Aubry, 1971; Barnes & Messdonghites, 1972; Doerr et al., 1967; Edwards, 1972; Eiseman, 1971/ Horan, 1972; Lawler, 1971; Lewis, 1972; Lockhead, 1969; Marin, 1972; Monk, 1969; Nowlis, 1970; Richards, 1970; Segal, 1972; Shelvin, Stuart, 1973; Swisher, 1970, 71, 72; To Parents about Drugs 1970, Wichita Public Schools, 1970). Generically the techniques can be divided into dependence upon conferences, symposia, workshops, lectures, journals, newsletters, grade specific curricula, other printed materials, and the use of tapes, films, and records.

The focus of ongoing drug education programs has been classified in the following way by Dr. Louise Richards of NIMH: "1) Appeal to authority, either traditional (i.e., medical) or experiential (i.e., ex-drug users); 2) Negative reinforcement through recall of bad consequences ("scare tactics"); 3) Logical argumentation or exhortation; 4) Induction of new cognitive structures ("factual approach"); 5) Self-examination and attitude confrontation; 6) Role or status enhancement, including use of peers; 7) Role playing and simulation; 8) Simulation through novelty, humor, drama, art and other unusual means (Richards, 1971). Unfortunately, none of those foci have predictable outcomes for either drug abstinence or any other drug prevention goals.

One of the problems inherent in contemporary drug education is the lack of delineation between goals, techniques, and content. All too often we settle for techniques, irrespective of the content and give little thought to the goals. We can call this the GCT approach – goalless, contentless techniques (Cohen, 1971; NCC DAEI, 1971; DeLone, 1972; Edwards, 1972; Einstein, 1975). Contemporary drug education programs are generally based on a number of assumptions that must be critically reviewed generally, and specifically done so as they relate to the nonmedical use of drugs. The first assumption is that the recipient of these programs is indeed involved in a continuous drug-related information dissemination process, which is associated with predictable outcomes. Secondly, that this is education. Thirdly, that the communication of specific information will result in drug abstinence, a change in drug choice, or a lessening in drug use.

It might be fairer to acknowledge from the onset that since most drug use prevention program participants have learned little about the many facets of the nonmedical use of drugs and their complex interrelationships that, at best, what they receive are fragmented facts rather than a continuous, challenging, enlightening, reinforcing, meaningful, and usable experience. Perhaps the most basic reason for this is that program developers are apparently myopic as to what factors are related to the contemporary nonmedical use of drugs and their relationships, what can realistically be expected of any one-time or even continuous program, and how and when to most effectively utilize various media in their effort (Barnes & Messolonghites, 1972; DeLone, 1972; Drug Abuse, 1969; Einstein, 1975; Einstein et al., 1971; Fort, 1969; Kolodny, 1972; Lennard & Assoc., 1971; Marin & Cohen, 1971; Richards, 1970; Segal, 1972; Smart & Feger, 1974; Swisher & Horman, 1970).

The premises that underlie most drug education programs, from the time that the temperance movement began to affect them to the present, are perhaps best stated by President Kennedy's Advisory Committee on Narcotics and Drugs:

> The teenager should be made conscious of the full range of harmful effects, physical and psychological, that narcotics and dangerous drugs can produce. He should be made aware that, although the use of a drug may be a temporary means of escape from the world about him, in the long run these drugs will destroy him and all he aspires to (DeLone, 1972).

Man's history clearly indicates that the conscious awareness of facts and their related consequences doesn't automatically become interpreted into daily, positive behavior changes. We all too often forget that man as a species readily enjoys the ability to rationalize, distort, deny, etc. A New York Times article on a project of Dr. Richard B. Stuart of Michigan University reported that drug education may lead to increased drug use (N.Y. Times, 1972; Stuart, 1973). After 600 junior high school students were part of a school-based drug education program, drug experimentation increased from 14 percent to 36 percent. This increase did not occur with a control group that had not been part of a drug education program. Dr. Stuart interpreted this as increased knowledge allaying fears that had previously served to deter drug misuse.

Not only have recent studies demonstrated that there is little relationship between drug-related knowledge and drug use, but some have even concluded that consumption of certain drugs may increase after a drug education program (Smart & Fejer, 1974). We also know that many drug users already know many of the facts. While it is true that they also believe many myths, it is questionable if we can easily correct these myths with the processes that we use, or that if we do, this will change their drug behavior and/or drug-related behavior. Indeed man's history again reminds us of the central importance that myths play in our present adaptations, our future plans, and our reverence of the past.

Swisher and his associates (Swisher et al., 1972) explored the thesis that giving a group just the facts about drugs would serve to dissuade drug use and/or diminish it. Since most contemporary drug education programs are based on this simplistic notion, this study merits perusal. Using a sample of 993 students (a private college preparatory academy, n=250; a Catholic high school, n=609; a regional campus of a major state university, n=134), the data indicated that:

1. There was a statistically significant correlation for all three samples between knowledge and attitudes toward drug use. The more knowledgeable the student the more pro-drug use were the attitudes.

2. Drug users (marijuana users) were significantly more knowledge- able about drugs than nonusers.

Obviously this study does not suggest that drug knowledge, which is associated with pro-drug use attitudes, will lead to drug use. But it seriously questions whether the presentation of drug "facts" is sufficient as a preventive measure.

Another study done by Warner & Swisher (1971) raises serious questions about the content of drug education programs. Along with the notion of programs simply presenting the facts, there is the assumption that if we can counter a student's sense of alienation we would eliminate or decrease the nonmedical use of drugs. Using an alienation and drug use scale with middle-class suburban high school juniors, the authors concluded that there was no significant positive relationship between a student's drug use and the extent to which his friends also use drugs. This study, notwithstanding its sample limitations, suggests that a preventive program must focus on the meaning(s) that the target population attributes to important factors, rather than the meaning(s) that program developers attribute to factors.

Another critical issue in drug education focuses on the attempt to change target group attitudes about drugs and drug use. Often this is combined with program budgetary limitations which result in short-term drug education programs. Swisher & Crawford (1971) offered four high schools different programs over four consecutive weekly sessions. The format was three one-hour, small group sessions (23 in a group), led by the same psychiatrist for all the ninth grades. Tenth and eleventh graders were given an initial large group (70 students), one-hour sessions, and then were split up into three small groups led by psychiatrists for the remaining two hours. Information was disseminated during the first hour and expression of attitudes and feelings were the focus of small group discussions. The twelfth graders' program was similar to the latter one, except that patients from an adolescent drug unit were included. The findings from this study were:

1. The varied programs did not have a significant effect on student drug-related attitudes. Obviously short-term programs are limited in their attitudinal effects.

2. The varied programs imparted equal amounts of information to all three grades. It would appear that the use of structured or unstructured programs will not differ in their information dissemination outcome. A similar finding was reported by Swisher and his associates in 1972.

3. A student's perception of what he got out of the program may be quite inaccurate when objective measures are used.

In essence this study suggests that many clear thinking people already know, short-term educational efforts do not result in long-term outcomes.

Swisher and his associates (1972) also investigated the effectiveness of using specific models as a technique in drug education programs. Ninth and eleventh grade students were randomly assigned to one of four groups: model reinforcement group counselling with an ex-addict as a model, model reinforcement group counselling with a nondrug user as a model, verbal reinforcement group counselling, and a standard health unit. None of these different techniques were found to have any impact on student attitudes toward drug abuse or the degree of drug usage. In summary it becomes patently obvious that prevention-education programs have to go beyond unevaluated techniques and simplistic and logical assumptions.

Information-Processing Issues

Smart and Fejer (1974) have suggested a rather simple but most useful series of steps which must be considered in drug education programs that are based upon an information-processing approach (Mcguire, 1970).

1. A relevant, persuasive message must be presented to the target person or group.
2. The target person or group must attend to this message.
3. The message must be comprehended.
4. The target person must yield to the conclusions of the message, and change his (or her) attitude.
5. He or she must then retain this change produced by the message.
6. He or she must change his (or her) overt behavior.

In order to achieve these steps, which Smart and Fejer list as dependent variables, a drug education program developer must be aware of at least five independent variables:

1. Source variables (e.g., credibility of the communicator (Bogg et al., 1968; Fejer et al., 1971; Houlard & Weiss, 1951; Lawler, 1971; Panzica, 1973; Smart & Fejer, 1972; Smart, 1972a).

2. Message variables (e.g, one-sided message) (DeLone, 1972; Glasser & Snow, 1969; Le Dain, 1972; National Commission on Marijuana & Drug Abuse, 1972; Richards, 1970).

3. Channel variables (e.g., medium specificity) (Kinsella, 1971; Smart & Krakowski, 1973).

4. Receiver variables (e.g., audience characteristics) (Horan & Swisher, 1972; Mcguire, 1970, 1969).

5. Distinction variables (e.g., behavior change) (Houlard & Weiss, 1951; Smart & Fejer, 1973).

An awareness of each of these independent variables, within the context of specific plans for a drug education program, should permit for the maximizing of goal achievements. From a programmatic perspective, such awareness should allow the program developer to set or reassess his goals realistically. Since there can be no drug education program that suits the variety of goals, audiences, media, sites of programs, etc., program development must be based on setting realistic priorities. The scope of a given program and the associated priorities should be set before the program is carried out and not rationalized retrospectively. Table 8.2 can be used as a simple guideline by drug education program developers, so as to assure them that they have indeed adequately considered those factors and issues that they are able to – given budget, staff, program site, and goal, temporal, and target audience considerations.

It should be obvious, given the complexities of each of these independent variables and the great difficulty in effectively controlling any of them, that awareness of what they are is not equivalent to a cookbook recipe approach to their most effective utilization. As has been discussed elsewhere in this chapter, education is not a controllable event; rather it is a continuously developing and unfolding process about which there is much that is still unknown. It may even turn out, in our age of needing to predict and control, that some parts of education are simply unknowable.

It is important that we recognize that facts per se are insufficient. Just as man does not live by bread alone, there is little evidence that he lives by facts alone. Indeed, if we did, not only should there be less drug misuse by now, bombarded as we are by drug prevention programs, but the drug education programs should have significantly changed by now. Instead we are simply doing more variations of the same fact-oriented theme. And we insist on calling it education or, at times, prevention.

Table 8.2. Independent Factors Affecting
Drug Education Program Effectiveness

Source Factors:	Expertness (knowledge, status, values, interests, ethnicity, age, drug use-misuse experience and status)
	Reliability
	Intentions
	Activeness
	Personal attractiveness
	The majority opinion of the listener's associates
Message Factors:	Content (one-sided, two-sided, multi-faceted, fear arousing, neutral)
Channel Factors:	Medium impact
	Exposure time
Receiver Factors:	Age
	Sex
	Intelligence
	Education level
	Anxiety
	Active versus passive participation
	Level(s) of suggestability
	Drug use-misuse status and experience
Destination Factors:	Longevity of effect and rate(s) of decay
	Sleeper effects
	Behavior committment
	Behavior change orientation
	Attitude change orientation

Much confusion continues to exist in distinguishing between education and training. In simplistic terms, education is a process by which a heterogeneous group becomes the focus of certain goals and techniques and terminates this process as a heterogeneous group. Training, on the other hand, is a process by which a heterogeneous group is aided in becoming a homogeneous one for specific skills, abilities, attitudes, values, etc.

This distinction is no minor one as programs attempt to reinforce certain patterns of drug use and inhibit others. Do we need or want heterogeneous or homogeneous groups of citizens in regard to the use and misuse of all drugs? Do we need drug aware and sensitized citizens or simply maximally functioning friends, neighbors, and family? What criteria should be developed, if any, to screen in and screen out individuals from drug-related education programs of any type? These are just some of the issues that must be confronted when we begin to consider drug related education programs for a given population.

The third assumption is that doing a one-time drug survey (which all too often passes for the epidemiology of drug use) on a selected and/or captive sample of high school or college students will put the stamp of research on the educational efforts (Berg, 1970). The reality is that the usable, longitudinal, epidemiological drug study is a rare entity (Einstein & Allen, 1972). Data from most current studies are most often used to bolster or challenge policy-making decisions and procedures and have little to do with developing usable prevention program content, or changing whatever is currently being used. At issue is using research as a scapegoat or holding operation in order to avoid coming to terms with what prevention programs can be and should be.

For example, discerning the current pattern(s) of and types of drug use, and the general and specific drug-related knowledge that a group of eleventh graders have may be useful in setting priorities for covering facts about certain drugs, correcting myths, etc., but does not really relate to developing a meaningful and necessary prevention process. This is basically so because the drug-related data that is collected is too limiting to be of use for the broader areas that prevention must necessarily cover.

At issue, then, is working out the usable relationships between research generally, epidemiological research specifically, and prevention (Johnson, 1968; Smart & Fejer, 1974).

The Funding-Program Syndrome

Drug prevention, education, and training programs have increasingly become commercialized, and more often than not have suffered as a result. There is little question that we are experiencing a drug education boom in terms of monies spent on salaries and materials (DeLone, 1972).

With the advent of the Federal Drug Education Act of 1970, the U.S. Office of Education spent $13 million in 1972 on drug education. A part of the one billion dollar budget of the White House Special Action Office for Drug Abuse Prevention (SAODAP) went toward drug education. Twenty-three million dollars was committed by New York state's legislature to school drug prevention programs during 1971/72. The United States Armed Services are presently running prevention programs for servicemen and their dependents as is the U.S. Veterans Administration System.

The field has become flooded with specialized newsletters and journals; film companies and book publishers are quite literally turning out drug related materials weekly, the "specials" on the mass media are so frequent that they no longer are special, and the drug scene has become a common topic of commercial films (Tagi, 1972). Corporations such as Lockheed Aircraft Corporation (Lockheed Education System,

1969), 3M and Westinghouse have invested heavily in drug education. Two trends have become quite clear —

1. If there is a message — written, spoken, or visual — and in some way it relates to drugs, we call it drug education and by extrapolation, drug prevention. In this process evaluation is blatently missing. Indeed, in what was a major ongoing evaluation of drug films, done through the National Coordinating Council for Drug Education by a rather large review team (of which I was a member), the vast majority of films were found to suffer from factual errors, stereotypy, irrelevance, racism, and age level inappropriateness. The council suggested that there be a national moratorium on the production of drug literature and materials. The National Education Association, after a yearlong study, concluded that the norm for drug education is "deplorable instruction," "teachers and administrators who fail to recognize the problem," and "misinformation" disseminated through "superficial education processes" (DeLone, 1972). Similarly in Great Britain, the publication in October 1972 of Drugs and the Schools, which was to be a major drug education resource for "teachers, lecturers in colleges of education and their students" was evaluated in the following ways: "not only unenlightening, but at times positively misleading" (DeLone, 1972).

2. If a program is not successful, it is because of inadequate funding rather than the processes, goals, techniques, staff, audience specificity, etc. This is generally based on the simplistic notion that one can buy one's way out of a problem. The irony of this is that, as we attempt to financially buy our way out of the nonmedical use of drugs, we often challenge the drug users effort to chemically buy his way into or out of particular lifestyle adaptations. As it turns out, both these ways are unrealistic because what we seek to buy cannot be bought with the exchange medium being used.

In order to most effectively harness the various media, both as process and technique for drug education efforts, we must understand what they can or cannot do and what roles they should and can play.

Media-Related Issues

Following is a brief overview of various media-related issues that should be taken into account in the planning and carrying out of media-based drug education efforts.

The appropriate use of any medium for drug education efforts must be based upon acknowledging —

1. The unique differences between each of the media, as well as the unique characteristics of the individuals utilizing specific media at specific times.

2. The relationship between the various needs that individuals seek gratification for, via the media, and the differential ability of the various media to gratify these needs.

3. That no one medium, by itself, should be expected to represent the total answer to serving the needs and interests of its many diverse audiences.

4. That the media has three primary functions – gratifying the individual, connecting him to society, and serving as a reality-based catalytic agent.

5. That there are functional alternatives to the more formal media.

The most appropriate use of any given medium, for any given goal, or set of goals, is contingent upon understanding what it does and how it functions. Within the context of this chapter "media" is construed to mean any formal process that disseminates information or entertainment to segments of the population, or that can affect their information needs.

A major criticism of most drug education efforts that have been carried out to date is that they have not been sensitive to the strengths and weaknesses of the techniques being used, the strengths and weaknesses of the audiences for which these programs have been developed, or the present and future needs of these audiences.

Classification of the Media

The choice of a particular medium for a drug education program can be immensely aided by classifying the various media. The following simple classification can serve as a guideline to help us understand which specific medium, or combination thereof, are best suited for the drug education goals and audiences one wishes to reach.

The media may be classified in the following ways:

1. Mode of transmission
   a. Electronic
   b. Print
   c. Personal communication, or group communication

2. Mode of reception
   a. TV and films – listening and watching
   b. Radio – listening
   c. Newspapers and books – reading
   d. Lectures, seminars, workshops, meetings – listening and watching

3. Extent to which distance is overcome (inner and outer orientation)

a. Books – self-orientation
b. TV and films – social orientation
c. Newspapers and radio – world orientation

4. Skills and abilities of recipients
   a. Educational abilities – TV is more important for the lesser educated
   b. Perceptual abilities (seeing, hearing, etc.)
   c. Mobility

5. Functions of the media
   a. Gratifier – attracts and holds audiences
   b. Contents effects – satisfies social, psychological, and cognitive needs
   c. Frame of reference effects – the media relates to the self, social environment, and society at large.

6. Agent of:
   a. Diversion
   b. Entertainment
   c. Information
   d. Influence

Needs and Functions to be Satisfied

The success of any specific medium, or combination of media, is dependent upon an understanding fo the specific types of audience or recipient needs that can and must be met, along with the previously mentioned factors.

The minimal needs and functions to be satisfied by the media are:

1. Cognitive needs – strengthening information, knowledge, and understanding
2. Affective needs – strengthening aesthetic, pleasurable, and emotional experiences
3. Integrative needs – strengthening credibility, confidence, stability, and status
4. Social integrative function – strengthening contact with family, friends, and the world
5. Separative function – weakening contact with self, others, and the world (i.e, escapism, tension-reduction, etc.)

Theoretically, as well as from a contemporary empirical basis, one can conclude that various individual needs are associated with different kinds of media, depending upon the specific functions that are involved.

Utilization of the media vis-a-vis issues and problems relating to the use and misuse of drugs must take into consideration the following generalizations:

1. Self-knowledge is best served primarily by books.
2. Pleasure and entertainment are mutually served by TV, films, and books.
3. Self-regulation and self-confidence are best served primarily by the press.
4. National and social issues are best communicated and integrated via the press and radio.

Major Characteristics of Specific Media

The following sections are meant to serve as a quick overview of the major characteristics of the various media that have been used in a variety of drug education efforts. An understanding of these characteristics should be helpful in making appropriate selections of specific media for planning a drug education program as well as to better comprehend why certain programs have succeeded or failed in their goals.

TV

The major characteristics of TV are:

1. combination of sight and sound
2. immediacy
3. intimacy
4. reliance upon the home for utilization
5. use as major source of entertainment, and a source of news
6. relatively high costs
7. time limitations
8. impossibility of involvement in other activities while viewing
9. creation and reinforcement of a passive role for the viewer
10. need for a large staff and high budgets for the creation and production of programs
11. possibility of more active community and individual program development with the advent of half-inch video, cable TV, and public access channels
12. general reinforcement of drug use and misuse-related stereotypes
13. general reinforcement, via advertisements, of the notion that there are chemical solutions to the problems of living

TV is the most diffuse contemporary media, dealing as it does with a wide range of functions.

Radio

The major characteristics of radio are:

1. utilization of sound — which makes it a preferred modality for

groups that must depend upon sound rather than visual images (i.e., segments of the aging population).

2. implantation of mental images in our minds – which permits a more extensive utilization of cognition and fantasy for the listener. This more often than not results in the creation of a sense of electronic companionship which is readily available.
3. nondemand for passivity from the listener.
4. flexibility of its utilization anywhere (i.e., home, work, street, recreational areas, etc.).
5. use as prime electronic medium in most parts of the world.
6. use as a primary source for news and information.
7. relative low costs.
8. minimal time limitations.
9. dependence upon smaller staffs and budgets for programming.
10. mobility and ease in creating and producing programs.
11. relative ease in developing mini-documentaries.
12. possibility of utilizing it as an electronic companion.

In many parts of the world, TV and radio are highly interchangeable.

Print (newspapers and books)

The major characteristics of print are:

1. durability
2. privacy of consumption
3. informative functions
4. cultural functions
5. general focusing upon issues rather than personalities
6. relative ease with which the reader can detach himself emotionally
7. facilitation of discussions and interchanges with others
8. opportunity to reexperience both past and contemporary events
9. function as a tool for daily living
10. use as primary source for news and information
11. relatively high costs
12. reliance upon fairly good eyesight and decent levels of literacy
13. habitual use in a person's lifestyle
14. need for concentration
15. utilization for depth analysis
16. dependence upon a relatively big and varied staff, as well as budget
17. possibility of an active role for the reader (i.e., newspapers)

The major function of the press vis-a-vis drug-related issues has generally been to focus on events and personalities, and has not been one of in-depth analysis of the various factors affecting the use and misuse of drugs and their complicated interrelationships.

Films

The major characteristics of film are:

1. relative durability
2. building and reinforcing social connections
3. primary role and goal of personal enjoyment
4. relatively minor goal vis-a-vis information dissemination (i.e., training and documentation)
5. general focusing upon stories and personalities, not issues
6. relative ease with which the viewer can identify with characters
7. dependence upon hearing and seeing
8. relative high costs to produce
9. dependence upon many skilled personnel to produce
10. reliance upon movie houses and specific centers for utilization
11. time limitations
12. creation and reinforcement of a passive role for the viewer
13. relative high costs to view
14. preferred modality for escapism and tension-reduction
15. impossibility for involvement in other activities while viewing
16. relative lack of tradition in many parts of the world to use as a tool for social documentation
17. general reinforcement of drug use-related stereotypes
18. general presentation of the image of social acceptance of the use of various chemicals (i.e., alcohol, cigarettes)
19. relative lack of scientifically reliable, well-put-together "drug" films that are audience specific (suitable for specific audiences and/or ages) and age specific

Adult education

The major characteristics of adult education are:

1. satisfaction of both new and old adaptational needs
2. dependence upon special time considerations
3. reliance upon factors relating to attention and literacy
4. reliance upon specific sites
5. budgetary considerations regarding: staff, sites, and materials
6. dependence upon well-trained, regionally available staffs for planning and coordination
7. dependence upon regionally available staff for the actual programs
8. possibility of utilizing the material again via electronic, film, or printed reproduction
9. dependence upon sufficient materials and tools that are in working order and that are kept in working order
10. use as source of information, training, education, and leisure time adaptation
11. selectivity of the audience
12. use as catalyst for individual and community change

Public lectures

The major characteristics of public lectures are:

1. satisfaction of sociopolitical needs
2. reliance upon factors relating to attention
3. reliance upon specific sites (i.e., centers, halls, etc.)
4. involvement of politicization, vested interests vis-a-vis sponsorship of many public lectures
5. relatively low costs
6. possible time limitations
7. dependence upon small staffs and budgets for planning and programming
8. dependence upon speakers who may vary greatly in terms of knowledge, credibility, and delivery
9. possibility of utilizing the material again via electronic or film reproduction
10. use as source of information
11. selectivity of the audience
12. use as catalyst for audience action

The major function of public lectures is that of topically related information dissemination. One should keep in mind, however, that participating in public meetings is very much culturally and experientially bound.

FROM DEFINITIONS TO EDUCATION-TRAINING TO PREVENTION

Just as many of the younger generation are now attempting to live a life that goes beyond drugs, we must go beyond definitions to key issues and toward tentative decisions and conclusions. The failure of most drug education-training intervention is due to the fact that evaluation of what is needed is almost nonexistent, goal setting for the program is most often a myth, the roles of the constituents of the program are not clearly thought out, or are confusing; the actual site of drug abuse education is rarely considered in the planning stages of a program, the modalities and materials being used may have little relevance to the initial evaluation or goals, and may be misunderstood by the program developers; there is little, if any, ongoing evaluation during the process, follow-up is a myth, and prevention, as a concept, most often has little to do with offering the participants and the people they serve viable alternatives to the pressures and pleasures that they experience or wish to experience chemically (Cohen, 1971; Edwards, 1972; Einstein et al., 1971; Goodstadt, 1974; Smart & Fejer, 1974).

Obviously there are different models of drug prevention and drug education that are possible, each one having its own associated set of processes and consequences. It is suggested, however, that there are common denominators to most drug prevention programs and that they should not be significantly different from other types of prevention programs.

Planning and carrying out a drug prevention program should include the following steps:

1. Determination of the scope of the program in terms of what is to be prevented and what is to be reinforced; the types of drugs to be focused upon; the patterns of drug use to be included, the viable alternatives that can realistically be offered; the drug and nondrug-related issues to be raised (i.e., drug misuse, social pharmacology, anomie, etc.); and the specificity of the audience that is to be reached. The greater the heterogeneity of the group, the greater the possibility of coming to terms with the various options and roles that are available for prevention specifically and intervention generally, including the problems associated with them, and the less likely that participants will go home continuing to feel bored, frustrated, helpless, isolated, or even exploited. A heterogeneous group should be better able to focus on issues rather than on dogma, which should result in openness rather than on parochialism.

2. Development of baseline data relevant to the incidence and prevalence of drug use and misuse, and attitudes about drugs, drug misuse, and drug misusers. Without this type of data, the program may get bogged down in concepts and theories that have little to do with the drug-related health needs and lifestyle adaptational needs of a given community or being able to anticipate them for the near future. Baseline data are also needed to assess the general strengths and weaknesses of a group and their community. Without this information, prevention efforts may be unrealistic or irrelevant.

3. Agreement upon data and the associated meanings that relate to the state of knowledge about what drugs do and do not do, and what people and communities can and cannot do. Prevention is not meant to reinforce mythology or dysfunctional, ritualistic intervention.

4. Development of a program goal system that pinpoints the various levels of acceptable program-related behavioral alternatives to drug misuse. The goal system should meet the minimal criteria of being meaningful, achievable, and acceptable to those being educated, acceptable to the educator and the general community, and flexible to all concerned. Selection of goals should be related to the value systems of a given constituency, their actual and imputed roles and status, and their needs in the present and the immediate future. A program without clearly delineated goals is not a program; at best it is systematized activity. A program that does not include in its format the concepts of roles, consequences, continuity of prevention-intervention, and responsibility is at best a gathering or meeting and not an educational experience. Table 8.3 is an example of one model of a goal system.

Table 8.3. A Proposed Goal System for Drug Education Programs

Types of Goals	Evaluation	Purpose/Consequence
Healthier Drug Misuse		Evaluation indicates that drug misuse pattern changes are unlikely in the present or near future. This goal focuses on training the individual and/or group in the most healthy use of the particular drug (i.e., sterilization of needles, etc.)
Drug Misuse Dimunition		Evaluation indicates that the level of functioning has become increasingly inadequate over time and is specifically drug related. The goal is minimizing the drug misuse in order to control the dysfunctional behavior.
Drug Substitution		Evaluation indicates that the level of functioning has been on a healthier level prior to drug misuse and that there has been a history of socially acceptable drug use. The goal is to achieve the previous level of satisfactory functioning with socially acceptable drug use through drug substitution.
Social Pharmacology		Evaluation indicates a generally satisfactory level of functioning with occasional drug misuse. The goal is to reinforce the present level of satisfactory functioning and to reinforce socially and medically approved drug use.
Going Beyond Drugs		Evaluation indicates unutilized strengths and skills within a context of rare drug use and/or misuse. Going beyond drugs will permit the learning of viable nondrug alternatives to the problems and pleasures of living.

5. Relating drug prevention to formal and informal education which prepares those being educated to a life of people-oriented issues and daily decision making that focuses on alternatives and values rather than on a life of drug-oriented issues that focus only on certain types of people and drugs and dangers.

6. Role definition for all the participants in the prevention program so that each one knows what is expected of him, and what his boundaries and limitations are to be. Concepts such as continuity of prevention and continuity of responsibility are associated with this step.

7. Determination of the techniques, modalities, and materials to be used so that choice of the media used is reality based and not chance or expediency based. That a coordinated effort is assured, the program's limitations can be made manageable, its strengths maintained or reinforced, and its outcome can be evaluated. This should be done in relation to the goals of the program and the strengths, weaknesses, and roles of the participants, the media processes, and techniques.

8. Selection of the appropriate site of prevention programs so that choice is related to the initial evaluation, goal selection, role definitions, and the techniques and materials being used rather than based on the notions of availability, captive audiences, institutional mandates, or other less than relevant factors.

9. Ongoing reevaluation in order to assess whether the program should be continued, modified, or terminated; goals maintained or changed; roles maintained or changed; techniques shifted or maintained; materials revised, maintained, or dropped; site of the program shifted or maintained; and whether the resources necessary for effective prevention are present and being utilized, are absent and are needed, or are adequate or inadequate.

10. Follow-up evaluation at specific intervals after the program has been completed in order to determine the effects of the program.

Table 8.4 is designed as a convenient checklist for program developers to aid them in remembering what program factors are to be considered.

All of the aforementioned is contingent upon our acknowledging that there is no such thing as the prevention program, and that all such programs are affected by temporal and geographical considerations. A program for here and now may be inappropriate for here and tomorrow, or for that matter anywhere else tomorrow. Obviously, since programs are man-made, they must be man-tailored, rather than viewed as being the oracles of Delphi, or, indeed, the Lord's design.

Table 8.4. Developing a Drug Abuse Prevention Program – A Schematic Checklist

	Goals	Content	Roles	Process-Techniques			Resources
		facts, attitudes, skills		printed media	electronic media	individual group presentations	
Participants:							
Strengths							
Weaknesses							
Needs							
Intervention and Teaching Community:							
Strengths							
Weaknesses							
Needs							
General Community:							
Strengths							
Weaknesses							
Needs							

A Framework for the Development of
A Continuing Drug Prevention Program

The initial, practical decision that has to be made in developing a drug prevention program has to do with the type of drug abuse we are most concerned about, or if we are concerned about all three types (abuse of laws and mores, self-abuse, abuse of others), giving priorities to each one, and the type and quality of individual and community functioning we wish to reinforce or inhibit.

The next step is to decide upon the focus of intervention. We have the choice of focusing our efforts on:

1. drugs themselves
2. abstainers, be they individuals who have never used or misused drugs, or those who have ceased their misuse
3. active drug misusers
4. intervention agents and programs, be they individuals doing treatment, teachers, school administrators, clergy, law enforcement representatives, media representatives, parents, peers, counterculture representatives, etc.
5. the general community

The next decision facing us has to do with the content of the possible intervention. Now that we have decided upon the type of drug abuse we wish to affect, and what our primary focus is to be, we can come to terms with the direction of our efforts. Acknowledging that the direction or content areas that we select are arbitrary ones we nevertheless should consider the following potential areas:

1. Physiological Health
2. Psychological Health
3. Social Health
4. Physical-Chemical Adaptation
5. Spatial Adaptation
6. Temporal Adaptation
7. Cultural Adaptation
8. Religious Adaptation
9. Political Adaptation
10. Economic Adaptation

These ten content areas serve to remind us that all of us must somehow come to terms with our physio-psycho-social selves and needs, as well as with the physical-chemical world, space and time, and the pressures of cultural, religious, political, and economic considerations.

Table 8.5 is created by this type of consideration and permits us to consider what we can and cannot do as we attempt to affect man's appetites and thereby effect a change in his modes of adaptation. It also permits us to consider what our responsibilities and limitations are for each cell, so that we do not become bogged down by the enormity of the initial task and then do the most current thing – turn to the drug expert.

Table 8.5. Alternatives to Drug Abuse by Type, Focus of Intervention, and Areas of Adaptation

	Physiological Health	Psychological Health	Social Health	Physical-Chemical Adaptation	Spatial Adaptation
Abuse of drug laws, mores, rituals	Drugs Abstainers Active drug users Intervention agents General community				
Self-abuse	Drugs Abstainers Active drug users Intervention Agents General community				
Abuse of others	Drugs Abstainers Active drug users Intervention agents General community				

Table 8.5. (cont'd.)

	Temporal Adaptation	Cultural Adaptation	Religious Adaptation	Political Adaptation	Economic Adaptation
Abuse of drug laws, mores, rituals	Drugs Abstainers Active drug users Intervention agents General community				
Self-abuse	Drugs Abstainers Active drug users Intervention agents General community				
Abuse of others	Drugs Abstainers Active drug users Intervention agents General community				

An analysis of this table allows us to understand that none of these ten content areas have inherent high priority attached to them. Rather, by choosing any of them we are serving notice that this is our arbitrary choice, as we seek to create meaningful, achievable alternatives to drug abuse. But once we have chosen a particular area, based on careful thought rather than a hope for a panacea or total solution, we should have better results with it than has been the general experience to date.

For example, that program planning is necessary and possible if our concern is an individual's or group's social health, while focusing upon active drug misusers, as we attempt to limit or eradicate drug related self-abuse? Obviously one possibility is learning how to challenge the active drug users ability to achieve those values or goals that are important to him through drugs only. It is the rare goal or value that can be achieved and/or experienced only through the use of drugs.

If a program that is being planned cannot come up with the content or the faculty for a particular cell, then we should plan to focus on areas or cells that permit us to effectively utilize the available expertise, time, and energy that is at hand. The rule of thumb is not that something is better than nothing. Nothing is nothing! This type of analysis of a continuous drug prevention program is no more than a suggested approach. It obviously is not a guide to the do's and don'ts of drug abuse prevention. Rather it offers all of us, with our many roles, statuses, and relationships a framework which we can add to or delete from, while permitting us to decide what role prevention can and may play in a contemporary problem area that continues to be colored by ambiguities and hysteria.

Drug Training Programs As Part of Prevention

Returning to the operational definition that training assumes the changing of a heterogeneous group into a homogeneous one, in terms of knowledge, attitudes, skills, etc., one has to consider that there are three major groups that can become the focus of drug-related training. These include the active drug user, intervention agents, and the general community.

The active drug user

Traditionally, the kind of information given to the drug user has concerned itself with either the dangers associated with drug use in general, the use of specific drugs, or the legal consequences related to drug use.

Given that many people may continue to use drugs for nonmedical reasons, irrespective of communities' intervention, drug training may impart other kinds of knowledge and skills. These include information concerning: 1) the kinds of private and community resources available in a specific area, and how to utilize them, 2) whether drugs have been adulterated with poisonous materials, 3) what entails a proper and effective referral, 4) the rights one has particularly in terms of protecting oneself from becoming jeopardized (i.e., urine testing, drug-related "eye tests," civil commitment). The priority prevention goal for active drug users is to prevent them from dying, physically, psychologically, socially, etc. We should be helped to delineate other issues by which we can be of significant help to the drug user.

Intervention agents

More often than not the knowledge imparted to the intervention agent has tended to reinforce the notion that there is a specific type of person known as a drug addict; that certain drugs are dangerous and implicitly others are less so; that a drug problem in a given community simply consists of certain people using certain drugs; and that the three avenues open for effective intervention are treatment, education, and the law and that any of these interventions are inherently logical and good and their failure should be attributed to the drug user. The training of intervention agents who are to be <u>permitted</u> to work in the field of drug abuse should go beyond the content areas of <u>drugs</u> (type, frequency, patterns, meaning), <u>characteristics</u> of the drug user, and <u>consequences</u> of drug use, to include a base level of knowledge of the following areas:

1. Research
   a. theories of drug use
   b. theories of drug action
   c. theories of treatment
   d. theories of human development
   e. theories of communication
   f. classification of medications – social substances
   g. classification of drug users
   h. classification of nondrug users
   i. the role of research in prevention

2. Treatment
   a. types of programs
   b. evaluation procedures
   c. goal systems
   d. available treatment modalities
   e. evaluation
   f. policies and procedures affecting treatment
   g. professional and nonprofessional roles, responsibilities, and obligations
   h. criteria for treatment agents
   i. drug misuser roles
   j. follow-up systems

3. Attitudes and Values Toward Drug Use, Misuse, and the Drug User
   a. intervention staff
   b. general community

     c. drug users and misusers
     d. policy makers and decision makers
     e. the media

4. Public Policy Relating to Intervention
     a. laws
     b. policies
     c. procedures

5. Economics of Drug Use
     a. licit factors
     b. illicit factors

6. The Politics of Drug Use Intervention
     a. intervention as a political activity
     b. drug misuse as a political issue
     c. the geopolitics of drug use and misuse

7. Education
     a. nondrug-related alternatives
     b. drug-related alternatives
     c. decision making
     d. respect for people
     e. respect for drugs
     f. respect for feelings
     g. built-in inequities of living
     h. role definitions, associated responsibilities, and consequences
     i. theories of education

8. Philosophy
     a. nondrug-related alternatives
     b. drug-related alternatives
     c. celebrating life

9. Religion
     a. nondrug-related rituals
     b. drug-related rituals
     c. celebrating life
     d. altered states of consciousness

10. Culture
     a. drug and nondrug-related and oriented literature
     b. drug and nondrug-related and oriented music and songs
     c. drug cultures

11. Patterns of Adaptation
     a. roles
     b. meanings
     c. decision-making factors
     d. consequences

    e. personal and community responsibilities

12. Mass Media
    a. people-oriented patterns of living
    b. drug-oriented patterns of living
    c. media modalities, processes, and variables

13. Other Intervention
    a. early case finding
    b. prevention
    c. drug user registration systems and consequences

These areas should not be covered simply in terms of empirically based facts relating each of them to the issues of drug use and prevention, but should also include the generic issues of roles, responsibilities, consequences, and meanings. The major outcome of this type of training is to be the creation of a cadre of intervention agents who know why they are doing what they are doing to whom, under what circumstances, and who have a realistic idea as to the kinds of outcomes, and what options are available if their original intervention is not successful. Only after an individual has himself been adequately trained in each of these facets, can he begin to take an active role as a source of information dissemination based on his areas of actual strengths and not based on his imputed strengths, status, or drug or nondrug-related history.

The general community

The general community has all too often been led to believe that drug abuse is a unique behavior which is best left to drug experts (i.e., physicians, law enforcement agents, ex-addicts, etc.) whose efforts the community must fund. Aside from receiving training similar to the intervention agent, the general community must be helped to understand:

1. In what ways does a community reinforce the use and misuse of drugs?

2. In what ways does a community inhibit the use and misuse of drugs;

3. What are the viable roles, and their associated consequences and limitations, open to a community as a whole as well as to its individual constituents, for a given type and quality of lifestyle?

4. What are the gaps in resources and services as well as what duplication of effort exists in a community?

In a sense the training for the general community should lead to one major conclusion: The community deserves the type of human, environmental, and chemical adaptation that it permits. The end result of such training should be a coming to terms with social pharmacology as well as drug abuse by defining and giving priorities to role definitions for all concerned, and for various intervention efforts (see Table 8.6).

The traditional assumption of focusing most prevention programs only on specific groups, such as the adolescent, the anomic, or populations-at-risk, can only interfere with the achieving of realistic goals. Adolescents, for example, as a psychosocial age group are involved in much testing of themselves, things, and people around them. It is not drug prevention that they need. Rather it is maturity facilitation with its major component of healthy identity. Secondly, it has yet to be demonstrated that adolescents are a given society's or community's major drug users and misusers. If prevention efforts are

Table 8.6. Drug-Related Prevention and Education-Training
Programs and Some Derived Consequences

	Models	
	Prevention	Education-Training
Process	Socialization and resocialization	Educational processes and training techniques
Drug-related focus	Social pharmacology	Drug misuse limited
General focus	Broad, nondrug related	Drug related
Theoretical assumption about types of drug users	Heterogeneous	Homogeneous
Theoretical assumptions about drug use etiology	Identification with social and religious rituals	Social-psychological pathology
Role of participants	Active	Passive
Types of staff	Socialization representatives	Skilled technicians
Successful outcome	Maximizing individual and community potential (i.e., going beyond drugs)	Specific types of drug abstinence (i.e., redefining drugs and drug use)

related to social pharmacology, as they should be, then the entire population is in potential need and is deserving of these efforts. Lastly, prevention is not meant to save particular people or groups. Crisis intervention, emergency care, and triage medicine are most appropriate for that. Prevention is meant to facilitate agreed upon desirable outcomes unencumbered by the real pressures for the immediate saving of individual or community life.

This chapter has presented an overview of various issues related to drug prevention, attempting to distinguish the process of prevention from those of education and the techniques and goals of training. It is purposely not a blueprint for the most efficacious drug prevention program since such a program could only be a static one when indeed the use and misuse of drugs, as well as the nondrug alternatives, are in a dynamic state of flux.

> Blessings often come in the disguise of a curse. A new curse threatens the life of America, the infatuation with drug culture. I interpret the escape to drugs as coming from the need for experiencing moments of exaltation. Man is in need of relaxation but he is also in need of exaltation. He cannot live on sedatives alone. He is in vital need of stimulants. In search of exaltation man is ready to burn Rome, even to destroy himself. It is very difficult for a human being to live on the same level, shallow, placid, repetitious, uniform, ordinary, unchanged.
>
> We, having shaped our lives around the practical, the utilitarian, devoid of dreams and vision, higher concerns and enthusiasms, are literally driving young people into the inferno of drug culture in search of exaltation.
>
> The sickness of our technological civilization has at last reached our consciousness, although the depths of that sickness still have not been plumbed.
>
> Man is born to be concerned with ultimate issues. When he refuses to care, he ceases to be human.

Abraham Joshua Heschel

REFERENCES

Aubrey, R.F. School-Community Drug Prevention Programs. Personnel & Guidance Journal 1, 1971, 17-24.

Barber, B. Drugs & Society. New York: Russell Sage Foundation, 1967.

Barnes, D.E. & Messolonghites, L. Prevention of Drug Abuse. New York: Holt, Rhinehart & Winston, 1972.

Berg, D. The Non-medical Use of Dangerous Drugs in the United States. International Journal of the Addictions, 5:4, 777-834, 1970.

Bogg, R.A., Smith, R.G. & Russell, D. Drugs and Michigan High School Students. Final Report of a Study Conducted by the Special Committee on Narcotics, Michigan Department of Public Health, 1968.

Cazalas, M.W. Addiction in the United States. A medical-legal history. Loyola Law Review, Vol XVIII, No. 1, 1971-72, 1-21.

Clark, W.H. Chemical Ecstasy. New York: Sheed & Ward, 1969.

Cohen, A.Y. The Journey Beyond Trips: Alternatives to Drugs. Journal of Psychedelic Drugs, 3:2, 16-21, 1971.

Common Sense Lives Here: A Community Guide to Drug Abuse Action. A Project of the National Coordinating Council on Drug Abuse Education and Information, Washington, D.C., 1971.

Dawtry, F., (ed.): Social Problems of Drug Abuse. New York: Appleton, Century, Crofts, 1968.

DeLone, R.H. The ups and downs of drug abuse education. Saturday Review of Education, November 11, 1972.

Doerr, Dale, Kabat, Hugh F., Sheffield, William J., and Skinner, William J. On the Campus — Drug Abuse Programs. Journal of the American Pharmaceutical Association, Vol. NS7, No. 9, September, 1967.

Drug Abuse: A Reference for Teachers. N.J. Department of Education, Trenton, N.J., 1969.

Edwards, G. Reaching Out: The Prevention of Drug Abuse Through Increased Human Interaction. New York: Holt, Rhinehart & Winston, 1972.

Einstein, S. Beyond Drugs. New York: Pergamon Publishing Co., 1975.

Einstein, S., & Allen, M. (ed.) Student Drug Surveys. Farmingdale, New York: Baywood Publishing Co., 1972.

Einstein, S. et al. The training of teachers for drug abuse education programs: Preliminary considerations. J. Drug Ed., Vol. 1 (4), December, 1971.

Eiseman, S. Education about Narcotics and Dangerous Drugs — A Challenge to our Schools. Journal of Drug Education, 1971, 1, 177-185.

Erikson, E. Identity: Youth & Crisis. New York: W.W. Norton & Co., 1968.

Erikson, E. (ed.) Youth: Change & Challenge. New York: Basic Books, 1963.

Fejer, D. Smart, R.G., Whitehead, P.C., LaForest L. Sources of Information About Drugs Among High School Students. The Public Opinion Quarterly, 35, 1971, 235-241.

Fort, Joel The Pleasure Seekers. New York: Bobbs-Merrill, 1969.

Glasser, D. & Snow, M. Public Knowledge and Attitudes on Drug Abuse in New York State, N.Y.S. Narcotic Addiction Control Commission, New York, 1969.

Goodstadt, M. (ed.) Research on Methods and Programs of Drug Education, Alcoholism and Drug Addiction Research Foundation of Ontario, Toronto, Canada, 1974.

Hills, S.L. Marijuana, Mortality & the Law. Crime & Delinquency, Vol. 16, No. 1, 57-66, 1970.

Horan, John J. and Swisher, John D. Effective Drug Attitude Change in College Students via Induced Cognitive Dissonance, Pennsylvania State University. Paper presented at annual meeting of Educational Research Association, April 6, 1972.

Houlard, C.I. & Weiss, W. The Influences of Source Credibility on

Communication Effectiveness. Public Opinion Quarterly, 15, 1951, 635-650.

Jeffee, S. Narcotics – An American Plan. New York: Paul S. Eriksson, 1970.

Johnson, Barbara B. A Junior High School Seminar on Dangerous Drugs. The Journal of School Health, Vol. 38, No. 2, February, 1968, pp. 83-87.

Kinsella, J.K. Confidentiality and Drug Education. The International Journal of Addiction, 6, 1971, 609-614.

Kitzinger, A. Drug abuse education in California. California Teachers Association, Southern Section, The Valuator, Spring, 1969.

Kolodny, J. Disagreement among experts leaves editors at sea.   The United Teacher Magazine, M-1-M4, May 7, 1972.

Lavenhahr, M. & Sheffet, A. Recent trends in non-medical use of drugs reported by students in two suburban New Jersey communities. Preventive Medicine, 2, 490-509, 1973.

Lawler, John T. Peer Group Approach to Drug Education. Journal of Drug Education, Vol. 1 (1), pp. 63-76, March, 1971.

Le Dain, G. Canadian Commission of Inquiry into the Non-medical use of Drugs, Treatment, Ottowa, Ontario, Canada, 1972.

Leech, K. & Jordan, B. Drugs for young people: Their use and misuse. Oxford, England: Religious Education Press, 1967.

Lennard & Associates. Mystification & Drug Misuse. San Francisco: Jossey Bass, 1971.

Lewis, Jerry M., et al. Evaluation of a Drug Education Program, Hospital and Community Psychiatry, April, 1972.

Lindesmith, A. The Addict & the Law. New York: Vintage Books, 1967.

Lockheed Education Systems. Drug Decision. Lockheed Aircraft Corporation, California, 1969.

Manheimer, D.I. & Mellinger, G.D. Marijuana use among urban adults. Science, Vol. 166, December 19, 1969.

Marin, P. and Cohen, A. Understanding Drug Use: An Adults Guide to Drugs and the Young. New York: Harper & Row, 1971.

Marin, G.L. & O'Rourke, T.W. The Perceived Effectiveness of Selected Programs and Sources with Respect to Preventing the Use of Dangerous Drugs. Journal of Drug Education, 1972, 2, 329-335.

Mcguire, W.J. Designing Communications to Change Attitudes Regarding Drug Abuse. In Wittenborn, J.R., Smith, J.P., and Wittenborn, S.A. (eds.) Communications and Drug Abuse Proceedings of the Second Rutgers Symposium on Drug Abuse. Springfield, Illinois: Charles C. Thomas Publishers, 1970.

Mcguire, W.J. The Nature of Attitudes and Attitude Change. In Lindzey, G. and Aronson, E. (eds.) The Handbook of Social Psychology, Vol. III, Addison-Wesley Publishing Co., USA, 1969.

Middlemiss, H.S. (ed.) H.S. Middlemiss. Narcotic Education, Columbian Building, Washington, D.C., 1926.

Monk, Mary; Tayback, Matthew; and Gordon, Joseph. Evaluation of an Anti-smoking Program among High School Students, Program Evaluation in the Health Fields. New York: Behavior Publications, 1969.

National Commission on Marijuana and Drug Abuse, Drug Use in

America: Problem in Perspective. Second Report of the National
    Commission on Marijuana & Drug Abuse, U.S. Government Printing
    Office, Washington, 1973.
National Commission on Marijuana & Drug Abuse, Marijuana: A Signal
    of Misunderstanding, U.S. Government Printing Office, Washington,
    D.C., 1972.
Drug Education is Linked to Use, New York Times, December 3, 1972.
Nowalk, Dorothy. Innovations in Drug Education. Journal of School
    Health, Vol. 38, No. 2, February, 1968, pp. 83-87.
Nowlis, S. Drugs on the College Campus: A Guide for College
    Administrators. National Association of Student Personnel Admin-
    istrators, Detroit, Michigan, 1967.
Nowlis, H.H. Some assumptions implicit in a variety of drug education
    and information programs. In Wittenborn et al. (eds.), Communica-
    tion & Drug Abuse, Springfield, Illinois: Charles C. Thomas, 1970.
Panzica, N. Effect of Communication Background on Credibility.
    Journal of Drug Education, 1973, 3, 95-106.
Polloch, Marion B. An Evaluation Instrument to Appraise Knowledge and
    Behavior Regarding Use of Stimulants and Depressants. The Re-
    search Quarterly, Vol. 39, No. 3, pp. 662-667.
Richards, Louise G. Evaluation in Drug Education. School Health
    Review, Vol. 2, No. 3, September, 1971.
Richards, L.G. Psychological sophistication in current drug abuse
    education in Wittenborn, et al. (eds.) Communication & Drug Abuse.
    Springfield, Illinois: Charles C. Thomas, 1970.
Segal, M. Drug Education: Toward a rational approach. International
    Journal of the Addictions, 7:2, 257-284, 1972.
Selected Drug Education Curricula Series, National Clearinghouse for
    Drug Abuse Information, Baltimore County Board of Education
    (Grades 6, 9, 12); Flagstaff Public Schools (Grades K-12): Great Falls
    School District No. 1 (Grade 6); N.Y. State Education Department
    (Grades 4, 5, 6); Rhode Island Department of Education (Grades K-
    12); South Bay Union School District (Grades K-12); Tacoma Public
    Schools (Grades 6-12); Resource Book for Drug Abuse Education,
    U.S. Government Printing Office, Washington, D.C.
Shelvin, Julius B. Effectiveness of Programmed Materials in Teaching a
    Secondary Health Education Unit. The Research Quarterly, Vol. 39,
    No. 3, pp. 704-707.
Smart, R.G. & Fejer, D. Drug Education: Current Issues, Future
    Directions. Addiction Research Foundation of Ontario, Toronto,
    Ontario, 1974.
Smart, R.G. & Krakowski, M. The Nature and Frequency of Drug
    Content in Magazines and on Television. Journal of Alcohol and
    Drug Education, 18, 1973, 16-22.
Smart, R.G. & Whitehead, P.C. The consumption patterns of illicit drugs
    and their implications for prevention of abuse. Bulletin on Narcotics,
    Vol. XXIV, No. 1, 1972.
Smart, R.G. & Fejer, D. Credibility of Sources of Drug Information for
    High School Students. Journal of Drug Issues, 2, 1972, 8-18.
Smart, R.G. Rejection of the Source in Drug Education. Journal of Drug
    Issues, Fall, 1972a, 55-60.

Smart, R.G.; Whitehead, P.J. and LaForest, L. The prevention of drug abuse by young people: an argument based on the distribution of drug use. Bulletin on Narcotics, Vol. XXIII, No. 2, 1971.

Stuart, R.B. Teaching Facts about Drugs: Pushing or Preventing? Unpublished report, University of Michigan, 1973.

Swisher, John D. & Crawford, James, L. An Evaluation of a Short Term Drug Education Program. The School Counselor, March, 1971, pp. 265-272.

Swisher, John D. and Horman, Richard E. Drug Abuse Prevention. The Journal of College Student Personnel, September, 1970, pp. 337-341.

Swisher, John D.; Warner, Richard W.; and Herr, Edwin L. Experimental Comparsion of Four Approaches to Drug Abuse Prevention Among Ninth and Eleventh Graders. Journal of Counseling Psychology, Vol. 19, No. 4, pp. 328-332, (1972).

Szasz, T.S. The ethics of addiction. Harpers, April, 1972.

Taqi, S. The Drug Cinema. Bulletin on Narcotics, 24, 1972, 19-29.

Teaching About Drugs, A Curriculum Guide, K-12. American School Health Association and the Pharmaceutical Manufacturers Association, 1971.

To Parents about Drugs. Metropolitan Life Insurance, Co., 1970.

Virgilio, Carmela Louise. A Comparison of the Effects of the School Health Education Study (SHES) Approach and the Lecture-Discussion Approach Upon Drug Knowledge and Attitudes of High School Students. Ed.D Dissertation, Boston University School of Education, 1971. (Photocopy available from Boston University Library at $.20 per page)

Warner, Richard W.; Swisher, John D.; and Horan; John. Drug Abuse Prevention: A Behavioral Approach. Pennsylvania State University 1972 (in press).

Warner, R.W., & Swisher, J.D. Alienation and Drug Abuse: Synonymous. NASSP Bulletin, 1971.

Waterford School's Guide to Drug Education, Waterford School District, Pontiac, Michigan, 48054.

Weil, A. The Natural Mind. New York: Houghton Mifflin, 1972.

Whitehead, P.E. and Smart, R.G. Validity and reliability of self reported drug use. Canadian Journal of Criminology and Corrections, Vol. 14, No. 1, 1972.

Wichita Public Schools. What Parents Should Know About Drugs. Withita, Kansas, Wichita Public Schools, 1970.

Zinberg, N.W. & Robertson, J.S. Drugs and the Public. New York: Simon & Schuster, 1972.

DRUG EDUCATION
ANNOTATED BIBLIOGRAPHY

Book Resources

Blum, R. and Associates Society and Drugs, Vol. 1; Students and Drugs, Vol. 11, San Francisco, Jossey-Bass, 1969.
This two volume series presents an overview of the various factors which are needed to understand the use and misuse of various psychoactive drugs. The reader is helped to understand, historically and currently, changing patterns of drug use by various segments of society.

Child Study Association of America Your Child and Drugs. New York: Child Study Press, 1971.
This slim volume serves to remind us that our concern in drug misuse intervention should be a person and not a stereotype.

DeRopp, R.S. The Master Game: Pathways to Higher Consciousness Beyond the Drug Experience. New York: Dell, 1968.
Written by a bio-chemist, this book explores the various avenues available to man to achieve the highest possible levels of consciousness, and thus to go beyond drugs.

Einstein, S. and Allen, M. Student Drug Surveys. Farmingdale, New York: Baywood Publishing Co. 1972.
The complete Proceedings of the First International Conference on Student Drug Surveys. Discusses why a drug survey should be initiated, how to make the survey, results of various student drug abuse surveys, implications for the student and the school. Contains authoritative papers and sample student drug abuse questionnaires.

Goddstadt, M. (ed.) Research on Methods and Programs of Drug Education. Addiction Research Foundation of Ontario, Toronto, Ont., Canada, 1974.
Based upon an international Symposia held in Toronto in 1973, this compilation of articles focuses upon drug education from both a conceptual and empirical perspective. It is not a "how to do it" book, but rather a "what was done" and "why it was done" work which can be a most useful resource tool for drug education planners and policy makers.

Lennard, H.C. and Associates Mystification and Drug Misuse: Hazards in Using Psychoactive Drugs. San Francisco: Jossey-Bass, 1971.
Sets forth the thesis that today's drug scene must be understood in terms of the mystification of drugs. Accuses the mass media, pharmaceutical industry, medical profession and the youth culture of creating belief in drug oriented life-styles.

Marin, P. and Cohen, A.Y. Understanding Drug Use: An Adult's Guide to Drugs and the Young. New York: Harper and Row, 1971.
The books' central concern is to help parents and other adults understand drug use and to develop realistic alternatives to it. The book focuses on the various meanings of a child's drug use.

Weil, A. The Natural Mind. New York: Houghton Mifflin, 1972.
The thesis is presented that man quite naturally attempts to alter

his state of consciousness through a variety of activities as well as by using various substances in a very convincing way. The challenge to drug education is how to meet this "natural need" in a world full of drugs.

III
Research

9 Methodology in Community Research

M.A. Lavenhar

The great tragedy of science — the slaying of a beautiful hypothesis by an ugly fact.

Thomas Henry Huxley

In response to the problem of widespread illicit drug use in the late 1960s, many communities perceived the need to do something, and to do it quickly. Numerous intervention and prevention programs were instituted in the absence of careful planning and tested hypotheses. A great amount of resources in time, energy, and money has been expended in preventive efforts. As the costs of these programs have spiraled upward, with few apparent successes, the trend has been toward critical assessment of the efficacy of these efforts. Most of the evaluative designs have not been based on objective scientific principles. In those limited cases where scientific methodology has been employed, for the most part the "beautiful" hypotheses of the 1960s have not been supported by the critical findings of the 1970s. As a matter of fact, there is currently little empirical evidence available to demonstrate that community programs have indeed been effective in reducing the problem of drug dependency.

A comprehensive community-based program to combat drug abuse addresses all three levels of prevention, where prevention is used in the epidemiological sense. The different phases of drug abuse prevention can be defined as follows (Smith, et al., 1973):

Primary Prevention: Prevention of drug abuse in a previously uninvolved population.

Secondary Prevention: Prevention of the progression of drug abuse in an involved population which does not as yet have residual disability from its drug usage.

Tertiary Prevention: Rehabilitation of the drug-abusing population which has significant residual disability as a consequence of its drug involvement.

The traditional approach to primary and secondary prevention has been through legislation and law enforcement designed to prevent or reduce drug misuse and through policies aimed at limiting the available supply of drugs. During the drug abuse epidemic of the 1960s, it became apparent that legal sanctions and efforts to limit the supply of drugs were not sufficient to stem the tide of illicit drug use, particularly among the young. Preventive drug education was proposed as a logical alternative or complement to the legal approach. A wide variety of drug education programs has been employed during the past decade, but their impact has rarely been rigorously tested.

Historically, up until the late 1950s, drug addiction was considered to be primarily a problem of "deviants" who could be handled by legal means, and incarceration was regarded as the only appropriate "treatment." In recent years, the trend has been toward treating drug abuse as more of a medical than a criminal problem. Various treatment approaches to tertiary drug abuse prevention have been instituted but few have been scientifically evaluated.

Community planners and policymakers must have knowledge of local drug use patterns in order to evaluate the impact of community drug abuse programs and to allocate resources in an efficient manner. However, at the present time we have no reliable means of estimating the number of people who use or misuse various drugs and their drug-using behavior patterns.

Many questions about drugs cannot be answered in the laboratory or in clinical research. Community research is needed. Unfortunately, it is seldom possible, in the community setting, to attain the level of control provided by scientific experimentation in the laboratory.

The following discussion considers the advantages and limitations of some of the research methodologies that have been or might be used in drug use intervention programs. The focus is upon the community rather than on drugs or drug users. Major emphasis is given to three aspects of community research in the field of drug use – estimating the magnitude of the problem, treatment evaluation, and drug education evaluation.

ESTIMATING THE MAGNITUDE OF THE PROBLEM: INCIDENCE AND PREVALENCE

The task of estimating the extent of illicit drug use, abuse, and addiction in any community has always been, and continues to be, extremely difficult. Because of serious reporting gaps, much of the data needed for estimates are not available; much of the available data are suspect. Other confounding factors include the large number of drugs that are being abused, the variable composition of illicitly produced drugs, the widespread deceptions in the illegal drug market, and the wide range of frequency of use and dosages employed. The latter points to another major obstacle to estimating the scope of illicit drug use — there is no general agreement on what constitutes drug abuse or addiction. Indeed, these terms defy precise definition. Smart (1971) studied the distribution of drug use scores among Canadian high school student drug users and concluded that the distribution was a smooth one (lognormal) with no discontinuities, implying that there is no clear-cut differentiation of drug users into discrete categories (e.g., users, abusers, addicts) on the basis of drug consumption alone.

The two measures most frequently used to characterize the extent of illicit drug use in a community are incidence and prevalence. Incidence pertains to the number of new drug addicts (abusers) that come into being during a specified period of time (e.g., one year). While point prevalence attempts to estimate the number of drug addicts (abusers) on hand at a given point in time, period prevalence describes the number of cases that were observed during a specified period of time (e.g., one year). All three statistics are usually expressed as a rate per 1,000 individuals.

Inasmuch as incidence rates are tied in with onset of illicit drug use, they are important in epidemiological investigations of cause and effect and in studies evaluating the impact of preventive drug education programs. On the other hand, prevalence data are most useful for effective planning and utilization of treatment and rehabilitation facilities. Since incidence and prevalence statistics may be derived from several different sources of information that may have different reporting needs, this leads to wide variability in reporting.

SOURCES OF INCIDENCE AND PREVALENCE DATA

Police Records

Historically this has been the major source of incidence and prevalence estimates even though drug-related arrest data obtained from police records represent only the visible or known drug abuser and provide no indication of those who may not be known to law enforcement agencies. Moreover, arrests are unevenly distributed among different socioeconomic classes and groups. They are concentrated in persons in the lower socioeconomic classes and therefore are likely to grossly underestimate middle and upper-class illicit drug use. Furthermore, police records cannot provide the data needed to estimate the extent of misuse of licit drugs.

Drug Registers

A case register is a system for collecting registration and follow-up information on a population with a particular disease or problem based on cases reported by agencies or individuals (Fishman, Conwell, and Amsel, 1971). Most drug registers have focused upon cases of narcotics addiction.

The U.S. Bureau of Narcotics and Dangerous Drugs (BNDD) maintains a national register of drug addicts that depends on voluntary reports. Since its prime contributors are law enforcement agencies, it is subject to the same limitations as police records as a useful source of incidence and prevalence data.

Growing concern over the problem of narcotics addiction in the 1960s led to the establishment of several localized, community-based narcotics case registers to provide incidence and prevalence information. Two of the most ambitious narcotics register projects were the ones developed by the New York City Department of Health (Kavaler, Denson, and Krug, 1968; Fishman, Conwell, and Amsel, 1971) and by the Narcotics Treatment Administration in Washington, D.C. (Dupont and Piemme, 1973). The kinds of case information reported to these registers include name, address, sex, age, ethnicity, birthdate, amounts and types of drugs used, occupation, marital status, and arrests and convictions.

The development of any register population for the purpose of providing meaningful indicators of incidence and prevalence requires a comprehensive reporting base (hospitals, addiction services, police and correctional institutions, private physicians, and other health and social services agencies). A register must also carefully define the criteria for reporting. For example, the New York City Narcotics Register defines an addict as any individual who is reported by a medical source or is accepted for treatment by a hospital, clinic, or established social service agency.

The three major requirements of an effective register are completeness, representativeness, and accuracy. Inasmuch as registers generally must depend upon unpaid reporters and on largely unenforceable reporting requirements, they are not likely to count all cases. For example, the New York City Register receives few reports from industrial physicians and from schools and agencies working with young people (Andima, et al., 1973). Moreover, a case register population is not likely to be representative of the entire addict population, but only of the known or visible addicts. The extent to which it is representative of the latter group depends largely upon the relative absence of errors introduced by inaccurate reporting, and by inadequate report processing and register maintenance. Some of these potential error sources are measurable and controllable, while others are not. Despite assurance of confidentiality, addicts may make a conscious effort to provide inaccurate information. In some instances, it is possible to verify responses by checking with external sources such as police records. Although the accuracy of most responses cannot be verified, it is feasible to evaluate the consistency of responses by cross-checking information reported on individuals by more than one source. A comparison of the first two reports submitted on 1,000 registrants of the New Jersey Medical School Narcotics Case Register in Newark revealed a high degree of consistency in reporting basic demographic characteristics such as sex, race, and date of birth, but the reproducibility of recall items such as age at onset of drug abuse was not nearly as good (Lavenhar, et al., 1975). Another potentially serious problem is that of duplicate registration of individuals. This possibility often presents itself in narcotics case registers because of the widespread use of aliases by addicts. Matching addicts by date of birth and other identifying characteristics is one way of minimizing duplicate registrations. Register clearance is another problem that is frequently ignored by most registers. It involves deleting from the files those registrants who have been "cured," have moved out of the registration area, or have died subsequent to registration. If individuals are never deleted from a register, this may bias any derived estimates of prevalence.

It is conceded, by even the staunchest supporters of the case register approach, that an addict register will never be able to provide a precise addict count. The major problem lies in estimating the number of addicts who do not come into contact with official agencies, and who manage to escape detection by reporting sources. Several attempts have been made to develop a workable method for estimating the total addict population in localities where there is some reporting of addicts to a central register. These efforts, designed to overcome incomplete reporting, are based on extrapolation from a register population on the bases of testing against an independent outside data system, i.e., one in which cases are reported to it on the basis of some criterion other than narcotics use.

Death certificates.

In New York City all deaths suspected of being attributed directly or indirectly to heroin are carefully investigated by the Office of the Chief Medical Examiner. The number of heroin-related deaths over the years was consistently about one percent of the number of reported addicts (Richards and Carroll, 1970). If it can be assumed that heroin-related deaths are distributed randomly among all users, then it is possible to estimate the size of the total addict population by multiplying the number of overdose deaths per year by 100. This approach, attributed to Dr. Michael Baden of the Office of the New York City Chief Medical Examiner (see Dupont and Piemme, 1973) requires a high degree of sophistication within the Medical Examiner's Office. Most cities are not equipped to identify all heroin-related deaths. Inasmuch as overdose deaths frequently occur in clusters, it is unlikely that they are randomly distributed among addicts. Moreover, the concentration of street heroin purchased in different localities is likely to be different, leading to considerable variability in the probability of death due to overdose.

Andima and coworkers (1973) compared the New York City Narcotics Register data with the narcotics-related deaths recorded in the Bureau of Vital Statistics to determine the degree of underreporting and to estimate the addict population in New York City. It was observed that approximately one-half of the people dying of narcotic-related causes in New York City were not previously known to the Narcotics Register. The conclusion was drawn that since the register did not have reports on half of the people dying of narcotic use, it therefore must also lack reports on half of the entire addict population. The actual number of addicts could then be estimated by multiplying the number of individuals reported by two. This estimation procedure assumes that the narcotics death rate is approximately the same for the reported and unreported addict population and that the percentage of deaths that are reported to the Bureau of Vital Statistics is the same for both groups. Andima and associates (1973) critically examined these underlying assumptions and conceded that known addicts, because of their contact with reporting institutions (including treatment facilities) may have lower death rates than the unreported addicts. They also recognized the possibility that the same factors inhibiting reporting of a given addict during life may inhibit reporting at death, leading to a higher proportion of deaths reported among register addicts than among unreported addicts.

Other data systems.

In an attempt to estimate the heroin-dependent addicts in Washington, D.C., Dupont and Piemme (1973) used a similar "Indicator-Dilution" estimation procedure by comparing the Narcotics Treatment Administration data with three independent and diverse populations: addicts presenting themselves voluntarily for treatment, addicts caught up in the criminal justice system, and addicts reported to the U.S. Bureau of Narcotics and Dangerous Drugs. Assuming that prior registration was independent of latter inclusion in any of these three groups, three estimates of the total addict population were derived, all falling within a narrow range.

Extrapolation based on tenuous assumptions are extremely risky. However, in the absence of more precise techniques, this estimation approach does provide a workable method for approximating prevalence in a community. Prevalence estimates should be used with caution and corroborated with as many independent external populations as possible.

Treatment Program Records

Estimates of the incidence and prevalence of drug addiction, obtained from treatment program records, are not only incomplete to an unknown degree but are also likely to be biased for a number of reasons (Hunt, 1974):

  a. Many treatment programs depend largely on voluntary admissions and attract only the highly motivated segment of the addict population.

  b. There is no standard definition of addiction — programs admit users of all description.

  c. Other factors such as the physical location of the program, the nature of treatment, admission policies, and program capacities all influence the number and types of addicts entering a program.

Hunt (1974) speculated that the above-mentioned biases are likely to be unselective with respect to year of onset, which is used as a measure of the incidence of "drug addiction." In other words, he assumed that a treatment modality would not tend to exclude either longer-term or more recent addicts. If this were the case, then relative incidence from year to year would be unaffected, and treatment incidence data could provide a good indication of local trends. However, this assumption may not be valid in some instances. For example, some methadone maintenance programs clearly concentrate their efforts on long-term addicts. Moreover, it has previously been mentioned that addicts' responses to recall items such as onset of drug use are not very reliable (Lavenhar, et al., 1975). Even though treatment incidence may not be representative of the entire addict population, it can provide an indication of trends in treatment demand which is of utmost interest to the health planner.

Polls and Surveys

Patterns of drug abuse in individuals not known or identifiable by any agency require study by the use of polls or surveys. Polls that include questions on the use of drugs (e.g., Gallup Poll) are seldom adequate for estimating the scope of the problem because they generally provide gross measures of drug use. Surveys tend to be more comprehensive and frequently elicit information about knowledge of and attitudes toward drugs in addition to drug-using behavior.

The survey is the most used (and perhaps most abused) means of estimating the incidence and prevalence of drug abuse in a given population. This data-gathering technique has been used to assess teenage substance abuse at a national level (Josephson et al., 1972; U.S. Department of Health, Education, and Welfare, 1972; Johnston, 1974) and to investigate drug use patterns of adults residing in diverse communities (George, 1972; Smart and Fejer, 1973). However, surveys have most frequently been employed in the more accessible "limited" populations such as military personnel (Callan and Patternson, 1973; Prendergast et al., 1973; Greden, Morgan, and Frankel, 1974) and high school and college students (Wolfson, et al., 1972; Hughes, Schaps, and Sanders, 1973; Milman, 1973 a, b; Porter et al., 1973; Smart, Fejer, and White, 1973; Anker, 1971; Goode, 1972; Corder et al., 1974). Glenn and Richards (1974) provided a comprehensive compendium bringing together statistics from recent published and unpublished surveys of nonmedical drug use reported in 1971 or later.

If properly designed and implemented, surveys can provide useful information to help assess the magnitude of the drug problem in a given population, and to generate baseline data essential for the evaluation of educational programs in drug abuse prevention. However, data obtained from surveys have frequently been rather superficial and especially vulnerable to bias introduced by one or more of the following:

a. inadequate sampling techniques

b. insufficient sample size
c. inclusion of loaded or leading questions
d. lack of standardization of interviewing techniques
e. large nonresponse
f. invalid responses

If these sources of bias are not controlled or accounted for, it becomes very difficult to interpret and draw inferences from survey data and the utility of survey results is of questionable value. Moreover, since drug use patterns tend to change rapidly, survey results become obsolete in a short period of time.

Reliable, valid estimates for generalization to wider groups and populations are possible only if the following requirements are met (Glenn and Richards, 1974; Lavenhar, 1973):

a. A random sample is selected from the target population (if 100 percent sampling is not considered necessary or is not feasible).

b. The sample size should be a compromise between the desired precision of estimates and the resources available, but should be sufficiently large to provide meaningful estimates of the extent of use of even the rarely used drugs.

c. It should be possible to estimate the potential bias due to nonresponse from statistically acceptable data.

d. The questionnaire should be carefully designed and pretested, on a population similar to the target population, prior to use in the actual survey.

e. Reliability and validity checks should be instituted to screen out misleading data.

f. The administration of the survey should follow a carefully worked out standardized protocol.

g. If survey results are based on responses elicited from a random sample of the target population then estimates of drug use should be accompanied by an indication of the range of variability (e.g., confidence intervals).

Randomization

Although many surveys of drug use have been conducted, all or most of the conditions listed above have rarely been satisfied. Relatively few surveys have been based on carefully conducted random samples. Random selection is generally feasible with small, closed populations such as students at a specific school or military personnel on a particular installation, where an entire list of the target population is frequently available. It is more difficult to implement when surveying larger, diverse populations. Nevertheless, several investigators have attempted to overcome many of the difficulties by utilizing well thought out sampling designs. In a national sample survey of teenage cigarette smoking, conducted by the National Clearinghouse for Smoking and Health (1972), telephone interviews were administered to a group of teenagers randomly selected from a bank of all possible combinations of area codes, telephone exchanges, and subscriber numbers. A previous survey, in which teenagers residing in nontelephone households were given personal interviews, revealed that the addition of nontelephone households to the sample resulted in very little change in the data obtained from telephone households. Johnston (1974) studied the incidence and distribution of drug use in a national sample of males in a particular age cohort by employing a stratified random sampling procedure designed to be representative of all young males beginning public high school in the United States in the fall of 1966. Josephson and coworkers (1972) reported on a national survey of adolescent marijuana use which was conducted with a national household sample of 498 youngsters 12 to 17 years of age. The sampling procedure was designed so that one youngster in each household in the sample was chosen at random to be interviewed. Weights were used in order to reduce the bias introduced by the unequal number of eligible adolescents in sample households.   An additional weight was applied to adjust for varying completion rates by sex, age, race, education, and geographical region.

Some innovative sampling techniques have been employed in smaller, community-based surveys. George (1972) instituted a drug use survey of residents of a beachside suburb of Sydney, Australia, by interviewing all members of randomly selected households between 14 and 65 years of age. Although it was recognized that a sampling of individuals would have been theoretically more acceptable than a sampling of households, the anticipated gain in accuracy was considered to be insufficient to justify either the additional expense or the reduction in sample size. Households were randomly selected from the 1971 electoral rolls. The dwelling actually chosen for inclusion in the sample was three houses to the right of that found on the electoral roll, allowing nonvoters an equal chance of being chosen. In a survey of marijuana use among adults residing in Toronto in 1971 (Smart and Fejer, 1973), all census tracts in both urban and suburban areas were sampled according to the percentage each comprised of the dwelling units in the city. Within tracts, dwelling units were selected at random. Persons were selected within households to obtain the correct age and sex proportions and to equalize the chances for persons from different family sizes to be chosen. In a study of drug use among students in grades 7, 9, 11, and 13 attending schools in metropolitan Toronto (Smart, 1973) each borough was represented by school districts in proportion to their part of the total; the schools used in the survey were randomly selected from the total number of high school districts within each borough. Within each school, classes were selected at random from each of the grades 7, 9, 11, and 13 until 120 students were obtained. Although, on theoretical grounds, it is more desirable to designate the individual (student) as the sampling unit rather than the group (class), this procedure is frequently not followed because of practical reasons. Failure to adhere to this principle is not likely to bias survey results provided that the groups are reasonably homogeneous or they are sufficiently large in number so that diverse groups will be adequately represented in the sample.

Sample size

In surveys of large, spread-out populations, sample size is more likely to be determined by available resources than by the precision desired in the estimates. Surveys of closed populations, such as students enrolled at a particular school, frequently attempt to include all members of the target population. Of course, the absolute size of the sample is a more important consideration than the proportion of the target population represented by the sample. If some prior indication of the variability of the responses is available, the sample size required to attain any given level of precision may be readily estimated.

Nonresponse

One of the most perplexing dilemmas encountered in surveys eliciting information sensitive issues is introduced by the phenomenon of nonresponse. Even when 100 percent sampling is attempted or a random sampling design is strictly adhered to, the data may be seriously biased if there is considerable nonresponse and if those who fail or refuse to respond behave differently from those who do respond. It would be reasonable to assume that drug users would be less likely to respond to a drug use survey than nonusers, so that a large nonresponse rate may very well lead to a large underestimates of the level of drug use in the target population. If the investigator has no information on those who did not respond, he cannot estimate the extent or the direction of the bias due to nonresponse. Nonresponse bias in school drug use surveys may be introduced by absenteeism on the survey day, or by lack of cooperation of those who are present. It is frequently difficult to determine how much bias is introduced by voluntary participation. Bias is also a potentially serious problem in household interview surveys. Aside from those who refuse to participate in the survey, a major concern is that of failure to include certain population groups such as the young, the single or divorced, the employed females, and others who are likely to be away from home when an interviewer calls. Underrepresentation of these groups will almost certainly result in underestimates of drug use. If the relevant characteristics (sex, age, race, education, etc.) of the target population are known, then it is possible to adjust the survey results to allow for varying rates of nonresponse within each population group.

There are many factors that influence the rate of nonresponse, including the manner in which the questionnaire is administered, the degree of involvement of the participants and the perceived confidentiality of the information provided by the respondents. Mail questionnaires seldom attract a high rate of response. Anonymous, self-administered, on-the-spot questionnaires generally do better. Personal interviews have had mixed success in surveying sensitive issues such as drug use. Response is likely to be best when the participants are well motivated and actively involved in the development and administration of the survey and/or they are informed about all relevant aspects of the survey. Response is also maximized when the respondent is confident that his answers will be held confidential and/or there is no way that he can be identified with his replies.

Questionnaire design

One of the most critical aspects of survey planning is questionnaire design. Of utmost importance is the necessity to pretest the questionnaire carefully on a population similar to the one being surveyed to eliminate ambiguously worded or slanted questions that are likely to bias the response in one direction. The pretest period is the ideal time to check for reliability or reproducibility of the data by determining the extent to which the same respondents will provide the same information with the same questionnaire on two separate occasions. In surveys employing the personal interview, the pretest period should also be used to train interviewers and to insure that the personal biases of the interviewer are not transmitted in the interview so as to affect the responses.

Utility of drug surveys

The proliferation of mainly one-time surveys of diverse populations in scattered locations using a wide variety of sampling techniques, data-gathering instruments, and survey methods has become a cause for concern among a growing group of researchers who have begun to raise questions as to the usefulness of drug survey data for program planning and development. The diversity of methods employed (e.g., categories of drug use) makes comparison among surveys difficult.

The basic questions are the extent to which sample survey data are generalizable to and representative of the population under study and the extent to which the data are applicable to other similar populations. In an attempt to answer these questions, attention has recently been focused upon the issues of reliability and validity of survey data. Reliability is defined as the degree to which a survey would yield similar estimates if repeated several times. Validity refers to the extent to which estimates drawn from a sample reflect the true characteristics of the total population.

Imprecise, ambiguously worded questions generally lead to unreliable responses. It has been previously mentioned that this can be minimized by careful pretesting of the questionnaire. An additional reliability check is achieved by retesting some of the survey respondents with the same data-gathering instrument. In a survey of drug use in Anchorage, Alaska (Porter, et al.,1973), results of a randomly sampled pretest were compared with those of the large survey to assess the reliability of the data. All 16 drug classifications that were included on both survey forms yielded total usage rates that were within the desired five percent precision level. Furthermore, a comparison between the pretest survey rank ordering of the number of students ever having used each drug yielded a Spearman rank correlation coefficient of 0.96, indicating a high degree of reliability. Similarly, Haberman and coworkers (1972), in a pilot study conducted in two east coast metropolitan area schools, requestioned 205 students two weeks after the initial administration of questionnaires and observed that the proportions reporting varying amounts of marijuana use were almost identical in the two waves.

Survey data are subject to two sources of error — random error which is readily measurable, and nonrandom error or bias which is frequently difficult to measure. Some of the main sources of bias and the measures that may be taken to minimize them have previously been discussed. In view of the legal and social implications of nonmedical drug use, a major concern in questionnaire surveys is the validity of respondents' reports of their drug use. Clearly, even the most sophisticated survey designs may yield invalid data if the respondents are less than truthful in their replies. The issue of response validity in drug surveys has attracted much attention in the recent literature.

The accuracy of self-reported drug use is influenced by many factors including the specific drug category involved, the respondent's memory, the ability of the respondent to correctly identify drugs taken on prescription or purchased in the illegal drug market, fear of reprisals, and changing peer group pressures which make some drugs more socially acceptable than others. In an effort to maximize response validity, researchers have taken several steps such as involving the respondents in the design and implementation of the survey, assuring confidentiality of the data via anonymity, and screening and editing of the data to identify and eliminate suspect responses. Respondents may also be asked to leave any questions blank that they do not feel they could answer honestly.

It is widely assumed that anonymity of respondents is essential for the collection of valid data regarding drug usage. This assumption was supported by a study conducted by Horan and associates (1973) that revealed that rates of self-reported drug use were higher when data were collected in a group anonymous interview situation and lowest when collected through individual interviews where the examiner addressed the subjects by name. However, the results of two other studies suggest that anonymity may not affect the validity of responses as much as expected. In a comparison of responses of secondary school students who either did or did not give their names (Haberman et al., 1972), drug use was no higher in the anonymous group. In a matched samples study of anonymous and identifiable questionnaires administered to college undergraduates (King, 1970), a comparison of the two groups revealed no significant difference between identifiable and unidentifiable forms. A study of university students, exploring the influence of anonymity on reported illegal use of marijuana (Luetgart and Armstrong, 1973), utilized the interview technique in addition to written questionnaires and concluded that reported lifetime use of marijuana was not affected by anonymity per se. However, the findings indicated that anonymity may be an important factor when the dimensions of frequency and recency of use are introduced. Assurance of anonymity may not be as critical as assumed for some groups, but it is still an advisable precaution to assure confidentiality.

A variety of checks have been employed to assess the response validity of survey data including the following:

a. Responses are screened to detect obvious overstatement or understatement of usage.

b. Questions are asked in more than one way to detect inconsistency of responses.

c. Respondents are asked to indicate the degree of honesty with which the questionnaire was completed.

d. Questions are included about usage of fictitious drugs.

e. Lie scales are used.

f. Rates of drug use derived from self-reported data are compared with an independent estimate that is not based on self-report.

Several investigators (Johnston, 1974; Porter, et al., 1973; Smart, Fejer, and White, 1973; Smart and Jackson, 1969; Haberman, et al., 1972; Petzel, Johnson, and McKillip, 1973) have used one or more of these validity checks in their drug use surveys of diverse populations and all agreed that dishonest responses were likely to have little effect on results. On the basis of a critical review of four studies that examined the question of validity and one study that focused on test-retest reliability in surveys of drug-using behavior among adolescents, Whitehead and Smart (1972) concluded that "there is reason to have confidence in the validity and reliability of self-reports of drug use."

Assessment of drug use trends

Most of the earlier surveys of drug use were small-scale, one-time studies conducted in widely scattered local schools and communities. They were useful in providing a direct estimate of the prevalence of drug-using behavior in a given population at a particular point in time. However, the one-time survey could not yield direct estimates of incidence and provided limited information on drug use trends over time. In recent years, the scope of drug use surveys has broadened and the trend has been toward more repeated cross-sectional surveys that can assess overall changes in the target population, and toward longitudinal surveys to assess changes in the individual.

The National Clearinghouse for Smoking and Health has conducted cross-sectional national sample surveys biennially since 1968 to assess trends in teenage cigarette smoking. The San Mateo County, California Department of Public Health and Welfare (1975) has sponsored annual drug use surveys since 1968 to evaluate trends in levels of use of various drugs by junior and senior high school students. A 1968 sample survey of drug use among metropolitan Toronto students in grades 7, 9, 11, and 13 was repeated in 1970 and 1972 by resurveying the same or similar school classes (Smart, Fejer, & White, 1973). It was not always possible to return to the same class that was surveyed in 1968 because the class numbering system was modified in some cases and some classes were no longer intact. Greden, Morgan, and Frankel (1974) surveyed a randomly selected sample of military personnel at a Fort Lee, Virginia, installation in each of three years beginning in 1970. Although every effort was made to survey each sample in the same fashion each year, the investigators attributed much of the increase in drug use to changes in the makeup of the population in the last two years of the follow-up period. Herein lies one of the limitations of the repeated cross-sectional survey approach – it may reflect changes in the composition of the population rather than changes in drug-using behavior of a given population.

Longitudinal studies, which provide an insight into changes in individual drug-using behavior, are much more difficult to implement than repeated cross-sectional studies because of the problems involved in following individuals over a period of time. One of the more successful large-scale longitudinal studies was reported by Johnston (1974) who followed a national sample of young men beginning public high school in the United States in the fall of 1966 by means of an initial survey and three follow-up surveys. Subjects were paid for participation in the follow-up surveys. By the time of the fourth data collection in 1970, 73 percent of the original sample remained in the study. Moreover, comparison between retained and original samples revealed few differences.

Although the longitudinal approach to trend analysis is theoretically desirable, it creates a major logistical problem in surveys of sensitive issues. Longitudinal studies require that subjects must be identified in some manner so that they may be periodically resurveyed, making it difficult to guarantee the privacy and confidentiality of the data. To address this problem, several attempts have been recently made to develop techniques for insuring data security and respondent anonymity. Haberman and associates (1972) proposed a relatively simple technique for matching respondents in successive survey waves while insuring their anonymity. Respondents were asked to construct a self-generated numerical code based on certain letters of their names and the dates of the months in which they were born. Kandel (1973) employed an extended version of this identification procedure in which each respondent was asked to construct an eight-digit number based on the two middle letters of his last and first names, his date of birth, and the last two digits of his telephone number. She observed that while most respondents were willing to construct self-generated numbers, this procedure introduced a bias since those who did not give a code number and could not be matched were more likely to be drug users than those who provided a code number. Astin and Boruch (1970), faced with the problem of developing a system for maintaining the security of data files in a continuing longitudinal study of college and university students, developed the Link System in which a computer data file (Link file), representing the only means of linking the subject's identity with his answers, was deposited at a computer facility in a foreign country. This system offers complete protection for the respondent against subpoena of records and/or unauthorized use by research staff members. The search for new approaches to this problem will undoubtedly continue until the overall question of the rights of the researcher, with regards to the protection of the privacy of his subjects, is resolved.

Panels

One of the methods used by Blum and associates (1970) to gain insights into student drug use patterns was the panel (chapter 10). Three subsamples of students were asked to keep a diary of their drug use over a period of six months. In two schools, the subsamples were drawn at random, using a random number table, from the larger randomly selected study sample at each school. In a third school, panelists were not selected at random, but were chosen because they reported use of illicit drugs. It was desired to learn more about the day-to-day drug habits of such individuals. A modified diary was employed which required that the panelists would keep a record of drug-using behavior during only one week each month. To avoid any systematic error due to recording the same week each month, the week of the month was rotated for each panelist. The two randomly selected panels, initially consisting of 36 and 28 members, each wound up six months later with 22 active participants. The drug-using panel ended up with 16 of the original group of 36 panelists. Because of the small sample size, the large drop-out rate, and the lack of anonymity it is frequently difficult to evaluate the validity of data provided by panelists when a sensitive issue such as illicit drug use is involved.

The Epidemic Approach

Because there are certain similarities between the spread of heroin use and the spread of infectious diseases, there has been some development of epidemic models that purport to describe the spread of heroin use. These models use sophisticated analytical techniques to examine the incidence of heroin use over a long period of time by geographical area. A detailed description of this approach is provided by Hunt (1973, 1974).

EVALUATION RESEARCH

Since the remainder of this chapter will focus upon the methodologies involved in the evaluation of drug abuse intervention programs, it would be useful, at this point, to consider a general theoretical framework for evaluation research.

Evaluation and Research

Evaluation is the process of determining the value or amount of success in achieving a predetermined objective (American Public Health Association, 1960). It has been argued (James, 1969) that evaluation differs from research in that, unlike research, it does not seek new knowledge and should not end with the presentation of results. Evaluation is viewed as a circular process that provides decision makers with immediate feedback that can be used to improve the program. Although evaluation studies do not specifically seek new knowledge, most well-designed programs will generate new information about the problem under investigation. Moreover, since evaluation employs the same general statistical and epidemiological methods as research, it can be classified as a research component.

Evaluation Models

There are at least three different models of evaluation research at the program level (Larkin, 1974):

1. Goal-Attainment Model (evaluation by objectives). A model for determining the degree to which prestated objectives are achieved. It is the most popular evaluative model. It consists of four separate phases (Schulberg et al., 1969):

   a. Formulation of the objectives
   b. Identification of the criteria to be used in measuring success
   c. Determining the program's degree of success
   d. Recommendations for program improvement

   This approach to evaluation utilizes methodology drawn from well-established research designs; it is closely related to classical experimentation. Although this model is conceptually simple, difficulties in implementation arise in accurately defining the program objectives, in determining the level of evaluation to be undertaken (evaluation of effort, evaluation of performance, evaluation of efficiency), in selecting the measures to be used to assess the program's success, and in choosing and instituting the appropriate research methodology.

2. The Systems Model. This model focuses upon the program resources needed to achieve its objective, and attempts to measure the degree to which these resources are allocated in an optimal way. The systems approach is less concerned with the determination of the present level of functioning, but is more concerned about increasing the level of achievement. The main advantage of this model is its strong emphasis on immediate feedback. However, since it is generally more expensive and more difficult to implement than the Goal-Attainment Model, it is not extensively used.

3. The Ackoff Model (Ackoff et al., 1962). This model is applicable when several different courses of action (treatment programs, educational approaches) are available. It involves the determination of the probabilities of specific outcomes for different types of subjects when exposed to different programs.

Status of Program Evaluation

Many of the evaluations reported in the literature suffer from a variety of shortcomings. While to some extent they reflect a lack of awareness of methodological principles, for the most part they are due to the inability to apply appropriate research designs. Schulberg and associates (1969) aptly described the state of the art by concluding that "evaluation studies are easy to formulate and criticize but exceedingly difficult to carry out."

Because of the difficulties encountered in fulfilling the requirements of true experimentation in natural settings, it is difficult to find many successfully completed program evaluations that incorporate the classical features of research design, including random selection of subjects, random assignment of subject to experimental and control groups, and opportunities for manipulating and controlling all relevant variables. Most investigators are able to attain, at best, a quasi-experimental approach to evaluation.

Research Designs in Program Evaluation

The choice of any one research design for evaluating the efficacy of a program will depend upon the relative importance of realism, precision of measurement, opportunities for manipulating variables, and other relevant features of the research situation (Schulberg, et al., 1969).

In any social research setting, program evaluation is frequently complicated by the presence of several extraneous factors that could, independently or, in conjunction with the experimental variable (i.e., treatment or educational program), influence the study outcome thereby making it difficult to interpret the results. The more rigorous research designs attempt to control these potentially relevant variables so that conclusions can be drawn with a high level of confidence.

Following are some of the more prominent categories of extraneous variables that the more sophisticated research designs seek to control (Campbell, 1969; Twain, et al., 1970):

1. History effects: Effects attributed to external events occurring in addition to experimental stimulus.

2. Maturation effects: Effects that are not related to specific events but are a function of the passage of time, that might have occurred in the absence of the experimental "treatment."

3. Testing effects: The systematic scoring effect produced by taking the same test on more than one occasion. Persons taking a test for the second time score systematically different from those taking the test for the first time.

4. Instrument decay effects: The effects caused by factors such as fatigue or experience produced when humans are used as a part of the measuring apparatus as judges, observers, raters, coders, etc., or when these individuals change over the course of a study.

5. Regression effects: Shifts toward the mean will occur due to random imperfections of the measuring instrument or random instability within the population.

6. Selection effects: Biased selection or recruitment of the study samples may produce differences independent of the effect of the experimental variable.

7. Mortality effects: Effects due to loss to follow-up of a biased subset of the experimental samples thereby changing the initial comparability of experimental and control groups.

8. Hawthorne effects: Effects which are produced by any change in policy or procedure, and are not necessarily caused by the experimental variable.

The effects of the extraneous variables may be exerted independently or in addition to the effects of the experimented variable, thereby influencing the internal validity of the experiment (i.e., the significance of the experimental variable in this particular setting) or may interact with the experimental variable, affecting the external validity (generalizability) of the experimental results.

Research designs may be categorized into three main groups: preexperimental, quasi-experimental, and true experimental. Following is a classification of some of the research designs in each of these groups that have been or might be used to evaluate social programs. In each case, the extent to which the design deals with the problem of extraneous variables is discussed.

1. Preexperimental Designs

a. Posttest Only Design: Measurements are made on only one group after it is exposed to a program and observations are attributed to that exposure. Since no measurements are taken prior to exposure, there is no indication that any change has taken place or of the magnitude of that change. Moreover, since there is no basis for comparison with an unexposed group (controls), there is no way of determining whether the results would have been the same with or without the experimental program. This design does not merit consideration as an experimental technique since it does not involve at least one formal comparison. It is particularly vulnerable to the history, maturation, selection, and Hawthorne effects.

b. One-Group Pretest-Posttest Design: This widely used design involves the measurement of one group on some behavior or characteristic prior to, and after, exposure to an experimental program. It allows for the determination of the magnitude of changes occurring during exposure to the program, but in the absence of an unexposed control group, it is not known whether the same changes would not have occurred without the program. This design leaves several categories of extraneous variables uncontrolled. Therefore, observed differences may be attributed to the effects of history, maturation, testing, instrument decay, regression and mortality, as well as to the Hawthorne effect.

c. The Static Group Comparison Design: This design compares a group that has been exposed to an experimental program with a group that has not, in an effort to evaluate the effect of exposure. This model does not imply equivalence of the two groups prior to exposure. Since equivalence cannot be assumed it is possible that observed group differences could be attributed to inherent preexposure differences and have no relationship to the experimental exposure (selection effect). For example, since admission to a treatment program is generally voluntary, those who seek treatment are likely to be systematically different from those who do not. Even if the groups were equivalent prior to the study, if a specific subset has been lost to follow-up, they may differ at the time the measurements are made (mortality effect).

2. Quasi-Experimental Designs

These designs are frequently employed when no control group is available, or when the relevant control group is comprised of people who do not participate in the experimental program or who are exposed to a different program. In the latter case, administrative considerations generally preclude random assignment to experimental and control groups. Quasi-experimental designs provide a means of controlling for extraneous variables without randomization, although, in comparison with true experimental designs, a lower level of confidence must be accepted with regard to interpretation of results.

a. Interrupted Time Series Design: This design is an extension of the One-Group Pretest-Posttest Design where the treatment group is utilized as its own control. The influences of such factors as external events, maturation, testing, and the Hawthorne effects can be accounted for, to some extent, by a design in which the experimental treatment is applied, withheld, and reapplied during the study period in order to distinguish the influences of treatment from those of extraneous variables. However, the possible effects of instrument decay, regression, and mortality are not controlled with this design.

b. Matched Assignment Design: This design is an adaption of the Static Group Comparison Design and is applicable to situations in which random assignment is not feasible. An attempt is made to establish similarity or comparability of the experimental and control groups by matching them so that they will have the same distribution with respect to all potentially important variables (e.g., age, sex, social characteristics). Unfortunately, the most relevant variables may not be known or may not be measurable. Moreover, it may not be possible to eliminate systematic differences between the experimental and control groups by matching.

3. True Experimental Designs

These are the most powerful experimental designs which attempt to insure control over all possibly relevant variables by means of random assignment of subjects to experimental and control groups, and also assume control of exposure to the treatment variable. These designs yield unbiased results and also permit estimation of the likelihood that an error has been made in the drawing of conclusions.

a. Pretest-Posttest Control Group Design: In this design, individuals are randomly assigned to a treatment or nontreatment group. Each group is tested prior to the experiment, the treatment group is then exposed to the experimental stimuli, and then both groups are tested again. Before and after differences observed in each group are compared and if the changes occurring in the treatment group are significantly different from the changes occurring in the nontreatment group, then it is assumed that the differential results can be attributed to the treatment.

This design has been highly regarded in the social sciences for many years. It controls for the simple or main effects of all the important categories of extraneous variables (history, maturation, testing, instrument decay, regression toward the mean, selection, mortality). However, it has recently been noted that this highly esteemed design may be seriously limited in its application because of the interaction effect of testing (Campbell, 1969). The main effect of testing implies that some of the changes observed during the course of an experiment may be attributed to the testing or measurement process. This main effect is controlled in this design because any differences due to testing found in the experimental group would also appear in the control group. However, interaction effects (effects occurring jointly with the experimental variable) may occur in the absence of main effects. As interaction effect would be present if the testing or measurement process had the effect of sensitizing the subjects to the experimental variable so that a change would take place only when the testing process preceded the experimental exposure, whereas testing or experimental exposure alone had no effect. While the Pretest-Posttest Control Group Design is internally valid, the possibility of interaction effects may seriously limit its generalizability from the pretested experimental group to the unpretested general population (Campbell, 1969).

b. The Posttest Only Control Group Design: This fully valid experimental design has not gained the recognition it deserves nor is it used as much as it might be in social research. It is similar to the Pretest-Posttest Control Group Design, with the primary difference being that testing is instituted only once, after exposure to the experimental variable. It is sometimes confused with the Static Group Comparison Design. However, that design does not assume equivalence between the treatment and nontreatment groups. The distinguishing feature of the Posttest Only Control Group Design is that even though no testing is done prior to exposure to treatment, the experimental and control groups are assumed to be initially equivalent because subjects are randomly assigned.

Like the previous design (3a), this one is capable of controlling the main effects of most of the important categories of extraneous variables. Its main advantage is that it eliminates any possibility of a testing interaction effect. However, while this design does control for the important extraneous variables, it cannot measure their effects. Moreover, although it enables one to compare the exposed and unexposed groups to determine whether the groups differ significantly with respect to a specific measurement, the elimination of the pretest requirement precludes the estimation of the magnitude of the change caused by the experimental stimulus. In addition, one can only assume that random assignment provides equivalency – without measuring there is no way of confirming this assumption. Finally, this design is particularly vulnerable to experimental mortality which can disturb the initial balance produced by random assignment.

c. The Four-Group Design: This elegant design, proposed by Solomon (1949), enables one both to control and measure the relevant simple and interactive effects. It has replaced the Pretest-Posttest Control Group Design as the ideal design for social scientists (Campbell, 1969). It is simply a consolidation of the two previously discussed experimental designs (3a and 3b). The four groups are arranged in this design as follows:

Group	Exposed	Measurements
1	Yes	Pre-Post
2	No	Pre-Post
3	Yes	Post
4	No	Post

This approach offers all the advantages of the two preceding experimental designs and also enables one to measure the combined main effects of maturation and history, and the main and interaction effects of testing in addition to the main effect of the experimental variable.   The major limitation to this design is that the four-group requirement is more costly to implement and more difficult to administer. However, in the usual practical application where sampling control is less than perfect, the Four-Group Design provides greater assurance against mistakenly attributing effects to the experimental variable.

General Guidelines in Evaluation Research

The following guidelines outline the essential requirements for an effective evaluative research undertaking:

1. Evaluation mechanisms should be built into programs at the time of their inception. Once a large amount of resources are committed to a program, it may be difficult to initiate the evaluation process. Ineffective programs should be discontinued or revised before a large amount of resources are expended on them.

2. Evaluations should be done extramurally by individuals who are not personally involved with the programs and do not stand to benefit from a negative or positive appraisal. These individuals should be given unlimited access to the program data. When budget cuts, staff reductions, or the very life of the program is at stake, the data made available by program administrators tend to be quite biased.

3. The evaluation team should formulate a precise statement of the objectives and scope of the program and the specific criteria to be used to determine whether or not the program objectives have been achieved. Evaluations may focus upon the level of effort or

activities generated by the program, the efficiency of that effort, or the adequacy or efficacy of performance. Measures of success may be direct indexes of the desired change (most useful) or indirect measures reflecting assumed change. Measurement should be made at some point sufficiently advanced in time so that changes affected as a result of the program can reasonably be expected.

4. Evaluation research must be objective and based upon sound, well-considered experimentation rather than upon speculation or a priori thinking. The methodology should be drawn from well-established research designs that require the imposition of as much control as possible on the many potentially influential extraneous variables in order to isolate the effect of the experimental variable. The key element in experimental research is random allocation of subjects to experimental and control groups. Moreover, instruments, tests, and procedures used in the collection of data should be valid, reliable, and objective.

5. If administrative considerations preclude random assignment of subjects, then some level of acceptable control can still be achieved through the use of quasi-experimental designs.

6. The internal validity of the evaluative findings should always take precedence over the external validity or generalizability of the results.

7. Evaluation should be viewed as a circular process providing immediate and useful feedback to program administrators.

EVALUATION OF TREATMENT PROGRAMS

In the late 1960s, the increasing incidence of drug dependence and the substantial recidivism among drug offenders demonstrated the ineffectiveness of the predominantly punitive approach to drug abuse and triggered the proliferation of newly established drug treatment facilities in an attempt to find a therapeutic solution to the problem. Although the medical professions have been studying and treating drug dependence for more than a century, there is still a great deal of uncertainty and confusion about the causes and nature of drug dependence and about the rationale behind treatment. Confusion about the nature of drug dependence has resulted in confusion about its treatment. Although a wide range of treatment approaches has been employed, no method of treatment has been proven generally effective.

While the earlier treatment programs tended to be limited in scope and generally focused upon a single treatment modality, many current programs offer a wide range of treatment methods and techniques to a large number of clients. The five most common types of treatment modalities are:

1. detoxification (mainly hospital inpatient)
2. outpatient drug-free therapy
3. therapeutic community
4. methadone maintenance
5. multimodality programs

Until recently, there has been little demand for scientific assessment of treatment programs. Evaluation in the past relied almost entirely on naturalistic observation of therapy as practiced. Systematic data collection and feedback have been, in general, nonexistent or extremely primitive. It has been assumed that reasoned judgment and experience were all that was needed to develop and administer treatment programs, and judgments as to program effectiveness have been based generally upon minimally documented evidence.

The recent proliferation of treatment programs has placed a strain on the public and private resources needed for their support. Therefore, it has become imperative to determine which programs are effective enough to warrant retention and further support. While much has been learned from naturalistic observation, there is a clear need for more scientific methods of evaluation which allow for manipulation and control over the wide range of variables interacting in the present-day treatment setting.

Although some progress has been made in recent years in the development of objective evaluative models, most attempts at program evaluation have taken the form of one-time intramural efforts at a definitive evaluation. This approach has generally had little practical impact on the administration, planning, or delivery of treatment services (Putnam, et al., 1973). In general there has been a lack of sound and detailed extramural evaluations of treatment efficacy.

The most pressing problems encountered in evaluative studies have generally been lack of funds for in-depth evaluation, a lack of expertise, and a lack of objectivity. There have also been, and still are, many specific obstacles to effective evaluation that are extremely difficult to overcome. Some of these, which merit further discussion, include:

1. limited generalizability of evaluative findings
2. lack of agreement on aims, objectives, and criteria for effectiveness of treatment
3. the unavailability of appropriate outcome measures
4. difficulties in obtaining objective and reliably measured data
5. practical difficulties in applying experimental designs
6. practical difficulties in patient follow-up

Major Difficulties Encountered in Treatment Evaluation

1. Limited generalizability of evaluative findings

It is difficult to generalize from reported evaluation efforts because of the wide variation in populations studied, research methodology, sample size, time span of observation, criteria for admission, and criteria for classifying clients as cured or relapsed. Generalizations are also hazardous since the research subjects are usually the hospitalized or institutionalized drug addicts, not the unknown or invisible street addicts who avoid contact with official agencies. Therefore, evaluative findings may only be relevant to a particular population in a given treatment setting.

2. Lack of agreement on aims, objectives, and criteria for effectiveness of treatment

Treatment may be broadly defined as "any intervention or technique applied to certain problems of an individual with the goal of affecting a specified change in the problem areas" (Annis, 1973). Treatments for drug dependence differ not only in method but also in rationale. Of course, all drug treatment programs are dedicated to the elimination of drug dependence as their ultimate goal, but they may pursue this goal in different ways. For example, the traditional approach to addiction is based on the assumption that abstinence must precede rehabilitation. However, the drug maintenance approach to therapy (e.g., methadone maintenance), which is gaining more and more supporters, is based on the opposite assumption, that rehabilitation must precede abstinence.

In the past, changes in drug involvement were used almost exclusively to assess treatment efficacy. More recently, it has been argued that no single criterion measure is sufficient to serve as evidence of treatment effectiveness. Sells (1973) categorized the goals and rationale of treatment into two major groups:

1. intrapsychic changes in attitudes, personality organization, character, and values
2. behavior changes including definers of lifestyle

Because of the difficulties in measuring intrapsychic changes, the first group of criteria has not been used extensively in evaluation studies.

The most generally accepted criteria for behavioral change are those defining lifestyle which include, in addition to drug use, such critical areas as employment, family relations, social adjustment, and participation in illegal activities. Contemporary treatment evaluation studies frequently employ multiple criteria in assessing treatment efficacy.

3. The availability of appropriate outcome measures

In treatment evaluation we frequently measure what we can, not necessarily what we would like to measure. In other words, the selection of outcome measures is often dictated by the type of information that is available. Two types of data may be generated in drug treatment programs – management information and research evaluation information. Management information tends to be cross-sectional and deals primarily with process outcomes, while research and evaluation information tends to be longitudinal and focuses upon product outcomes.

Inasmuch as it is generally easier to obtain management information (which is program based) than research information (which is patient based), evaluative studies frequently involve process analysis rather than product analysis. Process analysis monitors the extent to which a treatment facility utilizes its resources to pursue its program goals. Product analysis assesses the extent to which the facility's efforts achieve the desired ultimate goal or end product (e.g., reduction of drug abuse).

Effective process analysis depends on the development of a good management information system that is designed to achieve the following goals (Amos, et al., 1973):

    a. to build and maintain a registry of patients who have been or currently are in treatment

    b. to monitor the progress of patients during and after treatment

    c. to provide accurate, timely, and meaningful information needed for evaluation research

The key indexes of treatment efficacy provided by a management information system for process analysis include rates of intake, rates of termination, readmission rates, and retention rates. The use of retention rates as an indicator of treatment effectiveness is based on the assumption that the longer a patient remains in treatment the more likely that the treatment will have a positive effect. In order to represent retention rates in a meaningful way, life table methods are applied to the data (Gearing, 1971; Sheffet, et al., 1973) for the purpose of generating "survival" curves which indicate the probability that an individual or group of individuals will remain in a program for any given period of time.

A well-conceived process analysis could provide the basis for at least a partial judgment regarding the effectiveness of a treatment agency and could also provide an indication of its potential ability to achieve the ultimate or product goals (Kern, 1974). However, even though a program's performance goes as planned, there is no assurance that it will be effective in reaching its ultimate objectives. Therefore, despite the difficulties involved it is usually desirable to extend the evaluative effort to a product analysis.

The major outcome measures of a product analysis are generally elicited by personally interviewing the client, and sometimes his friends, members of his family, or program counsellors who are in close contact with him. These measures usually focus upon behavioral factors such as current substance use (e.g., relapse rates), family relations, employment status, housing environment, social involvement, and illegal activities. Intrapsychic patterns may be assessed by means of a wide variety of psychological tests administered to the patient. It is sometimes feasible to obtain corroborating data from official agencies (police, correction agencies, employers) or from local case registers (Amsel, et al., 1971). The actual number and types of criteria used in a particular evaluative effort depend upon several factors including the treatment goals and rationale, and the available resources. The most frequently used measures of product outcome are substance use, criminal activities, and employment status.

4. Difficulties in obtaining objective and reliably measured data

A good Management Information System (MIS) can be an effective management tool and can provide timely and meaningful data needed for ongoing evaluative research. It is most effective if it is conceived as an integral part of the day-to-day treatment routine and implemented at the very onset of a new program. Problems in collecting reliable data occur when the MIS is imposed upon an ongoing program and requires that forms be filled out in addition to the standard treatment forms employed by the program staff. In large programs, a good Management Information System generally requires access to a computer, and therefore it has not been available to management as much as it should be.

It has previously been mentioned that patient interviews must be relied upon for the bulk of the information obtained in evaluations of product outcomes. A continuing problem is that of assessing the truthfulness of addicts as respondents. In an effort to shed more light on the problem, Stephens (1972) compared the responses of 100 male formerly hospitalized addicts to a series of items concerning drug use, work experiences, and encounters with the police, with the responses of aftercare counsellors and relatives. Since the responses were in general agreement, he concluded that addicts tend to be truthful in research situations. Similarly, Ball (1967) compared the responses of 59 Puerto Rican addicts to questions on age, onset of drug use, current drug use, and arrest history with hospital records, FBI arrest reports, and urine sample assays and concluded that the data were highly reliable and valid. However, the findings of Summers (1970) suggest that alcoholics' self-reported drinking histories are highly unreliable.

The organization of reporting to assure reliable and valid data involves careful form design, thorough training of interviewers, and systematic built-in checks to minimize error. There are three ways of checking the truthfulness of addict responses:

a. Collect urine samples at the time of interview.

b. Interview family members and other persons who know the respondent well.

c. Check responses against official records.

Few evaluative studies of treatment effectiveness can withstand close scrutiny. Positive evaluations are readily accepted. Negative evaluations are frequently challenged – usually on the basis of reliability and validity.

5. Practical difficulties in applying experimental designs

Although the overall design for the evaluation of treatment effectiveness is fairly straightforward, the major difficulties arise in execution,
simply because the degree of control of all factors relevant to
treatment outcome that is needed to apply classical experimental
designs is rarely, if ever, attained in a treatment setting.

In evaluating therapy, it is ethically indefensible to deny treatment
to certain individuals in the name of research. Therefore, random
assignment of drug-dependent individuals to treatment and nontreatment groups can hardly be justified. Frequently, the classic experimental design must be replaced by, at best, a quasi-experimental approach
that utilizes a matched control group of individuals who never reach a
significant treatment stage (e.g., less than four weeks in treatment).
However, the findings of Sheffet and coinvestigators (1973) and Bale
and coworkers (1973) indicate that addicts who do not receive
significant treatment may be inherently different from those who do;
this potential selection effect may easily bias the results of evaluative
studies.

In most settings where more than one treatment is available, no
attempt is made to assign individuals to a specific treatment modality.
Instead, the choice among treatment alternatives is essentially hap-
hazard, influenced by a number of factors including the reputation of
the program, the type of facility (outpatient vs. inpatient, drug-free vs.
drug therapy, etc.), the proximity to the patient's place of residence,
and the criteria for admission. Random assignment to alternative
treatment regimens is technically feasible but difficult to implement
inasmuch as drug addicts frequently have preconceived ideas as to
which treatment is "best."

For evaluation purposes, several attempts have been made to
randomly assign incoming patients to treatment facilities, but only few
have met with any degree of success. Bale and coworkers (1973)
investigated the relative effectiveness of methadone therapy versus the
therapeutic community approach in Palo Alto, California, by assigning
incoming patients to these modalities at random from a central pool.
This randomized study was designed to determine whether the modalities were differentially effective for different types of patients and for
different outcome criteria, and also whether the modalities were
differentially acceptable to patients. After detoxification, those patients who requested a rehabilitation program were randomly assigned
to one of three therapeutic communities or to the one methadone
maintenance program. Those patients who refused to accept the
assigned treatment were required to wait a period of four weeks before
they would be considered for admission to another program. Some of the
preliminary findings of this investigation indicated that the methadone
maintenance program was twice as likely to be accepted by patients
than the therapeutic communities. However, few differences were
noted between the patients entering methadone maintenance and those
entering the therapeutic communities. Moreover, patients entering any
program differed from those who refused offered treatment.

A small, controlled Swedish study of the effectiveness of a simple hypnotic method for the treatment of alcoholism (Jacobson and Siffverskield, 1973) also utilized random assignment. Patients were given the opportunity to be included in a group where different treatment methods (e.g., hypnosis) would be tried. Of those accepting treatment, 40 were randomly assigned on their first visit to the hypnosis group, and a like number to a control group who received the usual therapy. The groups were compared with regard to objectively measured variables one year before the treatment started and again six months after the last treatment. Randomization is likely to be most successful in the small clinic setting in which there is considerable administrative control.

Statistical studies of treatment effectiveness involve many problems related principally to the large number of variables that may be considered relevant (Sells and Watson, 1970). In evaluations where no adequate control groups are available, it may be difficult to determine how much of the observed changes can be attributed to the treatment itself, and how much may be due to the interference of various types of extraneous variables. A treatment evaluation study should consider at least three major categories of variables describing (a) the patient population, (b) the treatment programs, and (c) other extraneous factors.

Agencies providing treatment frequently accept patients with different drug-using behavior and diverse personality traits regardless of the appropriateness of the services they offer. Comparative evaluations of treatment success have little meaning if they do not take into consideration differences in patient populations. For example, the overall success rate of any program can be artificially enhanced by accepting clients with minimal drug involvement. Since certain segments of the patient population may be disproportionately represented in some treatment programs, the patient population should be subdivided into homogeneous subgroups before comparisons of treatment efficacy are made. If it is desired to match patients with treatment for optimal results, a range of patient types should be examined across samples of agencies in which various treatment approaches are practiced.

Since there are so many differences within and between agencies in the pattern of treatment delivered, the treatment factor in itself is a variable that needs to be taken into account. Two programs offering the same treatment modality (e.g., therapeutic communities) may be miles apart in their philosophical approach to treatment. Treatment program labels are frequently misleading – the services actually delivered may be considerably different from what is supposedly being offered. The most challenging problem encountered in treatment evaluation is to identify the specific therapeutic agent or agents (i.e., the factors or processes involved in each treatment or those aspects of the treatment agent's skills, attitudes, and motivations) that affect measures of treatment outcome.

In the absence of adequate experimental controls, it is difficult to determine the extent to which various categories of extraneous variables may influence the measured outcome. Of particular concern in uncontrolled studies are the potential analytic problems introduced by the Hawthorne effects, and the extraneous effects of history and maturation. Without an appropriate comparison group it is generally impossible to determine how much of the change observed in the study group is achieved by special considerations and opportunities (Hawthorne effects) and how much can be attributed to the treatment itself. Moreover, the influence of environmental variables (history) may be so powerful as to obscure the effect of treatment.

The development of the "maturing out" hypothesis (Winick, 1962) added another dimension to the problem of evaluating treatment effectiveness. In a five-year follow-up study, Winick observed a sharp decline in drug-related activities when patients reached their mid-thirties. He hypothesized that drug addiction is a phase in some people's development that is outgrown. This hypothesis has been debated for many years. However, recent follow-up studies (Hunt and Odoroff, 1969; Stephens and Cottrell, 1972) revealed that patients under 30 years of age become readdicted at much higher rates than those over 30, providing strong support for Winick's "maturing out" theory. It is a factor that must be given serious consideration in the design and analysis of treatment evaluation studies.

One final problem worth mentioning is that of maintaining the original design of the evaluative study. Any change in treatment strategy can seriously complicate the interpretation of the experimental outcome. This creates a dilemma inasmuch as good evaluation is perceived to be a continuous process providing management with timely feedback that may frequently dictate policy changes, and often results in a conflict between the researcher and administrator that is difficult to reconcile.

6. Practical difficulties in patient follow-up

Most evaluation designs depend upon criterion measurement prior to treatment and at one or more points after the patient returns to the community. A major problem in implementing evaluation studies involves locating the study population subsequent to treatment (graduates and dropouts). Unless substantially all or a representative number of the subjects can be contacted, the results of evaluative efforts may be seriously biased.

An evaluation study of the effectiveness of the methadone maintenance program in Ontario, Canada (Krakowski and Smart, 1972), was hampered by the fact that within one year 57 percent of the study patients had been discharged and presumably lost to follow-up. In a five-year follow-up study of patients admitted to the methadone maintenance treatment program in New York City (Gearing, 1974), more than one-third of the study subjects were no longer under observation. Some excellent follow-up results have been reported. In a field follow-up study of patients discharged from the United States Public Health Service Hospital at Lexington, Kentucky (Hunt and Odoroff, 1969), the follow-up team, consisting of two psychiatric social workers and one public health nurse, was able to achieve some degree of contact with 98.4 percent of the discharged patients. In another follow-up investigation of patients discharged from Lexington, Vaillant (1966) succeeded in locating 94 percent of his study subjects until their death or until 10 years after hospital discharge. Unfortunately, the excellent follow-up results achieved in these two investigations are rarely attained in most longitudinal evaluations of treatment efficacy. Moreover, some evaluations omit from follow-up those dropping out in the early stages of treatment (e.g., the first three months) even though these individuals may represent more than one-half of the treatment population.

Representative Approaches to Treatment Evaluation

Since there are a multitude of approaches to treatment evaluation that have been, or might be employed in various treatment settings, it would be impractical to attempt to describe all of them. Instead, some of the more representative approaches will be outlined.

Perhaps the most comprehensive evaluations of a single treatment modality are those reported by Gearing and associates (Gearing, 1971; Gearing and Schweitzer, 1974; Gearing, 1974) who have carefully followed the progress of patients admitted to all methadone maintenance programs in New York City since 1964. The goals of the New York City methadone maintenance treatment program have focused on social rehabilitation of the patient, with major emphasis on assisting them to become employable by completing their formal education, by learning a vocational skill, or both. The major criteria used for measuring treatment success are 1) abstinence from heroin and other drugs (including alcohol), 2) decrease in antisocial behavior (as measured by reported arrests and/or incarcerations, and 3) increase in social productivity (as measured by employment, schooling, or vocational training). Discharge rates were examined by means of a modified life table method which was employed to generate and compare "survival" curves by length of addiction, by education, by age at onset of addiction, and by previous employment. The influence of treatment was assessed by means of a One-Group Pretest-Posttest Design in which the critical measures were noted for each patient prior to and at the end of the study period.

These evaluative studies were of major significance because they stressed the importance of extramural evaluation and were administered by Dr. Gearing under the direction of an independent evaluating committee. The studies were not entirely extramural since the data were gathered intramurally, but whenever feasible the data were validated by outside sources. There are two major limitations to this approach to evaluation:

1. The patient sample available for analysis was highly selected and is not likely to be representative of the total addict population. The patients had to be sufficiently motivated to volunteer for

treatment and many of them had to wait three to six months from the time of acceptance to admission for treatment. Furthermore, the patient population was likely to be older than the addict population since admission to the program was limited to patients with at least two years of addiction. Therefore, the evaluation findings could be applied only to a group of older, longtime addicts who voluntarily sought treatment.

2. In the absence of a scientific comparison group, the potential influence of the Hawthorne effects, the effects of maturation, and other extraneous variables were largely uncontrolled. A quasi-experimental approach was employed by establishing a contrast group from a New York City detoxification program by matching the men in the program by age and by ethnic group. The detoxification group was followed in the same manner over the same period of time that the methadone maintenance group was followed and the two groups were compared by means of number of arrests, death rate, employment status, and educational advancement.

The growth of multimodality treatment programs has added a new dimension to evaluation studies. The methodology employed in early evaluation efforts was not very sophisticated. In a 1971-72 survey designed primarily to identify and delineate all drug programs within the state of Pennsylvania, the assessment of quality of treatment was a subsidiary part of the study (Glaser, et al., 1974). Programs were visited by two or more members of a four-person professional team consisting of a psychiatrist, a criminologist, a social worker, and an epidemiologist. Each team member formed an impression of the quality of treatment being provided and independently arrived at a rating on a scale from A through F immediately after each visit. The investigators, in their report, acknowledged the limitations of this approach to evaluation, recognizing that in the absence of any standardized criteria, the ratings were both global and impressionistic.

Most community responses to the drug problem have been unsystematic and poorly planned. Schlenger (1973) proposed a systems framework for studying the impact of the provision of services to drug users. His computer model is based on four major structural components: the drug user population, the nonuser population, the service component, and the legal component. The model balances the costs of providing services associated with alternative strategies with the effects of each strategy on the size of the drug user population. It allows for the specification and stimulation of any desired combination of available services over any number of simulated years. The projected impact of each strategy on the system variables of interest can then be compared to identify the most effective strategy. This approach requires a high degree of sophistication in computer modeling as well as access to a computer.

One of the most ambitious large-scale efforts to systematically evaluate drug abuse treatment programs over a short period of time was launched by Johns Hopkins University for the Office of Economic Opportunity in July 1972. The project fieldwork was completed one year later and the final report was submitted in August 1973 (Johns Hopkins, 1973).

The primary objectives of this study were:

1. to provide a description of the types of programs being funded to rehabilitate drug abusers, and

2. to evaluate a sample of treatment and rehabilitation programs with special emphasis on measuring changes in client behavior.

Patient flow data were analyzed for 16 programs, the characteristics of treatment delivery were examined for 11 programs, and a total of 1,328 patients was interviewed from 10 programs representing four different treatment regimens. The sample of programs studied was not chosen to be representative of all programs in the country.

Outcome measurements included retention rates based on more than 12,000 patient records and patient outcome status based on more than 1,000 patient interviews. The interview questionnaire, which was administered only once, after exposure to treatment, attempted to elicit from the patient his or her status before and after treatment in the following five areas: drug use, criminal activity, economic productivity, health and psychological adjustment, and social coping.

The investigators observed a marked decrease in drug abuse and crime for those who dropped out of treatment as well as those who remained in treatment. This improvement was noted in patients exposed to all treatment regimens. However, in the absence of a no-treatment comparison group, no definitive conclusions could be drawn with respect to the efficacy of treatment. The researchers acknowledged the possibility that, in addition to treatment, many other factors may have contributed to the measured outcome including the accuracy of the responses (patients may have exaggerated their pretreatment drug involvement and minimized their present use), the self-selection of patients interviewed (only 60 percent of the sample population was interviewed), and the influence of environmental variables.

Since 1969, the Department of Preventive Medicine and Community Health of the New Jersey Medical School has administered a comprehensive narcotic addiction treatment and rehabilitation program for the metropolitan Newark, New Jersey, community in cooperation with six established and independent treatment agencies. A model for extramural treatment evaluation has been gradually developed (Sheffet, et al., 1973) that is, at best, quasi-experimental in nature, but is nevertheless likely to represent a prototype of what is attainable in treatment evaluation.

The New Jersey Medical School evaluation model is based on a computerized management information system which includes a narcotics case register providing descriptive data on all drug-dependent individuals who come in contact with any treatment component, and a patient monitoring system that records each patient's progress in treatment. The model has evolved into three distinct evaluation phases, each focusing upon different criteria for measuring treatment efficacy:

Phase I: Patient Retention Rates: Life table methods are used to calculate patient retention rates (survival curves) for each treatment modality, and for various homogeneous patient subgroups, based on the premise that the longer a patient remains in treatment, the greater the chances of successful rehabilitation.

Phase II: Psychosocial Variables: To permit a more comprehensive analysis of treatment success, a detailed psychosocial questionnaire is administered to each patient upon admission to treatment and repeated at six month to one year intervals. The psychosocial outcome variables measured include: duration, nature, and extent of drug involvement, peer relationships, occupation and employment, education, residential stability, social, political, and religious involvement, family stability, motivations and goals, self-image, daily time allotments, legal income, medical complaints and disabilities, involvement with community agencies, hospitalizations, arrests, convictions, and incarcerations, and social deviations and alienations.

Phase III: Treatment-Based Variables: On-site assessment of treatment programs to determine to what extent treatment success or failure is influenced by specific treatment regimens, the attitudes and/or skills of the program staff, the interrelationships between program staff and addict, and other aspects of the treatment environment.

The immediate goal of the New Jersey Medical School's evaluation efforts is to establish an objective and meaningful procedure for evaluating treatment efficacy. The ultimate aim is to identify those patient and treatment-related variables that discriminate between treatment success or failure, raising the possibility of predicting a prospective patient's likelihood of success in a given treatment program or modality.

The Medical School model attempts to address the analytic problems caused by nonrandom assignment of patients to treatment facilities. An early attempt to randomly assign incoming patients to treatment programs was unsuccessful and was abandoned. As a result, a self-selection process exists by which certain segments of the patient population are disproportionately represented in some treatment programs. Therefore, comparative evaluations of treatment success have little meaning if they do not take into consideration differences in patient populations. The patient population is divided into homogeneous subgroups before comparisons of treatment efficacy are made among various programs. Within programs, the relative influence of a wide range of variables upon treatment success is estimated by means of multivariable statistical techniques. Patients who have not been exposed to a significant period of treatment (i.e., less than four weeks) are utilized as a "nontreatment" control group for comparison purposes. These procedures are designed to achieve a quasi-experimental approach to evaluation.

Future Directions in Treatment Evaluation

Evaluation research in the treatment of drug abuse has, in the past, been primarily concerned with the impact of the total program. The trend has been toward focusing upon subcomponents of the treatment program to determine which specific intervention procedures produce the most desirable changes in which patients under which conditions. This requires greater explicitness in defining treatment goals and techniques, and also a clearer understanding of the specific mechanisms of change. The latter can only be achieved through the application of scientific methodology that permits isolation and manipulation of variables in order to evaluate their effect.

Since it has been clearly established that not all patients respond equally well to a given treatment, the focus of evaluation research has transgressed beyond assessment of treatment efficacy to a search for those patient characteristics that discriminate between successful and unsuccessful treatment rehabilitation. This approach assumes that if it is possible to identify demographic, social, and/or psychological indexes that, on the average, differ significantly in groups of successfully and unsuccessfully treated patients, then it may be possible to measure prospective patients on one or more discriminating variables and predict their likelihood of success in a given treatment program or modality. This approach and some of its limitations are discussed in the recent literature (Hunt and Odoroff, 1969; Chambers et al., 1970; Snowden et al., 1973; D'Orban, 1974).

Guidelines for Treatment Program Evaluation

Following are some recommended guidelines to be followed to obtain optimal results in treatment evaluation efforts:

1. Evaluation should be a continuous process providing timely feedback to program administrators and staff.

2. Any evaluation effort must start with an explicit statement of the treatment objectives and of the criteria for effectiveness.

3. There is no single criterion measure that is sufficient to assess treatment effectiveness.

4. Program evaluation should be systematic and objective and based on empirical data.

5. Systematic data collection should be conceived as an integral

part of the day-to-day treatment routine at the inception of the treatment program and should not impose an unreasonable burden on the program staff.

6. Assessment of treatment efficacy should be based on at least a quasi-experimental research design when true experimental methodology is not feasible.

7. Evaluation of treatment efficacy should be based on the measurement of criteria before, during, and after exposure to treatment programs.

8. Evaluation should focus upon the impact of specific components of the treatment program as well as the impact of the total program.

9. Extramural evaluation is generally preferable to intramural evaluation.

EVALUATION OF DRUG EDUCATION PROGRAMS

Until the last decade, community drug abuse prevention programs were identified exclusively with the law. Once it became apparent that the use of illicit drugs could not be effectively controlled by the exclusive use of harsh legal penalties, police surveillance, and efforts to curtail the influx of drugs, then communities turned to drug education as the best means of prevention. It was generally assumed that communication of information about illegal substances would dissuade people from trying drugs or cause them to stop if they were already using them.

Drug education is a relatively new field that gained momentum in the late 1960s when illicit drug use among adolescents and young adults reached epidemic proportions. In fact, most of the formal drug education programs have been directed at adolescents through the school systems. Little headway has been made in educating adults and nonschool populations — the vast potential of the mass media as an educational tool has not been fully exploited.

Most school drug education programs have focused upon primary prevention in young populations. Swisher (1974) defined drug education as "a series of activities and experiences with young people which occur before decisions have been made about drug involvement and which, if fully explored, will result in fewer negative consequences for the individual." The fact that most drug education programs are narrow in scope, focusing upon student groups rather than on the population as a whole, has detracted from their usefulness. Other problems that have prevented the field of drug education from realizing its full potential include: 1) lack of clearly defined goals, 2) competition from mass media and other sources, 3) lack of well-trained, effective teachers, and 4) lack of clear understanding of the individual's motivation to use drugs (Smart and Fejer, 1974b).

Despite the fact that a great quantity of resources in time, activity, and money has been expended in drug education efforts, several recent published reviews of research on these programs (U.S. National Commission on Marihuana and Drug Abuse, 1973; Braucht, et al., 1973; Goodstadt, 1974; Smart and Fejer, 1974b) reached the same conclusion – there is little scientific evidence available to assess the effectiveness of drug education. Few evaluative research studies have been undertaken, and most of these have been scientifically unsound. Compared to the large number of implemented drug education programs, it was recently reported that no more than a few dozen have undergone even a rudimentary evaluation, probably less than a dozen have employed the principles of scientific experimentation, no more than eight programs have utilized a no-treatment control group, and fewer than eight programs have studied their impact on drug use (Smart and Fejer, 1974b).

Not only has there been virtually no empirical evidence confirming the hypothesis that drug education can prevent or reduce drug use, but it has been suggested that under certain circumstances drug education may even encourage drug usage by allaying fears and by arousing curiosity (Bourne, 1972), and also may, in effect, prove to be a costly distraction from the more important moral and political issues underlying the drug problem (Halleck, 1971). In view of the uncertainty as to the impact of drug education, the U.S. National Commission on Marihuana and Drug Abuse (1973, p. 357) recommended a moratorium on all new school drug education programs until operating programs have been tested for effectiveness. The value of drug education is currently being seriously scrutinized in light of its generally questionable past performance. The answers to the critical questions regarding program effectiveness will not be forthcoming until the major problems in evaluative research are resolved. It has been argued that scientific evaluation is too costly in terms of effort, time, and funding. However, drug education itself is very costly and unless it is objectively evaluated, there is no way of assuring its effectiveness.

Research Shortcomings of Drug Education Evaluation Studies

Most of the research limitations attributed to treatment program evaluation are equally applicable to the vast majority of studies evaluating drug education programs. The methodological requirements for effective evaluation are frequently difficult to attain in real life situations. Most of the reported evaluative studies in drug education suffer from one or more of the following methodological shortcomings:

1. Educational goals and outcome criteria were not clearly defined.

2. Difficulties were encountered in measuring behavioral changes.

3. Subjects were not randomly assigned to experimental and control groups.

4. No provision was made for the use of control groups consisting of individuals who were not exposed to any educational program (or to the usual program).

5. No attempt was made to assess the validity and reliability of criterion measurements.

6. Possible selection bias was introduced by the use of volunteer subjects.

7. Possible response bias was introduced by the subject's awareness of the problem objectives.

8. Possible response bias was introduced by the differential loss to follow-up of subjects in the experimental and control groups.

9. The sample size was inadequate.

10. The program content was too brief.

11. Follow-ups were held too soon to measure lasting change in knowledge and behavior.

12. Preprogram baseline data were unavailable for comparison (Posttest Only Design).

13. Difficulties were encountered in matching subjects in long-range longitudinal studies.

14. The study design precluded the control of exposure of the study population to variables extraneous to the educational program (e.g., information obtained from the mass media, peer group pressure).

15. Questionable generalizations were made of the evaluative results beyond the study population.

16. Too much emphasis was placed on assessing the impact of the total educational effort, and not enough on the specific approaches to drug education.

The evaluator has not only been faced with significant methodological problems, but has frequently been confronted with strong opposition to scientific evaluation of school-based drug education programs by parents and school administrators. Parents may not react favorably to a program that assigns their children to a control group receiving no drug education. They may also object to requiring their children to answer questions on drug use, on the grounds that this constitutes invasion of privacy. School administrators may feel threatened by attempts to test the effectiveness of educational programs. Many evaluation efforts have been unsuccessful because the evaluators did not take the time to educate, motivate, and involve the community.

GOALS OF DRUG EDUCATION

Although it is well recognized that meaningful evaluation is impossible without a clear delineation of the goals of a drug education program, it is frequently difficult to obtain a consensus on what should be the ultimate aims of drug education, and on what constitutes a favorable outcome. Goals range from an emphasis on abstinence to a stress on decision making and the formation of values (Globetti, 1974). In light of the widespread experimental use of drugs among adolescents and young adults, the trend has been toward compromising the objective of total abstinence and accepting the more realistic goals of lessening heavy drug use or confining it to less dangerous drugs. One or more of the following general criteria have been employed to measure the success of drug education programs:

A. Drug-Related Criteria
1. <u>Knowledge</u>: increasing knowledge about drugs
2. <u>Attitudes</u>: developing healthier attitudes toward drugs
3. <u>Behavior</u>: preventing the use of illegal drugs or altering current use levels to achieve –
   a. total abstinence
   b. a decrease in drug use levels
   c. a change in drug choice to less dangerous drugs
   d. a slowing of the increase in drug use
B. General Criteria (Swisher, 1974)
1. Increasing participation in alternative activities
2. Enhancing mental health
3. Improving decision-making capabilities
4. Clarifying values
5. Reducing alienation
6. Improving interpersonal relations

The analytic framework that is most compatible with the traditional approach to drug education is the information-processing approach outlined by McGuire (1970) and by Swanson (1972). This approach essentially treats drug education as communication designed to change attitudes and behavior or reinforce existing ones if they are compatible with the educational goals. It assumes that the communication of information is the first phase of a continuing process that flows from knowledge acquisition to attitude change and results in behavior modification.

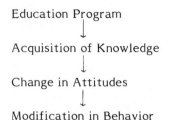

Education Program

↓

Acquisition of Knowledge

↓

Change in Attitudes

↓

Modification in Behavior

Using this approach, an antismoking campaign aimed at adolescents would be based on the assumption that, as the subject is exposed to more and more information on the relationship between smoking and health, he will eventually believe that smoking may adversely affect his health, he will therefore conclude that smoking is undesirable, and finally he will either quit smoking or reaffirm his intention to abstain in the future.

Recent studies have challenged the basic assumptions of the information-processing approach, demonstrating that there is little relationship between drug-related knowledge and drug-using behavior (Einstein 1973; Swisher, 1974). The relationships among knowledge, attitudes, and behavior are apparently neither simple nor consistent. After reviewing all published reports on drug education evaluation studies, Smart and Fejer (1974b) found that drug education programs of many types had increased knowledge, but they could identify only a few programs that produced changes in attitudes, and were aware of only one documented program that actually achieved a reduction in drug use. It now appears that attitudes are amazingly resistant to change and may not be easily affected by acquisition of knowledge. It also is questionable whether attitudinal changes necessarily result in behavioral changes. In fact, recent research tends to support the opposite hypothesis, suggesting that a person's behavior may change before his attitudes (Wicker, 1969; Swanson, 1972).

It is becoming more and more apparent that, to effect changes in behavior, a drug education program must do more than provide information about drugs. Educators are looking to develop a more meaningful overall educational experience that will focus upon preparing individuals to face a variety of problems and decisions throughout life, including those pertaining to the use of illicit drugs.

EXPERIMENTAL VARIABLES IN DRUG EDUCATION

Evaluation of drug education programs is complicated by the fact that there are a wide range of variables that can readily affect the measured outcome. These variables, which can be manipulated experimentally to determine what types of drug education programs have what types of effects on what types of people, may be classified into five separate categories (Smart and Fejer, 1974b):

1. Source variables: characteristics of the person or persons presenting the communication

2. Message variables: include type of approach, type of delivery, and message content

3. Channel variables: concern the medium or modality of communication (film, TV, radio, books, magazines, newspapers, face-to-face)

4. Receiver variables: characteristics of the target population (age, sex, educational level, socioeconomic status, drug involvement, etc.)

5. Destination variables: the goals of communication

These five categories of study variables must be clearly delineated before generalizations can be made beyond the study population. For example, the effectiveness of a specific communication may be due exclusively to the charisma and/or ability of the communicator – the type of approach may be irrelevant.

There has been much discussion in the literature on the choice of the most appropriate approach to drug education. At least eight different approaches have been proposed including: 1) the scare tactic approach, 2) the logical argument (exhortatory) approach, 3) the authoritative source approach, 4) the peer approach, 5) the cognitive or conceptual approach, 6) the encounter group approach, 7) the entertainment approach, and 8) the life problem approach (Richards, 1970; Zinberg and Robertson, 1972; Smart and Fejer, 1974b). Several recent studies have attempted to compare the effects of different approaches to drug education. Some of these studies will be described in detail.

Examples of Controlled Evaluations of Drug Education Programs

The relatively few evaluative research studies reported in the literature that have incorporated some degree of experimental control are of two types – those that attempt to measure the overall impact of a drug education program, and those that seek to compare alternative strategies. Following are some representative examples of each type of evaluative study:

Studies of Overall Impact

1. Evaluation of a two-day drug abuse prevention program in the Dallas Texas School District (Lewis, Gossett, and Phillips, 1972)

An anonymous questionnaire covering the use of 32 drugs or categories of drugs was administered to a random sample of 315 students at one of the larger senior high schools (experimental group), and to a random sample of 164 students at a smaller nearby school (control group). Except for size the schools were quite similar. Three days later a two-day drug education program was instituted at the experimental school. After a period of two weeks, the two schools were resurveyed during a district-wise study. The impact of the educational program was measured by comparing differences in drug use reported in the experimental and control group samples over a period of 19 days between the two surveys. The evaluators were unable to detect any significant program impact. However, the subjects were not randomly assigned to the experimental and control groups, and the elapsed time between the two measurements may have been too short to reflect the effects of the program.

2. Evaluation of a three-year antismoking program
in Winnepeg, Canada (Morison, Medovy, and MacDonnell, 1964)

The smoking habits of all Winnepeg school district students (grades five and up) were surveyed before and after a three-year program of health education on the hazards of smoking, directed to 8,300 out of 48,000 students. Two high schools were selected for the experimental program. All elementary and junior high schools that normally sent students to these high schools were included in the study. The results suggested that an intensive program of health education directed to teenagers in school was a potentially useful approach to decreasing the incidence of cigarette smoking. Although the experimental program was sufficiently long in duration to affect behavioral changes, it did not randomly assign subjects to the experimental group and made no attempt to match students to measure individual changes in smoking behavior.

3. Evaluation of a three-week drug education course in
Houston, Texas (Weaver and Tennant, 1973)

An intensive three-week drug education course was given to 452 eighth grade students from three schools in one school district in the greater Houston area. A group of 380 students from three schools in a different school district, similar in socioeconomic status, receiving minimal drug education, served as controls. At the conclusion of the three-week program both groups were administered anonymous questionnaires to measure knowledge and drug use levels. Nine months later the same questionnaire was anonymously administered to the experimental group only. Of the original 452 subjects, only 327 could be located for the nine-month retest. The study revealed that the students in the experimental group actually increased their drug use during the nine-month follow-up period. However, this study suffered from several research shortcomings including lack of random assignment, lack of baseline data, and lack of follow-up data on the control group.

Comparisons of Alternative Educational Strategies

1. Emotional vs. fact-giving appeals (English, 1972)

Two films were chosen to test the relative effectiveness of materials having different primary appeals in changing attitudes toward drug-using groups. The study population consisted of four male high school physical education classes. The first class was shown a drug film containing a high emotional appeal, the second viewed a factual, didactic presentation on drugs and the nervous system, and the third class witnessed an unrelated newsreel. No film was shown to the fourth class. All four groups were tested on a specially designed substance abuse scale developed to measure identification with and favorability toward certain drug-using groups. The first three classes were tested immediately after viewing their film. The effect of the emotional appeal film was not significantly different from the fact-giving film. However, both drug educational films produced the desired effect relative to both control groups. This evaluative model assumes that the four experimental groups were initially comparable, although there is no assurance that this was the case in the absence of random assignment.

2. High vs. low fear messages (Smart and Fejer, 1974a)

The impact of three levels of threat appeal about marijuana was measured by means of a 14-item anxiety scale. Each student in grades 9, 11, and 13 in North Bay high schools in Toronto was randomly given one of four questionnaires containing either a high-fear message, a medium-fear message, a low-fear message, or no message at all (control). After the message was read, each student was asked to respond to an anxiety scale and to indicate whether they had ever used marijuana and/or if they intended to use it. Of the total target population of 3,147 students, 82 percent responded to the anonymous questionnaire. The investigators concluded that the differences in anxiety produced by the varying levels of persuasion were very small and insignificant. The findings apply only to the short term – the long range impact was not measured. This study represents one of the few applications of the posttest only control group experimental design.

3. Lesser drugs vs. major drugs (Stuart, 1974)

This study attempted to evaluate two educational formats (student led, teacher led) and three content approaches (lesser drugs only, major drugs only, both types), employing a "no education" control group. Students in grades 7 and 9 (935) were randomly assigned by class to the various experimental or control groups. The experimental groups received their drug education during one class per week for ten weeks. The student-led sections had to be abandoned because of poor attendance; the educational formats could not be compared. The evaluation was based on three tests administered over a period of four months based on self-reported drug use and dealing in alcohol, marijuana, and LSD, items indicating "worry about drug use," and multiple-choice questions testing knowledge of pharmacology. No significant differences in impact were observed among the three content groups. Although the study purported to show an increase in drug use and dealing as a result of drug education, the findings are subject to question since only 106 of the original sample of 935 students could be matched for three test periods and the loss was greatest in the experimental group.

4. Comparison of four approaches to drug education
(Swisher, Warner, and Herr, 1972)

This investigation examined the relative impact of four different programs on drug-related attitudes, knowledge, and use. A total of 108 ninth grade and 108 eleventh grade students all received a standard ten-week drug education course as part of the basic health education curriculum. The students were stratified for intelligence and randomly assigned to one of four study groups. One group received no additional drug education (control group). Each of the other three groups received a different form of group counselling. Six intensively trained counsellors were randomly assigned to the counselling groups (two to each group), which met once a week for six weeks. The impact of the four programs was assessed by means of attitude, knowledge, and drug use scales, with measurements taken prior to and on the termination of the programs. The results showed no significant differences among the experimental and control groups in any of the areas of measurement, although the long-term impact of the programs could not be ascertained.

FUTURE DIRECTIONS IN EVALUATIONS
OF DRUG EDUCATION PROGRAMS

Despite the fact that drug education programs have proliferated during the past five years, it is still not possible to make an objective judgment as to whether or not they have been generally effective in preventing or reducing the use of illicit drugs or in controlling the indiscriminate use of various medically approved drugs and medicines. In order to make sound decisions as to the future directions of drug education, it is not only essential to be able to assess the overall impact of programs, but it is also critical to ascertain the relative levels of effectiveness of different approaches to drug education, with different target populations, in attaining different educational goals.

Clearly, more scientific research is needed to measure the effects of drug education programs. However, it is also important to gain greater understanding of the underlying factors that determine the effectiveness or ineffectiveness of these efforts. In particular, some of the specific questions that merit further consideration are:

1. What, realistically, should be the goals of drug education?

2. How do knowledge, attitudes, and behavior interact in the decision-making process?

3. What are the relative influences of source, message, channel, and receiver variables in the communication process?

4. How does the duration of exposure to an educational program relate to the longevity of its impact?

5. To what extent do largely uncontrolled environmental factors, such as parental and peer use of licit and illicit drugs, counteract the impact of drug educational efforts?

6. What are the potential risks of obtaining adverse effects as a consequence of drug education?

To provide the information that will be needed for future community intervention, two basic forms of study will be needed:

1. Large-scale, controlled longitudinal studies of intended outcomes to investigate the long-term (three to five years) impact of programs.

2. Smaller-scale experimental studies to measure the impact of different approaches to drug education, with emphasis on determining which components of successful programs contribute the most to producing the intended outcomes. It may be the case that the most effective approaches to education have already been discovered. If so, the task remains to isolate these from the large set of available approaches.

Guidelines for Drug Education Program Evaluation

1. All newly established drug education programs should have a built-in evaluation mechanism.

2. Goals should be well defined and realistic.

3. A variety of criteria for effectiveness should be considered with emphasis placed on changing attitudes and behavior in addition to increasing knowledge.

4. An attempt should be made to assess the reliability and validity of data-gathering instruments.

5. A strong attempt should be made to approximate experimental conditions.

6. Studies should be of sufficiently long duration to permit the assessment of long-range effects of education.

7. In addition to measuring overall program impact, studies should focus upon the specific effects of source, message, channel, and receiver variables.

SUMMARY AND CONCLUSIONS

There has been a plethora of newly established community drug abuse intervention programs during the past decade. Until recently, the effectiveness of most programs was not critically evaluated. While the costs of community drug programs have increased dramatically, there is little scientific evidence to demonstrate their efficacy. The trend has been toward more critical assessment of these programs to determine whether or not they merit continuing public and/or private support.

Some progress has been made in applying scientific principles to research and evaluation problems in the field of drug abuse, but much has yet to be done. Unfortunately, it is extremely difficult, in the community setting, to attain the level of control required for true scientific experimentation.

An attempt is made, in this chapter, to identify some of the difficulties encountered in applying scientific methodology, to suggest ways in which these difficulties may at least partially be overcome, and to recommend techniques and procedures that might be used in community research.

Major emphasis is given to three aspects of community drug research — estimating the magnitude of the problem, treatment evaluation, and drug education evaluation. The weaknesses and strengths of various sources of incidence and prevalence data are elucidated, and an analytic framework is developed and guidelines are established for the evaluation of community treatment and drug education programs.

Although the imposition of rigorous scientific control in community research may not often be possible, it is usually feasible to approximate the true experimental environment by means of quasi-experimental research designs which can yield useful information. If researchers take the appropriate steps to maximize the reliability and validity of their data, and to exercise some degree of statistical control, then workable estimates of the incidence and prevalence of drug abuse and addiction, and meaningful assessments of the efficacy of community intervention programs are attainable.

APPENDIX: OUTLINE OF CRITICAL CONCEPTS

Major Sources of Incidence and Prevalence Data

1. Police Records
2. Case Registers
3. Treatment Program Records
4. Polls and Surveys

5. Panels
6. Epidemic Models

Major Sources of Survey Bias

1. Inadequate Sampling Techniques (No Randomization)
2. Insufficient Sample Size
3. Poorly Worded Questionnaires
4. Lack of Standardization of Interviewing Techniques
5. Large Nonresponse
6. Invalid Responses

Classification of Research Designs

1. Preexperimental Designs
   a. Posttest Only Design
   b. One-Group Pretest-Posttest Design
   c. Static Group Comparison Design

2. Quasi-Experimental Designs
   a. Interrupted Time Series Design
   b. Matched Assignment Design

3. True Experimental Designs
   a. Pretest-Posttest Control Group Design
   b. Posttest Only Control Group Design
   c. Four-Group Design

Categories of Extraneous Variables
to be Controlled in Evaluation Research Studies

1. History Effects
2. Maturation Effects
3. Testing Effects
4. Instrument Decay Effects
5. Regression Effects
6. Selection Effects
7. Mortality Effects
8. Hawthorne Effects

Criteria for Evaluating the Success of Drug Treatment Programs

1. Behavior Changes
   a. Changes in Drug Involvement
   b. Other changes in Lifestyle

        Employment and education status
        Family stability
        Social, political, and religious involvement
        Illegal activities (arrests, convictions)
        Housing stability
        Medical problems

2. Intrapsychic Changes
   a. Attitudes
   b. Personality Organization
   c. Values
   d. Motivations and Goals
   e. Self-Image
   f. Alienations

Major Difficulties in Treatment Evaluation

1. Limited Generalizability of Evaluative Findings
2. Lack of Agreement on Aims, Objectives, and Criteria for Effectiveness
3. Lack of Appropriate Outcome Measures
4. Difficulties in Obtaining Objective and Reliably Measured Data
5. Difficulties in Applying Experimental Designs
6. Difficulties in Patient Follow-up

Criteria for Evaluating the Success of Drug Education Programs

1. Drug-Related Criteria
   a. Knowledge
   b. Attitudes
   c. Behavior
      Total abstinence
      Decrease in drug use levels
      Change in drug choice
      Slowing of increase in drug use

2. General Criteria

   a. Increasing Participation in Alternatives
   b. Enhancing Mental Health
   c. Improving Decision-Making Capabilities
   d. Clarifying Values
   e. Reducing Alienation
   f. Improving Interpersonal Relations

Major Shortcomings of Drug Education Evaluation Studies

1. Lack of Clearly Defined Educational Goals and Outcome Criteria
2. Difficulties in Applying Experimental Designs
3. Questionable Validity and Reliability of Outcome Measurements
4. Possible Response Bias Introduced by the Subjects' Awareness of the Program Objectives
5. Differential Loss to Follow-up of Subjects in Experimental and Control Groups
6. Follow-up Studies Held Too Soon
7. Difficulties in Matching Subjects in Long-Range Longitudinal Studies
8. Questionable Generalizability of Results Beyond Study Population
9. Inadequate Emphasis on Specific Approaches to Drug Education

Experimental Variables in Drug Education

1. Source Variables
2. Message Variables
3. Channel Variables
4. Receiver Variables
5. Destination Variables

BIBLIOGRAPHY

Ackoff, R.L., Gupta, S. & Minas, J.S. Scientific Method: Optimizing Applied Research Decisions. New York: Wiley, 1962.

American Public Health Association, Glossary of Administrative Terms in Public Health, American Journal of Public Health 50:225-226, 1960.

Amos, E.D., Dupont, R.L. & Lau, J.P. The Management of Large Multimodality, Multiclinic Drug Treatment Programs and Management Information Systems. Proc. 5th National Conference on Methadone Treatment 2:875-898, 1973.

Amsel, Z. et al. The Use of the Narcotics Register For Follow-Up Of A Cohort Of Adolescent Addicts. International Journal of the Addictions 6:225-39, 1971.

Andima, H., Krug, D., Bergner, L., Patrick, S., & Whitman, S. A Prevalence Estimation Model of Narcotics Addiction in New York City. American Journal Epidemiology 98:56-62, 1973.

Anker, J.L. Drug Usage and Patterns of Behavior in University Students: 1. General Survey and Marihuana Use. Journal of the American College of Health Association 19: 178-186, 1971.

Annis, H. Directions in Treatment Research. Addictions 20: 50-59, 1973.

Astin, A.W. & Boruch, R.F. A "Link" System for Assuring Confidentiality of Research Data in Longitudinal Studies. American Educational Research Journal 7:615-624, 1970.

Bale, R.N. Van Stone, W.W., Kuldau, J.M., Engelsing, T.M., & Zarcone, V.P. Methadone Treatment Versus Therapeutic Communities: Preliminary Results of a Randomized Study in Progress. Proc. Fifth Nat'l Conf on Methadone Treatment 2:1027-1034, 1973.

Ball, J.C. The Reliability and Validity of Interview Data Obtained From 59 Narcotic Drug Addicts. American Journal of Sociology 72: 650-654, 1967.

Blum, R. and Associates. Students and Drugs. San Francisco: Jossey-Bass, 1970.

Bourne, P.G. Is Drug Abuse A Fading Fad? J. Am. Coll. Health Assoc. 21: 198-200, 1973.

Braucht, G.N., Follingstad, D., Brakarsh, D., & Berry, K.L. Drug Education. A Review of Goals, Approaches and Effectiveness, and a Paradigm for Evaluation. Q. J. Stud. Alcohol 34:1279-92, 1973.

Callan, J.P., & Patterson, C.D. Patterns of Drug Abuse Among Military Inductees. Am. J. Psychiatry 130: 260-64, 1973.

Campbell, D.T. Factors Relevant to the Validity of Experiments in Social Settings In: Program Evaluation in the Health Fields, H.C. Schulberg, A. Sheldon, & F. Baker, editors, New York: Behavioral Publications, N.Y. 1969.

Chambers, C.D., Babst, D.V. & Warner, A. Characteristics Predicting Long-Term Retention In a Methadone Maintenance Program. Proc. Third Nat'l Conf. on Methadone Treatment, 1:140-143, 1970.

Corder, B.W., Dezelsky, T.L., Toohey, J.C., & Tow, P.K. An Analysis of Trends in Drug Use Behavior at Five American Universities. Journal of School Health 44:386-9, 1974.

D'Orban, P.T. A Follow-Up Study of Female Narcotic Addicts: Variables Related to Outcome. British Journal of Psychiatry 125:28-33, 1974.

Dupont, R.L. & Piemme, T.E. The Estimation of The Number of Narcotic Addicts in an Urban Area. Medical Annals D.C. 42:323-326, 1973.

Einstein, S. Drug Abuse Prevention Education: Scope, Problems & Prospectives. Prev. Med. 2:569-581, 1973.

English, G.E. The Effectiveness of Emotional – Appeal Versus Fact – Giving Drug Educational Films. J. Sch. Health 42:540-1, 1972.

Fishman, J.J., Conwell, D.P., & Amsel, Z. New York City Narcotics Register: A Brief History. Int. J. Addict 6:561-569, 1971.

Gearing, F.R. Evaluation of Methadone Maintenance Treatment Program. In Methadone Maintenance, S. Einstein, Editor, Marcel Dekker, Inc., 1971, pp. 171-197.

Gearing, F.R. Methadone Maintenance Treatment Five Years Later – Where Are They Now? American Journal of Public Health Supplement 64:44-50, 1974.

Gearing, F.R. & Schweitzer, M.D. An Epidemiological Evaluation of Long-Term Methadone Maintenance Treatment for Heroin Addiction. American Journal Epidemiology 100:101-112, 1974.

George, A. Survey of Drug Use in a Sydney Suburb. Medical Journal of Australia 2:233-237, 1972.

Glaser, F.B., Adler, F., Moffett, A.D., & Ball, J.C. The Quality of Treatment for Drug Abuse. American Journal of Psychiatry 131:598-601, 1974.

Glenn, W.A. & Richards, L.G. Recent Surveys of Nonmedical Drug Use: A Compendium of Abstracts. National Institute on Drug Abuse, Rockville, Md., 1974.

Globetti, G. A Conceptual Analysis of the Effectiveness of Alcohol Education Programs In Research on Methods and Programs of Drug Education, M. Goodstadt, Editor, Addiction Research Foundation of Ontario, 1974, pp. 97-112.

Goode, E. Cigarette Smoking and Drug Use on a College Campus. Int. J. Addict. 7:133-140, 1972.

Goodstadt, M. Research on Methods and Programs of Drug Education. M. Goodstadt, Editor, Addiction Research Foundation of Ontario, 1974.

Greden, J.F., Morgan, D.W., & Frenkel, S.I. The Changing Drug Scene: 1970-1972. American Journal of Psychiatry 131:77-81, 1974.

Haberman, P.W., Josephson, E., Zanes, A. & Elinson, J. High School Drug Behavior: A Methodological Report on Pilot Studies. In Proceedings of the First International Conferences on Student Drug Survey, Einstein, S. & Allen, S., Editors, Farmingdale, N.Y.: Baywood Publishing Co., 1972.

Halleck, S. The Great Drug Education Hoax. Addictions 18:1-13, 1971.

Horan, J.J., Westcott, T.B., Vetovich, C. and Swisher, J.D. Drug Usage: An Experimental Comparison of Three Assessment Conditions, Unpublished Report, The Pennsylvania State University, 1973.

Hughes, P.H., Schaps, E., & Sanders, C.R. A Methodology for Monitoring Adolescent Drug Abuse Trends. Int. J. Addict. 8:403-19, 1973.

Hunt, L.G. Heroin epidemics: A Quantitative Study of Current Empirical Data, The Drug Abuse Council, Inc., Washington, D.C., 1973.

Hunt, L.G. Recent Spread of Heroin Use In The United States. Am. J. Public Health 64:16-23, 1974 (Supplement).

Hunt, G.H. & Odoroff, M.E. Follow-up Study of Narcotic Drug Addicts After Hospitalization. In Program Evaluation in the Health Fields, Schulberg, H.C., Sheldon, A. & Baker, R., Editors, New York: Behavioral Publications, 1969, pp. 393-415.

Jacobson, N.O., & Silfverskiold, N.P. A Controlled Study of a Hypnotic Method in the Treatment of Alcoholism, With Evaluation by Objective Criteria. British Journal of the Addictions 68:25-31, 1973.

James, G. Evaluation in Public Health practice. In Program Evaluation In the Health Fields, H.C. Schulberg, A. Sheldon, & F. Baker, Editors, New York: Behavioral Publications, 1969.

Johns Hopkins University School of Hygiene and Public Health. An Evaluation of Treatment Programs for Drug Abusers. Volume 2. Summary, Baltimore, 1973.

Johnston, L.D. Drug Use During and After High School: Results of a National Longitudinal Study. American Journal of Public Health 64:29-37, 1974 (Supplement).

Josephson, E., Haberman, P., Zanes, A., & Elinson, J. Adolescent Marijuana Use: Report on a National Survey. In Proceedings of the First International Conference on Student Drug Surveys, S. Einstein and S. Allen, Editors, Farmingdale, N.Y.: Baywood Publishing Co., 1972.

Kavaler, F., Denson, P.M. & Krug, D.C. The Narcotics Register Project: Early Development. Brit. J. Addict. 63: 75-81, 1968.

Kern, J.C. Evaluating Community Drug Abuse Agencies. J. Drug Educ. 4:129-139, 1974.

Kandel, D. Adolescent Marihuana Use: Role of Parents and Peers. Science 181: 1067-1070, 1973.

King, F.W. Anonymous Versus Identifiable Questionnaires in Drug Usage Surveys. Psychology 25:982-985, 1970.

Krakowski, M. & Smart, R.G. The Outpatient Treatment of Heroin Addicts With Methadone. Canadian Journal of Public Health 63:397-404, 1972.

Larkin, E.J. Three Models of Evaluation. Canadian Psychologist 15:89-94, 1974.

Lavenhar, M.A. The Drug Abuse Numbers Game. American Journal of Public Health 63: 807-809, 1973.

Lavenhar, M.A., Sheffet, A., Duval, H., & Louria, D.B. The New Jersey Medical School Narcotics Case Register. I. Background, Methodology and Summary of First Four Years of Operation. Addictive Disorders 1:513-527, 1975.

Lewis, J.M., Gossett, J.T., & Phillips, V.A. Evaluations of a Drug Prevention Program. Hospital Community Psychiatry 23:36-38, 1972.

Luetgert, M.J., & Armstrong, A.H. Methodological Issues in Drug Usage Surveys: Anonymity, Recency, and Frequency. Int. J. Addict. 8:683-689, 1973.

McGuire, W.J. Designing Communications to Change Attitudes Regarding Drug Abuse. In Communications and Drug Abuse. Proceedings of the Second Rutgers Symposium on Drug Abuse, J.R. Wittenborn, J.P. Smith, & S.A. Wittenborn, editors, Charles C. Thomas, Springfield, Illinois, 1970.

Milman, D.H. Patterns of Illicit Drug and Alcohol Use Among Secondary School Students, Journal of Pediatrics 83:314-320, 1973a.

Milman, D.H. Patterns of Drug Usage Among University Students: V. Heavy Use of Marijuana and Alcohol by Undergraduates. Journal of the American College Health Assoc. 21:181-187, 1973b.

Morison, J.B., Medovy, H. & MacDonnell, G.T. Health Education and Cigarette Smoking. Canadian Medical Association Journal 91:49-56, 1964.

Petzel, T.P., Johnson, J.E., & McKillip, J. Response Bias in Drug Surveys. Journal of Consulting Clinical Psychology 40:437-439, 1973.

Porter, M.R., Vieira, T.A., Kaplan, G.J., Heesch, J.R., & Colyar, A.B. Drug Use in Anchorage, Alaska Journal of the American Medical Association 223:657-664, 1973.

Prendergast, J.J. Jr., et al. Drug Use and its Relation to Alcohol and Cigarette Consumption in the Military Community of West Germany Int. J. Addict. 8:741-754, 1973.

Putnam, D.G., McCaslin, F.C., Stewart, A., Senn, R.M., Bent, R.J., & Kiesler, D.J. A Model for Program Evaluation and Development. Proceedings of the 5th National Conference on Methadone Treatment 1:1285-1288, 1973.

Richards, L. Psychological Sophistication in Current Drug Abuse Education. In Communication and Drug Abuse, Proceedings of the Second Rutgers Symposium on Drug Abuse, J.R. Wittenborn, J.P. Smith, & S.A. Wittenborn, Editors, Charles C. Thomas, Springfield, Illinois, 1970.

Richards, L.G. & Carroll, E.E. Illicit Drug Use and Addiction. In the U.S. Public Health Rep. 85:1035-1041, 1970.

San Mateo County Department of Public Health and Welfare. Student Drug Use Surveys — San Mateo County, California, 1968-1975, June 9, 1975.

Schlenger, W.E. A Systems Approach to Drug User Services. Behavioral Science 18:137-147, 1973.

Schulberg, H.C., Sheldon, A., & Baker, F. Chapter I. Introduction In Program Evaluation in the Health Fields. H.C. Schulberg, A. Sheldon, & F. Baker, Editors, New York: Behavioral Publications, 1969.

Sells, S.B. & Watson, D.D. A Spectrum of Approaches in Methadone Treatment: Relation to Program Evaluation. Proc. Third National Conf. on Methadone Treatment, 1:17-21, 1970.

Sells, S.B. Evaluation of Treatment for Drug Abuse. Proc. Fifth National Conf. on Methadone Treatment 2: 1362-1368, 1973.

Sheffet, A., Hickey, R.F., Lavenhar, M.A., Wolfson, E.A., Duval, H., Millman, D., & Louria, D.B. A Model for Drug Abuse Treatment Program Evaluation. Preventive Medicine 2:510-523, 1973.

Smart, R.G., & Jackson, D., A Preliminary Report on the Attitudes and Behavior of Toronto Students in Relation to Drugs. Addiction Research Foundation, Toronto, 1969.

Smart, R.G. Illicit Drug Use in Canada: A Review of Current Epidemiology with Clues for Prevention. Int. J. Addict. 6:383-405, 1971.

Smart, R.G. High School Drug Use: A Survey with Implications for Education. In Resource Book for Drug Abuse Education, 2nd Edition, National Clearinghouse for Drug Abuse Information, 1973, pp. 13-18.

Smart, R.G. & Fejer, D. Marihuana Use Among Adults in Toronto. Br. J. Addict. 68:117-128, 1973.

Smart, R.G. Fejer, D., & White, W.J. Trends in Drug Use Among Metropolitan Toronto High School Students: 1968-1972. Addictions, 20:62-72, 1973.

Smart, R.G. & Fejer, D. The Effects of High and Low Fear Messages About Drugs. Journal of Drug Education 4:225-235, 1974a.

Smart, R.G. & Fejer, D. Drug Education: Current Issues, Future Directions. Addiction Research Foundation of Ontario, Toronto, 1974b.

Smith, D.E., Linda, L., Loomis, S., Jacobs-White, L., Bricker, B., and Singleton, J. A Community-Based Drug Abuse Rehabilitation Program in the Haight-Ashbury. Preventive Medicine 2:529-542, 1973.

Snowden, L., Wolf, K. & Panyard, C. Issues in Developing Useful Screening Indicators From Variables Which Discriminate Between Successful and Unsuccessful Methadone Treatment Patient. Proceedings 5th National Conference on Methadone Treatment 1:169-172, 1973.

Solomon, R.W. An Extension of Control Group Design. Psychology Bulletin 46:137-150, 1949.

Stephens, R. The Truthfulness of Addict Respondents in Research Projects. International Journal of the Addictions 7:549-558, 1972.

Stephens, R., & Cottrell, E. A Follow-up Study of 200 Narcotic Addicts Committed for Treatment Under the Narcotic Addict Rehabilitation Act (NARA). British Journal of the Addictions 67:45-53, 1972.

Stuart, R.B. Teaching Facts About Drugs: Pushing or Preventing? Journal of Educational Psychology 66:189-201, 1974.

Summers, T. Validity of Alcoholics' Self-Reported Drinking History. Quarterly Journal Stud. Alcohol 31:972-974, 1970.

Swanson, J.C. Second Thoughts on Knowledge and Attitude Effects Upon Behavior, Journal of School Health 42:363-365, 1972.

Swisher, J.D., Warner, R.W., Jr., & Herr, E.L. Experimental Comparison of Four Approaches to Drug Abuse Prevention Among Ninth and Eleventh Graders. Journal of Consulting Psychology 19:328-332, 1972.

Swisher, J.D. The Effectiveness of Drug Education: Conclusions Based on Experimental Evaluations. In Research on Methods and Programs of Drug Education, M. Goodstadt, Editor, Addiction Research Foundation of Ontario, 1974, pp. 147-160.

Twain, D., Harlow, E., & Merwin, D. Research and Human Services, Research and Development Center, N.Y., 1970.

U.S. Dept. of Health, Education, and Welfare, Nat'l Clearinghouse for Smoking & Health. Patterns and Prevalence of Teen-age Cigarette Smoking: 1968, 1970, and 1972. DHEW Publication No. (HSM) 73-8701, August 6, 1972.

U.S. National Commission on Marihuana and Drug Abuse. Drug Use in America: Problem in Perspective, 2nd Report, U.S. Govt. Printing Office, March 1973.

Vaillant, G.E. A 12 Year Follow-up of New York Narcotics Addicts I. The Relation of Treatment to Outcome. American Journal of Psychiatry 122:727-737, 1966.

Weaver, S.C. & Tennant, F.S., Jr. Effectiveness of Drug Education Programs for Secondary School Students. American Journal of Psychiatry 130:812-14, 1973.

Whitehead, P.C., & Smart, R.G. Validity and Reliability of Self-Reported Drug Use. Canadian Journal of Criminology and Corrections 14:1-7, 1972,

Wicker, A.W. Attitudes Versus Actions: The Relationship of Verbal and Overt Behavioral Responses to Attitude Objects. Journal of Social Issues 25:41-78, 1969.

Winick, C. Maturing Out of Narcotic Addiction. United Nations Bulletin on Narcotics 14:1, 1962.

Wolfson, E.W., Lavenhar, M.A., Blum, R., Quinones, M.A., Einstein, S., and Louria, D.B. Survey of Drug Abuse in Six New Jersey High Schools: I. Methodology and General Findings. In Proceedings of the First International Conference on Student Drug Surveys, Einstein, S. and Allen, S. Editors, New York: Baywood Publishing Company, 1972, pp. 9-32.

Zingberg, N.E. & Robertson, J.A. Drugs and the Public. New York: Simon & Schuster, 1972.

METHODOLOGY IN COMMUNITY RESEARCH
GLOSSARY

Bias:
>Any influence that systematically affects the accuracy of observations.

Case register:
>A system for collecting registration and follow-up information on a population of drug addicts, based on cases reported by agencies or individuals.

Control group:
>Subjects who are selected so that they are initially comparable to the experimental group, but are not exposed to the experimental stimulus.

Drug use survey:
>A data-gathering technique frequently employed to elicit information about knowledge of and attitudes toward drugs in addition to drug-using behavior.

Evaluation research:
>The process of determining the extent to which a program is successful in achieving a predetermined objective.

Experimental group:
>Subjects who are exposed to the experimental stimulus.

Extraneous variables:
>Factors that could, independently or in conjunction with the experimental variable, influence the study outcome if uncontrolled.

Incidence:
>The number of new drug addicts (abusers) that come into being during a specified period of time (e.g., one year).

Interaction effects:
>The effects of extraneous variables occurring jointly with the experimental variable.

Longitudinal surveys:
>Repeat studies of a specific group of individuals over a period of time.

Matching:
>A technique used to attempt to establish similarity or comparability of the experimental and control group by selecting them in such a way that they will have the same distribution with respect to all variables known to affect study outcome.

Period prevalence:
>The number of cases that were observed during a specified period of time (e.g., one year).

Point prevalence:
>The number of drug addicts (abusers) on hand at a given point in time.

Primary prevention:
>Prevention of drug abuse in a previously uninvolved population.

Process analysis:
>Monitors the extent to which a program utilizes its resources to pursue its goals.

Product analysis:
  Assesses the extent to which a program's efforts achieve the desired goal(s) or end product(s).
Random sample:
  A sample in which the probabilities of selection are known. (In its simplest form, each member of the population has an equal and independent chance of being selected.)
Reliability:
  The degree to which a measurement is reproducible.
Secondary prevention:
  Prevention of the progression of drug abuse in an involved population that does not as yet have residual disability.
Stratified random sample:
  The population is first divided into distinct subgroups or strata, and a random sample is drawn from each subgroup.
Tertiary prevention:
  Rehabilitation of the drug-abusing population which has significant residual disability.
True experimental designs:
  Studies that incorporate the classical features of research design, including random selection of subjects, random assignment of subjects to experimental and control groups, and opportunities for manipulating and controlling all variables that may affect study outcomes.
Validity:
  The degree of conformity of an estimate derived from a sample to the true value of the parameter in the total population of interest.

SELECTED ANNOTATED REFERENCES

Blum, Richard H. and Associates, Students and Drugs. Drugs II: College and High School Observations. San Francisco, Calif.: Jossey-Bass, 1970, 399 pp.
  This work represents some of the major findings of the studies conducted by the psycho-pharmacology group at Stanford University, focusing on drug-using conduct and social and psychological correlates of drug use among students in five western colleges or universities and in four California high schools.
  Several methods were used to analyze the study data. In each of the five participating colleges, a sample of undergraduates was randomly drawn from the registrar's list of matriculated students. Personal interviews were conducted by trained interviewers using a thoroughly pretested interview schedule. In addition, selected samples of students with intense interest in illicit drugs, left-wing politics, right-wing politics and religion were interviewed and given psychological tests. Other methods employed included rating scales of experience and attitudes, sociometric devices, a panel study, psychiatric interviews, and data gathering from records of institu-

tions, school administrators, school health services, and local and state police agencies. The data collected were processed by means of coding, quantification, computer processing, and, when appropriate, the application of statistical tests.

Braucht, G.N., Follingstad, D., Brakarsh, D. and Berry, K.L. Drug Education. A Review of Goals, Approaches and Effectiveness, and a Paradigm for Evaluation. Quarterly Journal of Studies in Alcohol 34:1279-1292, December 1973.

This paper outlines the controversy over the goals and educational methods currently used in alcohol and drug education. A review of the research on drug education programs indicates that there is almost no empirical evidence of the effectiveness of these programs. Strategies for future research are suggested to address some of the unanswered questions in drug education.

Campbell, D.T. Factors Relevant to the Validity of Experiments in Social Settings. In Program Evaluation in the Health Fields, Schulberg, N.C., Sheldon, A., and Baker, F., editors. New York: Behavioral Publications, 1969.

The validity of experiments in social settings is examined by identifying and analyzing seven categories of extraneous variables which experimental designs seek to control including history, maturation, testing, instrument decay, regression, selection, and mortality. The extent to which these variables jeopardize the internal and external validity of the experiment is discussed. The validity of three preexperimental and three true experimental designs is evaluated by considering the ways in which each design handles the problem of controlling extraneous variables. A case is made for the use of the Posttest Only Group Design in social settings.

Fishman, J.J., Conwell, D.P., and Amsel, Z. New York City Narcotics Register: A Brief History. International Journal of the Addictions 6:561-569, September 1971.

This paper traces the early history and the development of the New York City Health Department Narcotics Register Project as a research application of the cumulative case register approach to disease surveillance. The development of a comprehensive reporting system, based on nonmedical as well as medical sources, is correlated with successful long-range efforts to amend the New York City Health codes and the New York State Health Law to assure the confidentiality of register information. Improvements in the reporting system and the method of handling reports have increased the level of efficiency and have enhanced the research potential of the register contents.

Gearing, F.R., Methadone Maintenance Treatment Five Years Later – Where Are They Now? American Journal of Public Health (Supplement) 64:44-50, December 1974.

The results of a five-year follow-up of a cohort of 1,230 patients admitted to the Methadone Maintenance Treatment Program in New York City through 1968 are presented. The major criteria used for measuring success of treatment were increase in social productivity, decrease in antisocial behavior, and willingness to accept help for excessive drug use or for psychiatric problems. The data were analyzed using a life table method to account for the variation in the periods of observation.

During the study period, the percentage of patients who could be classified as socially productive rose from 36 percent to 72 percent and antisocial behavior, as measured by arrests and incarcerations, decreased from 201 per 100 person-years to 1.24. Inasmuch as the cohort followed was a highly selected group, the findings are likely to apply only to highly motivated individuals who volunteer for treatment after surviving at least two years of addiction.

Glenn, W.A., and Richards, L.G. Recent Surveys of Nonmedical Drug Use: A Compendium of Abstracts, National Institute on Drug Abuse, Rockville, Md., July 1974.

This useful compendium of recent drug use surveys not only contains summary data abstracted from published reports, but also offers a comprehensive critical review of survey methodology. The discussion is focused upon a consideration of sampling methods, sample size, nonresponse bias, response validity, and questionnaire preparation and administration. The specific methodological requirements needed to obtain reliable, valid estimates for generalization to wider groups and populations are outlined.

Goodstadt, M. Myths and Methodology in Drug Education: A Critical Review of the Research Evidence. In Research on Methods and Programs of Drug Education, Goodstadt, M., editor, Addiction Research Foundation of Ontario, Toronto, 1974, pp. 113-145.

This paper critically examines the scientific quality of the available evidence concerning the effectiveness of drug education programs. The discussion centers upon the limitations of three different types of investigations-survey studies, large-scale experimental programs, and smaller-scale experimental programs. It is concluded that there is an almost total lack of evidence indicating beneficial effects of drug education; the evidence is insufficient from a scientific viewpoint to permit one to conclude confidently, one way or another, about the effectiveness of drug education. The forms of study required for future research are outlined.

Lavenhar, M.A. The Drug Abuse Numbers Game, American Journal of Public Health 63:807-809, Sept. 1973.

This paper attempts to warn readers of the pitfalls and limitations in the collection and interpretation of statistical data relating to drug abuse, a subject where caution and circumspection are necessary. Four variations of the drug abuse numbers game are discussed – the Incidence and Prevalence Game, the Epidemiology Game, the Consequence Game, and the Treatment Evaluation Game. It is concluded that most of the deceptions in reporting in the field of drug abuse are unintentional, but due to lack of statistical expertise.

Richards, L.G. and Carroll, E.E. Illicit Drug Use and Addiction in the United States, Public Health Reports 85:1035-1041, December 1970.

This review article attempts to describe the difficult task of estimating the scope of illicit drug use, abuse, and addiction in the

United States. The authors found that most of the data needed for estimates simply do not exist and those that do exist cannot be used with full confidence because they lack validity or reliability or both. The limitations of various reporting sources, including nationwide polls and surveys of high school and college students, are discussed along with various approaches to estimating narcotic addiction. It is concluded that data from ongoing health surveys yield the best estimates of narcotic drug use since they do not depend on varied sources and forms of reporting.

Schulberg, H.C., Sheldon, A., and Baker, F. Chapter 1. Introduction. In Program Evaluation in the Health Fields, Schulberg, H.C., Sheldon, A., and Baker, F., editors. New York: Behavioral Publications, 1969, pp. 3-28.

This introductory chapter provides an overview of the basic concepts of program evaluation in the health field. The two most frequently used evaluation models, the Goal-Attainment Model and the Systems Model, are discussed. Major emphasis is given to the problems of choosing an appropriate research design and of selecting relevant evaluation or appraisal indexes. The shortcomings of various examples of program evaluation are enumerated.

Sheffet, A., Hickey, R.F., Lavenhar, M.A., Wolfson, E.A., Duval, H., Millman, D., and Louria, D.B. A Model for Drug Abuse Treatment Program Evaluation. Preventive Medicine 2:510-523, December 1973.

This paper describes the comprehensive narcotic treatment and rehabilitation program administered by the New Jersey Medical School for the metropolitan Newark, New Jersey community in cooperation with six independent agencies, and outlines a three-phase proposal for evaluating the program. Preliminary results focus upon characteristics of patients by treatment modality, treatment retention rates, and an analysis of program graduates. This evaluative effort is designed, not only to assess the efficacy of individual treatment programs, but also to investigate the feasibility of matching addicts to programs.

Smart, R.G. and Fejer, D. Drug Education: Current Issues, Future Directions, Addiction Research Foundation of Ontario, Toronto, 1974, 112 pp.

This comprehensive, critical review of the current status of drug education starts with a discussion of the major problems of drug education and the difficulties involved in deciding upon appropriate goals, targets, and methods. The information-processing approach to drug education is chosen as the analytic framework for the critical review. The results of research into what influences the effectiveness of drug information communications are presented. A description of the curricula, programs, and drug educational guides used in North American programs is provided. A critical analysis of all published and unpublished evaluations of drug education programs is presented along with a summary of current research needs and suggestions for ideal drug education programs, from the point of view of evaluation and content.

Swisher, J.D. The Effectiveness of Drug Education: Conclusions Based on Experimental Evaluations. In Research on Methods and Programs of Drug Education, M. Goodstadt, editor, Addiction Research Foundation of Ontario, Toronto, 1974, pp. 147-160.

The purpose of this paper is to describe the extent to which a variety of drug education strategies have been effective. The author starts with the premise that drug education, to be effective, must be more than simply education about drugs. It must provide germane education experiences to enhance mental health, improve decision making, clarify values, and increase participation in alternative activities. In other words, it must prepare individuals to face a variety of decisions, including those pertaining to the use of drugs.

The effectiveness of drug education programs is defined in the context of uniform and unique outcomes. Several conclusions are reached on the basis of a review of the published research. Although nearly any kind of educational program will result in an increase in knowledge about drugs, attitudinal change appears to be more difficult to effect and there is very limited evidence that any program has been successful in altering drug use patterns.

10 Addiction as a Community Disorder

I. Silverman

In response to their problems of drug addiction, our communities have made a commitment of their resources that is nothing less than amazing, inasmuch as it has happened so fast and in so many places and with so broad a penetration of the very fabric of our institutions. Less than a full generation ago, it was possible almost anywhere in this country to run a school or a hospital or a police department or a house of worship or even a family group without knowing or caring much about addiction. That has changed almost everywhere, and there is still no prospect in sight of its changing back. By now we have not only addiction but also a massive addiction services effort to be concerned about.

THE PROBLEM

Most observers would agree that the manner of our collective response has been muddled and unsure at every level, most noticeably at the local level. We have chronically lacked information on what happens in the fast-changing scenes of illegal drug consumption, scenes that we have driven underground by our heavy-handed reliance on legal machinery for control. Much of our information deficit, however, is not self-inflicted. We simply have not yet learned enough about the specifics of what causes addiction, or of what "cures" it, or just what we are buying through spending on programs to control it. Everyone who has worked on the problem – by now we are legion – has found it very tough to deal with.

If there is so much that we don't know, why are we doing so much? For all we know, might we not do as well or even better by doing much less about addiction – or perhaps much, much less?

That kind of question is raised both on the left and on the right, in that it occurs to some who like smoking marijuana and to some who hate "social programs." It is a valid question that should not be ignored in the political process that sets the level and the tone of our effort. To answer with dignity we need not only knowledge but wisdom. We need to find out not merely if we should do more of this or less of that, but also and above all: What is it all about?

My thesis here will be that addiction should be seen as a disorder of the community as a whole in the same formal way that heart disease should be seen as a disorder of the person as a whole. It is not enough to perceive that people get addicted or that hearts get attacked. A larger frame is needed to hold the most important questions.

In the following sections of this paper I will question each of the substantive terms in its title. What is addiction? What is community? What is disorder? The ensemble of the answers I shall offer is intended to form a "big picture," one that community leaders and second-guessers might care to hang on the wall as if it were a map of a theater of operations. To anticipate how the questions are intended and how they are to be handled, I will comment on each one:

Addiction is what? It is "enslavement to some habit."(1) By a stricter definition, addiction has a physiological basis, as distinct from habituation where the basis is merely psychological. This distinction is easy to imagine but hard to measure, especially for epidemiologic purposes of finding and counting cases. Therefore, the World Health Organization has suggested that the term "addiction" might be abandoned in favor of "dependency." For present purposes, however, the point is not what happens in the tissues but rather what happens in the community, where the term "addiction" has the power to disturb, and the term "dependency" sounds like a euphemism. Socially, there is much difference between some people's dependency on heroin or alcohol or gambling or golf, as opposed to everyone's dependency on air or water, or an infant's on parental care, or parents' on each other. I will try to define addiction in societal terms, finally producing a chart that locates addiction in relation to other comparable concepts of disorder within community.

Community is what? Literally, it means "together as one," a basic idea that is bound to collect many facets of meaning. For our purposes a community is a place to live (or visit) and know people and make a living (and perhaps get parking tickets). I will discuss the literature that has appeared at the intersection of "community" and "addiction"; and, as a point of departure, I shall offer a model to locate the concept of "community" for present purposes.

Disorder, finally, is what? It is a state in which "the shoe pinches." To remedy disorder, or even to become aware of it, there must be a conception of good order as it applies to feet and to shoes and to the fit between them. The concepts of disorder and order will occupy us between our points of departure and arrival.

COMMUNITY

In the large amount of learned literature that has accumulated on matters of addiction, there are many studies that are relevant to our topic, but I could find only two reports that I would place at the center of the domain of addiction as a community issue. What kinds of studies have been done? What are the two central studies about, and what do they have to say? What do we mean by "community" in the first place?

The Literature

To make a search for community studies on addiction, we might consider everything written on addiction and then proceed by elimination. We might first eliminate studies of physical, chemical, and biological properties of drugs. We also would eliminate those studies that are psychological or behavioral in nature, if they view addiction as a property of a personality system. The studies that do reach to higher levels of analysis usually have a story to tell about one or more of the following: programs, populations, and places. These are impressionistic classes, derived simply by considering the bulk of the work that is to be found.

Programs report on their designs and activities as part of their accountability to various interested parties. Most programs fall within one institutional sphere: medical, legal, educational, and so on. By extension, we may locate studies in this class if they deal with institutional history and analysis, a classic example being Lindesmith's work on The Addict and the Law.(2)

Publics are indispensable to programs, if only to provide pools of people – the patients and the healers, the robbers and the cops – who will directly take part. Programs also must consider the general matters of public opinion and public relations, and that is related to their presumed or actual impacts on public images and public health and safety. Most of the studies in this group are directed at the general public to learn about public knowledge attitudes, values, and activities. Studies of special publics as populations at risk are confined mostly to school situations.

Places are the locales of social action, and many community studies are designed as the study of a place of some kind and scale – a school or a school system, a town or a city, or an entire nation (England especially).   The story of a place with respect to a problem would include accounts of its programs and its publics, just as the story of either of the latter two would owe an account of the nature of the place in which it is located.

The two studies that I have judged as central fall into two of the above three rough classes. One of them focuses on "suburbia" as a type of place, and the other focuses on the "coordinating council" as a type of program. Without entering into their many detailed findings, we will be interested in how they begin and how they end. Despite their differences in focus, and even though they were done without knowledge of each other, the two studies are remarkably similar in their frames of reference and in their ultimate conclusions.

The studies appeared within a month of each other in March and April of 1973. The first was commissioned by the National Commission on Marihuana and Drug Abuse as "A Study of Decision Making," and the five authors (I being one of them) chose to study a baker's dozen of contiguous suburban towns in Bergen County, New Jersey.(3) The second, commissioned by the National Institute of Mental Health as A Guide to Community Action, studied drug abuse coordinating councils in 25 communities of varied size in 20 states across the country.(4) From their different vantage points, each of the studies went into the field to observe what was happening in the community and to draw both analytic and evaluative conclusions.

The theoretic framework of the suburban study is in terms of institutional realms of social control, with major emphasis on the four categories of law, treatment, education, and politics (the latter referring to the forming of public policy by government officials and other leaders).   The national study presents eight categories in an overview of a "comprehensive community-wide effort," and a close look discloses that these eight correspond to an expansion of the other study's four categories.

The final conclusions of the suburban study were that the response of the communities under study to the drug problem, after an initial period of alarm, had become routinized in a pluralistic and fragmented way. The authors were impressed most by what was missing from the picture they saw – any signs that people were still accepting the challenge of the problem. After instituting a variety of programs, they were simply accepting the problem and "living with it."

The national study concluded that to achieve an effective coordinating council in a community there was no one pattern to be applied and no cookbook approach to success, and that was because of great differences in histories and circumstances among communities. They did, however, point to one "key factor" that applied universally, and that was the very general matter of leadership. In the final summing up, the authors of the national study parallel those of the suburban study by pointing to a missing ingredient: "The ultimate task ... is doing something positive about the conditions in the community which may lead to drug abuse. The goal shall be one of creating a community where people can get turned on to all sorts of positive things and not just to drugs."(5)

Locating the Concept

What, then, is the meaning of "community" that I may point to in these two studies to justify my original intuition that they go to the heart of the matter? Part of the answer is made explicit in the studies themselves: They think about community institutionally. But "institution" is another term of many uses. Their usage focuses on institutional areas as the means of meeting functional needs of a social system. In the issue of drugs, the areas most vigorously involved are security (the cops), politicality (the pols) and – in between – productivity (the docs or service providers). The educators also are very active, but they tend in practice to borrow from the aforementioned three for curriculum and lectures. Moreover, one finds at the local level, once a line of policy has jelled politically, that most of the institutional participants most of the time become service (productivity) oriented in the area of drugs. A set of responses become conventionalized and routinized; and the cops, the docs, and the pols are concerned to produce their respective contributions in good order. Even when the pols tell the cops to lean on the teenagers who congregate to smoke pot in a local park (as reported in the suburban study), the intent is mainly to deliver service to an appropriate constituency of complaining adults.

The meaning of "community" as it applies to community studies of community problems can be further resolved, I believe, by a further turn of the screw — by an analysis of the productivity function in a locality; and that takes the form of a model of a political economy. This analysis (which follows a format that I have described elsewhere(6)) is predicated on the insight that no economy can consist merely of consumers and providers but must also include the policy inputs of what may be called "franchisers."

In a political economy as a system, I would distinguish three parties at interest. They are: (y) the Citizens (as a body of independent consumers), (x) the Community (as a body of established producers), and (r) the State (as the ultimate franchiser of producers).

The system as a whole works by an orderly set of relationships among parties. The Citizens depend on their Communities through the Civil Process. That is the everyday matter of voluntary participation based on needs, interests, and resources of the participants. The Community depends on the largest political authority, the State, through the Sovereign Process. That is the process that "lays down the law." It is the exercise of the State's monopoly on the legitimate use of compulsion. (In our pluralistic system, the states delegate some sovereign powers to local government and have ceded some to national government.) Finally, the authority of the State depends upon that of the Citizen by way of the Constituency Process — thus closing an overall feedback loop among the three parties at interest. Even in a State that is ruled absolutely by divine right, a ruler will lose his position, and perhaps his head, if he lacks an effective constituency.

The analysis just completed is intended to locate a conception of Community in system terms. That begins a line of reasoning to be pursued presently. The analysis gives us terms of reference, I believe, that are very useful in considering problems of addiction from a societal standpoint. In our national experience, we have often tried to rely on the Sovereign Process as a specific "cure" for our addiction problems, and we have learned painfully, notably in our national prohibition experiment, that such a course does not solve but only complicates the original problem. When addiction is regarded as a problem at the level of the Community, then we imply by our analysis that both the Sovereign Process and the Civil Process must be taken into account.

Our topic, however, is that of addiction not merely as a problem in a community but more specifically as a disorder of a community. For that perspective we must next turn to examining the concept of "disorder."

DISORDER

Our first task in this section is to develop a "key-factor" typology, one that is applicable to disorders in general and will help us to enquire into the nature of addiction. The second task is to offer a model of disorder that will help in the next section to locate addiction as a community disorder.

A Typology

To make a diagnosis is to get "through" in order to "know." It is a puzzle-solving activity, like finding a key to fit a lock to open a door and see what is on the other side. To use a diagnostic nosology is like having a ring of keys to choose from. We may generalize the notion of a "key" by defining it as an entity (meaning entirety or whole, i.e., a system) that compactly answers the "combination" of questions in an informational framework and thereby permits useful intervention in another entity by virtue of matching the configuration of the latter. By this definition we may state that the essential thing in diagnosing a morbid entity is identifying the key factor. In unblocking a door, to be sure, there may be other factors (complications) to consider (e.g., a frozen hinge, a barricade), but the factor that is most often most important (and aesthetically appealing) is the key factor.

The type of entity that is subject to disorders is an open system, one that can conduct exchanges between its inner world and the world around it. It is a tenet of general systems theory that a closed system must wind down to a state of maximum disorder (entropy), while an open system can counter this fate by its commerce with its environment, through its inputs and outputs of various kinds.

Because of its dependence on environment, an open system may suffer if things go wrong either outside or inside itself, and this raises the first of two distinctions we want to resolve: Is the key factor exogenous or endogenous? Thus an animal will suffer if it cannot get its food from the outside or if it cannot assimilate that food on the inside. The second distinction, independent of the first, is that a factor may do harm on either side of an acceptable range. An animal may hurt from eating too much or too little. We ask: Is the key factor excessive or abessive?

The combination of our two questions generates a fourfold typology of disorders on the basis of some hypothetical key factor with respect to the amount of the factor being too much or too little and its source being outside or inside of the affected system. In Table 10.1, the four types are labelled from A to D, and an example of each type is given.

Where on the table is addiction to be placed? By common understanding it is an A-type disorder, in that it is caused by an excess of an outside factor. Thus, it may be humane to give morphine to a patient, but overdo it, and addiction will follow. Or it may be expected that some youngster, experimenting with heroin, will overdo it, and addiction will follow. For all the logic of this position it is nonetheless

Table 10.1. A Key-factor Typology of Disorders

How Much?— Amount of Factor	Where From?— Source of Factor	
	Outside— Exogenous	Inside— Endogenous
Too Much— Excessive	Type A (Hypervitaminosis A)	Type B (Essential Hypertension)
Too Little— Abessive	Type C (Avitaminosis C)	Type D (Diabetes)

arguable that a patient who is addicted to methadone may be maintained on that drug, much as a diabetic is maintained on insulin, as treatment for a D-type disorder, compensating for too little of an inside factor. What might that inside factor be? Some thinkers, looking at addiction as a character disorder, say that it is "maturity." It is interesting that those who have this view usually oppose methadone in favor of a therapeutic community approach to treatment. Our interest here is in addiction as a problem of the community at large, and in that frame I also will conceptualize addiction as a D-type disorder. My reasoning will be consistent with the conclusions of the two studies discussed in the last section, that in a community's response to its addiction problems the key is not to take away what is there but rather to supply what is missing.

The key-factor table allows us to raise pertinent questions as to which type of disorder we are talking about, but it does not supply a model of what we mean by a disorder in the first place. I will define a disorder as a departure from the concept of an operative order. To clarify what that means, I will next locate and then analyze the concept of an operative system.

A Model

Systems theory, as I would have it, finds its starting point in "rationality" as an entity. The problem of how that entity "hangs together" is stated in terms of a general system format (used above in the analysis of a political economy), which requires us to nominate six system concepts (as levels of analysis). Then each concept may be regarded as a system type (a subsystem), and each type poses a problem of how it hangs together that is accountable in terms of its own six concepts, and so on. We locate the concept of operative order at the end of the following sequence. (O) Rational: (y) Structural, (xy) Logical, (x) Analytic, (rx)

Positive, (r) Functional, (yr) Operative. A full discussion of this analysis would carry us far afield, but we do want to note that the Operative concept (yr level) is located within it as a product of (y) the Structural and (r) the Functional. A further analysis of these three concepts as system types would yield the following concepts within each subsystem at the rx level (which corresponds to the level of the organism in biological systems): Structurally, the concept is "organizational arrangements." Functionally, the concept is "productive purposes." Operatively, the concept is "integration as a whole." Thus, to regard an empirical system operatively is to see its wholeness (the root of haleness or health) as based upon the interplay of how it is put together structurally and what it accomplishes functionally.

Having located the operative concept in an analysis of rationality, our next move is to analyze it as a system type. That may be done in parallel with a common-sense definition. An operative system is:

(y) a type (form) . . . (xy) of parts . . . (x) forming . . . (rx) a whole . . . (r) of a type . . . (yr) in a context.

The three ordinate terms in this statement are all variants of the idea of a type, and they may be referred to as (y) microtype, (x) mesotype, and (r) macrotype. An operative system concept may be nominated for each level of analysis. The level of the parts (xy) may be called participation. The level of the whole (rx) may be called integration. The level of the context (yr) may be called selection. Concepts also are nominated for the three ordinate levels. The microtype is for actuation; the mesotype is for regulation; and the macrotype is for specification.

To illustrate how these concepts may be applied, we may look at our earlier analysis of a political economy in operative terms and, for comparison, we will add the levels of analysis that would be applied to biological systems.

(y) The Citizen is for actuation, like the level of the cell in biology, by inputs of information and energy.

(xy) The Civil Process is for participation, like the level of the tissues.

(x) The Community is for regulation, like the level of the organs.

(rx) The Sovereign Process is for integration, like the level of the organism.

(r) The State is for specification, like the level of the species.

(yr) The Constituency Process is for selection (of leadership) like the level of natural selection in Darwinian evolution.

A model of disorder may be taken directly from this model of operative order. In common sense terms, disorder occurs when: Types of Departures Deform a Whole of a Type in a Context. Corresponding to each operative order concept is a disorder concept that is formed by adding the prefix "mal." These six basic concepts of a disorder model may be mapped to the three basic concepts of the classic epidemiologic model of agent, host, and environmental factors.

Malactuation and malparticipation correspond to agent factors.

Malregulation and malintegration correspond to <u>host</u> factors.

Malspecification and malselection correspond to <u>environment</u> factors.

The relationship discussed in this section are schematized in Table 10.2.

Table 10.2 Operative System Concepts and Disorder Concepts

Models & Concepts	Levels of Analysis					
	1 (y)	2 (xy)	3 (x)	4 (rx)	5 (r)	6 (yr)
A. Operative Model	Types	of Parts	Form	a Whole	of a Type	in a Context.
B. Operative Concepts	Actu- tion	Partici- pation	Regula- tion	Integra- tion	Specifi- cation	Selec- tion
C. Disorder Model	Types	of De- partures	Deform	a Whole	of a Type	in a Context
D. Disorder Concepts	Agent Factors			Host Factors		Environment Factors

ADDICTION

We want at last to draw the table that will locate "addiction as a community disorder," referring to a condition where there is something wrong with the community. I have foreshadowed many of the features of that table: It will regard addiction as a D-type disorder, where the diagnostic key is that there is too little of an inside factor; and it will regard "community" and "disorder" as system concepts whose levels of analysis may be represented by further concepts. We have discussed levels of analysis in disorder, but not yet in community. That is our last preparatory step, to be taken by regarding the community in question as a <u>social</u> (or sociocultural) system, an analysis that I have presented at some length elsewhere(7) and will only summarize here.

Three axial levels of a social system, corresponding to three parties at interest, are: (x) Individuals, (y) Collectives, and (r) Cultures. The process levels are: (xy) Interactional, (rx) Institutional, and (yr) Prophetic. Looking at a social system operatively, we may say that by design: Actuation is by Individuals (social selves); and that depends on participation in processes (scenes and situations) of social Interaction; and that depends on regulation by Collectives (group memberships); and that depends on integration by Institutional processes; and that depends on specification by Cultural values; and that depends on selection by Prophetic processes; and that in turn loops back to depend on Individuals as they accept or supplant received values.

Our "big picture" is shown in Table 10.3. The logic of that table is that each of the parties to a social system is analyzed row-wise as an operative subsystem, and each party is considered to be subject to an abessive disorder at each operative process level. The row and column headings are reduced from six to three concepts each; that is a simplification and a matter of rigging the table for an intended result. The intention is to systematize a set of concepts that are prominent in the literature of social science in general and of community studies in particular. The purpose of the table is to picture the problem of addiction in its largest aspect, not merely as a public health problem whose "vector" may be a ship from Marseilles and whose "reservoir" may be the poppy fields of Turkey, but rather as a community health problem whose key is our endogenous lack in a body politic.

Table 10.3. Types of Abessive Disorders Within Social Systems

Social System Levels: Parties	Operative System Levels : Processes		
	Participation (xy)	Integration (rx)	Selection (yr)
Cultural (r)	Accidie (inter-apathy)	Alienation (inter-estranged)	Anomie (inter-anarchy)
Collective (x)	No programs (-action)	No coordination (-leadership)	No public support (-constituency)
Individual (y)	Acedia (intro-apathy)	Addiction (intra-estranged)	Anomia (intra-anarchy)

The three Operative concepts that serve as column heads on the table are Participation, Integration, and Selection. At the Cultural level, the corresponding concepts are Accidie, Alienation, and Anomie; and these three classic concepts are associated (in parenthesis) with the leitmotifs of apathy, estrangement, and anarchy.

Accidie, a term borrowed from theology, means literally the absence of care, as in the deadly sin of sloth. Emile Durkheim developed the parallel concept of Anomie to refer to a condition of normlessness which has a devastating effect because of the failure to keep options within bounds. Durkheim insisted that Anomie was not to be understood as a psychological trait but rather as a reality of its own kind. I have placed Anomie on the Cultural level and have labelled its counterpart on the Individual level as Anomia, and I have likewise placed Acedia as the individual counterpart of Accidie. (It should be stressed that the level of the Individual is not intended as a psychological concept either. It refers to the sociological concept of the "social self," formed through social interaction.)

Alienation is the middle term on the Cultural level. It is defined as mal-Integration and identified with inter-estrangement, a "house of strangers" condition that comes from the weakening or absence of social bonds.

Addiction, our focus of interest, is located as the counterpart of Alienation on the level of the Individual. Addiction is defined as intra-estrangement, the rationale being that the addicted person pursues his "pretty poison" in a way that renders him "a stranger to himself." Addiction in this sense is not a matter of dependency per se but of what that dependency leads to in violations of social expectations which in turn work havoc on the bonds of the social self. A "dope fiend" is at least as vulnerable as the average person to the varieties of human anguish. The addict who "steals from his own mother to get a fix" is riven by a contradiction. To hold himself together he does things that tear him apart.

The table of "Abessive Disorders within Social Systems" locates Addiction between Acedia and Anomia. That is consistent with the general nature of the menu of pretty poisons. There are uppers to help to compensate for intra-apathy, and there are downers to compensate for intra-anarchy.

Addiction as a community disorder may be compared with hemophilia as a bodily disorder. The key to hemophilia as an abnormality is not the risk of occasional cuts and bruises, because normally these are expected and handled with ease. Rather the key is the absence of something that is normally present. The analogue of the missing somatic clotting factor is a missing social integrating factor that can bind up the social self and keep it together. The use of opiates, medically or recreationally, does not always lead to addiction any more than a cut finger always leads to interminable bleeding. When addiction does occur, an appropriate response must rise to the level of community, and it must think of providing what is needed, not merely of removing what is not wanted.

Leadership of the community's response to its problems is the central concept on Table 10.3 as it was the central theme in the conception and the conclusion of the national study discussed earlier. Insufficient leadership, an abessive disorder of social systems, has been noted more and more in recent years as a worldwide condition.

Leadership is more than a matter of some people coming forward because they have a flair and enjoy the limelight. Leadership is an integration of collective efforts, influenced on the one hand by the public supports that are its creators and on the other hand by the programs of action that are its creatures. As a collective force for integration, leadership must address itself (columnwise on Table 10.3) to the Cultural and Individual forces that work for integration as against estrangement. Addiction is not an incidental problem for collective leadership. Rather, Addiction and Alienation are Leadership's close and perpetual antagonists, each capable of potentiating the other. Have we not in this country become addicted to the personal automobile (as part of a broader addiction to affluence itself)? It would be very beneficial to alter our lifestyles to cut down on our personal driving for the sake of more exercise, cleaner air, fewer accidents, and so on. Shall we all do our part in such a movement? Perhaps, if there is leadership to marshal public support and to institute programs. But to the extent that we are alienated, it will be difficult to counter the addiction. And, to the extent that we are addicted, it will be difficult to counter the alienation. And to the extent that we are addicted-alienated, it is difficult to elicit strong leadership.

When we do get strong leadership we get the peril that goes with it, especially that of moral corruption. Those who are in a position to make public decisions must also try to appeal to the public — to do education and "image-making." Such purposes may easily degenerate into a game of cynical manipulation. And yet, it is "the only game in town." To keep it honest needs above all the concern and the sophistication of the community's members.

A personal disorder becomes a collective disorder if the community's response is either too hot or too cool. A personal disorder is especially threatening to the community if it affects the operative order on which social systems depend. By Table 10.3, the common idea that apathy about addiction leads to anarchy is quite valid. In the matter of addiction, it is important to do, and sincerely to do the best that we can, and to do so even when we cannot demonstrate a swift and sure eradication of our troubles. We must hope that in time our "addiction services" apparatus will wither away. At this time, I believe, our massive response does us credit.

NOTES

(1) Taber's Cyclopedic Medical Dictionary (Philadelphia: F.A. Davis Co., 1958).

(2) Lindesmith, A.R., The Addict and the Law (Bloomington: Indiana University Press, 1965).

(3) Brotman, R., et al., "Suburban Towns Respond to Drugs: A Study of Decision-Making in Contiguous Communities," in Drug Use in America: Problems in Perspective, The Technical Papers of the Second Report of the National Commission on Marijuana and Drug Abuse, Appendix II, March 1973.

(4) Wynne, R.D., et al., Effective Coordination of Drug Abuse Programs: A Guide to Community Action, DHEW Publication No. (HSM) 73-9047, Washington, D.C.: U.S. Government Printing Office, April 1973).

(5) Ibid., p. 46.

(6) Silverman, I., "Self-Help in Social Systems," in Stanley Einstein (ed.) Proceedings of the Conference on the Therapeutic Community and Other Self Help Efforts (in press).

(7) Ibid.

11 The Pharmaceutical Industry and Drug Use and Misuse
M. Falco

When we think about drug misuse, we usually think of illicit drugs like heroin, marijuana, or LSD. We may also think of organized crime, drug pushers, street corner junkies, and high school dropouts. When we think about drug use, we usually think of legal drugs like barbiturates and tranquillizers. We do not often think of them in the context of drug misuse despite the fact that they can be and are seriously misused. Unlike heroin and LSD, these drugs are officially recognized by the United States Food and Drug Administraiton as having medical uses and are legitimately manufactured and widely distributed for a number of therapeutic purposes. Similar governmental bodies in other countries are empowered under their laws to determine which drugs will be permitted in general medical practice and how their availability will be regulated. In Great Britain, for example, where heroin is used for medical purposes, the Committee on Safety of Medicines makes such determinations. However, the drugs are also used for nonmedical purposes, sometimes very dangerously, by people who obtain them from either legal or illegal sources. Although it is always difficult to gather accurate information on the extent of illicit drug use, it has been estimated that the numbers of people who misuse legally produced mood-altering drugs (including alcohol) far exceed the numbers of those who misuse illicit drugs.(1)

Whether the pharmaceutical industry which produces, promotes, and profits from mood-altering drugs should do anything to curtail the misuse of their products is a continuing subject of debate. Industry representatives have often pointed out that pharmaceutical companies have acted responsibly in the marketing and distribution of potentially abusable drugs: beyond warning the user to take the drug only under a doctor's supervision or in accordance with the label's directions, they argue, there is no effective way to prevent their products from being misused.(2)

*The views reflected in the article do not constitute an official expression of U.S. Government policy, nor necessarily reflect my officials views as the Senior Advisor to the Secretary of State.

In response to criticism of the extensive advertising and enormous profits generated by drug promotion, the industry has generally replied that the free enterprise system on which the American economy is based demands increasing sales and that large profits are necessary to support new drug research. Estimates of the cost of developing a new drug from initial research through animal testing and clinical trials to final government approval for marketing range from three to ten million dollars.(3) Even more important, industry spokesmen point out, is the fact that no direct causal link has yet been demonstrated between drug promotion and drug misuse, so why should drug advertising be limited?

Industry critics, of course, disagree, often vehemently, citing studies which show that drug promotion does result in increased drug use, a short step away from drug misuse.(4) The drug companies' eagerness for profits, they say, contributes directly to our rapidly developing "pill-popping" society. These critics point out as well that the industry annually spends about one billion dollars for promotion of prescription drugs but spends only a third of that amount on research. They infer from these figures that the drug industry is more concerned with selling its drugs than in conducting research.

This chapter will review the major issues in the debate over the role of the pharmaceutical industry in encouraging or inhibiting drug use and misuse. It will also explore ways in which the industry might develop its potential as an effective resource in community drug misuse prevention efforts.

In this chapter, drug misuse is defined to mean taking more than the medically prescribed dose of a mood-altering drug. Additionally, drug misuse is understood to mean taking drugs, even within prescribed doses, where no medical need exists. This problem can arise when an individual takes a drug for his own enjoyment or through careless diagnosis and prescribing by the physician. Some researchers have estimated, for example, that as much as 40 to 60 percent of drugs prescribed are medically unnecessary.(5)

Drug misuse differs from drug abuse in that abuse is defined here as the compulsive, chronic use of mood-altering drugs whether licit or illicit.

As general background for this chapter's discussion of the role of the pharmaceutical industry, using the United States as an example, current federal laws governing the activities of the industry pertaining to the production and distribution of mood-altering drugs will be described.

FEDERAL REGULATION OF MOOD-ALTERING DRUGS

The federal Controlled Substances Act of 1970 provides the comprehensive legal framework for the regulation of the supply and distribution of mood-altering drugs in the United States.(6) The act classifies drugs into five schedules according to their potential for abuse, physical and psychological dependence liability, and currently accepted medical use. Schedule I, the most strictly controlled category, includes drugs that are considered to have high abuse potential and that are not recognized for medical use in the United States, such as heroin, marijuana, and

LSD. These drugs can be dispensed only for limited research purposes.

Schedule II drugs, such as morphine, methadone, and the amphetamines, are primarily distinguished from Schedule I drugs by having limited but currently accepted medical uses. To be placed in this schedule, a drug, in addition to having high abuse potential, must also demonstrate severe psychological or physical dependence liability.

The drugs in Schedules III, IV, and V also have currently accepted medical uses; however, their abuse potential and dependence liability are considered to be relatively less in each descending schedule of control. For example, the sleeping pill, glutethimide (Doriden), which is presently classified in Schedule III, is considered substantially more dangerous in terms of abuse potential and dependence liability than the cough medicine Pertussin AC which is in Schedule V.

The reader should keep in mind that this typology, like all other drug typologies, is an arbitrary one. This is particularly so when we acknowledge that we don't know from an empirical perspective the relationship between a drug's experienced effects and action and a person's decision to use or not to use a specific drug.

The Controlled Substances Act is administered by two different federal agencies, the Drug Enforcement Administration (DEA) and the Food and Drug Administration (FDA). The DEA has primary enforcement authority under the act as well as the power to establish regulations governing the production, distribution, export, and import of controlled substances. The FDA is authorized to make scientific and medical evaluations and recommendations regarding drug scheduling decisions; these recommendations are binding on the DEA only to the extent that if the FDA recommends that a substance not be controlled, the DEA may not control it. While the issue has never been legally resolved, it is understood by the DEA and the FDA that the DEA may not exceed the level of control recommended by the FDA; at the same time, the DEA may take final action for a lower level of control than that recommended. In short, the two agencies must work cooperatively in the determination of which mood-altering drugs to include on the act's control schedules and what degree of control to impose.

The act assigns a key role to the pharmaceutical companies that produce controlled mood-altering drugs. As pivotal sources of drug supplies for the licit market as well as potential sources for the illicit market, they are required to comply with various reporting, security, record-keeping, and storage regulations. These controls are intended to provide accurate information regarding legitimate drug production and distribution as well as reduce the possibilities for theft and other diversion of controlled drugs into the illicit market. This information is made available to the DEA which is empowered to act if irregularities are observed in the production or distribution of these drugs.

The controls are more strict for the drugs that are considered to be relatively more abusable. For example, the controls imposed on the manufacture and distribution of Schedule II drugs, such as amphetamines and short-acting barbiturates, include production quotas, security storage, import and export controls, and nonrefillable prescription requirements. The controls imposed on Schedule V drugs are much less stringent, primarily record-keeping and reporting requirements and minimal prescription refill limitations. A table setting forth the major control differences among the five schedules is presented in Appendix A.

The act's control scheme assumes that eliminating the diversion of legal drugs from drug manufacturers and distributors will curtail nonmedical use of those drugs. In other words, the act attempts to insure that legally manufactured drugs will reach only those people who have medical need for them and who will use them under medical supervision.

Despite the act's best intentions, many people who legally obtain these drugs misuse them at some time or other. The housewife, prescribed amphetamines for diet control, may continue taking the pills after her diet is over because they make her feel good. Or the insomniac who has trouble sleeping may misuse his prescription for sleeping pills. Discouraged by his inability to fall asleep, he may take more than the prescribed dose. If he takes too many, especially if he has also been drinking alcohol, he may die.

The Controlled Substances Act does not attempt to control this sort of nonmedical drug use, except by the limitation of prescription refills. The theory behind this limitation is that if a person has a relatively small amount of these drugs at one time the likelihood of intentional or accidental overdose is diminished. Unfortunately, the thousands of overdose deaths resulting from legal drugs each year indicate that prescription refill restrictions are at best an imperfect safeguard against dangerous drug misuse, particularly if an individual is determined to acquire more than the prescribed amount of drugs. An often-used tactic is to obtain prescriptions at a number of drug stores, or through a number of doctors, and have them refilled more often than is medically required.

The most significant control imposed on the pharmaceutical industry by the Controlled Substances Act is the production quota requirement for Schedule II drugs, such as amphetamines, short-acting barbiturates, and methadone. For these drugs, which are considered to be the most "dangerous" in use for medical purposes, the DEA sets annual quotas. Under this quota system, those drug companies that produce Schedule II drugs are permitted to produce only the amount that the Drug Enforcement Administration permits. The DEA, in consultation with the FDA, sets the production quota by making a determination of legitimate medical need for a given drug. This is done by reviewing prescribing patterns for the drug and then estimating how much of the drug should be produced to meet this need.

Theoretically, if the act's control system worked perfectly from the point of initial production to final distribution, controlled drugs would not find their way to nonmedical users, unless of course those users obtained their drugs through legitimate prescriptions. In other words, if it were impossible for drugs to be diverted from legitimate production and distribution channels into the illicit market, quotas would not be considered necessary. However, experience has shown that many legitimate drugs do find their way to the illicit market.

A striking example of the impact of production quotas is provided by the amphetamines. Widely misused during the 1960s, the amphetamines were subjected to controls under the Drug Abuse Control Amendments of 1966;(7) however, these amendments only established minor record keeping requirements and had no effect on the amount of amphetamines produced. In fact between 1966 and 1970, despite increasing publicity about the drug's dangers, amphetamine production increased. During hearings held by the U.S. House Select Committee on Crime in 1969 it was estimated that the amount of bulk amphetamines legitimately produced annually was equivalent to 8 billion dosage units – which would provide 40 amphetamine pills for every man, woman, and child in the United States.(8) Researchers testified that there was an established medical need for only a tiny fraction of that amount. With the passage of the Controlled Substances Act in 1970, the federal government was given the authority to impose production quotas based on legitimate medical need, which it eventually did, despite opposition of the major drug companies producing the amphetamines. By 1973, subsequent to the imposition of Schedule II controls and production quotas on the amphetamines, annual production totaled 650 million dosage units, or less than ten percent of prior production.

GOVERNMENT ACTION AGAINST DRUG COMPANIES: CASE HISTORIES

By implication at least, the Controlled Substances Act assumes that production and distribution of mood-altering drugs cannot go unregulated without serious adverse consequences to individuals and to society. Companies that manufacture controlled drugs are required to report regularly to the DEA and the FDA and to comply with the regulations they promulgate. Companies that are developing new mood-altering drugs or that market drugs that are not yet included in the act's schedules recognize the possibility that their product will be controlled. Consequently, most companies work diligently to develop cordial relations with agency officials. Frequently, however, the interests of the companies and those of the regulatory agencies appear to be irreconcilable, particularly when the sales of a drug appear to be threatened by proposed controls.

The congressional hearings preceding and following the passage of the act were filled with examples of unethical and sometimes criminal conduct by various drug companies and wholesalers, indicating little if any concern for the public health and welfare. For example, Bates Labs of Chicago shipped one and a half million amphetamine pills in a period of eight months to an alleged drug distributor in Tijuana, Mexico.(9) Federal investigators discovered that the drug distributor's address was in fact the eleventh hole of the Tijuana Country Club golf course. As the hearings pointed out, the pills were coming back into the U.S. and falling into the hands of the black market for illegal sales. Upon revelation of this practice, Bates Labs ceased production of its amphetamines.

Another example of industry misconduct was Pennwalt Corporation, which in 1971 was the third largest amphetamine producer in the United States, with sales of $6.7 million a year.(10) Just prior to the imposition of Schedule II production quotas on amphetamines under the Controlled Substances Act, Pennwalt shipped 900 kilos of its amphetamine bulk — enough to make approximately 45 million 20 mg capsules — to its Mexico City plant. Soon after, Pennwalt amphetamine dosage units, known as Bifetamina in Mexico, began appearing illegally in large numbers in this country. In one six-month period in 1971, 173,000 Bifetamina capsules were either seized or purchased by federal drug agents. Following those seizures, a major federal investigation was initiated which led to additional seizures of nearly 900,000 Bifetamina capsules.

The federal investigation also revealed that Pennwalt's Mexican plant had shipped 13 million of the 17 million Bifetamina capsules it had manufactured in 1971 to eight small drugstores on the Mexican-American border, frequent stop-off points for smuggling into the U.S. What Pennwalt was doing in effect was following a policy that would make these dangerous drugs freely available for illicit use. In one of the strongest moves ever taken in a case of this kind, the federal government revoked Pennwalt's license to export amphetamines. The net effect on Pennwalt, however, was a sales loss of only one percent, since its license to produce amphetamines and other drugs in the United States remained untouched.

Perhaps the best known struggle between industry and the regulatory agencies over the imposition of controls involved the widely prescribed tranquillizers, Librium and Valium. Introduced to the United States market in the 1960s, they were extensively advertised: it is conservatively estimated that Roche Labs, their developer and manufacturer, has spent well over $400 million to promote these two drugs.(11) By 1973, Valium's wholesale sales exceeded $225 million and Librium's sales were approximately $75 million — in retail sales the total was in the neighborhood of a half billion dollars or about four billion pills a year. They were, respectively, the first and third most prescribed drugs in the United States.

Through a series of complicated and costly legal maneuvers, Roche Labs succeeded in keeping its two tranquillizers free from government control for nearly ten years, until July 1975, despite the fact that the drugs were widely misused and were shown to produce physical dependence after chronic, high dose use. A primary reason for Roche's resistance to controls was the potential loss of sales. They estimated the sales loss would be between $10 and $20 million a year.

The actual impact of controls on legitimate drug use has not yet been thoroughly documented; however, it is widely accepted that sales of a product are reduced by the imposition of controls. A primary impact of controls is the educative effect they have for the prescribing physician, who is alerted through the control designation and prescription limitation of the controlled drug's dependence and abuse potential. When Schedule IV controls were imposed on Librium and Valium, it was thought that sales would decrease because the practicing physician would become more cautious in the prescribing of these two drugs. Data on the actual impact of Schedule IV controls on Librium and Valium sales are not yet available.

While the history of Librium and Valium provides an example of industry successfully resisting minimal government controls for almost a decade, an example of somewhat precipitous government action to impose the strictest controls is presented by the drug methaqualone, marketed in the United States as Quaalude, Parest, and Sopor; in Great Britain as Melesedin and Mandrax; in Japan as Hyminal; and in Germany as Revonal. Introduced as a prescription sleeping pill and sedative in 1965, methaqualone was misused in various parts of the country by 1972, accompanied by widespread press and television coverage. However, the federal regulatory agencies made no attempt to impose any controls on methaqualone until late 1973 − more than a year after methaqualone had emerged as a highly popular nonmedical drug. Then the government recommended Schedule II controls, the strictest available for a drug with recognized medical uses. If the government had acted earlier, lesser controls would probably have been adequate to satisfy public concern. Even in 1973, many observers agreed with the methaqualone producers that Schedule III controls would have been more appropriate than those of Schedule II.(12)

The major methaqualone manufacturer in the United States, the William H. Rorer Company, challenged the Schedule II recommendation through the administrative review process provided by the Controlled Substances Act. The company argued that the government had not demonstrated that methaqualone abuse could lead to severe psychological or physical dependence. After three days of hearings, the administrative judge upheld the government's Schedule II recommendation.

The imposition of Schedule II controls on methaqualone indicates that drug companies theoretically may encounter occasional problems of overregulation of their products. The determining factors in the methaqualone control decision appear to have been the widespread media publicity and political and law enforcement concern engendered by the drug's nonmedical use rather than careful considerations of the scientific and medical properties of the drug. It is perhaps inevitable that in the emotionally charged area of "dangerous drug" control some objectivity and precision will be lost in the decision-making process. The very use of the term "dangerous drug" is a case in point. The reality is that there are no drugs that are not dangerous to some degree. Certainly, the vagueness of the scheduling criteria by which drugs are controlled enhances the importance of nonscientific and medical factors in the ultimate control decision. As public concern increases over the nonmedical use of drugs, and with the advent of increased social drug use, drug companies will probably face increasingly tighter controls over their products and increasingly complex relationships with federal regulatory agencies.

One lesson to be learned from comparing the case of Librium and Valium and the case of methaqualone is that a balance must be met. Drugs cannot be controlled too severely if their potential hazards do not warrant it, nor can they be controlled too leniently if the medical and scientific evidence suggests strong controls are needed. Moreover, the timing of the imposition of controls is crucial. Careless or hasty action by the government to control drugs is no less satisfactory than a company successfully resisting controls for a decade.

INDUSTRY PROMOTION OF MOOD-ALTERING DRUGS

Compared to the controls now imposed on the pharmaceutical industry in the production and distribution of mood-altering drugs, regulation of industry promotional activities designed to increase the demand for their products – and therefore sales – is almost nonexistent.

In recent years there has been much criticism of industry promotion efforts. As noted before, the industry justifies its conduct in terms of economic necessity: since the drug market, like any other, is essentially competitive, each company must seek to maximize its profits and to expand the number of its potential and actual buyers. The industry assumes quite correctly that the promotion of legal mood-altering drugs increases their use among the population; indeed, if promotion did not work to increase sales, it it unlikely that the industry would continue allocating more than one billion dollars a year to it.

It is important to remember that different regulations apply to mood-altering drugs which can be dispensed only on a doctor's prescription and to the less potent medications which can be sold over the pharmacy counter. Federal regulations allow prescription drugs to be advertised only to physicians and other health care professionals; advertisements cannot be placed in popular magazines, newspapers, or other mass media. However, over-the-counter drugs, such as Sleep-Eze, Sominex, No-Doz, and others, can be advertised to the general population, and frequently are, as any television viewer or magazine reader can attest.

Whether drug promotion contributes directly to drug misuse is an active area of controversy. To date there have not been empirical studies conducted to test the potential relationship between advertising and drug-taking behavior, although there are studies that show that advertising of a particular drug increases sales of that drug.(13) Whether these sales increases also reflect misuse of the advertised drug or tend to generate general increases in consumption and misuse of other drugs as well has not been demonstrated. However, there are studies that indicate an indirect link between drug use by parents and drug use by their children.

Three separate studies in California, Toronto, and New Jersey have shown that the use of legal mood-altering drugs by parents greatly increases the chances of their children using illicit drugs.(14) Dr. Richard Blum's California study found, for example, that 68 percent of the parents of those people who used illegal tranquillizers intensively were legal tranquillizer users. Only 38 percent of the parents of young people who did not use tranquillizers had used tranquillizers. Similar findings emerged in the Toronto and New Jersey studies. Furthermore, they found that if parents smoke one pack of cigarettes a day or more, the likelihood of their children using illicit drugs is two to three times greater than it is among parents who are not smokers.

In his Toronto study, Dr. Reginald Smart pointed out: "The conclusion is inescapable that the parents who are users of tranquilizers, barbiturates and stimulants are likely to have children who are users of drugs, such as marijuana, LSD, and speed, as well as prescription drugs and alcohol and tobacco."

While these studies do not demonstrate a direct link between drug promotion, drug prescribing, and drug use by parents and drug misuse by their children, they do indicate a strong connection between children's drug-taking behavior and parental attitudes toward drugs — attitudes that are presumably significantly molded by drug advertising and promotion.

Also, many observers believe that the widespread advertising of drugs contributes to general public acceptance of drug taking as a permissible means of making oneself feel better.(15) Consider, for example, the hundreds of television commercials promoting headache remedies and sleeping aids that depict people caught up in the everyday stresses of life and offer them a chemical panacea. The ads clearly imply that headaches and sleeplessness are inevitable daily occurrences for all of us and that taking the advertised pill will rapidly solve the problem. The ads never suggest that there might be deeper problems underlying the headaches and the insomnia and that there might be better solutions, like seeking medical or psychiatric help, or even changing one's lifestyle to relieve intolerable tension and pressure. Instead, drugs are offered as the exclusive — and sensible — remedy. Many people rely on the media as a primary source of information; it is hardly surprising that their views of drug taking are often critically shaped by drug advertising.

Promotion of prescription drugs is generally conducted through direct mailings to physicians, medical journal advertising, and personal visits to physicians by detail men. They are salesmen for the drug companies: more than 20,000 are employed industry wide. Detail men represent the largest share of promotional funds expended by the pharmaceutical industry — approximately $600 million a year of an estimated one billion dollars.(16) They visit doctors, drugstores, and hospitals on a regular basis in order to promote the drugs their companies sell. Not only do they build friendships with their prospective customers, they often also provide free drug samples. Drug companies, as has been documented in several congressional hearings, also provide expensive gifts, like radios, televisions, golf clubs, and vacations to physicians as part of their promotional activity.(17)

All of these promotional activities are designed to inform the physician of the company's drug product, convince him of its superiority over other similar drugs, and persuade him to prescribe it regularly. In 1973, the American Medical Association assessed the relative efficacy of these promotional methods in a study of a representative sample of physicians.(18) The study found that direct mail was reported to be a major influence on prescribing by 17 percent of the physicians while medical journal advertising was a major influence for 25 percent of the physicians questioned. However, 52 percent of the physicians reported that detail men were a major influence in their drug prescribing, and an additional 11 percent said the detail men were a marked influence. Thus, of the three promotional methods, detail men were reported to have the most influence.

The impact of drug promotion, as the AMA study suggests, is considerable. Numerous other surveys have shown that many if not most medical men are first induced to prescribe a new product not by a scientific report in a medical journal but by a drug advertisement or, most often, by the presentation of a detail man.(19) Among community pharmacists, there has long been the belief that by looking at the new prescriptions that come into the pharmacy each day, you can tell which detail man has been through town.

These promotional activities do perform a useful function to the extent that they inform physicians of drugs that might be helpful to them in their treatment of patients. However, advertising and detail men are often a physician's only source of information regarding a particular drug. Even the Physician's Desk Reference, the standard handbook for prescribing drugs, is written by the drug industry. Theoretically a physician could check the reliability of promotional claims by going to the library and looking up published reports concerning the drug in the scientific literature. In practice, however, this is generally impossible, particularly for the overworked general practitioner. As Dr. Harry L. Williams, professor of pharmacology at Emory University, notes, "It might be said that the physician has available to him the scientific literature and can make his judgment about the relative value of drugs from the literature. This is just not so – the physician does not have the time. I am a pharmacologist, and my professional role is to keep up with drugs, and I am unable to do so. I subclassify myself as a neuropharmacologist and I wonder if I even accomplish keeping up with this narrow field."(20)

Given the fact that these promotional activities are transparently self-serving, and given that physicians usually recognize this fact, the question is often asked, why then do physicians prescribe so many mood altering drugs? This question is all the more significant when we consider that about 250 million prescriptions for mood-altering drugs are written each year.(21)

First, as previously noted, because of his busy schedule and his very high patient case load, most physicians, particularly general practitioners, usually do not have sufficient time to analyze a patient's complaint beyond the patient's own description of his problem. Often, the problems are manifested as a physical complaint when there is actually an underlying psychological cause. In some studies, it has been estimated that perhaps as many as 60 percent of all patient complaints to physicians have no somatic cause.(22) In other words, patients are describing psychological problems to their physician even if they describe it in terms of a physical complaint. All too often, the physician's response is to prescribe a mood-altering drug, such as a tranquilizer or a mood elevator, to alleviate the patient's complaint. It should also be noted that many patients demand a mood-altering drug from their physician and the physician risks losing the patient if he fails to comply.

Another important factor to remember is that despite his lengthy and intensive medical education, the physician is not well equipped upon leaving medical school and completing his residency to evaluate and prescribe mood-altering drugs. Despite the wide medical reliance on these drugs to treat patients, psychopharmacology is a low priority at most medical schools. Medical students generally spend only three to six hours in formal psychopharmacology training at the best medical schools. At some medical schools the psychopharmacology training is even sketchier.

Dr. Peter Dews, professor of psychiatry and psychology at Harvard University Medical School, remarks on this problem.

> The teaching of antibiotic drug prescribing is far superior to psychopharmacology for the simple reason that you can pinpoint problems much more specifically in prescribing antibiotics. You can take a culture and refine your diagnosis, and you can then make a rational choice.

> Much less understood are the indications for psychoactive drugs. The prescribing physician has no hard and fast rules for prescribing a psychoactive drug. He has no objective correlations for these drugs; for example, we have very poor specific diagnostic criteria for minor tranquilizers. This lack of more specific diagnostic data is not really different at major hospitals than with practicing physicians, contrary to what we might expect.(23)

How does physician education — or lack of it — in pharmacology relate to the drug industry's promotional efforts? Simply because a physician's education ill prepares him to evaluate critically the accuracy of the direct and indirect claims made by the drug companies for their products. Advertisements for mood-altering drugs which appear in medical journals broadly reflect what the practicing physician is likely to encounter in his office in the way of patient complaints. (Some examples are provided in Appendix B.)

Ads for the stimulant Ritalin, for example, frequently pictured a tired or depressed woman, who, according to the ads, was in need of an energy lift. This was designed to conform to what the physician was likely to hear from a female patient. Such common complaints as household work were also introduced into these advertisements apparently to suggest that the housewife was tired because of overwork, and Ritalin was the suggested remedy. As women's groups in particular have pointed out, the companies' ads rely heavily on women — who have more nonspecific somatic complaints and use more mood-altering drugs than men — in their promotion of these drugs.

Another example is the tranquilizer Valium, the subject of perhaps the most intensive medical journal advertising campaign in the history of drugs. Valium presently accounts for about 55 million new and refilled prescriptions a year.(24) Valium advertisements were precisely tailored to reflect the stereotype that many physicians encounter in their offices – a woman apparently successful but anxious; a business executive, climbing the ladder of corporate success but unable to relax. According to the ads, the tension or anxiety would often be expressed in somatic complaints.

The promotion of psychoactive drugs has been designed to include virtually every conceivable complaint a physician could encounter in his office, in a simple, easy to recognize description. This is reflected not only in journal advertising and direct mailings, but also in the representations of the drug's efficacy by company detail men.

It is important to note that while the Food and Drug Administration has the power to regulate prescription drug advertising, it can do so only after an advertisement has appeared. The FDA resources and staff allocated to monitoring drug ads are very small, and the administrative procedures involved in revoking an ad are complicated and time-consuming. One ad that was retracted illustrates particularly well the tendency of the advertising companies to expand the definition of acceptable medical uses for their products. The ad was for Serentil, a major tranquilizer appropriate only for very serious mental and emotional disturbances. The ad was headlined "Serentil – for the anxiety of not fitting in."

This ad, and others for tranquilizers, stimulants, and sleeping pills, seek to encourage a broad-based, expanding concept of our understanding of "illness." At various times, we all feel depressed, anxious, tired, sleepless, but that does not mean that we are suffering from a clinical condition that requires drug treatment. As one former drug advertising executive described much of mood-altering drug promotion:

> It is a demonstration of the insidious way in which clinically significant anxiety once defined as "fear in search of a cause", has been broadened through promotion to include even theoretical anxiety, not exhibited to the doctor or even to the patient's family, but which is assumed to manifest itself when the patient is alone. And drug treatment has been broadened to include normal, life-caused tension brought about by situational stress; the job, the wife, the monthly bills.

> Today we see a 100 percent increase over the already high levels of just six years ago in the prescribing of so-called "anti-anxiety" and "anti-depressant" drugs.(25)

As noted above, the pharmaceutical industry has sustained much criticism of its promotional activities from many sectors of society – women's groups, consumer groups, the United States Congress, and physicians. The fact should not be lost, however, that promotional activities do provide a ready source of information about various drugs to physicians who, as already noted, are usually too busy to keep up with current pharmacological developments. The problem has been the disproportionate amount of industry promotion compared to more unbiased sources of information.

Also lost or overlooked amid the criticism is the vital role that mood-altering drugs play in the treatment of many clinically diagnosed illnesses. Without many of these drugs, our society would be a different place. Take, for example, one group of major tranquilizers, known pharmacologically as the phenothiazines. They have been used successfully for more than 20 years by many people suffering from severe mental illness who, before the advent of these drugs, would probably have to have been locked up for their own safety. Now they can often live at home or in their community and function reasonably well with drug therapy. Many of the minor tranquilizers perform the same role for individuals less severely disturbed.

Problems arise from the promiscuous, careless prescribing of these drugs, in particular the minor tranquilizers, sleeping pills, and some stimulants, which creates much of the current drug misuse problem in this country. As industry representatives point out, there is little that they can do to control how physicians choose to prescribe drugs. However, the industry itself could make greater efforts to impress upon physicians the potential hazards of these drugs and of the need to exercise greater caution in prescribing them. Although such an approach might not appear to be in the economic best interest of the drug companies, in the long run it might serve them and the nation better.

There are a number of steps the pharmaceutical industry can and should consider taking to demonstrate their commitment to reducing careless or irresponsible prescribing of mood-altering drugs.

First, the industry could agree to restrict its advertisements of these drugs to factual, verbal descriptions of the drug's uses, therapeutic range, and limitations. The use of pictures in ads and catchy titles (for example, "For the anxiety of not fitting in") could be eliminated and the physician's attention focused instead on the actual scientific findings regarding the drug's clinical uses.

Second, the industry should consider curtailing their promotional activities which involve free gifts and other emoluments to physicians. Presumably, if physicians are convinced of the merits of a particular drug, they will prescribe it regardless of other incentives. However, the practice of providing gifts, particularly expensive ones, at the very least suggests improper attempts to influence physician prescribing behavior. With regard to furnishing free drug samples, the companies could consider requiring that physicians request these samples in writing, as is now provided under California law.(26) By providing drug samples only on written request, the drug companies could avoid the criticism that their detail men flood physicians with samples in an attempt to encourage them to prescribe particular drugs.

Of course, the primary responsibility for physician overprescribing and misprescribing does not lie with the pharmaceutical industry but with the future of medical schools and the medical profession itself. Present drug promotion could not be so successful if physicians were not inadequately trained in psychopharmacology and so poorly informed of current scientific and medical findings on various mood-altering drugs. Furthermore, as already noted, the daily pressures on most physicians make difficult the careful diagnosis and extensive analysis of nonspecific complaints needed for psychoactive drug prescribing. It is too often much easier simply to give the patient a mood-altering drug and send him – and more often, her – on their way. Physicians must also recognize their role in fostering needless drug dependence in their patients and must be prepared to face patients who are displeased when they are told that they cannot always have a drug to solve their problems, and even more important, that drugs will not necessarily help them.

With regard to the industry's influence on the attitudes of the general public regarding drug taking, the industry could undertake a public education campaign on drug use and misuse. To balance somewhat the large number of television and other media advertising of drugs, public service advertisements – as attractive and catchy as regular drug advertisements – could be sponsored by the industry to inform people of the potential dangers of overreliance on drugs and to teach them to have a greater respect for the appropriate limits of drug taking. This has been done to a limited extent in the past by the Pharmaceutical Manufacturers Association. Although this sort of campaign might not directly or immediately reduce the overall amount of drug misuse, it would at least provide important information which would eventually affect people's attitudes about the role and purpose of legitimate drugs.

Too often, the drug industry is viewed as the corporate "pusher" of legitimate drugs in this country.

Indeed, there have been a number of dramatic examples of industry overreaching, whether through promotional activities that appear to be influence peddling, lobbying activities to prevent government controls to be imposed on potentially dangerous products, or through particularly aggressive attempts to increase profits through expanding sales beyond rational limits. However, the enormous potential of the pharmaceutical industry to provide vitally needed leadership in developing sensible public attitudes toward drug use and misuse is often overlooked. Some companies have already undertaken such efforts; hopefully, more will join in these efforts.

The pharmaceutical industry will become of ever-increasing importance in any consideration of drug use and misuse. Its influence has already gone beyond that of the simple purveyor of medications used in the treatment of illnesses to that of being able to affect, through psychoactive and other chemical substances, the quality and style of life of vast populations. Eventually, the tide of public opinion may turn against the use of these drugs, particularly if their power to modify psychological states greatly is perceived as a potential threat to individual freedom and integrity.(27)

APPENDIX A: Control Mechanisms of CSA by Schedule

Schedule	Registration	Record Keeping	Manufacturing Quotas	Distribution Restrictions	Dispensing Limits	Import/Export Narc. Non-Narc.		Security	Mfr.-Dist. Reports To DEA
I	Required	Separate	Yes	Order forms	Research use only	Permit		Vault-type	Yes
II	Required	Separate	Yes	Order forms	Rx— written; no refills	Permit		Vault-type	Yes
III	Required	Readily retrievable	No (but some drugs limited by Schedule II quotas)	DEA regis. number	Rx— written or oral; refills (w/M.D. auth.). Up to 5 times in 6 months	Permit		Surveillance	Narc.: yes Non-narc. no

331

Appendix A (Cont.)

Schedule	Registration	Record Keeping	Manufacturing Quotas	Distribution Restrictions	Dispensing Limits	Import/Export Narc. Non-Narc.	Security	Mfr.-Dist. Reports To DEA
IV	Required	Readily retrievable	No (but some drugs limited by Schedule II quotas)	DEA regis. number	Rx– written or oral; refills (w/M.D. auth.). Up to 5 times in 6 months	Permit	Surveillance	Narc.: no Non-narc. no
V	Required	Readily retrievable	No (but some drugs limited by Schedule II quotas)	DEA regis. number	OTC (Rx drugs limited to M.D.'s order)	Permit to import Notice to export	Surveillance	Narc. mfr. only Non-narc. no

APPENDIX B: AD PROMOTION OF MOOD-ALTERING DRUGS

What a difference a day can make

Your counsel and reassurance — and Ritalin.

A logical first step in treating mild depression,* and often all that's needed to bring quick symptomatic relief.

Indeed, your patient may begin to feel better within hours – her spirits boosted, her mood brightened. A single prescription may be all that's needed.

Ritalin is usually well tolerated even by older or convalescent patients. Note, however, that it is not indicated in the more severe depressions.

But whenever depression is mild, think of Ritalin — so your patient has a better chance of waking up to a brighter tomorrow.

Ritalin® hydrochloride Ⓒ
(methylphenidate hydrochloride)
TABLETS

INDICATION
Based on a review of this drug by the National Academy of Sciences-National Research Council and/or other information, FDA has classified the indication as follows: "Possibly" effective: Mild depression
Final classification of the less-than-effective indications requires further investigation.

CONTRAINDICATIONS
Marked anxiety, tension, and agitation, since Ritalin may aggravate these symptoms. Also contraindicated in patients known to be hypersensitive to the drug and in patients with glaucoma.

WARNINGS
Ritalin should not be used in children under six years, since safety and efficacy in this age group have not been established.
Sufficient data on safety and efficacy of long-term use of Ritalin in children with minimal brain dysfunction are not yet available. Although a causal relationship has not been established, suppression of growth (ie, weight gain and/or height) has been reported with long-term use of stimulants in children. Therefore, children requiring long-term therapy should be carefully monitored. Ritalin should not be used for severe depression of either exogenous or endogenous origin or for the prevention of normal fatigue states.

Ritalin may lower the convulsive threshold in patients with or without prior seizures; with or without prior EEG abnormalities, even in absence of seizures. Safe concomitant use of anticonvulsants and Ritalin has not been established. If seizures occur, Ritalin should be discontinued.
Use cautiously in patients with hypertension. Blood pressure should be monitored at appropriate intervals in all patients taking Ritalin, especially those with hypertension.

Drug Interactions
Ritalin may decrease the hypotensive effect of guanethidine. Use cautiously with pressor agents and MAO inhibitors. Ritalin may inhibit the metabolism of coumarin anticoagulants, anticonvulsants (phenobarbital, diphenylhydantoin, primidone), phenylbutazone, and tricyclic antidepressants (imipramine, desipramine). Downward dosage adjustments of these drugs may be required when given concomitantly with Ritalin.

Usage in Pregnancy
Adequate animal reproduction studies to establish safe use of Ritalin during pregnancy have not been conducted. Therefore, until more information is available, Ritalin should not be prescribed for women of childbearing age unless, in the opinion of the physician, the potential benefits outweigh the possible risks.

Drug Dependence
Ritalin should be given cautiously to emotionally unstable patients, such as those with a history of drug dependence or alcoholism, because such patients may increase dosage on their own initiative. Chronically abusive use can lead to marked tolerance and psychic dependence with varying degrees of abnormal behavior. Frank psychotic episodes can occur, especially with parenteral abuse. Careful supervision is required during drug withdrawal, since severe depression as well as the effects of chronic overactivity can be unmasked. Long-term follow-up may be required because of the patient's basic personality disturbances.

PRECAUTIONS
Patients with an element of agitation may react adversely; discontinue therapy if necessary. Periodic CBC, differential, and platelet counts are advised during prolonged therapy.

ADVERSE REACTIONS
Nervousness and insomnia are the most common adverse reactions but are usually controlled by reducing dosage and omitting the drug in the afternoon or evening. Other reactions include: hypersensitivity (including skin rash, urticaria, fever, arthralgia, exfoliative dermatitis, erythema multiforme with histopathological findings of necrotizing vasculitis, and thrombocytopenic purpura); anorexia; nausea; dizziness; palpitations; headache; dyskinesia; drowsiness; blood pressure and pulse changes, both up and down; tachycardia; angina; cardiac arrhythmia; abdominal pain; weight loss during prolonged therapy. Toxic psychosis has been reported. Although a definite causal relationship has not been established, the following have been reported in patients taking this drug: leukopenia and/or anemia; a few instances of scalp hair loss.
In children, loss of appetite, abdominal pain, weight loss during prolonged therapy, insomnia, and tachycardia may occur more frequently; however, any of the other adverse reactions listed above may also occur.

DOSAGE AND ADMINISTRATION
Adults
Administer orally in divided doses 2 or 3 times daily, preferably 30 to 45 minutes before meals. Dosage will depend upon indication and individual response.
Average dosage is 20 to 30 mg daily. Some patients may require 40 to 60 mg daily. In others, 10 to 15 mg daily will be adequate. The few patients who are unable to sleep if medication is taken late in the day should take the last dose before 6 p.m.

HOW SUPPLIED
Tablets, 20 mg (peach, scored); bottles of 100 and 1000.
Tablets, 10 mg (pale green, scored); bottles of 100, 500, 1000 and Accu-pak blister units of 100.
Tablets, 5 mg (pale yellow); bottles of 100, 500 and 1000.
Consult complete product literature before prescribing.

CIBA Pharmaceutical Company
Division of CIBA-GEIGY Corporation
Summit, New Jersey 07901   2 4891 17

Ritalin®
(methylphenidate)
acts quickly to relieve symptoms in mild depression

C I B A

This drug has been evaluated as possibly effective for this indication. See brief prescribing information.

TRIAVIL
containing perphenazine and amitriptyline HCl
a tranquilizer-antidepressant

for depression
with moderate anxiety

in many cases a result of the "empty nest syndrome"

The mid-life crisis: a critical crossroad

Preparation for change—intellectually, vocationally (or avocationally), and emotionally—can often help the menopausal-aged woman cope successfully with a new and different role after the children are grown and gone. Even when these changes have been anticipated and prepared for, a mid-life depression with moderate anxiety is not uncommon—a syndrome often uncontrolled by counseling or other appropriate measures and for which specific medication may be required.

**When depression
with moderate anxiety persists,
TRIAVIL can often help**

TRIAVIL provides a highly effective antidepressant and tranquilizer for symptomatic relief of *both* depression and coexisting moderate anxiety. The patient may be able to function more effectively in her daily life.

Many symptoms associated with depression and anxiety such as insomnia, fatigue, anorexia, and functional G.I. complaints, are frequently alleviated. More complete symptomatic relief is usually afforded than with an antidepressant or a tranquilizer alone. In fact, when anxiety masks the depressive state, treatment with just a tranquilizer may deepen the depression and delay symptomatic improvement.

**Advantages of the two components
in TRIAVIL taken together**

A single tablet containing both an antidepressant and a tranquilizer encourages patients to take medication properly and reduces the risk of dosage confusion and error. Cost of therapy to the patient is usually less. To date, clinical evaluations have revealed no undesirable reactions peculiar to the combination. Tablets TRIAVIL are available in four different combinations affording flexibility and individualized dosage adjustment.

Treatment with TRIAVIL—a balanced view

Contraindicated in CNS depression from drugs; in the presence of evidence of bone marrow depression; and in patients hypersensitive to phenothiazines or amitriptyline. Should not be used during the acute recovery phase following myocardial infarction or in patients who have received an MAOI within two weeks. Patients with cardiovascular disorders should be watched closely. Not recommended in children or during pregnancy. The drug may impair mental or physical abilities required in the performance of hazardous tasks and may enhance the response to alcohol. Antiemetic effect may obscure toxicity due to other drugs or mask other disorders. Since suicide is a possibility in any depressive illness, patients should not have access to large quantities of the drug. Hospitalize as soon as possible any patient suspected of having taken an overdose. **MSD**

MERCK
SHARP
DOHME

For additional prescribing information, please turn to the following page.

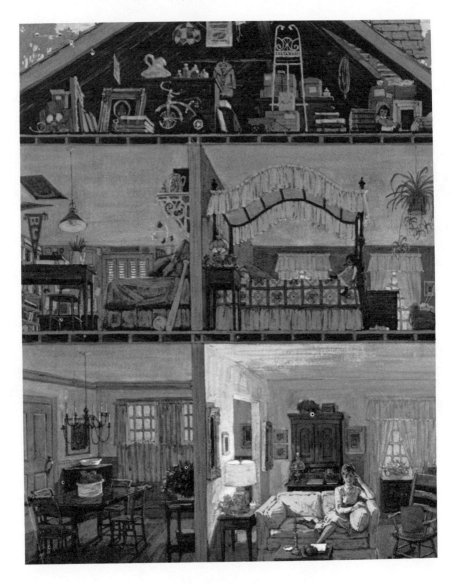

NOTES

(1) E. Brecher, <u>Licit and Illicit Drugs</u> (Boston: Little Brown, 1972), p. 475.

(2) C.J. Stetler, "The Pharmaceutical Manufacturers Association Responds to the Critics," <u>Journal of Drug Issues</u> 4: 274-282, 1974.

(3) Personal communication between author and officials of Parke-Davis Company, January 7, 1974.

(4) R. Bowes, "The Industry as Pusher," <u>Journal of Drug Issues</u> 4: 283-242, 1974.

(5) U.S. Senate Subcommittee on Monopoly; Hearings, <u>Competitive Problems in the Drug Industry</u>, Part 10 (Statement of Dr. George Baehr, p. 4061, December 19, 1968).

(6) 21 U.S.C. 801 et seq., P.L. 91-513 (1970). See also M. Falco, <u>Federal Drug Abuse Law Enforcement, Regulation, and Control</u> (Washington: Drug Abuse Council, 1975).

(7) 21 U.S.C. 360, P.L. 89-74 (1966).

((8) U.S. House of Representatives Select Committee on Crime, <u>Report on Amphetamines</u>, 1971.

(9) J. Pekkanen, <u>The American Connection</u> (Chicago: Follett, 1973), pp. 23-231.

(10) Pekkanen, ibid, pp. 311-325.

(11) J. Pekkanen, "The Tranquilizer War," <u>The New Republic</u>, July 19, 1975.

(12) M. Falco, <u>Methaqualone: A Study of Drug Control</u> (Washington: Drug Abuse Council, 1975).

(13) Council on Children, Media, and Merchandising: Petition for Rulemaking before the Federal Communications Commission, Washington, D.C., September 25, 1975.

(14) U.S. Senate Subcommittee on Monopoly: Hearings, <u>Competitive Problems in the Drug Industry</u>, Part 2 (Statement of Dr. Donald Louria, p. 507, July 22, 1971).

(15) Council on Children, Media, and Merchandising, <u>Petition for Rulemaking</u>, 12.

(16) Senator Gaylord Nelson,   "New Laws are Needed to Regulate the

Drug Industry," Journal of Drug Issues 4: 243-248, 1974.

(17) Senate Subcommittee on Health, Hearings on the Drug Industry, July 1975.

(18) American Medical News, American Medical Association, July 1973.

(19) R.W. Fassold, and C.W. Gowdey, "A Survey of Physicians' Reactions to Drug Promotion," Canadian Medical Association Journal 98: 701, April 6, 1968.

(20) M. Silverman, and P. Lee, Pills, Profits, and Politics (Berkeley: University of California Press, 1974), p. 50.

(21) Pekkanen, The American Connection.

(22) U.S. Senate Subcommittee on Monopoly, Competitive Problems in the Drug Industry.

(23) J. Pekkanen, "Drug Industry Promotion," Journal of Drug Issues, Winter 1975-76.

(24) Pekkanen, The Tranquilizer War.

(25) Bowes, "The Industry as Pusher," p. 239.

(26) Pekkanen, The American Connection.

(27) P. Selby, The Social Drug: Health in 1980-1990 (Basel, Switzerland, 1974).

12 Alternatives to Drugs: New Visions for Society

A.Y. Cohen

The concept of alternatives as a road to prevention and early intervention is based on increasing evidence that drug abuse represents an effort to achieve aspirations and fill experiential voids not being met for young people or adults in the context of today's social system. Thus the enhancement of opportunities for the kinds of rewarding experiences through which the human being achieves growth can in itself be a major effort in the direction of drug abuse prevention.

Robert L. Dupont, M.D., former director
National Institute on Drug Abuse, 1974

To penetrate into the essence of all being and significance, and to release the fragrance of that inner attainment for the guidance and benefit of others, by expressing in the world of forms, truth, love, purity and beauty – this is the sole game which has any intrinsic and absolute worth. All other happenings, incidents and attainments can, in themselves, have no lasting importance.

Meher Baba,
Discourses

INTRODUCTION

Social problems are also social opportunities.

Symptoms of social and personal malaise eventually provoke institutional responses, most of which are somewhat late and often ineffective. Perhaps it is the nature of modern civilization to deal with disruptions in its social fabric and public health after the fact. Perhaps it is also understandable if governmental and institutional responses leap toward political or legal solutions. It may now be unsophisticated to try to legislate morality, but mores are still considered fair game.

Persistent social hurt and individual suffering eventually bring about more compassionate and pragmatic responses. For example, the increasing economic and human costs of drug abuse have generated a new breed of programs and policies, focused more on underlying causes than symptoms, more on proaction than on mere reaction.

Thus, the emerging significance of drug misuse presents both a problem and opportunity. The problem lies in the alarming growth, acceptance, and persistence of all forms of social pharmacology, both licit and illicit.

The opportunity is greater than merely a dissolution of this potential cancer on the human spirit, for the use of psychoactive drugs is connected inextricably with other important social and personality dynamics. Often, it is both impossible and unwise to separate the problem of drug abuse from mental health issues, or juvenile delinquency from family problems or poverty. Thus, promising solutions to this most observable and emotionally charged symptom may have dramatic effects on other related disruptions of social and personal progress.

Thus, any comprehensive discussion of "alternatives" to drugs has major implications for a broad range of social alternatives. Because drug misuse can be so idiosyncratic and yet pervasive, principles of effective counterstrategies may be generalizable to other situations that have been treated symptomatically. In order to achieve precision, the use of psychoactive drugs will be the prime focus of this chapter, but readers are urged to extend the implications of the findings to other disciplines of interest and areas of social concern.

This chapter will feature an elucidation of a basic theoretical framework relating to drug use (a critique of traditional institutional responses), and a motivational model compatible with newer approaches. Then a survey of some important research and evaluation results will be presented, emphasizing the empirical evidence that may bear on alternative approaches. Finally, policy and program implications are discussed and extrapolated toward the future.

THEORETICAL FOUNDATIONS

Concepts

As applied to the abuse of drugs (including alcohol), the "Alternatives Model" is consistent with several other conceptualizations about human motivation, social dynamics, and social control mechanisms.

1. Supply and demand.

Although it seems obvious to any professional in the field, the mere availability of psychoactive drugs, though a probable factor in overall consumption rates, is not sufficient in explaining burgeoning drug use around the industrialized world. Neither are the physically addictive qualities of some substances (such as opiates) a sufficient explanation. It is likely that commercial advertising of drugs and excessive prescribing by medical practitioners has helped shape increasing demand. It is also likely that increases in supply, both licit and illicit, have manipulated prices downward, stimulating ease of acquisition. However, in most nations and localities, the stereotype "pusher" is not "pushing," but being "pushed" for their "products" by demanding consumers.

Because of obvious economic motives, demand creates greater supply. The growing acknowledgment of the role of demand reduction lies in the obvious failure of powerful supply reduction efforts to eradicate drug use. Except in the most totalitarian regimes, no matter how severe the laws, when the people desire psychoactive modification, supply channels exist to satisfy those desires.

Thus, although the reduction of supplies (through reduction of availability and manipulation of price) is a necessary component in control of social pharmacology, the motivational demand factors hold the key to ultimate solutions.

2. The motivational factors in demand for drugs.

If demand is the causative magnet for supply, it is critical to examine theoretical models explaining personal and social motivation. Such models are discernible both from the literature, and more practically, from the dominant social control mechanisms:

- Moral Model. Here the user is considered "sinful," of low moral character, a victim of "low forces," a person displaying immense characterological weakness. The solution proposed usually is confession, conversion, and/or personal reform.

- The Criminalistic Model. Here the user is seen as a conscious lawbreaker, as deliberately flaunting consensual codes of conduct, much as other common criminals such as burglars or sex offenders. The proposed solution is a law enforcement approach, offering some deterrence, but primarily prosecution and severe penalties to both clear the debt to society and to reform or rehabilitate the offender.

- The Medical Disease Model. Here the user is considered to be "sick," manifesting a possible disease process, especially when full chemical dependency sets in. At earlier stages, the user is likely to be considered psychopathological, drug use being a symptom of serious maladjustment. The solution comprises medical/psychiatric treatment, often with the use of substitute medications (e.g., methadone). Earlier intervention may involve early detection of symptoms.

- The Educational Model. Here the user is considered neither criminalistic nor sick, but "ignorant," devoid of the facts about the dangerous effects of drugs. Young persons especially are considered educable and various school, public health, and media efforts are used as channels for the flow of relevant information.

These, of course, are simplistic descriptions, but some form of their philosophies have tended to dominate traditional efforts of social control.

3. The Alternatives model of motivation.

The underlying theory of modern "alternatives" programming accepts some of the traditional concepts of motivation for psychoactive drug use, but chooses to emphasize less pathological and more volitional factors.

It is presumed that deep psychological or social deficiencies do exist in some personalities who become chemically dependent, and that pure physical addiction does take on elements of a quasi-disease process. However, it is argued that nonpathological personalities are also drawn to mood alteration, that drug use is not deviant for much of the public, that personal choice is strongly involved, and that the dominant medical model must be altered (if not replaced entirely) by a "consumer" model. This missing element in the motivational picture was summarized as follows:

According to recent interpreters of the Alternatives approach (Cohen, 1975; Jackson, 1975; Dohner, 1972), individual motives for drug taking, however diverse they may be, lead beyond experimental use because the drug experience somehow satisfies unfulfilled needs and aspirations. It is suggested that the most practical psychology of drug use should include a motivational common denominator: people use drugs primarily because they want to. Regular or compulsive drug use continues because people "feel better" as a result of the drug experience. "Feeling better" can incorporate a large range of mood or consciousness change, including anxiety-reduction, oblivion, mood elevation, consciousness alteration, mental or physical stimulation, and so on. Although desirable drug effects are invariably temporary, persons and peer groups, in the main, are trying to fill relatively legitimate personal or social vacuums. In the Alternatives Model, it is argued that persons will reduce their intake of intoxicants only when they find something better. The entire range of other possibilities for personal satisfaction are called alternatives to drugs. Alternatives are defined to include those constructive and viable attitudes, values, orientations, experiences, lifestyles, opportunities, activities, pursuits, and programs that can prevent significant drug abuse or diminish drug abuse by providing greater satisfaction than can drugs.

If some of its motivational assumptions are true, Alternatives theory comes into collision with the basic precepts of a public health model based upon the concept of "disease." Traditional strategies assume that the drug users come from a deviant population, susceptible to epidemic infection from a new kind of quasi-virus in the form of psychoactive drugs. Whatever the benefits of the medical model for humanizing legislation and whatever its empirical justification, it has created significant obstacles to effective drug abuse prevention.

In the most practical sense, drug abuse does not fit the model of contagious disease or personality disorder. The "deviant" population of drug misusers is nearly a majority of the population, especially in certain age groups. Particularly in the 13-21 age range, it is significantly more deviant not to experiment with psychoactive drugs (Johnston, 1978).

The Nature of Alternatives

The theoretical assumptions of this approach imply that there are certain qualities of alternative (nondrug) responses to unfulfilled needs or aspirations that maximize personal growth.

An overall, simplistic interpretation of the Alternatives concept tempts one to think of "alternatives" as "substitutes." In the definition proposed in this chapter, the concepts are not synonymous. Delinquent behavior may be a substitute for drug dependency, but it is certainly not a superior alternative. One easy criterion on which to discriminate constructive alternatives involves incompatibility with states of intoxication. The superior alternative involvement is obstructed by a person's being "stoned" or "loaded." Another measuring stick for a competing alternative is the degree to which the drug effect becomes unnecessary in fulfilling personal goals and objectives.

Suppose, for example, an alternatives program allows a "high risk" high school student to become a tutor in mathematics to an elementary school student. Suppose he/she finds this service role extremely fulfilling. The concomitant use of drugs would tend both to be incompatible (drugs make it more difficult to communicate about abstractions) and unnecessary (there would be no need to get high).

When successfully implemented, positive alternatives have effects on the individual that specifically contrast with the effects of psychoactive substances. In general, positive alternatives call for action and personal effort; drug use is passive and requires no responsibility. Positive alternatives heighten self-esteem; drug use lowers it. Positive alternatives build permanent knowledge, skills, and personal resources; intoxicants tend to leave only temporary experience. Positive alternatives increase an individual's social utility; drug use is essentially selfish.

Types of Alternatives

Displayed in Table 12.1 Cohen (1971) shows the relationship among areas of motivation for drug use and potentially positive nonchemical alternatives for each area.

In the broadest sense, there is a wide range of Alternatives activities, attitudes, lifestyles, philosophies, and programs that can

Table 12.1. Alternatives to Drugs*

Level of Experience	Corresponding Motives (Examples)	Possible Alternatives (Examples)
Physical	Desire for physical satisfaction Physical relaxation Relief from sickness Desire for more energy Maintenance of physical dependency.	Athletics Dance Exercise Hiking Diet Health training Carpentry or outdoor work
Sensory	Desire to stimulate sight, sound, touch, taste Need for sensual-sexual stimulation Desire to magnify sensorium.	Sensory awareness training Sky diving Experiencing sensory beauty of nature.
Emotional	Relief from psychological pain Attempt to solve personal perplexities Relief from bad mood Escape from anxiety Desire for emotional insight Liberation of feeling Emotional relaxation.	Competent individual counseling Well-run group therapy Instruction in psychology of personal development.
Interpersonal	To gain peer acceptance To break through interpersonal barriers To "communicate," especially nonverbally Defiance of authority figures Cement two-person relationships Relaxation of interpersonal inhibition Solve interpersonal hangups.	Expertly managed sensitivity and encounter groups Well-run group therapy Instruction in social customs Confidence training Social-interpersonal counseling Emphasis on assisting others in distress via education Marriage
Social (including sociocultural & environmental)	To promote social change To find identifiable subculture To tune out intolerable environmental conditions, e.g., poverty Changing awareness of the "masses."	Social service Community action in positive social change Helping the poor, aged, infirm, young, tutoring handicapped Ecology action.
Political	To promote political change To identify with antiestablishment subgroup To change drug legislation Out of desperation with the social-political order To gain wealth or affluence or power.	Political service Political action Nonpartisan projects such as ecological lobbying Field work with politicians and public officials.

Table 12.1 Alternatives to Drugs (continued)

Level of Experience	Corresponding Motives (Examples)	Possible Alternatives (Examples)
Intellectual	To escape mental boredom Out of intellectual curiosity To solve cognitive problems To gain new understanding in the world of ideas To study better To research one's own awareness For science.	Intellectual excitement through reading, discussion Creative games and puzzles Self-hypnosis Training in concentration Synectics—training in intellectual breakthroughs Memory training.
Creative-aesthetic	To improve creativity in the arts To enhance enjoyment of art already produced, e.g., music To enjoy imaginative mental productions.	Nongraded instruction in producing and/or appreciating art, music, drama, crafts, handiwork, cooking, sewing, gardening, writing, singing, etc.
Philosophical	To discover meaningful values To grasp the nature of the universe To find meaning in life To help establish personal identity To organize a belief structure.	Discussions, seminars, courses in the meaning of life Study of ethics, morality, the nature of reality Relevant philosophical literature Guided exploration of value systems.
Spiritual-mystical	To transcend orthodox religion To develop spiritual insights To reach higher levels of consciousness To have divine visions To communicate with God To augment yogic practices To get a spiritual shortcut To attain enlightenment To attain spiritual powers.	Exposure to nonchemical methods of spiritual development Study of world religions Introduction to applied mysticism, meditation Yogic techniques.
Miscellaneous	Adventure, risk, drama, "kicks," unexpressed motives Pro-drug general attitudes, etc.	"Outward bound" survival training Combinations of alternatives above Pro-naturalness attitudes Brain-Wave training Meaningful employment, etc.

*From Cohen, A.Y., "The Journey Beyond Trips," *Journal of Psychedelic Drugs*, vol. 3, no. 2, Spring 1971 (with permission).

function as positive alternatives to drug misuse. In another publication (Cohen, 1975), the author has catalogued over 100 different positive alternatives that show promise in satisfying the motive force for serious intoxication with psychoactive substances. Such alternatives range from physical recreation to nutrition to emotional awareness; from positive peer group activities to parent effectiveness training to stimulating hobbies; from artistic involvement to political action; from peer counselling to social service activities; and from values clarification to meditation.   Obviously, the possible types of nonchemical alternatives will vary substantially from nation to nation, from urban to rural populations, from the young to the elderly, from the poor to the wealthy. However, the concept is cross-culturally transferable.

In treatment modalities, one might suggest that the most successful treatment and rehabilitation programs for severely addicted and for drug dependent people supplant chemical dependency with powerful and positive alternatives. Appropriate examples might include such mutual help groups as Alcoholics Anonymous, Day Top, and Delancey Street, and nonresidential programs featuring spiritual conversion or ethnic and cultural pride. Earlier in the dependency cycle, programs that attempt to stop social drinkers or drug users from becoming serious users are relatively ineffectual if they have nothing else to offer.

A rich survey of promising positive strategies in primary prevention (an Alternatives approach in the broad sense) is found in Balancing Head and Heart (Schaps, et al., 1975). Eleven prevention techniques are described, analyzed, and examined for research evidence. Naturally, the authors conclude that even the best strategies must be implemented well, but there seems immense promise in programming that attempts to build personal and social resources, creating a higher "immunity" to a later demand for drugs.

As pointed out in Balancing Head and Heart, it is useful to draw a distinction between programs featuring alternative activities and other positive approaches that are consistent with Alternatives theory. The latter encompass many prevention strategies that seek either to supplant the demand for drug use with a more constructive orientation or to build positive internal and social resources that make drug use less satisfying. In the narrower sense, Alternatives programs seek to facilitate involvement in meaningful activities (from dance to medita- tion to work apprenticeship). Ideally, Alternatives programming should offer options that are acceptable, attractive, realistic, attainable, and meaningful. Aside from assisting persons to find self-understanding, improved self-image, feelings of significance, and/or expanded aware- ness, the alternatives provided should, as much as possible:

- contribute to individual identity and independence;
- offer active participation and involvement;
- offer a chance for commitment;
- provide a feeling of identification with some larger group of people or larger body of experience; and
- (at times) offer experience in the realm of the noncognitive and the intuitive.

When Alternatives programs are implemented, two subtle principles are often lost. First, in a successful alternatives approach, the <u>product</u> is often less important than the <u>process</u>. The power of a meaningful life involvement is more in <u>being</u> than in <u>becoming</u>. In an Alternatives program featuring dance or meditation, for example, the emphasis should be more on the inherent enjoyment and challenge of learning and mastering of the skills and experiences involved, not on the goal of becoming the best dancer or meditator.

A second important principle suggests that Alternatives program participants (particularly the young) be cast as responsible colleagues in the process, not as patients. The patient, or dependent role, suggests passivity and low self-esteem to the participant, exactly those traits compatible with drug use. Program leaders should not feel they are "giving" participants anything; rather that they are creating a limited environment for participants to reach their higher potentials.

EMPIRICAL EVIDENCE

Given the dominance of traditional approaches to drug abuse, it is hardly surprising that the body of research and evaluation data on the Alternatives approach is somewhat limited. However, recent years have shown a promising increase both in the quality and quantity of such basic research and program evaluation. Two types of studies appear most relevant to include in this chapter. On the one hand, several studies appear to bear on the utility of the motivational assumptions behind Alternatives theory. In addition, other studies reflect the varying effectiveness of programmatic strategies based on an Alternatives Model. Let us take them in turn.

Research and Evaluation: The Theory

1. Characteristics of drug nonusers.

The Alternatives Model necessarily generates interest in the nonpathological elements of drug abuse. Because of the dominance of the medical model, the vast majority of research in the area has focused on characteristics of drug users, usually seeking psychopathological or sociopathological correlates. Even when researchers contrasted heavier with lighter users of drugs or even discussed comparison groups with nonusers, the dimensions of measurement were heavily weighted toward negative traits. An implicit assumption of early research may have been that nonusers merely possessed an absence of pathological "causogens," in the same way that medicine previously defined health as the mere absence of disease. Another prominent reason for the focus on the user was the hypothesis that drug users belonged in the statistical and normative minority, thus having the focus of a special group in society, to be contrasted from the majority. However, as incidence and prevalence increased, the research emphasis changed little, perhaps specializing more in more severely chemically dependent individuals, still a minority of the population.

Only recently has the examination of nonusers gained significant new interest. One of the earlier studies (San Leandro Study, 1969; reported in Cohen, 1975) was designed by a high school faculty and the students. A drug use questionnaire, anonymous and distributed by trusted peers, was collected from approximately 800 students at a suburban high school in the San Francisco Bay area. In addition to other questions, the nonusers (about 400) were asked the question, "If you did not use drugs, what has been the biggest deterrent for not using them;" The 260 completed responses to this open-ended question were categorized and generated the following results seen in Table 12.2.

If the total percentage of apparently negative reasons for avoidance are totaled (categories 3, 6, 8, and 9), the figure is 18.6 percent. Explicitly positive categories (i.e., expressing the primacy of positive alternatives or values in contrast to fear of something) total 44.2 percent (categories 1 and 7). Responses in category 2 were not fully analyzed, but many students worried about health problems in relation to goal inference, i.e., not being able to continue some valued activity, like athletics.

These results are entirely consistent with growing observational data suggesting that legal constraints plus scare-oriented education are only very limited deterrents. Even in this population, where Alternatives programs were not specifically generated in the school, the bulk of nonusers reported that some kind of alternatives orientation (even if it only meant satisfaction with nonchemical life) was the decisive preventive factor.

In a more recent study (Barnes and Olson, 1976), the usage patterns of nondrug alternatives in students from 11 to 18 years of age were studied in Texas. Among other findings, the investigators discovered that illicit drugs and alcohol were used most frequently to achieve positive states of consciousness or feeling. They also concluded that, "The information from this study suggests that the nondrug alternatives which satisfy a nondrug usermight also satisfy a reformed drug user."

A significant contribution to the study of nonusers was sparked by a survey of nearly 3,200 public high school students in St. Louis County (MO) done by the County's Office of Drug Abuse Prevention (O.D.A.P., 1976). Statistical tests were performed to compare the 549 nonusers with users of alcohol and marijuana (861) and the users of alcohol, marijuana, and other drugs (640). Statistically significant differences on the survey instrument showed that, contrasted to the user groups, nonusers:

-   tended to say they have strong religious values and find religion helpful in solving their problems;

-   tended to be involved in extracurricular activities, hobbies, clubs, and the like; and

-   tended to have relatively fewer friends who use drugs.

Table 12.2 Reasons for Not Using Drugs

Biggest Deterrent	Percentage
1. No need (life is fine, I'm happy, I turn on other ways, etc.)	39.8
2. Physical or mental health or athletics	22.4
3. Laws (respect for the law and fear of getting busted)	7.1
4. Brains and good judgment (i.e., having them)	6.2
5. Fear of the unknown	6.0
6. Seen results in other people	4.9
7. (Out of) Love and respect for parents	4.4
8. Fear of addiction	3.4
9. Friends (i.e., peer pressure against it)	3.2
10. Other (not yet been contacted to take drugs, personal values or religion, unfavorable past experience, poor quality of drugs, and don't know)	10.2

*N = 260 students, percentage adds up to over 100% because of some combinations of reasons

Schwartz and Bodanske (1977) followed up this survey with depth interviews on 178 nonusers. In one sense, the researchers found it difficult to stereotype the typical nonuser. For example, some had friends who currently used alcohol and marijuana; others did not. Thirty-six percent said they were satisfied with their grades; 18 percent reported they were not.

However, data confirmed some extremely suggestive commalities. First, as predicted by Alternatives theory, only two percent said they were deterred by no opportunity for drug use, only nine percent by a fear of legal consequences or a fear of becoming addicted. Sixty-eight percent mentioned the possibility of physiological or psychological consequences. Other key findings included the following:

— Ninety percent of the nonusers described themselves as close to their parents. Nearly 70 percent said they were "very close" compared with their classmates.

— Approximately 80 percent of the teenagers said their parents checked up on them when they left the house; 60 percent said this occurred "almost always."

— Eighty percent reported that their high school grades averaged A or B.

— Almost 80 percent described religion as either very or moderately important to them.

— Seventy-five percent reported involvement in extracurricular activities; 28 percent reported spending more than six hours per week in such activities.

On other important dimensions, relatively little importance was attributed to being popular. Less than 20 percent of the nonusers considered themselves "very popular" at school, but eight in ten said they were satisfied with their status. Congruently, 95 percent described themselves as more independent than their classmates, with more than half ranking themselves as "very independent."

The investigators summarized and highlighted the findings as confirming the attitude that there are alternatives to drugs. Bodanske commented, "What we've found here is a student who appears very well adjusted, eager to remain busy at school or church, who just doesn't see the necessity for drinking or taking drugs. . . . And chief among these alternatives seems to be a strong identification with family, church and school and all the activities that go into making up those strong ties." Schwartz, commenting on the findings that only two of the subjects reported they could not obtain drugs if they wanted, said, "We found that these students apparently have certain strengths to withstand the obvious high degree of peer pressure that exists for youngsters to take drugs or drink. More than half said they felt 'no need' to take drugs."

2. Correlates: another look.

Despite past grounding in the traditional medical model, recent analyses of drug use correlates seem to be moving more toward a behavioral health orientation and away from the concept of de facto deviancy. In summarizing findings on adolescent health and behavior, Jessor (1978) observed that, ". . . there seems to be little evidence that the notions of psychopathology are very useful in these areas. . . . As far as personality is concerned, engagement in these behaviors is part of normal development. . . .What emerges in my view is the central importance of personality control factors that have traditionally involved the attitudes, orientation and values that serve to control against transgression or risk-taking behavior — the 'rightness' or 'wrongness' of various behaviors." Jessor concluded that illicit drug use behavior serves a specific and rational role for the adolescent, that it represents the means by which he or she attempts to establish independence, autonomy, control over the environment, and the like.

Jessor reported also that growing findings that alcohol and marijuana use among adolescents tends to be very highly related, subverting the expectation that marijuana use would act as a substitute for heavy drinking. In Jessor's work, those adolescents who are involved in "problem behaviors" such as illicit drug use, drinking, and sex also tend to reflect certain nonconformance personality characteristics, such as a greater degree of social criticism; a reluctance to take as nonproblematic the way society is put together; a tendency not to accept the status quo; a lower degree of religiosity; and a greater tolerance of deviant behavior. They also tend to place "a much greater emphasis on independence and autonomy," on rebelliousness, etc., on self-assertion, self-determination, and to put a lower value on achievement and striving. Also reflected in another cluster of attributes were frustration related to school and other traditional societal goals and institutions, a high value on spontaneity, openness to experience, and an especial vulnerability to peer pressure and support.

Some of the characteristics mentioned by Jessor related strongly to the findings of Schwartz and Bodanske, and are reflected in other recent studies. Research done in Boise, Idaho (C_2ODAC, 1976), showed a highly significant inverse statistical relationship between marijuana use and grade averages (only 3.7 percent of students with A averages smoked marijuana; all of those with D averages reported current use). A similarly powerful finding in the San Francisco Bay area was reported by Churgin (1978), finding surprisingly high current use of marijuana and cocaine in a control group, and very little current use in an academic honors class. The Boise study also confirmed the religiosity finding: only 2 percent of those attending church regularly used marijuana; of those who never attended, the figure was 24.5 percent. Again consistent with previous findings and Alternatives theory, the study found an extremely strong correlation between marijuana use and agreement with the statement "There's nothing to do." The critical role of the family was also confirmed, showing particular power in the role of parental modeling. There was a high direct correlation between parents' consumption level of marijuana, beer, or hard liquor and the usage patterns of their children.

The possibility that personality and drug use correlates based on the locus of control (internal vs. external) was recently brought up by Hochhauser (1978). The author observed, "To counteract the frustrating perception of external control, the individual may resort to drug use, since the self-administration of drugs provides some measure of internal control, as well as feelings of predictability and controllability. Furthermore, as drugs become a dominant mode of control, the drug user will probably develop a more active motivational state, insofar as drug-seeking and drug-using behaviors demand increased activity, rather than inactivity. Through these behaviors the adolescent drug user is able to control his/her own psychological state, establishing a degree of controllability over his/her existence that was previously unobtainable. . . . Unfortunately, while this pattern may provide an initial measure of control, the individual soon finds himself/herself returned to the helpless situation, as long-term drug use begins to establish control over his/her behavior. The successful internal control that was initially obtained with drugs has now shifted to a form of external control, and the individual may find himself/herself returned to a position of learned helplessness." Hochhauser further reports Segal's (1974) finding that nonusers of drugs tended to score higher on internal locus of control, with higher scores on external locus of control for alcohol, marijuana, and multiple drug users.

In the same way that internal control appears to be reasserted for the successful client of an alcohol or drug dependence program, so does the Alternatives Model posit a personal growth factor in the discontinuance of drug use. In a small study of former "moderate" users of psychedelic drugs (Cohen, 1968), 11 of 32 subjects reported discontinuing drugs because they were beyond it spiritually or psychologically. Two subjects cited goal interference and the remaining nineteen pointed to health concerns. It was noted that even where health concerns affected discontinuance, most interviewees related these concerns to some valued activity or pursuit of existing relationship that necessitated adequate physical or mental health. Very few subjects reported physical pain, mental agony, or general discomfort as being a prime motivating factor for their discontinuance. Substantially richer data is expected from a study of 100 former opiate addicts who discontinued use without treatment or coercion (Waldorf and Biernacki, Pacific Institute for Research and Evaluation).

3. Comments.

Certainly the proliferation of research relating to the etiology of drug use is anything but clear and consistent. A recent ambitious annotated bibliography, The Aetiology of Psychoactive Substance Use (UNESCO, 1977) states:

> ... the dominant approach, in terms of research effort invested, still seems to be the continued search for the drug dependent personality. Thus, personality traits or characteristic personality functioning have been described, though not agreed upon, for opiates, amphetamine, barbiturate, hallucinogenic and cannabis users. Although a prolific area of research, there are very few studies which have increased our understanding of the reason for drug use. . . . The main conclusion must be that while, on the one hand, we are being inundated with research "findings" we are, on the other hand, making little progress in our understanding.

Yet, the findings reported above, and many recent observations by professional researchers appear to be consistent with the essential hypotheses of the Alternatives Model. A significant attitude shift to the "coping mechanism" approach and away from the psychopathological approach is observed. Research seems to indicate the growing recognition of importance of volitional issues in psychoactive drug use, of lifestyle correlates, and of the positive factors influencing nonuse of drugs.

Program Evaluation: The Effectiveness of Alternatives

Much recent empirical work in the substance abuse field has turned to evaluation of program effectiveness. Social problems do not wait for theorists to establish closure on causation or correlates. As cost-effectiveness becomes a more important consideration in prioritizing social responses, funding agencies have been more insistent on applied research. Program evaluation, although a difficult form of investigation to sufficiently control, nevertheless offers data that can shed more light on the viability of the Alternatives approach.

1. Focus on treatment.

Evaluations of treatment and rehabilitation programs, where entering clients often display severe dependency on chemicals, rarely measure variables explicitly relevant to Alternatives theory. Outcome variables usually involve limited goals such as continuance of program participation, relative cessation of dependency, and various signs of potential for rehabilitation. There has been an implicit assumption and finding that practical life alternatives — vocation, positive family relationships, and/or meaning and purpose — were desirable elments for successful rehabilitation. However, given the priority on meeting the immediate needs of severely disabled clients, most treatment programs have not had the mandates nor resources to follow up on graduated clients. Indeed, generally, recidivism rates are rather high.

There has been new interest in aftercare services for chemical dependents. In a way, models such as Alcoholics Anonymous feature follow-up alternatives for members; perhaps as important for the recovering alcoholic is the ability to help others with drinking problems than to have helpers for those problems. One of the more promising research-evaluation projects involving aftercare is a three-year, controlled study of three approaches to aftercare services for opiate addicts being conducted in Alameda County, California (Pacific Institute for Research and Evaluation). Generally, however, it might be safe to suggest that eventual success in treatment and rehabilitation is linked to "something better," new roles, identities, or modes of coping that are more satisfying than the rather easy return to habits of dependency.

2. Focus on prevention and early intervention.

It is perhaps fair to observe that a higher proportion of early intervention and primary prevention programs feature the "new wave" of strategies — positive alternatives and inner resource development. Thus, a higher ratio of program evaluations tend to be of direct relevance to the theme of this chapter.

Broadly, "prevention" can be said to involve the stage of substance abuse precedent to regular use — i.e., abstention, experimentation, and occasional use. Primary prevention programs usually involve target populations manifesting these nondependent use patterns. Of course, prevention programming is particularly difficult to evaluate, since the object of measurement is something that will not occur. The earlier the stage of intervention (e.g., in primary school children), the more pressure on the longitudinal nature of the research. Especially in this youthful population, where the incidence of substance use is likely to be low, researchers must concentrate on the "intermediary variables" thought to be linked with a probability of later substance misuse. Thus, many program impact studies look at changes in measures of self-esteem, communication skills, values, etc. In studies of early intervention, researchers have attempted to measure changes in drug use or intention to use, as well as the attitudinal and affective variables thought to be intermediary. It might be helpful to describe briefly the findings of some representative studies that have relevance to the discussion of alternatives.

Murray and Coltoff (1977) reported on a drug prevention program (Children's Aid Society) based explicitly on Alternatives theory. The program clients were inner city youth, from 8 to 17, exposed to program strategies aimed at helping clients to improve their problem-solving abilities, develop a better sense of self, improve their social, academic, and creative skills, and to expose them to a wide range of cultural activities. A study comparing youth in the drug prevention program with youth in other Children's Aid Society programs found that prevention youth reported significantly more drug use at the beginning of the program year as compared with youth in other Children's Aid Society programs; however, at the end of the program year, this pattern had been reversed. A 1977 follow-up study showed that the overall use pattern seemed much less than comparable New York samples. Twenty-four of the 31 interviewees were not using any illicit drugs following the follow-up study. Of these, 22 stated that they avoided drugs because they did not want to ruin their health. This motivation was particularly strong among males and females who enjoyed vigorous sports. Similar findings in predicted directions were reported for the series of studies in the areas of self-image and attitudes toward drugs.

Another broad-based intervention program in New York City schools, SPARK, features peer counselling and leadership training for adolescents as well as a range of drug abuse prevention activities and services. Provision of alternatives – recreational, social, and intellectual activities – is also included. A 1977 review (New York State Office of Drug Abuse Services) reported that overall use of drugs dropped by at least 40 percent. For example, while one-third of the students used marijuana daily before entering the program, only 15 percent reported daily use after participating. Alcohol use also declined.

A California-based program, Project Community, targeted students 14 to 18 years old. The aims involved helping adolescents become more effective in dealing with personal problems, gain a sense of value, and thus decrease drug use. The strategies used were humanistic and effective, including components explicitly dealing with alternatives to drugs. Results were reported by Soskin et al. (1975). Changes in peer relationships, self-image, and drug use were generally very encouraging. Of special interest was the application of the strategies both in a community drop-in center and in two different school systems.

A program oriented more toward effective alternatives, specifically the clarification of values about drug abuse, was reported by Slimmon (1974). Comparing high school students exposed to specially adapted values clarification classes versus controls, the evaluation found differences in the predicted direction for 32 of 36 comparison variables reflecting drug use. The importance of comparison groups in such age populations was reinforced in this study. First year students, experimentals and controls, showed higher drug use during the year (being exposed to a new, high use environment). However, the experimental group tended to show a smaller increase in incidence and prevalence.

Other empirical data is available from studies investigating particular programs or methods and incidentally looking at substance abuse variables. Using a questionnaire survey, Shafii (1974) et al. investigated the effect of meditation on marijuana use. They reported that 15 percent of a nonmeditating control group decreased or stopped their marijuana use during a three-month period, and 50 to 75 percent of the experimental group had decreased or stopped their use during the first three months after initiation into meditation. The authors found further that the longer a person had practiced meditation, the more likely that he/she had decreased or stopped marijuana use. A similar later study (Shafii, 1976) showed the same trends for alcohol use, particularly the use of hard liquors. Meditators decreased use more than controls, results being statistically significant.

a. A review of impact studies. The program evaluations cited above are but a few examples of salient research. Other specific studies are mentioned in the bibliography. However, an overall perspective on findings relating to primary prevention and early intervention was strongly enhanced by a review of 75 such studies (Schaps, et al., 1978). The review report covered studies that evaluated a total of 127 primary drug abuse prevention programs. Eligible studies were those that measured program effects on drug use, intentions to use drugs, and/or attitudes toward drug use. The studies were gathered through an intensive and extended search, possibly the largest collection of prevention impact evaluations available in early 1978.

As part of the review process, each study was described along 70 programming and research dimensions. The descriptive data were coded for computer analysis, and various cross-tabular and correlational analyses were conducted. Although the review described and analyzed characteristics of prevention strategies, program settings, target populations, and research methods, the most important findings concerned program effectiveness. The authors concluded, "Taken together, the 127 programs were judged to be slightly effective on the average in influencing drug use behaviors and attitudes."

Of more interest was an intensive substudy of the eight best-researched and highest "intensity" (degree of program input over time) programs. As seen in Table 12.3, six of the eight such rated programs yielded positive drug-specific outcome ratings. One program showed no effect and another showed a negative effect on attitudes toward drug use.

Table 12.3 Outcomes in Exemplary Evaluation Efforts

Program ID	Constituent Strategies[1]	Intensity Score	Evaluation Quality Score	Findings[2]					
				Use	Intentions	Attitudes	Knowledge	Affective	Performance
A	4,5,7,14	8	15	−	−	0	−	0	−
B	3,5,8	11	14	+1	−	−	−	+1	+1
C	4	10	13	0	−	+2	+1	+1	+1
D	1,3,7,14	10	14	−	0	+1	+1	−	−
E	3,14	8	13	+1	−	−	−	+1	−
F	1,2	8	12	−	−	−1	−	−	−
G	3	9	12	−	−	+1	−	−	−
H	1,3	8	15	−	−	+2	−	+1	−

[1] Constituent Strategies:
  1 information
  2 persuasion
  3 affective-skill
  4 affective-experiential
  5 counselling
  7 peer group activities
  8 family relationships
  14 alternatives

[2] − not measured
  +2 substantial positive effect
  +1 slight positive effect
  0 no effect

This pattern of findings was regarded as very encouraging, especially in light of the fact that the only program showing a negative drug-specific impact was the one information-only type program in the group. The remaining seven programs were comprised of affective strategies alone or in combination with other strategies, and six of these seven yielded positive drug-specific effects. (It should be noted that Schaps, et al., defined "alternatives" programs in the narrowest sense, relating specifically to activities.) Despite the methodological difficulties in proving a preventive effect, the authors were encouraged that the newer effective-cognitive approaches to prevention showed promise.

At the very least, it seems fair to conclude that the newer, more positively oriented program strategies, cited in the review study and in other studies mentioned in previous pages, demonstrate a more desirable impact than earlier strategies that focused on the negative (scare education, symptomatic approaches, etc.). Indeed, a general review of studies involving rehabilitation, treatment, early intervention, and primary prevention has indicated that results are generally consistent with the theoretical assumptions behind the alternatives model.

IMPLICATIONS AND CONCLUSIONS: GOING BEYOND DRUGS

The empirical evidence for a "positive alternatives" approach to drug abuse appears promising, even in primary prevention, the most cost-effective stage of prevention. Given the tentative implication that this basic thrust deserves more attention in social policy and program planning, certain observations seem in order.

Social Strategies for Public Health

A major conclusion that appears warranted from theory and research involves the limitation of threat or fear as truly effective social reinforcers. An instructive parallel lies in attempts to control the smoking of tobacco.

Smoking shares almost all of the personal dynamics of other drug use except for blatant psychoactivity. Armed with overwhelming evidence regarding the physiological damage wreaked by cigarettes, health educators around the world found remarkable resistance to cessation and a disturbing threat of new incidence in the young. Although the dramatic case against smoking and the extraordinary effort in delivering the message are beginning to have its effects, the resistance offers a cautionary note to other drug and alcohol health preventors.

Although, for smokers, cigarettes may be equally addictive as in heroin or alcohol for dependers, the potential population of psychoactive drug abusers are not likely to get presented with such formidable information. Indeed, based on current pharmacological evidence, it is likely that mental-emotional side effects will prove to establish the most potent case against psychoactive substances; lethal physical effects are less easily demonstrated.

Thus, the recreational mythos surrounding psychoactive drug use makes the fear, legal, or moral approaches relatively undependable. As suggested by some of the research, even "fear" of physical or psychological functioning is often dependent upon the inherent valuing of body or mind, on a basic level of self-esteem and hope, on a central conception of meaning and purpose in life.

Return to the Natural

As 1980 approaches, we hear more reference to "health promotion" as a method of "disease prevention." This subtle shift of emphasis toward the primacy of "wellness" as contrasted with the focus on "illness" is in line with a more holistic approach toward public health and social problems. It reminds one of the intensely logical ancient Oriental practice where the physician was paid only if the patient remained well; all treatment for illness was free.

Behind this emerging holism is a latent respect for the "natural," for the superiority of life and lifestyle without toxin or pollution. For many years, the intense political concern with ecology did not transfer to the human body. More recently, there has been substantial interest in the carcinogenic characteristics of various chemicals in foods. Even so, the link of this concern with purity has not been clearly established in the mind of the psychoactive drug user. Too many times young people are found shopping natural food stores themselves quite "stoned" on psychoactive chemicals.

The naturalist ethos, as applied to the individual, is usually an optimistic one. At the same time that intoxication becomes a more and more prevalently accepted condition, a backlash of thinking and behavior is reaffirming the inherent beauty and growth potential of the human body, mind, and spirit. Those comfortable with positive models of alternatives tend to elevate human nature; those comfortable with the necessity of a medicated society take a more pessimistic view. To some extent, expectations create reality; those who are willing to experiment with the possibility that satisfaction in life can be had without changes in the biochemical environment are more likely to experience those change in a consciousness that produces freedom from biochemical manipulation.

It is perhaps no coincidence that some of the apparently most effective intervention strategies — religious experience, service to others, positive family environment, meaningful relationships, and work — all tend to imply a high estimation of human potential and purpose. Likewise, if we broaden our perspective to other social and health problems, from poverty to mental illness, we may be able to extract the same hypothesis that the celebration of life can occur in the face of severe difficulties and injustices. Indeed, the most perplexing problems of persons and societies may well generate the most creative new energies. It has been said of plants that "nothing grows without a resisting medium."

Thus, we have come full circle from the beginning of this chapter. It has been suggested that the paradox of increasing psychointoxication of industrialized society forces action, much of it ill-advised. Given the pressure of pragmatics, however, professionals and citizens groups have turned to the nontraditional, to an orientation apparently contradictory with the negativistic approach common in combatting the so-called "victimless crimes."

In the area of drug abuse, it would be well, however, for social liberals who support a laissez faire attitude not to buy into the same negative assumptions implied by severe prohibitionists, assumptions that doubt individuals are capable of making a choice toward their growth and not toward their dissolution.

Ending his book Beyond Drugs, Einstein (1975) quotes from Abraham Joshua Heschel: "We, having shaped our lives around the practical, the utilitarian, devoid of dreams and vision, higher concerns and enthusiasm, are literally driving young people into the inferno of drug culture in search of exaltation." However, as long as exaltation is possible in its natural and unfettered form, and this chapter has argued that it is, it will be continually rediscovered. The expansion of consciousness and the spirit cannot be stopped; it can merely be detained. The immense challenge in the prevention of substance abuse is but one effort to make that delay ever so much shorter.

BIBLIOGRAPHY

Barnes, C.P. and Olson, J.N. Usage Patterns of Non-Drug Alternatives. Texas. University of Texas of the Permian Basin. 1976.

Carp, J.M. and Goldstein, M. Better Living Without Chemistry. Some Program Alternatives to Drug Abuse. Journal of Drug Issues. 4(2), pp. 149-161. 1974.

C$_2$ODAC. Community Youth Development Survey 1975-6. Boise, Idaho. Community Youth Development Project of C2ODAC. 1976.

Churgin, Shoshanna, Satariano, William and DiBartolo, Russell. An Outcome & Process Evaluation of the Center for Human Development. Walnut Creek, CA. Pacific Institute for Research & Evaluation. 1978.

Cohen, A.Y. Alternatives to Drug Abuse: Steps Toward Prevention. Rockville, Maryland. National Clearinghouse for Drug Abuse Information. 1975.

_____. The Journey Beyond Trips: Alternatives to Drugs. Journal of Psychedelic Drugs, 3(2), pp. 16-21. 1971.

_____. Relieving Acid Indigestion: Educational Strategies Related to Psychological and Social Dynamics of Hallucinogenic Drug Abuse. Unpublished research report, Bureau of Drug Abuse Control, 1968.

Dohner, V.A. Alternatives to Drugs — A New Approach to Drug Education, Journal of Drug Education, vol. 2, no. 1, pp. 3-22. 1972.

Einstein, S. Alternatives to Drug Abuse: An Analysis. In Einstein, S. and DeAngelis, G.G. (Editors). The Non-Medical Use of Drugs: Contemporary Clinical Issues. Farmingdale, N.Y. Baywood Publishing, pp. 79-83. 1972.

_____. Beyond Drugs. New York: Pergamon Press, 1975.

Emrich, R.L. Alternatives: The Key to Drug Abuse Prevention and Rehabilitation, Unpublished paper, National Council on Crime and Delinquency Research Center, Davis, California, 1971.

Fazey, Cindy. The Aetiology of Psychoactive Substance Use. UNESCO, Paris. 1977.

Goodstadt, M.S. Myths and Methodology in Drug Education: A Critical Review of the Research Evidence. In Goodstadt, M.S. Research on Methods and Programs of Drug Education. Toronto, Canada. Addiction Research Foundation, pp. 113-145. 1974.

Hochhauser, Mark. Drugs as Agents of Control. Journal of Psychedelic Drugs, Vol. 10(1), pp. 65-69. Jan-March, 1978.

Hyde, M.O. and Clark, R.A. Turning on Without Drugs. Pp. 127-134. In

Hyde, M.O. (Editor). Mind Drugs. New York, N.Y.: McGraw-Hill, pp. 127-134. 1968.

Jackson, L.S. "Alternative Pursuits: Implications for Drug Prevention." In: Senay, E., Shorty, V. and Alksne, H. (Editors). Developments in the Field of Drug Abuse. Proceedings 1974 of the National Association for the Prevention of Addiction to Narcotics. Cambridge, Massachusetts: Schenkman, pp. 719-723. 1975.

Jessor, Richard, 1978. Address given at National Academy of Medicine Conference, as reported in Washington Drug Review, Vol. 11, No. 7, July 14, 1978.

Johnston, L., Bachman, Jerald G., and O'Malley, Patrick M. Highlights from Drug Use Among American High School Students 1975-1977. Rockville, Maryland. National Institute on Drug Abuse. 1978.

Mann, J. et al. The Alternatives Approach, Stash Capsules, 8(4) (April, 1976).

Marin, P. and Cohen, A.Y. Understanding Drug Use. New York: Harper and Row. 1971.

Messolonghites, L. (Editor). Alternative Pursuits for America's Third Century. A Resource Book on New Perceptions, Processes, and Programs – With Implications for the Prevention of Drug Abuse. Washington, D.C. U.S. Government Printing Office. 1974.

Murray, L. and Coltoff, P. Drugs and Urban Youth. The Children's Aid Society, New York, 1977.

New York State Office of Drug Abuse Services, Administrative Evaluation Report of SPARK, New York City High School Drug Prevention and Education Program, Division of Cost Effectiveness and Research, October, 1977.

Payne, B. Getting There Without Drugs. New York: Viking Press. 1973.

Schaps, E. et al. Primary Prevention Evaluation Research: A Review of 75 Program Impact Studies, National Institute on Drug Abuse, 1978.

Schwartz, S. and Bodanske, E.A. Environmental Strategies for Primary Drug Abuse Prevention Programs, Study made for the Office of County Youth Programs, St. Louis County, MO., 1977.

Segal, B. 1974. Locus of Control and Drug and Alcohol Use in College Students. Journal of Alcohol and Drug Education, Vol. 19(3), pp. 1-5.

Shafii, M.; Lavely, R.; and Jaffe, R. Meditation and Marijuana, American Journal of Psychiatry. 131(1), pp. 60-63. 1974.

_____. Meditation and the Prevention of Alcohol Abuse. Alcohol Health and Research World. Summer, 1976.

Slimmon, L. Annual Report: Alternatives and Values Clarification. San Rafael, California. Department of Mental Hygiene. 1974.

Soskin, W.F.; Korchin, S.J.; and Stein, K.B. Project Community: Therapeutic Exploration With Adolescents. Final Report 1971-74. University Extension, University of California, Berkeley.

Ungerleider, J.T., and Burnford, F. DARE – A Demonstration Project of a Meaningful Alternative to Substance Abuse. Drug Forum. The Journal of Human Issues. 2(1), pp. 55-64. 1972.

Index

Addiction
  and the community, 304,
     306-7, 308
  defined, 305, 314
  enforcement model of
     handling,
     Canada, 91-2
  history of, 17-8
  a model of, 310-2
  to opiates, 6-7, 12
  rehabilitation, U.S., 139-43
  in Singapore, 67-71, 72-3
  treatment of, Israel, 181-5
  typology of, 309-10
  in the U.K., 153, 155
Addicts, drug registers of,
  247-9
Alcohol, nonusers and users,
  346, 349
Alcohol use in Canada
  epidemiologic interest in,
    94-5
  among students, 96, 97-8
  See also Australia
Alternatives
  nature of, 342
  types of, 344-5
  as model in research and
    evaluation, 351-5
America. See United States

Amphetamine use
  in the U.K., 152, 161
  and the U.S. government vs.
    drug companies, 320-1
  See also Australia
Analgesic use. See Australia
Australia
  alcohol, 31-32, 36-9
  alcohol and the aboriginal
    male, 32-3
  alcoholism, 34, 55-6, 58-9
  amphetamines, 35, 45, 51
  analgesic use, 43, 45, 48
  hallucinogens, 45
  heroin addicts, 43
  hypnotics, 40, 43
  marijuana, 45
  methaqualone, 43
  multiple drug use, 51, 55
  narcotic addiction, 57
  narcotics, 51
  sedatives, 40, 43
  tobacco, 40
  tranquilizers, 40, 43
  treatment facilities for
    drug dependence, 56-7

Barbiturate use in the U.K., 148,
  152, 158, 162, 163
Britain. See the United Kingdom

Canada
addict defined as criminal, 92
addiction, treatment model,
91-2
alcohol use, 94-5, 96, 97-8
cannabis and drug use, legal
control, 108-20
drug misuse as disease, 154-5,
157
drug problems, remedial
approach, 93-4
heroin addiction, 92, 100
Le Dain Commission, 91,
95, 99, 100-5
marijuana use, 96-7, 98
narcotic legislation, 108,
110, 113, 114, 116,
120-1, 122, 126-7n 37
Cannabis
in Canada, an indictable offense, 110, 113, 114
history of use, 9-12
and the Le Dain Commission,
103, 105
See also Le Dain Commis-
sion; Marijuana
and selective decriminalization in Canada, 115-20
and the U.K., 154, 155
use in Canada defined, 108
China, opium trade, 152
Cocaine use in the U.K., 154,
155-6, 160
Community
concept of, 13-14, 307-8
and drug training programs,
233-5
Community research, survey
methodology, 251-9
Community response to drug
use and misuse in the
U.K., 148-9, 150
by doctors, 163-4
by psychiatrists, 165-6
in youth, 151-2
Criminalization, 22, 115, 122

Decriminalization
cannabis, Bill S-19, 120-1,
122, 126-7n 37

Decriminalization (cont.)
defined, 115-6, 119
of drug abuse, U.S., 135, 136
selective, 116-7
DeQuincey, Thomas, and opium
use, 7, 150
Deviance theory of drug use,
17, 22
Drug abuse, 17, 18, 35
alternatives to, 339-42
control and treatment in
the U.S., 133, 139-43
deviant-criminal concepts
of, 206, 207
education, critical issues,
209-12
influence of hypodermic
needle, 7, 147, 154
levels of defined, 245-6
motivational models for,
340-1
program evaluation and
research design,
261-6
programs, 202-3, 212
treatment, the issues, 87-8
varieties of, 86-7
See also Incidence and
prevalence; Israel and
drug abuse; Singapore;
United Kingdom;
United States
Drug companies, government
action against, 320-3
Drug consumption, Australia
and New Zealand, 34-6
Drug control and the League
of Nations, 131-2
Drug definitions
legal, 206-7
medical, 205-6
scientific, 207-8
social-religious, 203-5
World Health Organization,
146
Drug dependence
disease concept, 154-5
treatment facilities,
Australia, 56-57, 59

Drug education
    defined, 279
    experimental variables in,
        283-4
    goals, 282-3
    and increased drug use, 210,
        211
    and media, 216-8, 219-22
    program development, 213
    program evaluation, 284-6,
        288-9
Drug legislation. See Britain,
        Canada; Singapore
Drug misuse in the United
        Kingdom
    government reports on, 155,
        157, 159-60
    medical disease approach
        to, 154-5, 157
    treatment centers for, 165
Drug nonusers, characteristics
        of as research focus,
        345-8
Drug prevention, 208
    and early intervention pro-
        grams, 351-5
    and training programs, 230-5
Drug prevention program re-
        search
    content, 215
    framework, 227
    planning, 223, 225
Drug prevention programs, edu-
        cation vs. propaganda, 86
Drug problems, remedial ap-
        proach in Canada, 93-4
Drug program evaluation, ef-
        fectiveness of alterna-
        tives, 351-5
Drug program funding, 215-6
Drug registers, requirements
        for effective, 248-9
Drug repression, American
        campaign for, 135-6
Drug use
    assessment of trends, 257-9
    correlated with personality,
        349-50
    methodology for study of, 95

Drug use (cont.)
    and misuse, abuse, 316-7,
        324, 341.
    as social problem, 12, 17-22
    See also Incidence of drug
        use; Israel and drug
        use
Drug use in Canada
    among adults, 98, 9
    nature and extend, 94-5
    among young persons, 95-8
Drug use in Israel. See Israel
        and drug abuse; Israel
        and drug use
Drug use in the United Kingdom,
        151, 159-160, 161, 162,
        163
Drug user, active, 230
Drug-related definitions, 203-8
Drug traffic in the United
        Kingdom, 151, 159

Education, concepts of, 210, 213,
        214
England. See United Kingdom
Evaluation of drug education
        programs, 279-82
    comparisons of alternative
        strategies, 286-7
    guidelines, 288-9
    studies of overall impact,
        284-5
Evaluation of drug program
        effectiveness, Alterna-
        tives approach, 351-5
Evaluation of drug treatment
        programs
    examples, 276-8
    methodology and community
        research, 289
    patient follow-up problem,
        274-5
    studies, process vs. product
        analysis, 270-1
Evaluation research, 259-267,
        278
Experimental designs
    difficulties in applying, 272
    in drug abuse evaluation,
        261-6

Experimental designs (cont.)
in drug use surveys, 255-6

Federal Drug Education Act
(1970), U.S., 215
Food and Drug Act (FDA),
Canada, 118
Food and Drug Administration
(FDA), U.S., 318, 327

Goals
of drug education, 282-3
therapeutic, 74-5
and values, 97
Great Britain. See United
Kingdom

Hallucinogens, 45, 100
Hashish in Israel, 176, 189
increased demand for, 174-5
smuggling, 172-3
Heroin
addiction, Canada, 92, 100
addicts and methaqualone, 43
deaths from, 249
in the U.K., 158, 160
Hypnotic use in Australia,
40, 43
Hypodermic needle and drug
use, 7, 147, 154

Impact studies, a review of,
353-5
Incidence of drug use
and community research,
246-7
sources of data, 247-67
Israel and drug abuse
by Israeli youth, 175, 176,
180, 184, 192
as law enforcement problem,
173-4
maintenance programs,
186-7
methadone programs, 193, 195
public attitude toward,
189-94
scope and social char-
acteristics, 172,
178-80

Israel and drug abuse (cont.)
search for explanation, 190
treatment, 182-3, 191, 193-4,
195-6
Israel and drug use
addicts, 185-6
prevention, 187-8, 191, 192-3
in prisons, 179
research, 176, 193-4
smuggling as political security
problem, 174, 183
spread, 171-3, 175

League of Nations and international drug control,
93, 131-2
Le Dain Commission, Canada
(Le Dain Commission of
Inquiry into the Non-
Medical Use of Drugs),
91, 95, 99
legal recommendations,
103-4
origin and functioning, 100-3
recommendations and reac-
tions to, 104-5
Legal control of drug abuse
in Israel, 181-5
Legal definitions of drugs,
206-7
Legal sanctions and drug abuse
in Singapore, 83-4

Marijuana Tax Act of 1937, U.S.,
10, 12, 16, 134
Marijuana use, 18, 19
in Australia, 45
in Canada, 96-8
characteristics of users, 349
National Commission on
Marijuana and Drug
Abuse (1973), 306-7
reasons for use, 86
in Singapore, 71-2
study of nonusers, 346
See also Cannabis
Medical definition of drugs,
205-6

Medical literature, cannabis
    and opium, 6, 10
Methadone
    and addiction control, U.S.,
        141-3
    and addiction treatment, the
        U.K., 160, 161-2
    and narcotic dependence,
        Australia, 57
    programs in Israel, 193, 195
Methaqualone, 43, 322
Models
    in evaluation research, 260-1
    in evaluation of treatment
        programs, 276-8
    for motivation in demand
        for drugs, 340-1
Mood-altering drugs
    and federal regulation,
        318-20
    and pharmaceutical industry
        promotion, 323-9
    and the prescribing
        physician, 325-6,
        328-9
Morphine, 72-73, 153

Narcotic legislation in Canada,
        91, 93
    Bill S-19 (1974), cannabis,
        120-1, 122, 126-7n 37
    Food and Drug Act (FDA),
        108
    Narcotic Control Act of
        1961, 110, 113, 114,
        116, 120
    Opium and Drug Act of
        1911, 92
    Opium and Narcotic Drug
        Act of 1920, 92
Narcotic legislation in Singa-
        pore, 70
Narcotic legislation in Southeast
        Asia
    Dangerous Drugs Ordinance,
        1951, 83
    Drugs (Prevention of misuse)
        Act, 1969, 83
    Misuse of Drugs Act, 1973,
        84

Narcotic legislation in the U.S.
    Boggs Act (1951), 12, 135
    Comprehensive Drug Abuse
        Prevention and
        Control Act (1970),
        137
    Controlled Substances Act
        (1970), 317
    Harrison Act (1914), 18,
        134-5
    Marijuana Tax Act (1937),
        10, 12, 16, 134
    Narcotic Addict Rehabilita-
        tion Act (NARA),
        1966, 140-1
    Narcotic Control Act (1956),
        136
    Porter Act, 139
Narcotic use
    in Australia, 51
    in New Zealand, 35-6
Narcotics Treatment Adminis-
        tration (U.S.), 248, 250
New York City Narcotics
        Register, 248, 249
New Zealand
    alcohol as drug problem, 29
    Alcoholism and Drug Addic-
        tion Act (1966), 57
    drug consumption in, 34-6
Nonmedical drug use, 18, 102
Non-medical use of drugs in
        Canada, the Le Dain Com-
        mission, 91, 100-3
Nonresponse in surveys as prob-
        lem, 254-5

Opiates
    history of use, 3-9
    and the U.S. government, 16
    use and control measures,
        the U.K., 147-62
Opium addiction treatment
        centers in Southeast
        Asia, 78-80, 81
Opium control
    Harrison Act (1914), U.S.,
        134-5
    League of Nations, 93, 131-2

Opium farms, Singapore, 68-9
Opium as medical problem, 18
Opium smoking, 8, 70, 77
Opium use
    in America, 8-9
    in Britain, 147-9, 152-3
    in the nineteenth century,
        7, 150-1
    in Singapore, 67-71

Pharmaceutical industry
    and the Controlled Substances
        Act, 319-20
    and drug misuse, 316-7
    promotion of mood-altering
        drugs, 323-9
Pharmaceutical literature and
        opium, 6-7
Philippines
    drug dependence treatment
        centers, 82
    drug abuse programs, 85
    Drug Abuse Research Founda-
        tion, 85, 88
Polls. See Surveys
Prescription drugs, promotion
        by pharmaceutical
        industry, 324-5
Prevention of drug abuse in
        Israel, 187-8, 191, 192-3
Prevention of drug use,
        defined, 245-6
Psychedelic use, 150, 152

Randomization in surveys, 252-4
Reliability
    in drug use survey data,
        255-6
    in evaluation of drug use
        treatment program,
        271
Research
    and drug prevention program
        content, 215
    and drug training programs,
        231
    and evaluation, the theory,
        345-351
    in Israel, drug use and mis-
        use, 193-4

Research design. See Experi-
        mental designs
Research studies
    cross-sectional and longi-
        tudinal, 257-8
    of drug nonusers, 346-8
    of drug users, 345-6
    in evaluation of drug educa-
        tion programs, 280-2
    forms needed for drug inter-
        vention, 288
Responses
    of addicts in drug program
        evaluation, 271
    in drug use survey data,
        256-7

Sedative use in Australia, 40, 43
Singapore
    control of drug problem,
        83-6
    history of opium use, 67-71
    opium treatment centers,
        78-81
    pill taking, 76-7
Social problem of drug use, 17-22
Social problems, sociological
        theories, 14-7
Social reformer and social prob-
        lem, 15-16
Southeast Asia
    cannabis (ganja) use, 75-6
    drug abuse programs, 85-6
    drug treatment centers,
        81-2
    drug use and dependence, 77
    heroin use and trafficking,
        73-5
Surveys as community research
        methodology, 251-9

Thailand, drug-dependence
        treatment centers, 81-2
Tranquilizers
    misuse and federal control,
        321-2
    use in Australia, 40, 43
Treatment
    defined, 269
    of drug abuse, 87-8, 231, 351

Treatment (cont.)
  of drug abuse in Israel,
      182-3, 185-7, 191,
      193-4, 195-6
  evaluation of, 267-79
  modalities, 267-8

United Kingdom (U.K.)
  addiction, 153, 155
  amphetamine and hallucinogen
      use, 152, 161
  attitude toward drugs,
      162-8
  barbiturates, 148, 158, 162,
      163
  cannabis, 154, 155
  cocaine, 155-6, 160
  community response to drug
      use and misuse, 162-8
  drug abuse, 151-2
  drug legislation, 150-1, 160,
      161, 165
  government reports on drug
      misuse, 157, 159-60
  heroin, 158, 160
  laundanum. See opium
  methadone, 160, 161-2
  opium, 147-9, 152-3
  psychedelics, 150, 152
United States (U.S.)
  cannabis, 10, 12
  community response to drug
      use, 130
  drug abuse treatment and
      rehabilitation, 139-43
  drug control
    criminal sanctions, 133-9
    Federal Drug Education
      Act (1970), 215
    promotion of interna-
      tional action,
      131-3
  government action vs. drug
      companies, 320-3
  narcotic legislation, 134-5,
      136, 137, 139, 140-1
  opium, 8-9

United States, federal drug
      regulatory agencies
  Drug Enforcement Adminis-
      tration (DEA), 137,
      138, 318
  Food and Drug Administra-
      tion (FDA), 318, 327
  Treasury Narcotics Bureau,
      134
  United Bureau of Narcotics
      and Dangerous Drugs,
      136

Validity
  of drug use survey data,
      255-6
  in evaluation of drug treat-
      ment programs, 271
Variables
  in drug education program
      development, 213
  in evaluation of education
      programs, 283-4
  in evaluation of treatment
      programs, 273-4
  in research designs, 261-2

About the
Contributors

STANLEY EINSTEIN (Ph.D.) is Executive Director of the Institute for the Study of Drug Misuse, Inc., New York City. He is also Correspondent for "As It Happens," Canadian Broadcasting Corporation; and the Editor of several publications: International Journal of the Addictions, Drug Forum, Altered States of Consciousness, The Non-Medical Use of Drugs, Living, Growing & Dying, Decisions, Issues and Alternatives, and An Israeli Forum.

MENACHIM AMIR (Ph.D. in Criminology, University of Pennsylvania) is the Director of the Institute of Criminology, Faculty of Law at the Hebrew University of Jerusalem. He was a Visiting Professor at Pittsburg University (1963-65); the University of California at Berkeley (1969-71); and Ottawa University (1976-77). He has written papers on delinquency, runaway youth, and suicide among youth and is a member of government committees on prostitution, rape, and organized crime.

DAVID S. BELL (M.D.) is associated with the Hale Clinic, Mosman, New South Wales, Australia.

ALLAN Y. COHEN (Ph.D.) is Executive Director of the Pacific Institute for Research and Evaluation (California and Maryland) and Professor of Psychology and Philosophy, Department of General Studies, John F. Kennedy University, Orinda, California. Dr. Cohen is a licensed clinical psychologist in private practice in Lafayette, California. His most recent book is entitled The Mastery of Consciousness (Harper & Row, 1977).

PATRICIA G. ERICKSON was a criminologist in the Evaluation Studies Department, Addiction Research Foundation, from 1973 to 1977, where her special interest was in the social and legal effects of criminal sanctions against cannabis use. She is currently a Research Associate and Ph.D. candidate at the Department of Social Administration, University of Glasgow, Scotland.

MATHEA FALCO is a lawyer who served for three-and-one-half years at the Drug Abuse Council as Special Assistant to the President of the Council.

MAX M. GLATT (M.D., D.Sc., FRCP, FRCPsych., DPM) is Honorary Consulting Physician, Department of Psychological Medicine, University College Hospital; Member, Academic Board of Medical College, St. Bartholomew's Hospital; Medical Director, Galsworthy House, Kingston; Visiting Psychotherapist at H.M. Prison, Wormwood Scrubs; and Editor-in-Chief of the British Journal of Addiction. Dr. Glatt has been active in the field of alcoholism and drug dependence since starting the first National Health Service Unit for alcoholism in England in 1952.

ALBERT G. HESS (Ph.D.) is Professor Emeritus of Sociology at the State University of New York at Brockport. He has written several books, among them Chasing the Dragon (on drug abuse in Hong Kong), and articles on various forms of deviancy.

LEONG HON KOON is Associate Professor, Department of Social Medicine and Public Health, University of Singapore; and Senior Health Officer, Ministry of Health in Singapore. He was formerly Medical Officer-in-charge of Outpatient Services in Singapore, and has also served with the World Health Organization as a consultant to the 14th WHO Expert Committee on Mental Health.

RUFUS KING is a member of the District of Columbia, Maryland, and New York bars and practices in Washington, D.C. He was chairman of the Joint ABA-AMA Committee on Narcotic Drugs in 1956, consultant to the President's Commission on Law Enforcement and Administration of Justice from 1966 to 1968, and is the author of The Drug Hang-up; America's Fifty-year Folly (Charles Thomas, 1974).

MARVIN A. LAVENHAR (Ph.D.) is Professor of Preventive Medicine and Director of the Division of Biostatistics, Department of Preventive Medicine and Community Health, College of Medicine and Dentistry of New Jersey, New Jersey Medical School. Since 1969, Dr. Lavenhar's research interests have focused upon the problem of drug abuse, resulting in the publication of approximately 15 scientific papers in this subject area.

IRVING SILVERMAN (Ph.D., Columbia University) is Director of Research and Evaluation of the Divison of Community Mental Helath and Center for Comprehensive Health Practice, New York Medical College; and Associate Professor, Department of Psychiatry, New York Medical College. Dr. Silverman has written extensively on drug abuse and community intervention including an article in 1977 DHEW publication no. (Adm) 77-480 entitled "Investigating Treatment Outcomes: A Who-Done-It Model."

REGINALD G. SMART (Ph.D. in psychology from the University of Toronto) is Associate Research Director at the Addiction Research Foundation in Toronto. He has worked in the field of addictions for more than 20 years, specializing in epidemiology, program assessment, and the effects of legal change on alcohol and drug problems.